Doe's Book
PRESENT F
JERRY

Thank you
JERRY

THE ROLE OF THE HORSE
IN MAN'S CULTURE

THE ROLE
OF THE HORSE
IN MAN'S CULTURE

HAROLD B. BARCLAY
*Department of Anthropology, University of Alberta,
Edmonton, Alberta*

J. A. ALLEN
LONDON & NEW YORK

J.A. Allen & Co
1 Lower Grosvenor Place, London SW1
1980

British Library Cataloguing in Publication Data

Barclay, Harold B
    The role of the horse in man's culture.
    1. Horses – History
    I. Title
    636.1'009   SF283

ISBN 0–85131–329–9

Filmset by Inforum Ltd, Portsmouth
in 10 on 12 point VIP Palatino
Printed in Great Britain by
St Edmundsbury Press
Bury St Edmunds, Suffolk

Acknowledgements

The author wishes to acknowledge his indebtedness to the following:

Lewis Atherton (The Cattle Kings, University of Nebraska Press); J. Auboyer (in Animals in Archaeology, Barrie and Jenkins); L. Cabot Briggs (Tribes of the Sahara, Harvard University Press); J. Bronsted (The Vikings, Penguin Books); Francois Chevalier (Land and Society in Colonial Mexico, University of California Press); V. Childe (A History of Technology, Oxford University Press); J. Clebert (The Gypsies, Penguin Books); H. Dickson (The Arabs of the Desert, Allen and Unwin); Mountstuart Elphinstone (An Account of the Kingdom of Cabul and its Dependencies in Persia, Tartary, and India, Graz); John Ewers (The Horse in Blackfoot Indian Culture, Smithsonian Institute); Edit Fel and Tamas Hofer (Proper Peasants, Aldine Press); C. Forde (The Cultural Map of West Africa, Random House); J. Frantz and E. Choate Jr (The American Cowboy, University of Oklahoma Press); Mariya Gimbutas (The Slavs, Praeger); Ronald Gregson (Ethno-history); Francis Gummere (German Origins, Scribner); Herodotus (The Histories, Penguin Books); M. Howey (The Horse in Magic and Myth, Castle); Miklos Jankovich (They Rode into Europe, Harrap); Karl Jettmar (The Altai before the Turks, Museum of Far Eastern Antiquities, Stockholm); Waldemar Jochelson (The Yakut, American Museum of Natural History); V. Kenrick (Horses in Japan, J.A. Allen); Owen Lattimore (The Inner Asian Frontiers of China, Beacon Press); Owen Lattimore (Nomads and Commisars, Oxford University Press); M. Littauer (Antiquity); Philip Longworth (The Cossacks, Holt, Rinehart and Winston); Robert Lowie (The Indians of the Plains, Natural History Press); M. Mallowan (The Excavation at Tel Chagar Bazar, Iraq); Ammianus Marcellinus (The Roman History, H.D. Bohn); Marco Polo (The Travels, Penguin Books); Tamara Rice (The Scythians, Thames and Hudson); George Simpson (Horses, Doubleday Natural History Press); Charles Trench (A History of Horsemanship, Longmann); W. Tweedie (The Arabian Horse, Routledge & Kegan Paul); G. Tylden (Discovering Harness and Saddlery, Shire Publications); Varro (Roman Farm Management, MacMillan); Ernest Wallace and E. Hoebel (The Comanches, University of Oklahoma Press); Xenophon (Cyropaedia, Harvard University Press); Xenophon (The Art of Horsemanship, Vintage Press); Percival Yetts (The Horse: a Factor in Early Chinese History, Eurasia Septentrionales Antiqua).

Contents

Illustrations

Note: All illustrations have been drawn by the author from illustrations in the texts cited.

Introduction

SOME 45,000 books have been published on horses over the last few generations and nearly all of these can be classed as courses on horsemanship and horse husbandry or works on the history and description of horse breeds and types, or as combinations of these. This book is primarily concerned with none of these issues. It aims rather at a cultural historical survey of the role of the horse in human society. That is, this is a review of the uses to which the horse has been put, and the techniques for horse management and handling through time and space, with the intent of indicating explanations for the specific patterns which emerge.

Certain generalizations can be drawn from the assembled materials. Chief of these is that people who have employed the horse have invariably held it in high regard, primarily because out of the relationship between man and horse has come an admiration by men of certain qualities of the horse, and what may be termed a "centaur effect". That is, the control of the horse, particularly in riding, enhances the feeling of power, freedom, and mobility. There is the exhilaration derived from working with and from being part of a powerful, supple live force. Thus, the horse is recognized as a very unique kind of animal deserving of special treatment and concern. Depending upon ecological, economic, technological and other cultural and geographical forces, the resultant esteem for the horse may be directed towards associating the animal with more "patrician" forms of employment or, in contrast, with more "plebian" usages.

A limited number of horse 'complexes' – patterns of horse husbandry and use – have developed over the ages. Each complex emerges from the interdependence of culture (ideology, values, knowledge, orientation of economy, social organization and technology) with physical environmental factors of climate, vegetation and terrain as well as with human psychological factors. The purposive, intelligent, willing and creative force of man seems no less important than the forces of natural environment. And knowledge, values and ideology are as fundamental as technology and economy in comprehending the role of the horse in human culture as they are in comprehending anything else relevant to man.

Certain topics relevant to the role of the horse have been largely ignored in this book primarily because they would greatly extend the size of the volume. Thus, the subject of the horse in myth and magic has been introduced only where it is necessary to clarify what people do with the living animals. Veterinary care has also been neglected, in part because this is a matter on which most of the sources are silent. It also becomes a highly specialized and technical subject. Finally, all peoples who have used the horse have not been included. Rather there has been a selection based on the availability of source material and on an attempt to avoid unnecessary repetition due to the close similarity among some groups. At the same time the investigation has aimed at being as thoroughly cross-cultural as possible.

Important gaps exist in the material presented, but they are, I trust, because the data are not available without extensive and costly world-wide field research, although some would undoubtedly have been filled if all sources had been in English, French or German. The bulk of this book is based on previously published materials by historians, travellers, anthropologists and professional horsemen. A subject such as this creates several major methodological problems which I do not claim to have answered. One is that the data involve a variety of different disciplines and fields of endeavor, all of which one person can hardly expect to control adequately. Thus, on this basis alone this book is in no sense a definitive work. A second point is not unrelated to the first. Namely, the subject of the horse generates experts in horseman-ship, riding and gear who are novices and amateurs in history or ethnography, as well as historians and ethnographers who write of the horse, but are not horsemen. Each has his proper contribution and I have attempted to exploit the expertise of the several authors appropriately. Clearly there is a need for closer interaction between the non-academic professional horseman and the historian or anthropologist. The horse journals and popular horse books are too full of gross historical and ethnographic errors and the historians and anthropologists who deal with the horse sometimes hardly know the difference between a crupper and a collar.

My personal and first hand knowledge and acquaintanceship with the several cultural areas dealt with are limited to the cattle ranching area of Western North America, the North-eastern United States, parts of Europe, North Africa and Turkey. This book is largely inspired by the many enjoyable hours I have spent with horses and my own interests and training in anthropology. I am not a professional horse-man; neither show ring nor bronco rodeo rider. My association with the horse started over three decades ago when as an adolescent I worked with farm draught horses. For a number of years since then my main recreation has been in pleasure riding.

I
Some General Characteristics of the Horse

WITH the possible exception of the dog no animal has attracted man more than the horse and with no other animal has man developed such an intimate relationship. Of all species, the horse can make a greater claim to directly affecting the course of human history, largely because of its unfortunate widespread employment as a machine of war. The horse is alert, agile, and sleek in form and movement, making it one of the most aesthetically appealing of beasts. In addition it possesses sufficient intelligence to respond to man, to trust him and work willingly with him.

The domesticated horse is one of six living species of the genus Equus. The other species include the ass, both domesticated and wild, the onager, and three species of zebra. Equus is the only surviving genus of horse-like creatures; at least twenty other genera "are known only as fossils" (Simpson, 7).

Horse-like animals are classified among mammals within the order of Perissodactyla, an order of animals, usually hoofed, "with the weight mainly carried by the middle hoof when there [is] more than one, that eat plants, and that have various other peculiarities showing that all are descended from an eohippus-like common ancestry" (Simpson, 5). The equid's closest living relatives are the two other surviving perissodactyles, the tapir and the rhinoceros; from the point of view of the layman rather unlikely candidates for such a role. Some ancient, now extinct, kinsmen of the equines are of even more unlikely appearance, such as the huge and ungainly titanotheres and chalicotheres.

Millions of years of the evolutionary process have produced the basic horse design which "is adapted to roaming and running on the hard soil of plains, eating harsh grasses and escaping enemies" by quick start and flight. "A horse", writes Simpson, " . . . is a beautiful example of functionalism. The living species of Equus are almost perfectly designed to meet the needs of their ways of life, and most of the features in which they differ from other animals can be interpreted as functional adaptations to their special habit" (Simpson, 9).

For centuries men have employed horse symbols to signify speed, a practice which continues in modern times with horse names applied to various models of automobiles. Such symbolising is only appropriate since the body of a horse is designed for speed. Beneath its compact and sleek exterior the bones and muscles are arranged and developed for this end. "The great running muscles are bunched at the upper part of the legs, where they give maximum motion of the leg with relatively short motion of the muscles. The legs are long and slender and insure extra speed by the fact that the lower parts, more distant from the body, are particularly elongated. To increase the stride still more, the horse stands permanently on tiptoe, with only the point of the one toe, with its stout, hard hoof, touching the ground" (Simpson, 10).

Man in somewhat radical contrast possesses legs which "are longer in the upper part than in the lower and the muscles are distributed far down the leg and even bunched heavily (if at times, prettily) in the calf" (Simpson, 10). While the horse's heel – that is, his hock – is half-way up the leg and never touches the ground, that of man's rests upon the ground. Standing on tiptoe like a ballerina is difficult for man, the natural thing for the horse.

The elongated head and neck of the horse permit it to graze on short grass and at the same time remain alert to danger. Horses depend to a considerable extent upon their vision and the eyes, which are far back in the head, are sufficiently high to spot approaching danger while the animal is cropping grass. At the same time, the eye is of extremely large size, the largest of any land animal in absolute dimensions. (Simpson, 13). As any horseman knows, the horse is keenly sensitive to movements both to the side and to the rear. This is because each eye has a wide semicircular sweep without the eye or head having to be moved.

The horse's brain provides him with good sensory motor coordination, which among other things, permits him to perform certain tricks. How intelligent this animal might be is a matter of dispute. Some veteran horsemen argue that the horse is among the most stupid of creatures; others, possibly allowing their sentiments to prevail, attest to its great intelligence. But, as Simpson indicates, intelligence is a relative matter. Compared to the most doltish of humans a horse is miserably stupid; compared to other animals he does not fare badly. He is alert and skittish and quick to react, all of which gives the appearance of intelligence particularly when contrasted with the dull, slow ox.

The horse's teeth and hooves are both features well adapted to its traditional habitat. The teeth are useful in cropping grasses which are particularly harsh on them because of the silicious material in the grass as well as the grit and sand inevitably taken up in grazing. The hooves make for ease and swiftness of movement on hard, flat surfaces such as grassy steppes. They are also useful in pawing the snow away to recover the grass beneath. But they are not efficient mechanisms for soft swampy or sandy soil nor do they contribute to surefootedness in steep rough mountain country. It is however, incorrect to assume that the horse in the wild state is solely a steppe animal. On the contrary, this species has proven itself highly adaptable to forest and tundra as well, as its distribution and numbers in these areas demonstrate.

Horses are gregarious or herd-type animals. Left to their own devices they form in small herds composed of one stallion, from a half dozen to twenty mares and the immature offspring. The stallion defends the herd from predators. He is a polygynist who tolerates no competition within his own band. Consequently, he is ever vigilant, driving and herding his harem and warding off intrusions from other stallions and, where possible, seeking to attract mares from other herds. Because of this situation there are invariably bachelor stallions who graze on the peripheries of the territories of the predominantly female herds. These are outcasts either because of youth, age or infirmity, the young stallions among them being especially alert to the possibility of building their own harems.

On reaching maturity young stallions are driven from the herd by the ruling stallion – invariably their own sire – not because of any instinctive conception of incest, which is absent, but because the stallion desires exclusive access to the mares. At the same time he will seek to retain as many of the young mares as he can manage. Most frequently these are his own daughters. Within the herd there is a dominance structure in which, ordinarily, the stallion is at the top. It is more correct to say he *drives* his herd rather than leads it. Dominance is based upon size and age, with the former being more important. While poultry have their pecking order and baboons their "mounting" order, horses have a biting-kicking order in establishing dominance, so that the one who is able to bite and kick all the others in a herd is at the pinnacle of the hierarchy and the one who is kicked and bitten by all others is at the bottom. Among primates grooming is an important form of harmonious social interaction; among horses this takes the form of mutual nibbling.[1]

There is a consensus among specialists that the contemporary and post-Pleistocene, pre-domesticated horses constitute a single species – *Equus caballus* – which appeared during Pleistocene times. One interpretation of the early development of the species argues that in late Pleistocene times races of horses appeared due to specific adaptations to differing habitats. Another view, expressed by Zeuner, holds

---

[1] There is a considerable body of literature on the behaviour of horses and other equines. "The Behaviour of Horses" by G. Waring, S. Wierzbowski and E. Hafez presents a summary statement and bibliography (1975). Two more recent studies of specific horse populations are Stephanie J. Tyler's *The Behaviour and Social Organization of the New Forest Ponies* (1972) and F. Bruemmer's "The Wild Horses of Sable Island" (1967).

that differing habitats produce ecological variations so that it is possible for any type to develop wherever the appropriate habitat exists. Thus horses introduced into and remaining in desert or semi-arid steppe conditions tend to become lighter boned while those in forest environments develop a heavier form.

The dividing line between the concept of race and that of ecotype is a very fine one since an ecotype can become a geographical race "wherever a type of environment reigns exclusively over a large area. But the concept of the ecotype makes it possible for apparently racial types to co-exist in close proximity and to evolve independently in discontinuous areas" (Zeuner, 310).

Even if we were to agree that there were distinct races among pre-domesticated horses this still does not permit one, as several have tried to do, to derive contemporary types of domesticated horses from presumed archaic races. As Simpson has indicated man has been breeding horses for thousands of years so that the types of breeds "established by man were such mixtures and recombinations of the original wild stocks that the idea of derivation of each main domestic type from a particular, natural wild population may be unrealistic or meaningless" (Simpson, 33–4).

Domestic horses are of three major types: hot-blooded or light breeds utilized primarily for riding, cold-blooded or heavy breeds for draught purposes, and ponies. There are also mixtures, of "hot" and "cold" which are referred to as warm bloods. The light breeds have always been the most numerous both in terms of number of breeds and number of individuals. Simpson reports that there are perhaps sixty "recognized" breeds of horses in the world today, while among dogs there are over 200 and the difference between dog breeds is much greater than any between horse breeds (Simpson, 57). Summerhays, on the other hand, describes some 124 horse breeds and types including the tarpan and Przewalski's horse (Summerhays, 1968). Thus, the total number of breeds may in fact be well over a hundred.

It is usually claimed that the oldest existing breed of horses is the Arab which certainly goes back to the early centuries of the Christian era and prior to Muhammad. The Mongolian pony is likewise an ancient breed of indeterminate age as are some of the ponies of western Europe. Particularly since we know more about recent times and since selective breeding has become much more sophisticated in the last few centuries, it is to be expected that there would be a greater proliferation of new breeds in the course of the last half a millenium as compared to earlier times.

We must grant that climatic conditions and the availability of appropriate feed contribute considerably to making for the variety of different types of horses. Nevertheless, horse-breeding, like stock-breeding generally, is another monument to the ingenious creativity of man. The wide variety of breeds owes most to man, who desiring animals for specific purposes, sought to mould what nature had offered into something more suitable for his use. Thus, by selective, purposive breeding, by special care and treatment, men have created the numerous breeds.

Today the horse has been introduced into every part of the world except the High Arctic, the Antarctic, the tsetse fly-infested regions of Equatorial Africa and the thick tropical jungles of the Amazon and New Guinea. It is man who brought the horse back to the Americas, who introduced the first horses to Australia and the islands of the Pacific and who planted them in the inhospitable Sahara and Arabian desert. Thus, it is through man that the horse has become so wide-spread. It is likewise through the hand of man that the survival of wild and feral horses, as well as some of the breeds of horses developed by man himself, has been put in jeopardy.

In certain circles it has become fashionable to conceive of men as helpless marionettes whose every move and every thought is "determined" by some external "force". Sometimes these "forces" are held to be creatures of men which on being created assume a life and power of their own and, in fact, come to rule their creators. Man, as the livestock breeder, is certainly a major example attesting to his capacity to manipulate and modify his environment and to achieve important innovative goals which he has purposively chosen by his own will.

II

The Origin and Early Spread of the Domesticated Horse and its Role in Early Tribal-cultivator Societies

THE impetus for animal domestication has been a matter of some speculation leading to opposing hypotheses. One argues for a religious-ideological explanation. Initially enunciated by Edward Hahn (1896) it has more recently been given some credence by Carl Sauer (1952) and much more strongly endorsed by Erich Isaac (1970). This point of view rightfully indicates that earliest domesticated forms of cattle, sheep and goats would not have been milk producers, nor would sheep have been wool producers. At most they would have been a source of meat. Poultry, it is noted, exist in many parts of the world not for their egg production or their flesh but for use in divination. It is speculated that this was the original motivation for the domestication of poultry and, further, that the first cattle were in all likelihood also first domesticated for religious-ideological ends, to provide a reliable and readily available supply of animals for sacrificial purposes.

Another hypothesis derives domestication from economic motivations. A most reasonable expression of this thesis has been made by Charles Reed, namely, that domestication begins when a growing population changes over to a more settled and culturally more complex form of life so that domestic animals appear from the necessity of insuring regular food supply for a larger population (Reed, 1960).

Wilkinson among others has proposed a more general ecological explanation of domestication. He suggests that domestication is related to changes in ecological conditions where, in order to hold animals in an area from which they are leaving, they are enclosed by man (Wilkinson, 1972, 23–35). The significance of enclosures as well as decoy animals and castration in the domestication process had been noted by earlier writers. Lattimore believes that when wild animals tended to draw into oases from the open steppe some were captured and used as decoys to attract others in still further. The decoys would be made more tractable by castration which probably originated in fertility magic. Enclosing the animals would, of course, facilitate the process of control and taming (Lattimore, 1962a, 159–160).

The motivation for the domestication of animals was undoubtedly complex. While the economic factor appears to be a paramount one, some animals were undoubtedly domesticated for ideological reasons while others for both economic and ideological reasons. Such secondary or, that is, later domesticates as poultry and the cat probably had a non-economic origin, while the horse, another secondary domesticate, might have been initially domesticated for a meat supply. It was an animal which can make efficient use of pastures year round and under heavier snow cover than any other common domesticate and as such was a good producer of meat for people residing in temperate steppe country. The extent to which horse flesh was reserved for sacrificial purposes in contrast to utilitarian consumption is, however, a question.

Another issue pertaining to domestication of animals concerns the type of people who first undertook the practice. One early theory held that animal domestication was the achievement of hunting nomadic peoples while an opposing view was that it was primarily the workmanship of Neolithic cultivators dwelling in sedentary villages and shifting residence only when necessitated by the exhaustion of their soil.

The first thesis was given prominence in the cultural historical theory of W. Schmidt (Sieber & Mueller, 1941). In his scheme, elaborating on the earlier cultural historical theory of F. Graebner, bearers of a patrilineal, patriarchal nomadic hunting cultural "circle" developed the first animal domestication as a result of following wandering or nomadic types of animals – reindeer, sheep, goats. In due course, these initially wild animals became used to the company of man and interrelated with him to the point that domestication resulted and such specialized hunters following wild herds now were transformed into nomadic pastoralists maintaining domestic herds. Among the arguments brought forward to support this thesis is that of animal psychology. It is held that hunter nomads would be in a better position to domesticate and control herds, since they would have a greater understanding of the behaviour of animals.

The general argument for nomadic hunters as the first animal domesticators receives limited support from the archaeological evidence. For example, the eleven thousand year old site in north-eastern Iraq, Zawi Chemi, suggests the presence of domesticated sheep and no domesticated plants. Coon's work at Hotu Cave in Iran where domesticated sheep and goats were found in what appears to be a camp of early Neolithic nomadic hunters endorses the thesis. However in the great majority of sites remains of domesticated animals are always found in conjunction with remains of domesticated plants.

Those who believe that animal domestication commenced with Neolithic cultivators argue that pastoral activity implies husbandry, breeding, control – all constituents of a cultivator's world view and quite foreign to a hunter's. The pastoralist is engaged in the cultivation of animals just as the farmer engages in the cultivation of plants. In addition pastoralism is probably a highly specialized development out of the Neolithic cultivator community. In many parts of the world today herdsmen take care of pasturing a community's livestock. Such specialization may have developed several thousand years ago and led segments of the population to take up livestock breeding exclusively. Since these herds exploited the less fertile and more marginal lands, these pastoral nomads remained on the edges of cultivated zones following their herds from pasture to pasture. Their nomadism resulted from the necessity to maintain good pasture and water supply on marginal lands. Other patterns of pastoralism developed in a form that has become known as transhumance involving the exploitation of high mountain meadows in the summer and low elevation pastures in the winter.

Certainly the ultimate origins of animal domestication are lost in the mists of the past. It is most likely that the dog and reindeer and possibly, in some locations, the sheep, were originally domesticated by hunter-gatherers. Other animals seem to have been domesticated by those who were already plant cultivators.

In the case of the horse, we are dealing with an animal which was domesticated rather late in time compared to most others. Some recent estimates give the following approximate dates for domestication:

Dog	12,000 B.C. (Iraq)
Sheep	9,000 B.C. (Iraq)
Goat	7,000 B.C. (Turkey)
Swine	7,000 B.C. (Turkey)
Cattle	6,500 B.C. (Greece)
Horse	3,000 B.C. (Ukraine)

(Harlan, 93–94).

Obviously these datings must be viewed as tentative and some are controversial. Thus, another dating places the domesticated horse as early as the fifth millenium B.C. (see below). The lateness of the horse raises a question regarding the influence of the domestication of other animals on that of the horse. It is highly improbable that any people unfamiliar with the idea of domestication would independently seek to domesticate an animal like the horse which is large in size, skittish in temperament, and often independently minded or unruly – depending upon one's point of view. Mankind first domesticated smaller, more tractable creatures such as sheep and goats.

It seems likely that cattle would serve as an appropriate model for the domestication of the horse. They were domesticated at least two thousand years before the horse. They are large animals and were apparently the first beasts of burden. Further, the people who are associated with the first domesticated horses already possessed domesticated cattle and swine.

Of all the animals other than cattle a most likely candidate for a model for horse domestication would appear to be the onager. It is, however, difficult to fix the date for the first onager domestication. Bone finds as well as pictures of the animal in archaeological sites dating to the sixth and the fifth millenia B.C. could be either wild or domesticated onagers. Undisputed evidence of onager domestication does not actually appear until the third millenium in the form of paintings, models, and inlays depicting the employment of the animal for drawing four wheeled vehicles. At the very best it seems one could only argue that onager domestication is approximately coterminous with that of the horse. Further, all early domesticated onagers are confined to Anatolia, Mesopotamia and Iran, a region well out of the much more northern range of earliest horse domestication. Incidentally, it should be noted that the type of harness and method of guidance on the onager clearly indicate that draught cattle were the model for the use of these equines.

The donkey might be suggested as another model for horse domestication. However, its place of earliest domestication – Egypt – coupled with the date of about 3500 B.C., make this most unlikely. A similar argument applies regarding the camel which was apparently domesticated in South-west Asia between 2000 B.C. and 3000 B.C. That camel saddlery may have been transferred and applied in a modified form to the horse is another issue.

For several decades some authorities suggested that the reindeer was, after the dog, the earliest animal domesticate. A revision of this view held that while reindeer domestication might not precede that for sheep, goats and cattle, it did have priority over the horse and functioned as the major stimulus for horse domestication. Franz Hancar in what is clearly the most exhaustive review of the early culture history of the horse helped to perpetuate this view and a recent popular book on the history of horsemanship reasserts Hancar's argument (Jankovich, 1971). Hancar of course produced his magnum opus at a time when the evidence indicated that horse domestication commenced some time in the third millenium or at best in the late fourth millenium. At the same time he conjectured that reindeer domestication might have begun before this time and placed the beginnings of reindeer breeding and riding before 3000 B.C. although he presented no firm archeological data to substantiate these early dates (Hancar, 447). Since he wrote, the date for the initiation of horse domestication has been pushed further back in time.

Jettmar in several articles has well demonstrated that reindeer domestication is relatively late and that the earliest evidence for it does not precede the first millenium B.C. (Jettmar, 1951, 1952, 1953). In a more recent and lengthy review of the cultural history of reindeer herding, Vajda rejects the priority of reindeer breeding over that of the horse and the influence of the former upon the latter. He holds, on the contrary, that horse husbandry provided the model for reindeer breeding and agrees with Jettmar that the earliest reindeer domestication is within the first millenium B.C. (the second half of the first millenium B.C.) (Vajda, 400–402).

The archaeological evidence, then, does not support the priority of reindeer domestication over the horse, but on the contrary, one might suggest, the reverse of this. In addition, those who support the reindeer theory apparently overlook the fact that reindeer are neither domesticated nor treated in any way near the same fashion as other domesticated herd animals. Both Laufer and Hatt have shown that reindeer-and horse-husbandry are quite dissimilar which would not be expected if horse domestication was modelled on that of the reindeer. The best conjecture is that cattle might have been the model for horse domestication.

The Beginning of Horse Domestication: The Ukraine and Environs

The determination of whether an animal is domesticated or wild from archaeological bone remains is often a difficult task and especially so with the horse. Domestication in its earlier stages resulted in few distinctive morphological changes compared to other domestic animals. In particular, prehistoric techniques of horse keeping meant that the horse's way of life was hardly different from the wild form. In the case of horses, little is known about any decrease in size normally associated with domestication. During the Iron Age in Europe Celtic horses had become noticeably smaller, but since the end of the first millenium B.C. with more controlled animal breeding horse size has increased. "[T]he horse belongs to the few species of domestic animals of which certain present breeds exceed the size of the wild ancestors" (Bökönyi, 1974, 236). Domestication of the horse has resulted in "a decrease in the volume of the brain case, a broadening of the forehead, a shortening of the facial part and a narrowing down of the muzzle

. . ." as well as a decrease in the size of the teeth (Bökönyi, 1974, 236). Bökönyi concludes that "osteologically the remains of domestic and of wild horses can hardly be separated from each other in the material of archaeological sites" (Bökönyi, 1974a 236).

Certainly the most telling evidence is objects associated with animal husbandry such as bridles, halters and bits, but very little of this sort has been preserved from earliest times. Other clues of domesticated horses are, however, available. A domesticated population reveals much greater variation, lacks old animals, and has an overwhelming majority of mares. Furthermore, domestication is suggested by the presence in a site of complete skeletons since domestic animals would be slaughtered on a settlement site and so all the bones would be found in the settlement (Bökönyi, 1974, 237). Hunters of wild horses would be more apt to kill and butcher an animal on the spot leaving those bones with little flesh on them at the killing site so that some bones would be absent from the place of settlement (Bökönyi, 1974, 237).

The earliest record of the domesticated horse is in the Eurasiatic steppes. Huppertz has argued for the domestication of the horse in the Turan-Altai area holding that there was a horse breeding centre around the mid-third millenium in the Siberian wooded steppes (Huppertz, 1961a, 22). Herre believed the original horse domestication was in central Europe (Bökönyi, 1968, 6). For Bökönyi domestication took place "more probably in several places simultaneously" on the steppes of Asia and eastern Europe "for it was only there that a substantial material of wild horses, which had survived the Pleistocene Age, was found from the Neolithic Age" (Bökönyi, 1968, 7). From there the first domesticated horses entered central and western Europe. However, in the greater part of central Europe "domestication never reached a serious level, and it was always the horses introduced from the East that were prevailing" (Bökönyi, 1968, 7).

The archaeological sites most significant to the first horse domestication are those associated with the Cucuteni-Tripolye culture in the Ukraine north of Kiev on the river Dniepr and extending westward into present day Rumania. The Tripolye people were preliterate, tribal[1] people independent of any urban civilization. They were settled hoe cultivators dwelling in small villages composed of beaten clay houses in each of which probably lived large extended families. They raised wheat, barley and millet, but were probably more concerned about

---

[1] "Tribal" refers to a group who are united by some ultimate, if fictional, kinship as the descendents of a remote common ancestor. In contrast to the nation-state, in the tribe kinship and politics tend to be one. Its "several communities are not united under a sovereign governing authority, nor are the boundaries of the whole thus clearly and politically determined" (Sahlins, viii).

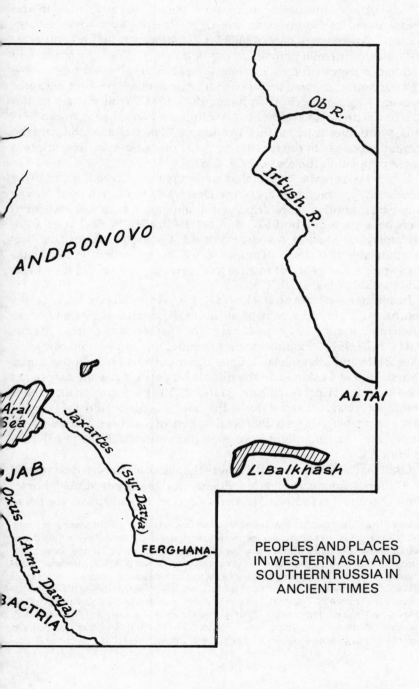

PEOPLES AND PLACES
IN WESTERN ASIA AND
SOUTHERN RUSSIA IN
ANCIENT TIMES

stock breeding, keeping in addition to horses, cattle, sheep and swine.

Very early domesticated horses are possibly associated with the Tripolye site of Dereivka on the river Dniepr, near Kremenchug, Ukraine. An assigned date of 4400 B.C. is, however, highly controversial. Mid-fourth millenium B.C. may be a "safer" date.[2] An amazingly high percentage of domestic animal bones found at this site were horse – 68 per cent, compared to 21 per cent cattle bones, 9 per cent pig and 7 per cent sheep and goat (Gimbutas, 1970, 157). Detailed examination of a complete horse skull with a jaw found among the remains ascertained its domesticated status. In addition "The great variability in the extremity bones" in the remains support the thesis of a domesticated horse population (Bökönyi, 1974, 238).

Gimbutas reports "perforated antler pieces, curved, straight or bifurcated" in the materials of the Dereivka site as well as at Novye Russeshty, another early Tripolye settlement, and considers them to have been parts of a bridle (Gimbutas, 1970, 158). While horses were probably first used as a source of meat, Gimbutas argues that it is "unthinkable that herds of horses could be controlled on foot" and thus apparently feels that even at this early date they could have been ridden (Gimbutas, 1970, 158).

In another early site on the lower Volga, Khutor Repin, horse bones comprised eighty per cent of all domestic animal bones and were discovered in rubbish heaps along with other remains of meals (Gimbutas, 1970, 157). "Equids" are represented on painted ceramic from Bilce Zlote and among clay animal figures at Kosilovcy in the upper Dniestr and at Suskovka in the middle Bug area. They are associated with the late Tripolye culture (Hancar, 72). Hancar classifies these animals as onagers, and if this is the case, it is of considerable significance in that it suggests that in this part of southern Ukraine both horses and onagers might have been domesticated in the fourth millenium B.C.

Usatovo (3400 B.C.–3000 B.C.) was the site of a Tripolye type people and affords interesting early evidence for the domesticated horse. Bone cheek pieces testify in Hancar's view "to the early use of the horse

[2] Aside from the specific disagreement about the reliability of the dating of these Dereivka remains, recent developments in new dating techniques have resulted in a radical revision of dates attributed to Neolithic and Bronze Age Europe. In general, European sites earlier believed to be between 1000 B.C. and 5000 B.C. are now recalibrated as between ten and thirty per cent older, so that for example a radio-carbon date of 1012 ₿.C. is now believed to be in fact 1152 B.C. while, similarly, a dating of 3512 B.C. is now believed to be 4207 B.C. In the following discussion, dating of sites, where possible, follows the latest reinterpretation. Prior to 1970 Dereivka was placed at 3500–3000 B.C. The new calibration would alter these dates to 3500–4200 B.C. In either case Bökönyi believes Dereivka is more recent (Bökönyi, 1974, 238).

for pulling" (Hancar, 72). There is also a picture on a limestone slab of one of the kurgans, or burial mounds, of a man with three horses and a stag (Hancar, 72). Usatovo, located in the steppes, shows a high percentage of sheep, goats, and horses and a low percentage of swine suggesting more emphasis on pastoral activity (Smith, 61).

Gorodsk, culturally similar to Usatovo and of about the same period, contains a high percentage of cattle and horse remains, perhaps because these animals could more adequately cope with the snow cover in the area. Gorodsk also provides a cheek piece from a bit (Smith, 61).

The culture of the Ukraine and surrounding area in eastern and central Europe from the mid-fourth to the last quarter of the third millenia B.C. is referred to as *Kurgan*. It is characterized by burials in house-like structures usually built of timber covered by a low mound, and "pastoralism with some agriculture, hilltop forts, small villages with small rectangular houses and simple unpainted pottery . . . " (Gimbutas, 1971, 20). In its early stages it had a Chalcolithic (copper and stone) technology, but in the end in most places it had become a Bronze Age culture.

The Kurgan people, whom Gimbutas believes are proto-Indo-Europeans, expanded widely in Europe, the Caucasus and eastward across central Asia. Their spread is associated with the diffusion of horse domestication (Gimbutas, 1970, 158) and thus we must follow their presumed influence into these regions.

In the lower Volga, the northern Caucasus, Ukraine, Moldavia, Transylvania and southern Yugoslavia, figurines of horses' heads made from semi-precious stones have been uncovered and are dated from the first half of the fourth millenium. "Some of them clearly show decoration of the horse's head by grooves or ridges around the nose and along the top of the head", features which according to Gimbutas are "the earliest pictorial representations of bridled horses" (Gimbutas, 1970, 158), although they might certainly also be representations of halters or hackamores.

From the third millenium B.C. a pit grave at Storozhova Mogila, on the Dniepr, contained remains of two wheeled carts (Gimbutas, 1965, 206). Elsewhere in the lower Dniepr and Volga two and four wheeled vehicles and models of them in clay have been recovered. However, these wagons may have been drawn by oxen rather than horses since they appear to have only solid oak wheels. The presence of spoked wheels would suggest a design for speed and hence the employment of horses. In addition, small figurines of yoked oxen cast in copper have been found in the Transcaucasus 3700 B.C. (Gimbutas, 1970, 161). Still, one cannot rule out the possibility that horses were used on these carts as well. In Mesopotamia onagers pulled solid-wheeled war "chariots" for several centuries.

Cheek pieces made of a bronze-copper wire with a loop in the middle were taken from Kurgan sites in Transylvania and dated as the third quarter of the third millenium B.C. (Gimbutas, 1970, 161). Several sites in Hungary in the vicinity of the Tisza River suggest that the domesticated horse was in central Europe in the fourth millenium B.C. in conjunction with the so-called Tiszapolgar culture. A presumed bone bridle bit from Hodmezovasarhely, Hungary, probably of this time period has been judged a fisherman's arrowhead by one investigator (Bökönyi, 1974, 238–239).

The Hungarian Bronze Age culture known as Otomanli in Transylvania (early second millenium B.C.) is of Kurgan origin, and sites contain figures of horses and clay models of four wheeled wagons. An earlier type of wagon had high sides and is a direct descendent of the Chalcolithic type known from Budakalasy, Hungary, associated with the Baden culture (third millenium B.C.). Later carts have lower sides and were probably brought to central Europe by Kurgan people (Gimbutas, 1965, 206–7).

For Hancar, the archaeological record provides proof of Neolithic European horse breeding. At Föllik near Gross-Höflein, Austria, a late Neolithic grave contained a goat with a kid, a ewe and a lamb, a cow with a calf, and a twenty year old mare with a foal, a young mare and another 20 year old of which only the severed heads were placed in the graves. Hancar believes the nature of the graves, the amount of effort involved, the presence of mothers and young of all forms of ordinarily domesticated animals definitely points to these animals all being domesticated. He further maintains that the larger number of horses suggests the increasing economic significance of that animal, but no clue is provided as to what they might be used for (Hancar, 39). Behrens, who stresses the rarity of horses in Neolithic and early metal-using sites, considers this Gross-Höflein grave to be the only significant horse burial so far discovered in middle Europe (Powell, 1971).

Antler tine cheek pieces come from Austria and Silesia in Early Bronze Age sites (Childe, 1954–6, 724), and from Late Bronze Age lake dwellers in Switzerland a bit of "sheep's marrow bone fixed between two sawn off antler tines" was found (Childe, 1954–6, 722).

Ritual burials of horses are located in several Danubian sites in southern Poland including Jordansmühl, Zlota, Potyry District, Plons, and Bodzaspart (Hancar, 40). It is however not at all clear that these are definitely domesticated animals.

Further south in the Balkans, aside from the Cucuteni culture of

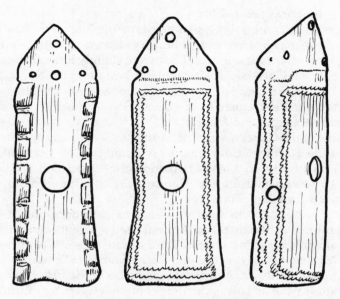

THREE VIEWS OF BONE CHEEK PIECE FROM
TIMBER GRAVE CULTURE
EARLY SECOND MILLENIUM B.C.

From Barrow at Komarovka, Middle Volga
Note notched edges on inner view at left
From Piggott, 1965, 96

Moldavia which is an extension of the Tripolye of the Ukraine, the domesticated horse is reported from other Rumanian Early Bronze Age sites as well as from a great number in Bulgaria (Bökönyi, 1974, 241). In eastern Macedonia, in the Drama Plain, excavation produced "a horse head figurine with a possible indication of a horse bridle" from layers associated with the Gumelnita culture dated to the fourth millenium B.C. (Gimbutas, 1970, 158).

Carbon 14 datings of the Cernovoda culture, located north of Troy III in the far north-west corner of Anatolia, are for 2330 B.C. The remains show pastoralism is "very marked" and domesticated horses appear from the beginning of this culture (Mellaart, 1966, 175). It does seem rather unusual, however, that the horse should be in Macedonia in 3000 B.C. and take another six or more centuries to get across the Bosphorus. Several horse graves have been discovered in Greece and date to the second millenium B.C. Bökönyi believes the custom of horse burial may have been introduced by the Achaean settlers about this time (Bökönyi, 1974, 240).

Two third millenium B.C. sites north of the Black Sea (the North Pontic area), Kobjakovo and Babino contained remains of horses among other domestic animals. They were slightly less common than in Usatovo or Gorodsk. According to Gimbutas the North Pontic cultures of the Bronze Age are the predecessors of the Cimmerians whom we shall encounter in the discussion of the development of equestrian nomadism in Eurasia.

Turning to the Caucasus area Maikop is an early metal age site (2500 B.C.) in the Northern Caucasus. Here among silver and gold ornaments was a horse on a silver cup shown in association with cattle, sheep, swine and wild animals. Hancar claims it to be a representation of Przewalski's horse (Hancar, 125).

A large vessel deposited with the skeleton of a horse in one of the burial grounds in Shakhtakhta, Armenia, shows multicoloured paintings of animals including a horse. The dates for these are controversial, some claiming as early as the end of the fourth millenium B.C. and beginning of the third. Others place the date in the fifteenth century B.C. and Mongait as late as the fourteenth to eleventh centuries B.C. (Mongait, 132).

The so-called Catacomb Grave people of the Ukraine and northwest Caucasus (late third millenium B.C.) were mainly sheep breeders, but they also kept cattle and horses. Since the bones and skulls of horses are found in their graves, horses appear to have been used in sacrifice (Gimbutas, 1956, 92).

Fatyanovo in the Volga-Klyazina distirct of central Russia provides remains of horses from the third millenium B.C., although they seem to have been unimportant, probably because of the more heavily forested nature of the country. Fatyanovo is believed to have been an extension of the Lower Dniepr culture (Smith, 71).

In the classic Timber Grave period (1800–1100 B.C.) north-east of the Black Sea, horses appear as prominent animals in religious cults and military life. Bone bridle parts, mostly elongated cheek pieces and round ornamental plates were laid in men's graves. At Komarovka (1100–800 B.C.) there were burials of bridled horses beside chieftains' graves, and at Bykovo (1450–1300 B.C.) near Stalingrad twelve horses were buried in one grave, lying on the ancient surface on their sides with legs outstretched. "The cheekpieces found in Komarovka are the usual types for the late Classical period and recur in several cemeteries and habitation sites. All of them were made of a rectangular bone plate, semicircular in cross-section. In the middle there was a hole through which to thread the bridle, and in the projecting triangular or rectangular upper part there were from two to five holes to fasten the cheekpiece to the leather belt of the bridle. The edges of the under part were notched so that the horse would feel the slightest pull of the bridle" (Gimbutas, 1965, 540). It is quite likely that horses were used for riding, although M.A. Littauer has remarked "the late use of bone and sinew bits . . . in cultures already practicing metallurgy . . . implies a far less exacting use of the horse among them than in the ancient civilizations" (Littauer, M.A., 300).

A late Timber Grave site in the Middle Volga area at Lake Moechnoe showed 53.8 per cent of the bones were cattle, 23.7 per cent were sheep and goats, 15.6 per cent were horses, and 6.9 per cent were swine. The horse bones were usually those of young animals (Gimbutas, 1965, 533). Thus, we may suspect that they were used for food consumption.

Another development in the course of the second millenium B.C. appears to the north of the Timber Grave peoples on the Volga and Kama rivers extending eastward to the Urals. This Turbino culture is believed by Gimbutas to be an expansion of central European peoples. Hoe cultivation and stock breeding appear by about 1500 B.C. (Gimbutas, 1965, 611ff.) and along with these came the domesticated horse. The Sejma culture (mid-second millenium B.C.), not far from the present city of Gorki on the Oka River, has left a find of a dagger with two horses represented on the handle (Hancar, 214–5).

Towards the end of the third millenium or beginning of the second horse domestication probably spread into the western extremities of Europe (except for the British Isles where it was not introduced until the Iron Age – 700–800 B.C. (Piggott, 189)).

By the beginning of the second millenium B.C. the horse was found in the Baltic area and Scandinavia. Domestic horse bones were discovered in hearths in sites around the Courish Lagoon (south coast of Latvia). In Poland, graves contained horse remains among other animals. These sites are associated with the Globular Amphorae culture centred south of the Lagoon in present day Poland) (Gimbutas, 1956, 144). Curwen puts the horse in Denmark in the Megalithic period (ca. 1900 B.C.) (Curwen, 1938) and it may have been in Sweden about the same time.

For the European Bronze Age there is no direct evidence that the horse was employed for riding purposes. Childe, however, has argued that the typical weapon of the time was the battle axe and that this is more adapted to a mounted warrior than to a foot soldier and, thus, from this supposes the central European "Battle Axe" peoples to have been mounted on horseback (Childe, 1929, 269). Clark has questioned this idea and at best it appears to be a good hunch (Clark, 1941).

In and of themselves the cheek pieces and bits so widely found in conjunction with Bronze Age Europe are no direct indication of riding;

they may more readily imply the employment of the horse and chariot or cart. But following Gimbutas' line of argument it seems that horse herders particularly in archaic steppe herding conditions would soon have to resort to riding. This would mean a pre-Bronze Age origin for the practice. Perhaps the implied belief that one cannot have horse riding unless there is some military role for it overlooks more mundane equestrian activities and, hence, a considerable antiquity for such endeavours as riding.

The Altaian Area

Afanasevskaya is a late Neolithic culture beginning about 2500 B.C. on the Upper Yenisei River in the Altai. Shared by Europoid peoples, this Altaian culture was another centre of horse use. Grave sites, which were low earthen works, yielded pottery, wooden vessels and articles of fur and perhaps skin (Gryaznov, 47). Rare remains of animal bones do show the presence of domesticated cattle, horses, sheep and the wild bison, roe deer, fox, chipmunk and fish. Gryaznov concludes that hunting was as important an enterprise as stock breeding. The people lived in earthen structures in permanent settlements of up to ten families. There were enclosures near the houses for keeping livestock and these animals were apparently for providing meat (Gryaznov, 49). Afanasevskaya culture shows close affinity with the pit cultures in the Volga and Don steppes regions (Gryaznov, 51). Indeed, Jettmar states: "The conjunction of cattle and horse breeding with this culture, coming from the South, points decisively against any possibility of a local origin in Siberia, and against horse breeding having sprung from reindeer breeding." Kurgans, domestic cattle, sheep, horses, perhaps yaks, copper, painted pottery vessels all are traits which separate Afanasevskaya from all surrounding Taiga cultures. "The simultaneous appearance of so many new elements" suggests an origin in the South (Jettmar, 1951, 140).

Around the end of the third millenium Afanasevskaya gave way to Okunev people who seem to have had few, if any, horses. More important to horse breeding is the Andronovo culture (1700–1300 B.C.). Bronze Age sedentary farmers of the Minussinsk Basin, south of the Afanasevskaya on the Yenisei. Andronovo people dwelt in large earthen houses and lived on a staple diet of dairy and vegetable products. They probably slaughtered horses on ritual occasions in connection with funerals, and possibly also at weddings and at the reception of guests (Gryaznov, 92). Hancar suspects that the Andronovo peoples associated with the grave fields of Fedorovsk (1700–1200 B.C.) used the horse exclusively for meat (Hancar, 392).

The number of bones from two different late Andronovo dates shows wide differences in animal use.

Comparative evidence indicates to Hancar that a definite transition was in process in late Andronovo culture from an economy based on stock breeding and hunting to one based more definitely on a nomadic pastoral way of life (Hancar, 395). This interpretation corroborates the hypothesis that pastoral nomadism begins to emerge around the end of the second millenium, although precisely how nomadic the late Andronovo people were has not been clarified. Both the promotion of horse and sheep breeding by Andronovo and later Karusuk peoples is related by Hancar to their needs for metal and metal objects and for carrying on a regulated trade. The sheep were for consumption, while the horses were more for transportation purposes (Hancar, 397).

Andronovo people apparently made some use of two and four wheeled covered wagons since a model of this type was found at the Tri Bata site in the Kalmyk steppes. Also at Minussinsk there are rock drawings of a variety of animals and equestrian figures and a covered two wheeled cart with shafts being pulled by a camel (Tarr, L., 102–3).

Further south in Turkmenia, domestic horses first appear in the Namazga site east of the Caspian and just north of the present Iranian border near Anau. There are "clay models of four wheeled carts with the heads of harnessed animals attached to the beam . . . Though these mostly took the form of camels, representations of horses also occur" (Masson and Sarianidi, 120).

At Tazabag'jab, a variant of the Andronovo culture, bones of horses were found as well as a clay model of a horse "with a hole through its mane" suggesting "it was part of a model horse drawn cart" (Masson and Sarianidi, 149). During the second millenium Andronovo traditions spread over central and eastern Kazakhstan and influenced inhabitants of Kirghizia and the Ferghana Valley (Masson and Sarianidi, 153). There appears to be no evidence of an entrance of the domesticated horse into Bactria and Afghanistan region at these early times – before the first millenium B.C.

Between the North Pontic cultures, (of the late Neolithic peoples north of the Black Sea) and the Andronovo, there is a major connecting link: the Timber Grave culture which appeared at the end of the second millenium B.C. in the lower Dniepr and adopted much of the North Pontic culture. Timber Grave peoples extended over to the Urals and are reckoned by Gimbutas to be so similar to Andronovo and to the Tazabag'jab culture between the Caspian and Aral Seas that she calls the Andronovo the south Siberian branch of the Timber Grave people and the Tazabag'jab the western Kazakhistan branch (Gimbutas, 1965, 528).

To sum up, it appears that from the fourth to the end of the third millenium B.C. a common type of culture spread over a wide area of the Eurasian steppe. With this cultural type the domesticated horse was carried out of its original Ukrainian homeland radiating in all directions so that by the middle of the third millenium B.C. it was well known from western Europe to the Altai, from central Russia south through the Caucasus. Horse breeding was associated with tribally organized cultivator-stock breeders and never became part of the paraphernalia of the urban-agrarian civilizations to the south until the end of the third millenium B.C.

Over this early horse keeping area, the animal seems to have had some importance as a source of meat; it is likely that it was early employed as a mount for horse herding and probably early in the fourth millenium B.C. was harnessed to carts of some kind. There seems to be no evidence for the milking of mares at this time. However, cattle were being kept for dairy purposes in the Near East and may have been similarly exploited in the steppes about this time as well. If this is so one might reasonably speculate that the idea of milking was soon transferred to the horse.

Bitting devices were invented before 3000 B.C. and had within a short space of time thereafter a wide distribution. For Afanasevskaya at any rate there is some evidence of stabling and hence the necessity to collect fodder for feed. The horse became widely involved in sacrificial and burial rites and even its importance in military undertakings may have been recognized. Ultimately, the eastern peoples involved in this complex became mounted equestrian nomad herdsmen. The North Pontic peoples may be the ancestors of the Cimmerians and the Timber Grave people of the Scythians whom we shall encounter in Chapter V. In the West other Kurgan groups became the ancestors of the Celts, proto-Germanic and proto-Slavic peoples.

III

The Spread of the Domesticated Horse and its Role in Early Urban-Agrarian Societies

WHAT is popularly referred to as civilization first arose in the Near East almost six thousand years ago and eventually spread over a sizeable portion of Eurasia and North Africa. This early civilization was considerably different in many crucial respects from modern civilization and we may therefore distinguish between the two by referring to the earlier as an urban-agrarian type of society and the latter as an urban-industrial type. Urban-agrarian societies all share a common socio-cultural pattern and this prevailed over much of the world until the nineteenth century when it began to decline in favour of a growing industrial society. It survives in part in much of Asia, Africa and South America today.

Urban-agrarian societies are hierarchical and pyramidal in structure; upward social mobility is extremely difficult and there is considerable sub-cultural variation based on regional differences, rural-urban differences, and social class distinctions, among other things. A nation-state apparatus is autocratic and invariably imbued with imperial designs and a martial flavour.

Horses were not introduced into such societies until after their class-oriented, autocratic and martial character had been well and long entrenched. As a result almost from the beginning horses were viewed as important machines of war. They came into great demand for chariots and later for cavalry and these equestrian branches of the military were from the start the most aristocratic. Peasants and others of the lower echelons were too poor to purchase and maintain good horses and often there were restrictions imposed from above as to who could in fact keep horses or ride them. For all intents and purposes horses were denied to the lower classes, a fact which also denied them an effective weapon if they desired to revolt. The horse was essentially an animal identified with the ruling powers; it was a symbol of power and special privilege. Only the poorest nags and the worn-out cavalry or chariot horses were sold off to draw carts and taxis, haul water and serve as pack animals, turn mills and olive presses, or thresh grain and harrow fields.

There were, of course, eventually exceptions to this situation, as in northern China and northern Europe where technological changes (the invention of the breast strap and horse collar) and the development in Europe of large heavy horses modified this pattern. But even with these innovations the attitude towards the horse altered slowly. A utilitarian role for the horse as an ordinary mundane work animal seems to become more important with the rise of capitalist society and the extension of a Protestant world view with its emphasis on practicality and frugality.

THE HORSE IN ANCIENT MESOPOTAMIA AND ANATOLIA

Salonen claims that horses were known in Babylonia in the mid-third millenium B.C. Animals, he says, in the Ur necropolis were ass and horse and horse and ass crosses. "Tamed" horses were apparently known in northern Mesopotamia about 2300 B.C. (Salonen, 12) and as will be recalled, were presumably domesticated in the extreme northwest part of Anatolia in 2330 B.C.

A recent excavation dated about the late third millenium B.C. north of Mari, at Tell Selenkahiye, Syria, has provided osteological evidence of the horse and what may be figurines of horses (Moorey, 49). The earliest example of a chariot drawn by a horse may be an illustration on a baked clay plaque from Uruk, from the beginning of the second millenium B.C. (Moorey, 49).

From Central Anatolia of the early second millenium evidence shows the use of the horse as a pack animal and possibly a draught animal as well, harnessed in the same fashion as the onager of Mesopotamia (Moorey, 49). At Kültepe, in the same area, a seal of the god Pirva standing on a horse was recovered and is dated at ca. 1950 B.C. (Hancar, 485). There are also clay figurines of horses, a box ornamented with horses' heads, and a beaked pot showing a horse. The nearby early Hittite site at Boghazköy yielded a copper rein-terret of the end of the third millenium B.C. portraying a man attempting to tame a horse (Rostovtseff). Representations of horses on copper rein-terrets from Boghazköy and surrounding areas are often ambiguous. Thus, the rein-terrets illustrated in Rostovtseff's article portray animals which are equine, but might be onager or horse.

Terra cotta models of equines from Chagar Bazar and Brak in the northern extremities of Syria are also dated to the end of the third millenium B.C. One model from Brak seems clearly a horse and is dated to 2300 B.C. It "is closely comparable with a figure from Tepe Gawra, stratum VI", presumably early dynastic (Mallowan, 1947, 215). Other horse figurines from Chagar Bazar are dated at 2000–1900 B.C.

They are often represented with harness and headstalls and found associated with remains of models of chariots. "The frequency with which these models occur suggests that the chariot and draught horse was a common feature of everyday life on the Khabur (river) in the upper half of the second millenium B.C. Such a picture well accords with the records of chariot warfare as practiced by the military dynasty of the Mitanni rather later in the middle of the second millenium B.C." (Mallowan, 1937, 96). All of these data indicate a horse breeding and using area from central Anatolia to northern Syria four thousand years ago. The similarity of the harness of the Hittites and the second millenium Elamites and Kassites with that of the Sumerians shows these people acquired the harness from the Sumerians (who had it first) (Dussaud, 256).

Hancar places the source of the horse in Mesopotamia as either in southeastern Asia Minor or "perhaps in an area of eastern Asia Minor – Armenia-Transcaucasus" (Hancar, 487). He believes "the oldest and most detailed written sources" all point to the latter direction (Hancar, 502). "At the same time the West Asian evidence for horse-breeding from the centuries immediately preceding the age of the war chariot follows a north-south route important to world transport" (Hancar, 524). This route commences in the wooded steppe region of central and southern Russia, thence to the Caucasus, to central Anatolia and into northern Mesopotamia (Hancar, 524).

Legrain believed that he had found "rare examples of horseback riding in (Mesopotamia of the late third millenium B.C.) . . . on two stone cylinder seals of the Post-Sargon type, and on a gold fillet discovered at Ur in a grave of the Royal Cemetery, also dated in the same Sargonic age" as well as three reliefs on clay plaques (Legrain, 28). Actually only four of these items show anything which could be classed as horses. Yet it is extremely difficult to determine whether they are in fact horses, hinnies, or mules or even donkeys or onagers. In the case of two of the examples, some animal other than an equine could readily be suspected.

The clay plaques of the first quarter of the second millenium described by Moorey are much more distinct. Here, apart from plaques showing onager riding, are obviously portrayals of horse riders. In one case the rider sits well back towards the rump of the horse while in another the rider is astride the centre of the back. Reins are held in the left hand and attach to a ring which passes through the animal's nose.

It was once hypothesized that Mesopotamian equids were guided by lip rings. However, the portrayals upon which interpretations are based are not always that clear and would seem to allow for viewing them either as lip or nose rings. It is, however, much more likely that they are nose rings, since equids use the upper lip in eating. Therefore, a lip ring would interfere with this process (Antonius, 1938).

One plaque described by Moorey presumably shows the rider holding the top of a girth as well as reins with the left hand while in the right hand he grasps a stick and the root of the horse's tail. In another the right hand clutches the girth. Legs in both cases are sharply bent at the knee. A bell or tassle is attached under the base of the horse's neck. Moorey says the reins "either pass round, or across, the neck or are held high over the animal's head, as if they passed between its ears when at rest" (Moorey, 42). The horses are males and of pony size, about twelve or fourteen hands. The style of riding and the harness clearly indicate an adaption from the use of cattle and onagers. What is more they betray a poor riding style with minimal control of the mount, demonstrating as Hancar noted in commenting on the Legrain cylinder seals, that riding, if it did occur in this period, was most unusual (Hancar, 551). Moorey, however, believes riding could have been common in the Ur III period at the end of the third millenium (Moorey, 48).

Probably the earliest written reference to horse riding is contained in a letter to Zimri-Lin, King of Mari, written by one of his officials.

"My lord should not ride on a horse," the official Bahdi-Lim advises, "Let my Lord ride on a chariot or indeed on a mule, and let him honour his royal status" (Saggs, 195). This suggests there was some question at this early date as to the propriety of horse riding. Yet Moorey warns us that the statement may be misleading. Royalty is generally conservative and one may readily suspect that horse riding was more acceptable among the lower ranks where the practice would be readily adopted if it appeared more efficient (Moorey, 48). In addition, it is not unlikely that horse riding for the King of Mari was scorned because it was already a well established mode of travel for neighbouring nomads and it would be deemed wholly improper for a king to be in any way identified with such people (Powell, 1971, 2).

Letters of the Mitanni Kings reveal most of the little that is known about horses in Mesopotamia during the first half of the second millenium B.C. Hancar states that from 2000 to 1700 B.C. there are three written references to the use of horses with the war chariot (Hancar, 487). One of these cuneiform references to the horse contains an order of Samsi-Adad of Assur (1749–1717 B.C.), a contemporary and opponent of Hammurabi, to his son Jasmach-Adad to send to Assur horse teams with racing and war chariots from Til-sha-annim (i.e. Chagar Bazar) for the procession of the New Year Festival.

Evidence for riding between the fifteenth and twelfth centuries B.C. from Mesopotamia and Anatolia is provided by four sources:

1. "Orthostats from Tel Halaf and other" Syrian and Mesopotamian sites portraying horsemen and dated at the fifteenth to fourteenth centuries B.C.
2. "A reference in a Hittite text to a king mounting a horse (fourteenth century B.C.) and Hittite references to messengers on horseback."
3. Kassite seals of "centaurs" from the end of the thirteenth century B.C.
4. "A reference to riding horses from the reign of Nebudchadrezzar I of Babylonia (end of twelfth century B.C.)" (Epstein, 1971a, 510, Hancar, 554).

The primary use of horses was for the war chariot to which they were hitched in pairs by throat bands. While the horse and chariot appear rather abruptly in Anatolia around 2000 B.C., they did not become important in south-west Asia until after 1700 B.C. Before that time the horse does not appear to have a great deal of value. It is not even mentioned in the famous Code of Hammurabi (1724–1682 B.C.). A Hittite codex as late as the fifteenth century which Hancar says is apparently based on an older version "and is considered a cultural mirror of the old Hatti empire" (Hancar, 486) provides some idea of relative values. A draught horse was worth twenty (thirty?) half shekels of silver; an "ordinary" horse fourteen; a yearling stallion, ten; a half yearling stallion four; a yearling pack mare fifteen; a half yearling pack mare four; while ploughing cattle were fifteen and mules, sixty (Hancar, 487).

With the development of the war chariot and the horse, the value of the animal was greatly enhanced. The increased status of the horse is indicated by an old Mesopotamian fable in which the horse boasts to the ox of how he lives near kings and great men, eating elegantly, and without himself being eaten. (Aynard, 65).

The horse and war chariot are of prime significance to the military expansion and history of the Mesopotamian and Asia Minor states during the second millenium. "The core of the Hittite army consisted of two armed categories: chariot warriors and foot soldiers. The decisive battle strength of the Hittite army as well as all other armies of the Near East of the second millenium B.C. was concentrated in the chariot warriors" (Hancar, 481). Wars were decided by the chariot battles (Hancar, 482). The size of the chariotry is shown by the following figures: Among the Hittites in one case there is a proportion of 100 bridled horses to 1000 foot soldiers (fifty chariots, or one to twenty foot soldiers). In another case there is one war chariot to thirty-five foot soldiers. The Hittite commitment against the Pharaoh's army amounted "to 17000 foot soldiers and 3500 chariots (one chariot to about every five foot soldiers.)" (Hancar, 481).

Cavalry came into importance after the beginning of the first millenium B.C. Apparently Mycenaeans in Crete preceded the Assyrians in its use since Childe reports a representation of "a mounted warrior on a sub-Mycenaean burial urn from Muliana," Crete (Childe, 1954–6, 728). This probably dates to before the beginning of the first millenium B.C. Any genuine reference to cavalry in Assyria is not before 890 B.C. During the reigns of Assurbanipal (885–860 B.C.) and Shalmaneser III (859–824 B.C.) Assyrians are depicted hunting and fighting on horseback. Hancar points out that the earliest mounted divisions of the Assyrian army were not truly cavalry, but rather more correctly a "riding infantry" which replaced a "driving infantry" of charioteers. This is because the Assyrian armies of the ninth to seventh centuries included mounted archers each accompanied by a shield bearer for his protection and also for controlling the horse in battle. Later these shield bearers were also equipped with lances (Hancar, 554). True cavalry did not appear until after the seventh century B.C.

Riding and Riding Gear

Assyrian riders of the ninth century B.C. either sat very far back on the croup like an Egyptian peasant riding a donkey or close to the withers and for probably similar reasons: the animal was not large enough to sustain the full weight of an adult man on his back for any length of time. It is, of course, perfectly possible for an adult to ride a pony or donkey astride, directly over the animal's back, but any prolonged trip would necessitate having an additional mount so as to change off periodically, as is done by Icelanders and Mongols. Ancient Near Easterners would not have had such an abundance of horses to do this. However, they soon resolved this problem by the practical solution of acquiring bigger horses.

These early Assyrians also rode very "short" with bent knees, and as we have mentioned, were accompanied by shield bearers who guided the mounts. Their horsemanship was not particularly good, since they did not grip with the upper part of the leg, but from the knee down, a practice which throws one off balance (Hancar, 554).

The armoured cavalry of Tiglath-Pileser II (747–727 B.C.) Trench accredits with being much better horsemen. They "ride fairly 'long', gripping from knees to crutch, not with the lower part of the leg" and ride "well bred, light-weight horses." They are shown riding bareback, but this could not have been universal since "both before and after them Assyrian warriors and shown using fringed saddle-cloths," fastened by breastplate and crupper. They may have used a kind of snaffle bit and bridles had headbands and throatlatches (Trench, 16).

According to Childe "crescentic cheek-pieces depicted on Assyrian scuptures certainly look like sections of antler-tine, and such tines, pierced with three holes, have in fact been found serving as cheek-pieces for bits, and that not only for the bone-bit (of Bronze Age Swiss lake dwellers), but for jointed metal mouthpieces, particularly in the region of the Caucasus" (Childe, 1954–56, 724). "Bits with curved metal cheek-pieces that might be translations of the antler ones occur very widely about, or soon after, 800 B.C. not only in Assyria but in temperate Europe, on both sides of the Caucasus, in Iran, and in Central Asia" (Childe, 1954—6, 724).

The cavalry of Sennacherib (705–681 B.C.) rode on quilted saddle cloths girthed to the horse. It should be borne in mind that at this time neither wood frame saddle, stirrups, nor buckles had been invented. Toggles were used in lieu of buckles where harness was not sewn. Long before this time, the Kikkuli texts had already shown that a distinction had been made between halter and bridle with a metal bit in which the horse worked. These texts also indicate that horses were trained to amble and to gallop (Kammenhuber).

Horse Care and Management

The most important single document on horse husbandry from ancient Mesopotamia is written in Hittite in the fourteenth century by a Mitannian named Kikkuli. It contains details of feeding, care and management, and breaking and training. Other similar horse texts have been uncovered in the Boghazköy archives and at Ugarit and there are Assyrian correspondences as well (Hancar, 482). The Kikkuli text has been interpreted variously as a veterinary treatise, as a training course for racing and as a tract about the acclimatization of imported war chariot horses. Hancar inclines to the latter view (Hancar, 479) although he recognizes it also as a military-hippological handbook (Hancar, 480).

These chariot horses were fed on barley, wheat, alfalfa (lucerne) and chopped straw. There was concern for when and how much water a horse should be allowed to drink. Grooming the horse was important, including washing it with warm and cold water and rubbing it dry and bathing with oil. There are recommendations about keeping the stables at proper temperatures. There was also a rigid 184 day training programme for a pair of horses pulling a two wheeled racing chariot (Kammenhuber).

Hittite stables were constructed of boughs and the Mesopotamian ones were reed huts. With the increased use of the horse for military purposes stalls superior to those of other animals were made. A stable in Anatolia ca. 1200 B.C. was better constructed than the dwellings for the stable master and the grooms (Salonen, 167–8).

From the animal lists of Tel Halaf, Syria a private riding stable of the governor of Guzana records two stall masters and eighteen animals including three mares, two female mules, and eight hinnies. The stable of the Babylonian king, Itti-Marduk-balatu, included twenty-two horses (Salonen, 168).

Assyrian grooms were expected to keep their master's horse in good condition and one illustration from the ninth century B.C. depicts a groom using a curry comb (Salonen, 169).

Early Kassite "horse texts" classify horses according to colour and breeding stallions in particular appear to be given personal names. Examples of names include Foxy, Starry, White, Piebald. "The name of a sire was often added (to the given name) (X, son of Y), showing that pedigrees were remembered and perhaps stud-books kept." "White horses were especially prized" since "they were destined to draw the chariots of kings and of gods and in Assyria were accorded divine honours" (Drower, 474). Foals were allowed to run freely with their dams on the chariot (Salonen, 24–26).

The Nuzi and Alalakh horses belonging to Hurrian peoples were all listed according to sex, colour and age (Drower, 473).

Central and eastern Anatolia and northern Mesopotamia were apparently important horse breeding areas. In early second millenium Cappadocia horses were grazed in the open country. Herds numbering in the thousands prevented their being corralled or put in stables. Breeding stock was grazed while the breaking of remounts required corralling (Herzfeld, 1968, 4). In the vicinity of Hattusa (modern Boghazköy, in central Anatolia) 100,000 head were kept for breeding purposes (Hancar, 487). Karkemish, on the upper Euphrates was well known as a major distirbutional centre for horses by the time of Hammurabi (1700 B.C.) (Hancar, 487).

Eastern Anatolia in the mountainous vicinity of Lake Van, later known as Armenia, was a region which had strategic significance for horse breeding to both the Assyrians and later for the Iranians. In the latter part of the second millenium B.C. it became organized as a kingdom by the Urartu who had apparently only just given up a pastoral nomadic way of life. The Urartu king retained the title of "herdsman" although his people became sedentary and took up serious agricultural endeavours. By 900 B.C. their domain had become a most important breeding centre for rather large size horses. Hancar believes it may even have become important in this respect sometime earlier in the second millenium B.C. (Hancar, 190).

That the horse was associated with religious cults in Urartu and Chaldee is indicated by a find of an Urartaic fortress burned down by the Scythians in 585 B.C., near Eriwan, Turkey. "In the centre of the citadel in the middle of a room and hidden under a heap of grain and twigs there was a collection of valuables, apparently for sacrifice in the temple: shields, quivers, and arrows, and armour and helmets, most of them with dedications to the god Chaldi." In addition there were horse ornaments and a bronze snaffle of Trans-Caucasian type belonging to King Menna. Among the remains of domesticated animals were a few complete horse skeletons (Hancar, 186).

The high position of horses in the armies of the time is shown by a victory monument which enumerates 106 war chariots, 9374 riders and 22704 foot soldiers used in a campaign by King Ispuini and his co-regent, Menna, against Man-Busttu-Bursus east of Van. "Lists of war spoils characteristically name the number of horses. Beyond this there is the enumeration of tributes demanded by Menna from the van-quished king of Diauchi:[1] 1000 riding horses, 41 mines of gold, 37 silver mines, 10,000 copper mines, 300 large horned cattle, 10,000 small horned cattle; an annual tribute of 300 riding horses was added" . . . (Hancar, 186).

A survey of the evidence suggests that during the second millenium B.C. and early first millenium B.C. the main centres of horse breeding and horse use in southwestern Asia were to be found in central and eastern Anatolia and the western extremities of Iran (in the domains of Hittite, Hurrian, Kassite, and Urartu peoples). Of no little importance is the clear appearance during this time and in this region of individual treatment, conscious selection, and purposeful breeding of the horse. As Bökönyi states, the horse was the first domesticated animal to be treated in this manner and because of its role as a comrade-in-arms (Bökönyi, 1974, 230).

EGYPT

It is generally agreed that the likeliest explanation for the introduction of the horse into Egypt is with the Hyksos invasions of the eighteenth century B.C. Possibly the Hyksos, who were stock breeders, are derived from either the Hatti (Hittite), or the Hurri or Mitanni who dwelt by this time in Anatolia and northern Mesopotamia. And, as we have mentioned above, all of these peoples were important horse

[1] Diauchi was the name of a kingdom in south-eastern Anatolia.

breeders and users. Albright indicates that during the Hyksos rule of Palestine town gates were so constructed as to provide for chariots (Albright, 89), but on the whole, the direct evidence for the Hyksos as horsemen is rather meagre.

The earliest record of a horse in Egypt is the so-called Buhen horse unearthed at Thebes, dated to the seventeenth century B.C., possibly the eighteenth, and thus about the beginning of the Hyksos period. What is more, this animal could be interpreted as being used for serious riding. It was larger than a pony. On its back was a rectangular piece of linen and leather which might be considered a saddle cloth. And this was attached to pieces which went around the horse's neck and other pieces which formed a girth (Chard, 1937).

After the Buhen horse the oldest Egyptian record of the horse is a wodden figure of a groom riding a horse dated at 1550 B.C. Wentworth mentions two other extremely early Egyptian finds. One is an engraving on the Tomb of Pihiri of "a perfect Arabian" type horse which she claims dates to 2000 B.C. (Wentworth, 178). If this engraving is in fact what she purports it to be, it is indeed odd that others have not often referred to it, but this is not the case. Further, the date of 2000 B.C. would place the horse in Egypt, probably about the same time it appeared in central Mesopotamia well before it appeared anywhere in Africa and as already a "perfect Arabian type," a claim which is certainly unacceptable when associated with such antiquity.

Wentworth also reproduces a picture of an Egyptian royal scarab presumably dated at 1503 B.C. of a man riding a horse. The rider sits far back on the animal's croup without a saddle in a manner similar to the more famous wall relief from Horemheb's tomb at Saqqara of a groom riding horseback (1342–1303 B.C.). However, on the scarab there are no noticeable reins and the rider appears to have his arms upraised holding a sword and shield (?). In fact the rider's legs appear to be hanging on one side of the horse almost over the hind legs (Wentworth, 133).

Possibly the earliest Egyptian example of a horseman is found on a plaque dated to the reign of Thutmose III (1490–1436 B.C.). Schulman lists eight examples of horsemen portrayed on materials from the XVIII Dynasty (1570–1303 B.C.) (Schulman, 264 ff.). Riding was probably not common in second millenium B.C. Egypt. It has been claimed that the earlier illustrations mainly depict grooms and stable boys riding, suggesting it was more of the order of a lark and not a practice of nobility. Schulman, on the contrary, believes the riders are mounted scouts since the representations are largely in a military connection and there would be a demand for scouts by the military (Schulman, 271). On the other hand, several illustrations show riders sitting bareback near or over the horse's croup – a rather insecure seat, especially if moving with some haste. As in Mesopotamia, riding could not acquire significance in hunting or warfare until there were horses large enough to bear men on their backs at a sustained canter or gallop.

The paramount use of the horse during the second and first part of the first millenium B.C. was as a chariot animal for which there is a great abundance of evidence after 1500 B.C.

At least from the time of Horemheb (14th century B.C.), horses were directed through a snaffle bit, either a straight or a jointed mouthpiece. Cheek pieces were sometimes fitted with spikes which stuck into both cheeks when the reins were pulled. A dropped nose band was used on early Egyptian chariot horses so that when the reins were pulled the band tightened across the soft tissues of the nose and impeded breathing. Reliefs from Amarna portray the dropped noseband as well as slit nostrils. Littauer believes this operation was an attempt to compensate for the impaired breathing caused by the low noseband. When the low noseband disappeared in antiquity, she notes, so do slit nostrils (Littauer, M.A., 293).

Horses in ancient Egypt were stabled and hand-fed and closely attended by grooms, owned as they were exclusively by nobility. Egypt provides the earliest evidence for branding of livestock, about 2000 B.C.; the idea may have spread from here to other parts of the Middle East and eventually into Europe after the beginning of the Christian era.

THE HORSE IN EARLY NORTH AFRICA AND THE SAHARA

The Sahara contains a number of rock paintings pertaining to horses dating from 1500–600 B.C. Thus it was not long after the introduction of the horse to Egypt that it spread across Saharan Africa. Over three hundred representations of chariots have been found in Tassili in the Hoggar district, Adrar in southern Morocco, and in south-western Algeria and into Mauritania. Such a wide and scattered distribution proves the employment of the chariot by widely separated peoples in the Sahara. The use of the chariot in the Sahara is further substantiated by texts of the XVIII Dynasty and by later Greek and Roman authors.

The rock carvings more commonly depict racing scenes rather than military ones, since chariots have no quivers or bow pouches and shields and lances are rarely noted in the hands of charioteers (Lhote, 1953). The fact that reins lead directly to the horse's mouth without rein rings, the style of the human figures, their dress, the use of the flying gallop art style in portraying the horses all suggest connections with the early island civilizations of the eastern Mediterranean, such as the Minoans, Mycenaeans and Achaeans. Lhote attributes the introduction of the horse chariot and the art complex connected with it to these island peoples who landed in Cyrenaica in 1230 B.C. with the intention of conquering Egypt. Lhote believes that when they failed in this endeavour, they settled in Libya from where their art and horsemanship diffused throughout the Sahara (Lhote, 1953).

Over seventy years ago Ridgeway propounded the theory that the ancient inhabitants of Libya had independently domesticated the horse, developing a light breed from among indigenous wild horses of the Sahara. He argued that it was from them that the Egyptians acquired both the horse and the chariot. Ridgeway laid a great deal of stress upon a light chariot with two wheels, each having four spokes, found in a tomb at Thebes of a period not later than the fourteenth century B.C. He believed this to be a Libyan chariot and that "it is therefore probable that the Egyptians obtained their light four spoked chariot from the Libyans and along with it the horse" (Ridgeway, 227). He claimed the chariot is not of Egyptian manufacture, and it has been observed that the wood was of "northern origin".

It has since been determined that the wood was from the Caucasus and the chariot was indeed of Egyptian manufacture (Tarr, L., 74). We know that both horse and chariot were employed by a variety of peoples in south-west Asia by 1600–1700 B.C. and about this time the horse was introduced into Egypt. The earliest substantiated dates for the horse in Egypt and south-west Asia are older by centuries than any dates for Libya. The major thrust of diffusion of the horse into North Africa is from the north-east. Further, Lhote offers fairly strong evidence that the Libyan horse complex was introduced by proto-Greek settlers, but only after the horse had already come to Egypt. Lastly there is no trace of any African horse in Paleolithic or Neolithic times out of which a possible Libyan horse might be derived. It would appear that Ridgeway's thesis, as a result of several decades of further research can no longer be upheld.

From the Roman and Greek authors we know specifically of two Saharan peoples who were horsemen: the Garamantians and the Numidians. The country of the Garamantians encompassed the region north of Darfur and the Wadai in the middle Sahara and included the Fezzan. They were once nomadic herders who travelled in ox carts, but were presumably taught irrigation by the Romans and became settled farmers. Herodotus says their warriors drove four-horse chariots; he recognized that the Greeks had acquired such a rig from them. However, the rock engravings show only two- and three-horse chariots except for one discovered not too many years ago which according to Bovill is "a crude but unmistakable drawing of a four-horse chariot . . ." (Bovill, 16). Herodotus also tells us that chariot use among the Garamantians eventually gave way to cavalry (Herodotus, 301–4). It may be that horse riding was actually not introduced into the Sahara until about 600 B.C.

The Garamantians became the middle men in the trade of ivory, slaves, and carbuncles between Rome and sub-Saharan Africa. They lived along the central trans-Saharan chariot route that went west from Egypt to the Fezzan, then apparently south-west via Tassili in the Hoggar to the Niger (Law, 1967).

The Numidians lived in what is present-day Algeria and were Berber neighbours of the Carthaginians. Strabo says both men and women rode small, spirited horses although Ridgeway believes they must have been docile, no doubt because of the technique of control. They were guided by a switch turning left when struck on the right side of the neck and right when struck on the left, and stopping when being swatted on the nose just like a donkey is guided in North Africa today. But the horse was also fitted with a neckband from which hung a leading rein. The neckband acted as an aid in stopping the horse and the lead rein as an aid in catching him if one is dismounted (Strabo, VIII, 167; Livy, XXXV, 11). These devices are employed by many Arab horsemen today, although reins are used for controlling the horse while riding.

The Numidians were aware of the bridle and bit from the Carthaginians and used them for their mules; a fourth century B.C. vase shows a Numidian riding with bridle, reins and bit (Trench, 22). It is therefore likely they employed a variety of devices for horse control.

In Northern Darfur men mounted on saddled horses are painted on rocks. Yet there is a problem in dating these finds. Balfour-Paul writes that it is reasonable to attribute them to "Neolithic people" but "most of the paintings in the Tagabo and Furnung Hills are evidently later, since the horse and even the camel make their appearance. But the dating of cave paintings is notoriously dangerous; the writer has seen a horse on the wall of an ancient cave in the Tagabo Hills whose red ochre was still wet!" (Balfour-Paul, 4).

ARABIA AND THE HORN OF AFRICA

Despite the fact that Arabia is renowned for its famous saddle horses, it is not only a land of few horses, but one in which the horse was a relatively late comer. The earliest possible evidence for horses in the

Arabian peninsula is for the eighth century B.C. and this does not indicate how widespread they were. Sargon II (722 – 703 B.C.) of Assyria recieved in 715 B.C. from "Samsi, queen of Arabia, It' amara (Yith'i-amara), the Sabaean chief, and from other kings of Egypt and the desert 'gold, products of the mountain, precious stones, ivory, seed of the maple (?), all kinds of herbs, horses, and camels, as their tribute'." (Hitti, 1953, 38). Until about the time of Srgon II no Arabians were ever portrayed with horses; they were always riding camels.

Archaeological investigations of the ancient Himyaritic and other kingdoms in south-western Arabia reveal no evidence of early use of the horse. Indeed, the horse is a very rare animal and all portrayals and statues of them seem to be of the post Christian era. A bronze horse bears the inscription: "Hawf'atat Yuha'din Gayman, the ruler of the tribe of Gayman dedicated to Rahman these two horses and their saddles in the temple called Qantan of the clan of Madrahum for the protection of himself and for the protection of the country of Gayman and of the camels he has . . . " There has been one suggestion that this bronze statue dates from 450 B.C., but another interpretation is that it is fourth to seventh centuries A.D., on the basis of the claim that Rahman an is the name of the Christian god (Jamme, 318).

Ahmad Fakhry reproduces three small objects presumably from Marib which show horses of a light oriental type, but they are not dated and probably do not go back before the Christian era (Fakhry, 133). South Arabia as well as other parts of Arabia contain rock drawings of men mounted on horseback, but again they are not dated and most seem to be since the beginning of the Muslim era.

It may be then that horses were introduced into the Arabian peninsula as early as the eighth century B.C. and probably gradually percolated southward, but as today they have never been anything but rare and precious animals. Judith Wentworth's claim, therefore, that Oriental stock originated in Arabia, specifically, in the Nejd, as a totally separate and ancient race and that such stock was introduced into Africa from Arabia is not tenable.

The horse probably never entered Ethiopia until after the beginning of the Christian era. Stiehler places the introduction of the horse as late Axumite times, (the Axumite period extended from the 1st–2nd centuries B.C. to the 7th century A.D.) (Stiehler, 260). Epstein puts the date of introduction even later into the eleventh century at which time they were introduced by Arabs. "Massudi, who travelled at the coast in A.D. 917, found only riding oxen for military use." (Epstein, 1971a, 428).

THE HORSE AMONG THE MEDES, PERSIANS, AND PARTHIANS

Horses had been introduced early into ancient Iran and were used for chariot purposes by the Kassites and Elamites in western Iran in the second millenium B.C. Horseback riding occurred by the end of the second or beginning of the first millenium B.C. since a cylinder seal from Sialk B in western Iran shows horseback riders (Barnett, 2998–9; Ghirshman, 1961, 71). Ghirshman believes Sialk B at this time represented the culture of the first Iranian tribes who about 1000 B.C. reached western Iran (Ghirshman, 1961, 71). The Luristan bronzes including rein rings, cheek pieces and bits have been variously dated from as early as the mid-second millenium B.C. to as late as the eighth century B.C. (Porada, 1964, 9–10). Porada believes that some of the cheek pieces are before the eighth century B.C. (Porada, 1964, 27).

In particular, the northern Luristan region was considered good horse breeding country. In the heat and drought of summer horses and cattle could be driven into the mountains and foothills for pasture (Porada, 1965, 75). Ancient Media was also important for horse rearing in the first half of the first millenium B.C. Here alfalfa grew, providing the best quality fodder for horses (Herzfeld, 7). Diodorus, in reporting the marches of Alexander, writes: ". . . on pastures of 'Medean grass' (alfalfa), the Nesaen horses were bred, only 60,000 instead of 160,000 of old" (Herzfeld, 9). Generally, north-western Iran and south-eastern Anatolia (Urartu or, later, Armenia) comprised an extensive horse breeding area from the second millenium B.C. The famous Nesaean horses raised in western Iran were not clearly distinguishable from those of Turkestan. This and other data appear to support the view that the Nesaean horse belongs to the horse breeding tradition of lower Asia and to the steppe type (Hancar, 370).

The Assyrian kings undertook to protect the horse breeding of western Iran (Nawar area) by prohibiting the import of stallions and mares apparently to keep horse breeding in the hands of the local population.

Herzfeld believes the ethnic name for the Persians – Fars – derived from a word for horse. Ancient Mesopotamian texts record ANSU-KUR-RA, "ass of a foreign land", as the word for horse. In Sumerian the word *sisu* from Indo-European was used by 2000 B.C. (Herzfeld, 2,5). Later, *si.su. u pa. ra. si.i* becomes horse and from *pa. ra. si.i* we get Farsi. A modification of this also became an Arabic word for horse and from that we have our word "farrier", or horseshoer (Herzfeld, 186).

Ownership of horses carried great prestige in ancient Iran and the number a man owned was a sign of his status. The landowners, as the Persian nobility, constituted the source for the Persian cavalry. No gentleman would ever be seen on foot (Xenophon, *Cyropaedia*, IV, iii, 23). Horses were primarily in demand as cavalry mounts and for chariots. Persian military superiority in the early centuries of the empire was no doubt in part due to the employment of the Nesaean horses which were apparently the largest then known to the "Western" world (Herodotus, 219).

The horse provided an early means of rapid communication which is essential to the maintenance of an extended empire. Not only did the ancient Persians build the first major empire, but they at the same time developed a network of roads and an elaborate system of royal messengers. Posting stations were placed at intervals of a day's ride. "Nothing stops these couriers from covering their allotted stage in the quickest possible time – neither snow, rain, heat, nor darkness. The first at the end of his stage, passes the dispatch to the second, the second to the third, and so on along the line . . . " (Herodotus, 531). The first part of these famous remarks of Herodotus describing the Persian courier system has become the motto of the United States postal system.

Herodotus claims the Persians were the inventors of the postal service. In any case it seems likely that no empire so enormous as the Persian could long be held together without the rapid transport provided by the horseback riding courier. Thus, as horse and chariot and cavalry became the primary devices for imperial conquest, so also the horse provided an essential means for maintaining that realm by efficient communication.

Horses were important to the Persians in games and racing. There were yearly races on a course in the shape of an ellipse. One circuit was about 1440 yards long and circuits were "made three, five, seven, and nine times". Nine times equalled about seven miles (Herzfeld, 21). Such courses were much longer than the Roman circuses.

Polo is a game of central Asiatic origin obviously closely related to bagai and buzkashi still played in Afghanistan and Turkestan. The name polo comes from the Tibetan word f ball, "pulu," but the earliest record of polo playing is from ancient Persia in the 6th century B.C. It probably spread eastward and westward from Iran and the Tibetan name has come to us because polo was introduced to India from Tibet and in India was learned by British colonialists in the early nineteenth century, who in turn introduced it to Europe; thence, it spread to other parts of the world. In its most ancient form the game was played at major festivals and the ball itself was a fertility symbol.

As many as a thousand men were on each team (Editorial Research Reports, 1971). Thus, in its earliest form it had closer similarities to the game of bagai and was also a religious rite.

Another role for the horse in ancient Persia was for payment of tribute. Part of the tribute of the Medean satrapy of Persia was pasturage for 50,000 Nesaean horses for the king. The Armenian satrapy provided 20,000 Nesaean foals each year for the king at the Mithra feast (see below). And Cilicia provided a white horse for each of the 360 days of the year as a "gift" (Olmstead, 291–5).

Finally, the Iranians, like their other Indo-European relatives, incorporated the horse into their system of religious sacrifices. Mithra, as a god of light, truth and integrity appears in the ancient Vedas and the Avesta as well. He is identified as "the lord of the wide pastures" – the one who renders them fertile. Zoroaster reduced Mithra to being one of several lesser genii, in his attempt to elevate Ahura Mazda as a supreme god. But the Persians continued to honour Mithra and other similar genii, particularly since they associated Mithra with many personified abstractions they had come to worship – as protector of warriors, defender of truth, justice, etc. Thus Mithra worship was reintroduced into Persia after Zoroaster (Cumont, 1–3). Mithra drove a chariot of four white horses who were shod in gold, were immortal and fed on ambrosia. The Nesaean horses came to be sacrificed to Mithra on New Year's day as representatives of these sacred white horses of the solar chariot (Olmstead, 25). At Persepolis thousands of animals were slaughtered daily for food at the royal court, including horses, camels, asses and ostriches (Olmstead, 183). On Cyrus' death, once a month thereafter a horse was given for sacrifice (Olmstead, 66).

For riding, a bit which apparently had the function of a curb was frequently employed. The sidebars extended around under the lower jaw. On the basis of illustrations depicting Persian horses, Trench argues that curbs were employed since a snaffle "acting on the corners of a horse's lips pulls his head up" while the curb holds the head down and the Persian horses are shown "over bent and over the bit" (Trench, 19). Snaffles with sharp edged discs and spiked rollers were also used by both Persians and Greeks and these, particularly with a hard-handed rider, produced a bloody foam (Trench, 23). Some riders guided their mounts with nose bands which contained small metal barbs. Bridle throatlashes were secured by toggles. Martingales were used but not spurs (Berenger, 132).

According to Strabo the pace of Persian horses was the amble. In reference however, to Pliny's statement that Spanish horses ambled as a natural gait, Anderson has said that Spanish and Parthian horses travelled instead at a fast, short-stepping, high-actioned trot (Anderson, 29). Presumably this alternative interpretation might likewise apply to the Persians rather than describing their gait as an amble.

In the middle of the first millenium B.C. in western Iran plantations and palm groves were all fenced, indicating to Herzfeld that horses grazed in open pastures (Herzfeld, 28). This was especially the case in the Nesaean area where there were so many horses, stabling would have been impossible. Hobbles were employed (Xenophon, *Cyropaedia*, III, iii) and at least one branch of the Persians used lassos, but apparently mainly as an implement of warfare (Herodotus, 443). Both Armenians and Persians roached the manes of their horses and apparently devoted considerable time to grooming at least some of them.

The culturally creative role of the ancient Persians is generally underestimated and unappreciated in the western world. At the same time they have been too often represented in Western history as a fearsome barbarian host, overlooking the degree to which Greece, and thus Rome and the West in general, were enriched by Persian culture. This applies not only to the uses of the horse, but to the less mundane realm of the religious ideology as well.

The Parthians, who followed after the Persians, were equally great horsemen. They were originally semi-nomadic herders deriving from a branch of the Scythians in north-eastern Iran. In the third century B.C. they founded a kingdom and proceeded to conquer Iran. Their cavalry was of great note and constituted the main part of their armies. It was divided into two types: horse archers and heavily armed cavalry (sagittarii and cataphractii). From the horse archers we get the term "Parthian shot" or "parting shot". That is, these warriors would feign flight from an opponent. As they withdrew with the enemy in pursuit, they would turn in their seats and shoot arrows back at their pursuers. The general technique of the mounted archer is, it should be noted, not an invention of the Parthians themselves, but is culturally and histori-cally related to the prior development of equestrian pastoral nomadism and the horse archer among many peoples in central Asia during the first millenium B.C.

The other wing of the Parthian army, the cataphractii, wore plaited armour from head to foot and the horses were armoured as well. Since the riders had no stirrups and gripped with their knees, the armour could not be too heavy. Nevertheless, all this extra weight necessitated larger mounts which were acquired from Nesaean breeders and also from the famous Ferghana area in Turkestan. The cataphractii antici-pated the heavily armoured Medieval knight. This heavy cavalry could effectively attack fully armed infantry, but with enormous losses of men and horses (Colledge, 65). They were more readily thrown from their horses than Medieval knights, but almost as helpless when dismounted.

Like the Persians, the Parthians had a class society based on irrigation agriculture and pastoral activity and a religion involving the practice of horse sacrifices. The aristocracy were described by Justin in the Epitome of Pompeius Trogus: "On horses they go to war, to banquets, to public and private tasks and on them they travel, stay still, do business and chat." Only slaves went on foot (Colledge, 93). By the second century A.D. the aristocrats probably played polo (Colledge, 94).

INDIA

It seems likely that the first Indian horse is to be associated with the Indo-European migrations and conquests in north and western India about the mid-second millenium B.C. Any evidence of horses before this time is extremely scarce and suggests that if there were horses they were most rare and uncommon animals. Possibly the horse was present in late Mohenjo Daro times (ca. 2000 B.C.). Terracotta figurines presumed to indicate the horse in Harappa culture in Punjab, at approximately the same time, are considered by Allchin to be "at best equivocal" (Allchin, 1969, 319–320). At Hallur, in south India, horse bones and rock paintings of horses and riders have been found and dated at between 1400 – 1050 B.C. (Allchin and Allchin, 165).

Indo-European peoples have the primary responsibility for the diffusion of the horse and the chariot in India. The spoked wheeled chariot drawn by a pair of horses was originated by them in the early second millenium B.C. on the northern fringes of Sumer and Akkad before their invasion of Mesopotamia (Piggott, 1950, 274).

In ancient India the horse seems to have been almost exclusively a chariot animal and reserved as well for occasional sacrifice. There is only a single reference to horse riding in the Rig Veda "and then it was described in such a way as to indicate that it was exceptional" (Ridgeway, 151).

The chariot corps was the elite of the army and all the best horses were taken for it. If it were defeated in a battle, so was the entire army. Drivers were recruited from the aristocracy (Auboyer, 130). The ancient Indo-European chariot in India was a spoked wheeled vehicle and the horses were harnessed to a central pole with a yoke, an arrangement similar to other early chariots. Piggott believes "[t]here is some evidence for the use of traces on the outer sides, and one word (*vani*) might have the significance of a swingle-tree or splinter-bar to which these were fastened" (Piggott, 1950, 279). If so, this would be the earliest suggestion of this sort of device.

Chariot racing became an important sport in India and took place on a course to a marker around which the driver turned and returned over the same route. It is possible that the idea of the Roman Circus and of Greek courses descended from such Indian examples (Piggott, 267). On the other hand it would seem more probable that the Greeks acquired the idea more directly from the Persians. That the Persians acquired it in turn from India is not unlikely, although, given the fact that both peoples are Indo-European, it is not unreasonable to suspect that each could have separately evolved the race course from a common ancient practice of competitive chariot racing.

Sacrifice was a third role of the horse in ancient India although it was not a common practice. From early Vedic times "the horse was associated with the idea of universal sovereignty" (Auboyer, 128). When through conquest a king had enlarged his realm to attain "the dimensions of an empire" he undertook a ceremony extending over a year in which he sacrificed a horse who had to be a carefully selected stallion, "a splendid racer . . . with no physical defects". Between February and March the horse was let loose in a herd of geldings. He was set off to move freely under the guard of a party of nobles. At the end of a year the king took possession of the area that had been covered by the horse and the claim was enforced by the accompanying warriors. The horse was then returned to its starting point. Twenty-one sacrificial posts were erected in an open space. To these various animals were tethered and then sacrificed. On the second day the stallion was sacrificed by strangulation, since his blood should not be shed. The stallion was offered to the personification of the universal "Self", Prajapati.

Parts of the stallion were held to correspond to specific seasons and divisions of the universe. "[T]he consecrated horse contained in himself the Year and its divisions, the cosmos and all its spatial and terrestrial components. By sacrificing the stallion the king identified himself with it, he recomposed the great, dispersed Whole so as to render himself master of it, and from thenceforth he was the Universal Sovereign" (Auboyer, 128). Such a sacrifice was very costly and limited to such occasions. It is obvious that it was actually a rare occurrence in ancient India. The sacrifice "was performed by the Maurya emperors in the third century B.C." It fell into dususe after 176 B.C., but was restored by the Gupta dynasts in 333 A.D. The last horse sacrifice was probably in the ninth century A.D. (Auboyer, 129). Joseph Thaliath describes a present day Hindu ceremony in which he feels there may be relics of the past horse sacrifice. However, no horses are employed in the ceremony (Thaliath, 1952).

Early Indian horse riding techniques and technology in many respects followed the general pattern of the Near East, but by the late second century B.C., as is indicated on sculptures at Sanchi, Pathaora Bhaja and Mathura, the Indians began to use the stirrup loop, an important predecessor to the true stirrup. It remains a question as to whether these leather loops were merely used as an aid in mounting or if they were employed as toe or foot supports in riding. If they were intended as foot "stirrups" they were probably not very safe devices since it would be too easy to get one's foot entangled in the flexible leather loop at the wrong moment. On the other hand, it is possible they were toe stirrups. Indian riders were barefooted, whereas those of the north wore boots. Thus, such a device would be practicable and we know that toe stirrups soon became common in India and later in south-east Asia.

A find of a pair of iron bars with looped ends from Nagpur in central India and dated just prior to the beginning of the Christian era has been interpreted as being iron stirrups. Also a Kushan seal dated at the first century A.D. is believed to show stirrups (Leshnik, 147). If the latter are stirrups, they suggest an effort on the part of peoples in Northern Pakistan and Afghanistan to adapt the toe stirrup to the need of boots (White, 15).

While toe stirrups were most likely common in India proper before the first century A.D., full foot stirrups are not recorded there until the tenth century, which is rather curious since they appear in Java at Borobudur in the eighth century (White, 140).

Arrian, a Greek historian of the second century A.D., reported that the ancient Indians used a noseband fixed with pointed pieces of iron or brass which were "moderately" sharp. The rich used ivory points and in the horse's mouth was a "piece of iron like a spit, to which the reins are fitted". Thus, both spit and noseband controlled the horse when the reins were pulled (Anderson, 46).

Indian archaeological remains have also yielded various types of snaffle bits and in the early centuries A.D. bits with curblike features appear probably ultimately resultant from Roman diffusion (Leshnik, 149).

Horses as prized possessions of an aristocracy were kept in stalls and carefully attended by grooms. When put out to graze they were hobbled. A king's stable maintained a large staff and horses were fed barley, peas, and oats; sometimes they were fed "root vegetables steeped in honey" or, on military campaigns, "wine to 'dope' the animals" (Auboyer, 130). They might also be given peas boiled in sugar and butter (Berenger, 133). Each horse had his own name and one was selected as the royal steed. Stallions were sometimes gelded, although mares were preferred for the chariots (Piggotss, 1950, 266).

King and nobles were trained at an "early age, to become 'horse experts'." Indian technical treatises give some information on how a horse was broken. It was tethered to a post by a cord and forced to trot and gallop round and round the post, so that the rope's length was gradually reduced and the circumference of the circle shortened (Auboyer, 130).

In ancient India the horse represented the epitome of aristocracy, the warrior's valour and a mark of great wealth and prestige. And in central and southern India it continues to be so associated, being retained almost exclusively as a riding animal.

CHINA

Huppertz reports finds of horse teeth ca. 3000 B.C. in excavations of Yang shao culture in Shansi province, north China (Huppertz, 1961b, 193). Whether these are supposed to be wild or domesticated animals is not specified since the remains were subjected to no systematic analysis (Huppertz, 1961b, 193). It would appear more likely that they are teeth of wild horses since the next indication of horses in China is not until the Lungshan culture period (2400 B.C. – 1850 B.C.) in north-east China. Here their remains are extremely rare. What is more, there is a question again as to whether the animals found even at this date were domesticated. If they were, they were in all likelihood used for chariots since riding was not known in China until a thousand years later, and there is no record of extensive horse flesh consumption in early China, nor any great likelihood they were at this time used in sacrifice (Creel, 1938, 219). At the same time, remains of chariots have never been found in Lungshan sites (Chang, 237).

Interestingly enough Lungshan culture shows some affinities with northern Iranian and east Caspian cultures. Certainly the horse was introduced to China from the west or more likely the north-west and the central Asiatic steppes (e.g. areas of Afanaseyskaya and Andronovo cultures of the third and second millenia B.C.).

Unquestionable evidence of the domestic horse is associated with the Shang Dynasty (1850 or 1766–1122 B.C.). The Shang were farmers and cattle breeders controlling north China. They were a direct development out of a sedentary Neolithic farming culture (Creel, 1937, -81). At the Anyang site associated with Shang culture there were uncovered a large number of horses, cattle, sheep, pigs and dog bones, with cattle and pig the most numerous (Creel, 1938, 183). The Anyang site contained thirty-eight horses all wearing bridles, all apparently sacrificed. Thus we may surmise that the horse was part of a sacrificial or funerary cult, although Creel states that on the whole the horse was rarely sacrificed. Oracles were asked what was desired for sacrifice and these were invariably animals, but the horse was not common (Creel, 1937, 200).

We may also surmise that the horse was used as a chariot or cart animal at least by mid-second millenium B.C. In Shang times the chariot was probably not prominent in war, but used more in battle to transport commanders and to direct fighting rather than in actual battle encounters (Creel, 1937, 153). The chariot was also employed in hunting expeditions and in the capture of wild horses for purposes of domestication (Creel, 1937, 74). Of over 10,000 pieces of published materials of this time, the character for chariot occurs only nine times (Creel, 1937, 149). This character (*chhe*) is really a picture of a chariot drawn from above and in the Shang Dynasty it was rendered thus:

In later Chinese writing it is modified and becomes the symbol for vehicle:

The early chariots required two horses, but four became common by the Chou Dynasty (1027–233 B.C.) and even six horse hitches were not unknown. With the four horse team, the centre horses were hitched to a shaft and the other two were added on either side of the centre horses, hitched a little further back from the centre ones with a loose trace, thus producing a fan-like appearance (Creel, 1938, 186). Creel believes this method originated from initially employing a third horse to help pull the chariot out of mud. An ingenious device of six reins to guide four horses was developed and the chariot carried a driver who stood in the middle of the vehicle, with an archer on his left (the chief place) and a lanceman on his right for balance.

Vassal lords were expected to provide definite numbers of horses and chariots according to their estate and rank. The number of chariots available to a ruler was the measure of the power of his state. The great importance attached to the chariot as a machine of war and to other wheeled vehicles in the Chou period is underlined by the development of roads and the classification of roads into pathways, roads for vehicles of narrow gauge, roads for broad gauge vehicles, "roads wide enough for wagons to pass one another (and) highroads taking three wagons abreast" (Tarr, L., 92).

Horse sacrifice persisted into Chou times. At Hsün Hsien seventy-two horses and twelve chariots were interred in royal tombs. When they were buried the horses were apparently hitched to the chariots from which the wheels had been removed (Creel, 1937, 335).

During the Chou Dynasty as well, horse meat was eaten rather generally but the practice later disappeared. "Tribes west of China bred and fed horses specifically for the purpose" (Epstein 1971b, 96).

Chinese scholars are known to have concerned themselves with the conformation of the horse. An account in an encyclopaedia of agriculture from the Han period (130 A.D.) provides the earliest surviving statement on horse judging (Epstein, 1971b, 99).

Horsemanship in China appears to have been in a rather static condition until the fourth century B.C. at which time a major revolution occurred. As a result of experiences with the Hunnish nomad horsemen to the north and the defeats of Chinese chariotry at their hands, the Chinese adopted horseback riding and abandoned the war chariot. This, it should be noted, was some four centuries after cavalry had replaced chariotry in the Near East. Along with riding, the Chinese adopted the Hunnish horses, riding gear and the boots and pants of the nomads which were more suited to riding than flowing robes. This original horseman's attire has become the general pattern of Chinese national costume surviving to this day.

The Chinese taught their horses the ambling pace which is still popular there. This gait was natural among a few horses, but for the most part had to be taught, by the practice of training them to walk with the legs of each side tied together. Ambling, Jankovich writes, was unknown in central Asia and probably originated in south-west Asia in imitation of the camel (Jankovich, 125). Such a view seems questionable. Although we do not know the kinds of gaits employed by the ancient Scythians and others of the early Eurasian steppes, the amble was perhaps the gait used by the ancient Persians and it is a perfectly common gait amongst contemporary central Asiatic horsemen, while on the other hand it is less common today in south-west Asia. If, further, the Chinese adopted the riding horse, riding gear and dress of the Huns and their kinsmen, it is only reasonable to expect that they adopted their riding gaits as well. Thus, the amble of the Chinese would be derived from their equestrian pastoral neighbours.

The amble is so widespread mainly because it is an easy gait for the rider, but Trench believes it is especially hard on the horse since he feels "the horse's equilibrium is maintained better by a diagonal than by a lateral pace" (Trench, 67). Summerhays states it is tiring for the horse (Summerhays, 1952, 18). These observations may have some credence especially in regard to a horse inadequately trained to an amble. Yet for some horses and for all camels it is the natural gait, which would raise the question of why a natural gait should be harder on an animal than another it must learn. Historical, travel and ethnographic accounts of central Asia are replete with reports of the great distances covered by steppe horses and of other testimonies to their great endurance as riding animals. Presumably a good part of their travel was at an ambling gait.

It is possible the first stirrups were introduced in China during the Han Dynasty (202 B.C. –221 A.D.). Needham considers them linked to the spread of Buddhism from India where loop stirrups were known in the second century B.C. and may have been used as toe stirrups for barefoot riders. The Chinese as booted riders had to modify the latter into full foot stirrups and these seem to be present in a clay model of a mounted figure excavated from a tomb dated to the fourth century A.D. in Changsha. Also, Wu Liang shrine reliefs (147 A.D.) *might* indicate a foot stirrup. On the other hand, the earliest sure evidence for the foot stirrup in China comes from Hunan Province in the early part of the fifth century and during that century a considerable number of clear demonstrations of the use of this device occur in China (White, 15).

Jope accredits the Han Dynasty Chinese as having a padded saddle but not a wood frame one (Jope, 556). Maenchen-Helfen states categorically that the Chinese of this period possessed "wooden saddles": "The riderless horses on some reliefs from Shantung undoubtedly were saddled: the front and back bows and the saddle tree are clearly delineated". He admits, however, that there are also representations of horses with padded saddles. "It has become almost a dogma," writes Maenchen-Helfen, "to derive everything in the equipment of the cavalry of the Chinese from their barbarian neighbours", but the archaeological evidence indicates the Huns had pad saddles when the Chinese had wooden ones (Maenchen-Helfen, 209).

In Han times horses were ridden regularly as cavalry in war, and combat was transformed by the introduction of long iron swords. At the same time there arose an interest in spirited horses and ones which were apparently bigger than those of the nomads, so as to fight them more effectively.

A superior breed of blood sweating,[1] "heavenly" horses in the Ferghana Valley on the Syr Darya (river) in Turkestan was reported to the Emperor Wu in 126 B.C. Yetts argues that the Emperor resolved to acquire horses of this type purely for practical reasons. "We may assume the reason was not that he was merely a lover of horses, but that he saw a means of countering the ever-present Hsiung-nu (Hun) menace. By mounting his cavalry on horses larger and fleeter than the small steppe breed, which apparently was the only kind known in the Far East, he hoped to beat the nomads at their own tactics" (Yetts, 232).

Arthur Waley has proposed a different explanation. He claims nothing in Chinese sources suggests Ferghana horses were needed for military expeditions. The Emperor Wu simply wanted "Heavenly Horses which would carry him to Heaven" (Waley, 103). Chinese stories of legendary monarchs being carried up to heaven by magic steeds go back to the fourth century B.C. and it is on the basis of such beliefs that the emperor searched for a magic horse "born from" a stream to carry him to the abode of the immortals (Waley, *passim*). Since Chinese expeditions to the Ferghana region resulted in the acquisition of thousands of horses – thirty superior horses and 3000 of "middling or lower quality" – it would appear that both presumed motives would be satisfied: the "superior horses" would go to the Emperor Wu and the remaining added to the Chinese cavalry (Waley, 96).

Creel takes Waley to task for not explicitly recognizing that the Chinese used Ferghana horses in battle in Han times. He also contradicts Waley's statement that Ferghana horses were not larger than Chinese horses and, while crediting him with pointing to the religious-ideological aspects of the Ferghana expeditions of the Emperor Wu, believes Waley has far overrated their role (Creel, 1965).

In any case the cost of these horses was enormous to the Chinese. As a result of their military expeditions to acquire them they lost in three or four years "several hundred thousand human lives and a vast expenditure of material" (Yetts, 234), and in one year (119 B.C.) a loss of 100,000 of their own horses (Yetts, 243).

Yetts insists the historical records leave no room for doubt but that these horses were desired to improve the cavalry. From the tomb of the statesman Ch'ao ts'o we read: "Chinese horses cannot vie with [the nomad's horses] in climbing rocky heights or fording mountain tor-

[1] Blood sweating results from a parasite which is under the skin and causes bleeding when the horse is active in the summer months. Sweat mixes with the tiny amounts of blood and produces a pink colour. The parasite is still common in Central Asia (Epstein, 1971b, 96).

rents, nor our horsemen with theirs in galloping over steep paths or shooting arrows while in rapid motion" (quoted in Yetts, 236). "These words emphasize the fact that the environment of the Chinese and their mode of life as settled farmers had not encouraged horsemanship. Indeed, there seems to be no certain evidence that they took to riding before the latter part of the fourth century B.C. Even then the creation of cavalry and consequent adoption of nomad dress and equipment were measures probably confined for some time to the States of Chao and Ch'in which adjoined the Hsiung-nu and had to bear the brunt of nomad raids" (Yetts, 236).

Yetts believes that until the end of the second century B.C. the Chinese shared with their nomad northern neighbours one type of horse, a breed closely akin to the wild steppe breed which he identifies as Przewalski's horse (Yetts, 242). Zeuner among others has pointed out, however, that the horse of Mongolia is more a tarpan, if one can make a distinction between tarpan and Przewalski's horse (cf. Epstein, 1971a, 414). Nevertheless, what Yetts intends to convey is the existence of a single breed of what we would now recognize as the Mongol horse and, after this time, with the introduction of the Ferghana horses, a different type is added to the Chinese retinue (Yetts, 242). Hayashi discounts this view, holding that he has evidence that in the period of the Warring States (late Chou Dynasty 450 – 221 B.C.) the Chinese already possessed horses similar to the Ferghana type (Hayashi).

In addition to bringing the new horses from the west, the Emperor's expeditions also resulted in the importation of their trappings and, more important, the introduction of the growing of alfalfa as horse fodder. Yetts stresses the ancillary consequences for the Chinese as a result of these expeditions. "Conquest of the Ferghana resulted in the opening up of free communication between China and the West. A flood of importations, through commerce and otherwise, ensued, profoundly modifying Chinese civilization. A signal outcome was that the way became clear for the introduction of Buddhism, which probably occurred in B.C. 2" (Yetts, 255).

While the chariot was essentially abandoned by the Chinese after the fourth century B.C., during the Han Dynasty the horse was applied increasingly to freight wagons. Yet it was still sufficiently rare that it proved difficult to raise four of the same breed for the state carriage of the Son of Heaven, and simple folk as well as generals and high officials continued to ride in ox drawn wagons (Tarr, L., 96).

In Chhin and Han periods horse drawn chariots with two shafts appear (Needham, 248). A breast strap with two traces is characteristic of the Han period. The pressure from the breast strap is on the sternum, thus removing the obstruction to breathing created by the throat strap. The Chinese carriage depicted on a relief on the I-nan tombs from the end of the second century A.D. culminates the Han technique. A tomb relief shows breast strap harness with a girth which Han chariots did not often have. There are bifurcated shafts with traces "attached to the mid-points of the shafts". In heavy carts for baggage and timber lugs the traces attached "to the body of the vehicle itself . . ." (Needham, 309).

The breast strap was such an improvement over the throat strap that it rapidly replaced the throat strap in China, although amazingly enough, it was extremely slow in diffusing to the rest of the world. There is a possibility that the Ostrogoths introduced it to Italy as early as the fifth century. Another source of entry to Europe may have been the Avars in 568 A.D. (Needham, 319).

Another important innovation of the Han Chinese was the invention of breeching, as a device for backing a vehicle or slowing it down. The breeching strap passes around behind the horse under its tail and is hitched to the shafts at mid point. It is ordinarily supported by straps passing over the animal's back. In the fore part the shafts are attached to the collar or breast band.

Both Chinese and Romans are accredited with independently inventing the use of shafts on carts. The Romans, however, never made much use of them so that they do not become common in Europe until Mediaeval times (Jope, 554).

To the Chinese as well goes the credit for inventing the horse collar, the earliest record for which dates to the first century B.C. Later indications appear in the third century A.D. and in the Tunhuang frescoes in a cave temple in Kansu province dated between the fifth and eleventh centuries A.D. (Needham, 320).

Recently Bulliet has argued that the existing theory of the introduction of modern harnessing to Europe from the East may be "incomplete" if not wrong. He notes that the adoption of the camel by peasants of Roman Tunisia necessitated the invention of new devices for harnessing since the ox yoke did not work satisfactorily on camels. Experimentation with camel harnessing may have led here to an independent invention of the breast strap and possibly some kind of collar for horses. The breast strap applied to the horse may then have spread from Tunisia into Southern Europe (Bulliet, 1975, 194 ff.).

The central significance of the Chinese in the evolution of technology is well substantiated in their connection with the development of horse harnessing. In all likelihood they are responsible for modifying the loop and the toe stirrups into a full foot stirrup. There is a possibility that they were the inventors of the wood frame saddle. Most important of all they did invent the breast strap, the horse collar, traces, and breeching. Yet, the Chinese never seem to have developed large, heavy draught breeds which could more effectively utilize this kind of technology. The harnessing of large draught horses with shoulder collars and traces was an achievement left to northern Europeans.

From China horses were spread to Manchuria and Korea, where they were introduced during the early part of the Ki-ja Dynasty (1122 – 193 B.C.) for military purposes (Osgood, C., 215). The Vietnamese adopted the horse after their subjugation by the Chinese in 207 B.C.

Beginning in the third century A.D. a number of central Asiatic peoples reached Japan via Korea and left earth-covered burial mounds. In the tombs are *haniwa* figures, realistic hollow terra cotta figures of retainers, sentinels and horses, placed in rows around the slopes of the mounds. These may betray an earlier practice of burying the followers, servants and horses of the deceased. The *haniwa* show saddles, ring stirrups and reins and so demonstrate a knowledge of horsemanship and the attachment of some importance to it (Fairservis, 156).

The Indians, like the Chinese, spread the horse beyond their realms into south-eastern Asia at a similar time. Thus probably, in the first three centuries of the Christian era horses were introduced by the Indians to Burma, Thailand and the Indonesian islands. Yet, certainly the Arab Muslim traders who arrived several centuries later are primarily responsible for the diffusion of horse use and the expansion of their numbers in Indonesia.

GREEK AND ROMAN HORSEMANSHIP

The oldest well documented data on horse husbandry and horsemanship come from the Greeks and Romans. The Greeks were ostensibly great horse lovers, but there is thereby no reason to suppose they were any better horsemen than the Persians, Gauls or Assyrians; certainly they were superior to the Romans. Since most of Greece is comprised of extremely rocky and steep mountain and hill country there is little that is suitable for horse rearing. The Plains of Thessaly became the main centre for this pursuit.

Because of this natural constriction of horse breeding and the close identification of the animal with the warrior aristocrat, the horse in Greece commanded great prestige as a symbol of honour, valour and luxury. Horses and dogs were the only animals viewed with any sentimentality by the ancient Greeks (Brodrick, 109). As such horse use was limited fairly exclusively to the chariot and, later, increasingly to riding to war, to the hunt and in equestrian sports. The Greeks took a great deal of pride in the development of equestrian sports but they are by no means the originators. Most likely an unknown earlier central Asiatic people have a greater claim to this, as do the Persians and Indians.

While horsemanship as an art has earlier roots in Persia and Assyria, it was the Greeks who left the world the major legacy of this art, epitomized in Xenophon's *Art of Horsemanship* which not only gives us information on horsemanship but on horse management and husbandry as well. More will be said about this work below.

The Romans, being more "practical", expanded the use of the horse to more utilitarian ends, especially to using it as a pack animal and to a lesser extent on carts or carriages. They also had greater access to horses since with their empire they could draw them from areas better suited for their production.

Uses of the Horse by Greeks and Romans
The Military Role:

The earliest Greeks employed the horse and chariot, but Philip of Macedon began the transformation to cavalry, and by the time of Alexander, the Greeks had become horse riders. Romans were more definitely charioteers, reluctant to ride horseback into a military campaign. "This role they delegated to auxiliaries drawn from the non-Roman inhabitants of the provinces" (Jankovich, 50). They initially adopted the Greek style of riding, although they soon became amblers, gait unfamiliar to the Greeks.

After the Punic Wars Roman horsebreeding received a great impetus. Numidian horses introduced into Spain resulted in production of larger animals and "from then onward Iberia became the most important province as a source of remounts for the Roman cavalry arm, and also for the dissemination of good quality horses throughout the western part of the Empire" (Jankovich, 50). Roman cavalry, however, met defeat especially at the hands of the Parthians, and, in facing the Germanic tribes to the north, the Emperor Gallienus (260–8 A.D.) introduced major reforms in the cavalry. Until his time only the Roman legions had a staff of officers and hierarchy of command and the cavalry was under the legion officers. Jankovich believes such a situation was not conducive to military efficiency so that Gallienus established the cavalry as a separate corps with its own chain of command (Jankovich, 51). Nevertheless, Roman power does not seem to have profited much from this reform.

The Greeks and Romans both rode without stirrups and, for most of their history, without a true saddle, thus making it easier for a cavalier to be knocked off in battle. Lefebvre des Noëttes believed that a cavalry with a lance but without stirrups could not be used as shock troops. Vigneron however points out that combat between two warriors without stirrups is possible and one can with a good seat withstand a moderate shock without stirrups: if necessary one can, as Xenophon recommended, grasp hold of the mane. Vigneron refers to documented cases of both Greek and Roman cavaliers engaged in single combat and of the use of cavaliers charging with lances in a squadron or collective group (Vigneron, 239–240). Nevertheless these charges were only carried out at the crisis of battle. More important than stirrups in this kind of encounter would seem to be a saddle with a high cantle, but there is no early evidence of this. How then such riders were not pushed off the back ends of their horses on their lances' contact with an enemy is difficult to see.

Greek and Roman cavalry also made use of the javelin, and for shock troops this would seem to be a more efficient use of a cavalry which was mounted on stirrupless pad saddles or mere horse cloths. But, as the Romans learned, a massive cavalry composed of mounted archers as developed among the Parthians was an even more formidable war machine.

Greek horses were initially quite small and were later improved when horses similar to the Ferghana type were introduced from the East. Thus, Philip of Macedon imported 20,000 Scythian mares and Alexander took a spoil of 50,000 eastern horses from the Persians. These horses when crossed with the local European ones produced the larger horses used by the Roman cavalry (Bökönyi, 1968, 40). The foundation of the Eastern stock was formed by Scythian horses which spread "from Northern Iran and Southern Russia, by Scythian expansion and by trade" into Central Europe, North Africa and eastward to the Altai Mountains and, eventually, with the Yakuts, to the Arctic Ocean (Bökönyi, 1968, 41).

The Romans enhanced the horse's military significance by using mounts capable of bearing a rider at great speed, and in conjunction with close quartered lance shock attack and javelin throwing. While the Central Asiatics advanced the role of cavalry with the introduction of the mounted archer technique, full development of the most efficient and most effective cavalry still awaited the invention of the stirrup and the saddle tree. With a large horse and a saddle with a wooden frame and stirrups, a bowman had the support necessary for a better shot. Such a lethal combination of elements made all earlier forms of cavalry obsolete.

Finally, the importance of the horse to the Roman postal and courier services should be noted (Vigneron, 160–1). As was mentioned in connection with the elaboration of this system by the Persians such an arrangement was crucial to the maintenance of a far flung empire.

Greek and Roman Sport

Horse racing was developed into an important sport by both Greeks and Romans. They constructed hippodromes for this purpose but these were not so large as those of the Persians. Chariot racing and mounted racing were both enjoyed. There were acrobatics on horseback of which so-called Roman riding – standing one foot on the back of each of two horses – is most famous, although it was introduced by the Greeks. Another technique found in ancient Greece was to choose four horses and, as they trot or gallop, the rider jumps from one to the other. In the Roman circus riders mounted on horseback performed standing upright, springing from one horse to another, lying down on their backs, and picking up things from the ground at full gallop (Berenger, 68–9). Such acrobatics have remained little changed down to modern times in their contemporary role in the circus.

There were also military equestrian sports such as throwing javelins or darts from horses or riding with a lance to stick a post fixed in the ground. These may constitute the background for Mediaeval jousts, and tilting tournaments. Demonstrations of manoeuvres by groups of horsemen were featured at the hippodromes and in the agoras and sanctuaries of Athens as well. There were demonstrations of the horse's training although this was not as sophisticated as the "high school" dressage which developed in Europe in the seventeenth century. Vigneron believes that since the ancient bits were simple snaffles and there were no severe mouthpieces the rider was not permitted to perform the delicate nuances of action which are made possible by the modern bridle (Vigneron, 213). Anderson finds no evidence of horse jumping by the Greeks and concludes it was "probably not practiced in the schools" although one would have to jump ditches and the like in riding in the countryside (Anderson, 106).

The Romans not only expanded upon and extended the spectator sport aspect of horsemanship but added to it spectacles of violence. The Greeks had already engaged in bull fighting from horseback and the Romans fought other animals from horseback as well, including elephants. They also engaged in gladiatorial fights from horseback and from chariots. Out of this Graeco-Roman background we have, on the one hand, the continuation of bull fighting from horseback in Portugal and the refinement of Spanish bull fighting as it is perpetuated in south-western Europe and Spanish America. Even the bull riding in the modern rodeo has an archetype in ancient Minos, although this is not the direct source of that idea.

The ass was employed in Greek and Roman occasions for buffoonery as it is today in circuses and rodeos. Here again the Romans elaborated on the use of the ass for comedy purposes and sometimes brought asses to their banquets, especially one accustomed to eating from dishes, so that he would join in and entertain (?) the guests. (Vigneron, 215).

Horses were used by the Greeks and Romans for hunting sports, following the pattern of Mesopotamia and Egypt in hunting from the chariot and later on horseback.

The Greeks apparently rarely rode horseback for pleasure. We "never read of a Greek taking a ride for pleasure". "Their horses were bred and reared primarily to be machines of battle, or for the scarcely less fiercely contested struggles in the hippodrome" (Morgan in Xenophon, 1893, 100).

Vigneron says that because of the absence of stirrups one had to be in good condition to ride horseback; thus older people and women, and those not accustomed to riding never rode and it was a mode of transportation almost limited to the military, although all Roman aristocracy were expected to know how to ride (Vigneron, 160–1).

Draught and Pack Horses

Vigneron challenges Le Febvre des Noëttes' thesis that the Greeks and Romans were constrained in the development of adequate transportation techniques because of the lack of the horse collar and dependence upon the throat band for drawing carts and chariots. He believes that only the army would have faced difficulties because they required transportation of materials at great distances and at maximum speed. Since the Chinese, who invented the horse collar, persisted in extensive use of human porterage for moving goods it becomes a question as to how much that invention resulted in the freeing of human labour. Both the Greeks and Romans also depended upon human porterage; they made extensive use of a variety of other transport devices such as river boats, mules and oxen to tow river boats and mules, asses and occasionally, horses as pack animals.

Again Vigneron believes Le Febvre des Noëttes is in error in attributing lack of horse cartage to the absence of a proper shoulder or collar piece. To Vigernon the main reason horses and carriages were not developed was because of the conditions of the roads. In Mediterranean countries pack animals, he observes, were important in many regions (such as the Pelopennese, Crete, Sicily, the Apennines,

Arcadia, and Bosnia) down to the twentieth century. Thus for him the horse and carriage was limited by conditions of the highway especially when affected by wet weather (Vigneron, 149–150). On the other hand, in defence of Le Febvre de Noëttes, it is also obvious that a horse or mule pulling from a chest band or shoulder collar has much better traction than with the throat band and so could more readily draw a cart over bad roads. Also, note that horses with collars were used to draw carriages and carts in Mediaeval and Renaissance Europe and, later in America, when the roads could not have been better than in Roman times.

It seems fairly clear that horse cartage on the part of the Romans was impeded not by one factor alone, but by several: lack of efficient harness, lack of proper roads, and in pre-Christian Roman times the prevalence of small horses. Further, one must not overlook the influence of the conception of the horse as properly associated with noble deeds and not normally intended for common labour. This view, especially strong throughout the Circum-Mediterranean area, militates against developing strains of horses better suited for draught purposes and the inventing of improved techniques for making use of horse power. Related to this issue was the fact that horses were in such regular demand for the Roman cavalry, they were too expensive to consider for common cartage.

Asses and mules worked in the mines; they turned presses and mills and horses too old for the race course were sold to spend their remaining days driving mills to grind grain or pressing out olive oil (Vigneron, 182). There was apparently a limited use of the horse in farm labour: they as well as mules and asses treaded out the harvest. As among many other peoples, horses were preferred in this because they moved faster and it was also believed that it was good exercise for them (Vigneron, 177). Thus, in this case employment of the horse for common labour could be seen as equally a device for exercising horses.

On occasion horses were used in harrowing, but never in ploughing. Again Le Febvre des Noëttes claims this is because they had no proper harness and were ineffective as drawers of ploughs; Vigneron counters that it was too expensive to employ horses in this manner. Both may be correct, yet both overlook once again the point that developments for more efficient use of the horse as a draft animal may have been impeded by the attitude towards the horse as a noble animal.

Horse manure and urine were valued by farmers as fertilizer. Varro claimed horse manure was best for meadows where it resulted in heavy stands of grass, but of little value for grain fields (Varro, 141).

The Romans developed different categories of horses, each for specialized purposes. Thus there were animals for travel, for pack, for circus performances, for racing, as well as ambling horses for easy riding and multi-purpose geldings.

Horse for Meat and Milk

Horsemeat was consumed largely by the poor in ancient Rome and animals slaughtered were most often mules, asses and horses too old and about to die, so that the meat was not wasted. Other than this horsemeat was not consumed.

Mare's milk was considered one of the best of purgatives followed by ass's milk. Varro wrote: "As a purgative mare's milk ranks first" (Varro, 262). In addition both mare's and ass's milk were used in beauty baths (Vigneron, 184).

Cult of the Horse

As with other Indo-European peoples the Greeks and Romans incorporated the horse into their religious symbolism and ceremonial and occasionally made sacrifices of horses to their gods.

Among the Greeks, the goddess Demeter had a temple which housed her image – a black mare's head – and "[i]ts priests were known as 'foals' " (Brodrick, 91). Poseidon may have originally been a horse being the "embodiment of all horses, their god and their lord." Later, as god of the sea he created horses. "He struck his trident on the ground and the first horse sprung out of the earth" (Brodrick, 106). Poseidon also invented the art of riding. He was especially honoured at Thessaly, the major Greek horse breeding centre. Horses also appear frequently in other respects in Greek and Roman religion as centaurs and winged animals.

Horses were too valuable for sacrifice, but were on occasion offered to Poseidon at which times "they were drowned and not slaughtered". This is reminiscent of the Indian pattern where the offered were strangled rather than being slaughtered so that blood would not be spilled. At an annual ceremony at Rhodes a white horse (another common Indo-European theme) "harnessed to a chariot on fire was cast into the sea" to drown in order to help revive the sun "after his winter weakness" (Brodrick, 107).

Riding Style

The Greeks seemed to have preferred to ride stallions, but the Romans desired geldings. Greek riding gaits included the walk, trot and gallop, while the amble, unknown to them until after the time of Aristotle, became the favourite pace of the Roman rider. The Romans did not trot their horses, but called such animals *Successatus* or Shaker, also *Tortores*, Torturers. This has a parallel to an old British usage where trotters were ironically referred to as Bone-Setters (Berenger, 80).

The Romans trained horses to amble and also tied rollers of wood on the pastern joints to compel them to lift their feet so they were sufficiently high stepping for desired elegance of form (Berenger, 78).

Mounting in Greece and Rome without stirrups involved a variety of techniques. One could jump on or vault on with the aid of a spear or staff, use a horse block, teach a horse to kneel, use a rope ladder which was thrown over the horse's back and discarded after mounting, or stand on the bent back of a slave. In Roman Italy highway superintendents were expected to provide piles of stones along the road in suitable form for use as mounting blocks (Anderson, 83). Xenophon recommends that to mount from the left side the rider take the reins in the right hand at the withers holding on to the mane so as not to jerk the horse's mouth, and in the left hand take the lead rope, leaving it slack so as not to jerk the horse with it either. The left hand either grasps the mane behind the ears or holds the spear, if armed, and, then, one jumps or vaults on. The lance might have a hook or loop fastened to the shaft some distance above the butt in which the rider could place his foot while at the same time throwing the other leg over the horse's back (Xenophon, 31). Xenophon also recommends that the groom teach the horse to lower itself. Apparently like the other peoples of the time, Greeks ordinarily mounted from the right side since one held his spear in that hand. Also since most men are right handed it might be expected that this would be the more natural side from which to mount. It should be borne in mind that while mounting was obviously a more difficult task without stirrups, the Greeks and earlier Romans had smaller horses than those which were developed later; most were barely fourteen hands.

In dismounting the Greeks observed a technique again in contrast with modern riding. The rider regularly slid off the horse's back with his back to the horse. Anderson says that dismounting as is common today is seldom shown in Greek illustrations, but this does not mean it was not done. He also points out that riders may have been portrayed dismounting face to a picture, so that the artist's subject would be shown face front. However, dismounting in this fashion, especially without stirrups, is no more unreasonable than modern practice; a warrior getting off his horse to confront an enemy would not have his back to him, but would be facing him (Anderson, 84).

Reins in ancient Greece passed from the bit over the forefinger and so downward through the hand, the opposite of the modern English style. A slack rein held in the left hand, as in modern American Western riding made for less contact with and "feel" of the horse's mouth (Anderson, 62). But the ancient rider had otherwise more contact with his mount since he had no saddle and at most a saddlecloth.

Illustrations reveal differences in riders between the ninth and seventh centuries B.C. The earliest ones are reminiscent of ninth century B.C. Assyrian riders "crouched awkwardly on their horses' backs, with thighs horizontal and lower legs gripping their horses' sides instead of hanging free" (Anderson, 68). Some "are escorted by companions holding" the reins. Anderson supposes the bit was not sufficiently powerful for full control. Riding, he contends, was not made possible "by severe bits, but . . . as men took to riding instead of driving in battle the extra control given by severe bits was found to be necessary, at least to men mounted on the fiery breeds of horses that had been developed in south-western Asia and parts of southern Europe" (Anderson, 77).

Xenophon recommended riding "long" with almost a straight leg. "I definitely cannot praise a seat such as one on a chair with knees pulled up high. The rider sits correctly if he sits with both thighs spread, and straight as though he were standing. This way he will be able to hang on with both thighs, will have a firmer grip, and, since he is in an erect position he will have more power to throw the spear or hit the enemy" (Xenophon, 31). Straight legs became the general style for all stirrupless riding and represented a considerable improvement over the earlier "style" by which a man with bent knees attempted to stay on by gripping with the lower leg. Trench reminds us that Xenophon's recommendations for riding were applied by European horsemen until the twentieth century and they are still orthodox Western practice (Trench, 28).

Roman riding followed the Greek pattern, but by the time of Vespasian (69–79 A.D.) the Roman cavalry had started mounting from the left or near side since cavaliers were now armed with swords which hung from the left hip. Finally the introduction of larger horses especially after the second and first centuries B.C. provided for an improved seat.

Riding Gear

Most early Greek riding was done bareback, but in time the saddlecloth became more common. Anderson believes Xenophon may have looked on the saddlecloth as more of a "protection for the horse than as an aid to the rider". His 'saddle' was "to be padded where the rider

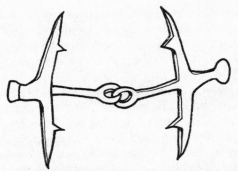

SNAFFLE BIT WITH BARBED SIDE PIECES
FROM KUBAN AREA, CAUCASUS
Fourth Century, B.C.
From Vigneron, Plate 19

sits, so as to make his seat more secure and avoid hurting the horse's back" (Anderson, 81).

The use of the saddlecloth apparently began in Greece about the sixth or fifth century B.C. Both Greeks and Romans used it, although Jope states the Romans did not employ it until the first century B.C. (Jope, 556). For obvious reasons, they preferred a broad backed riding horse. A crupper, breast piece and cinch were used to keep the saddlecloth in place. The Greeks from about the fourth century B.C. and the Romans from at least 200 B.C. used prick spurs. This form prevailed in Europe down to the thirteenth century (Ridgeway, 501).

Eventually the Romans adopted a wooden frame saddle, usually covered with leather, and placed over the horse cloth. These saddles, known as *sella*, or chair, Vernam compares to the McClelland type saddle with its low fork and cantle, light weight, and pommel which usually had no horn (Vernam, 64). But there appears to be no evidence that the Romans had such saddles until the fourth century A.D. It is widely held that the true riding saddle was introduced to the Romans by Asiatic elements, "probably in the Imperial cavalry" (Jope, 556). Bulliet, however, has developed the interesting hypothesis that the wooden frame saddle was first developed for the camel in North Arabia certainly by the first century B.C. and later adapted to the horse (Bulliet, 91 ff.).

In Greece mules usually pulled carts without the use of a bit (Anderson, 66). Halters were applied for tying horses in the stable, for leading pack animals, and on donkeys for riding. Riding horses sometimes had halters on under their bridles, "so that the rider, when he dismounted, would not have to use the reins to tie the horse up or to lead it"

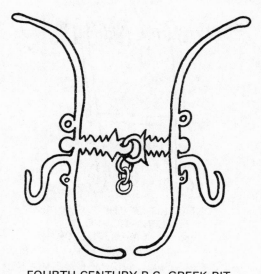

FOURTH CENTURY B.C. GREEK BIT
WITH CHEEK PIECES
(when placed on the horse cheek pieces fit flat against outside of animal's
mouth)
From Vigneron, Plate 23

(Anderson, 44). The use of the halter also protected the animal's mouth
so it would not get too hard being pulled by a bitted bridle when led
(Anderson, 42).

In some cases nosebands were employed and some of these were
constructed of metal. In one example, an all metal frame attached to a
metal nose piece and passed along the cheek and under the throat
(Vigneron, 58). Vigneron interprets Xenophon as saying that snaffle
bits and cavessons were used in combination, but admits that other
authors have different interpretations (Vigneron, 66). Bits were of the
snaffle type – straight bar or jointed two piece snaffles. As we noted in
connection with the Persians, some Greek snaffles of the sixth century
B.C. had sharp edged discs and spiked rollers. The Greeks also
attached short pieces of chain or a smooth roller to the mouthpiece for
the horse to play with in order to discourage his taking the bit in his
teeth (Anderson, 74). Xenophon recommended that for training a
horse one employ a bit with sharp discs and that later the animal
should be equipped with one having rounded discs. It is fairly clear
that he intended that a horse should be guided by a light hand (Taylor,
L., 72).

Curb bits were unknown in classical Greece, but could have been

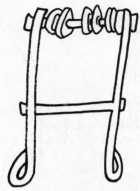

"CURB" BIT OF THE THRACIAN
HELLENISTIC EPOCH
From Vigneron, Plate 26

introduced by the Gauls (Celts) who entered the Balkan Peninsula
from central Europe in the third century B.C. (Anderson, 52). But
Taylor is of the opinion that the first true curb bits appear in Celtic
Britain and were carried to Rome by Caesar. He contends that many
scholars have considered any bit a curb which works on the outside of
the lower jaw in which case many Assyrian and Egyptian bits could be
so classified. A true curb operates on the fulcrum principle and Taylor
does not see this as being present in any bits in Graeco-Roman civilization until after the time of Julius Caesar (Taylor, L., 75). Le Febvre des
Noëttes believed the Byzantines invented the curb, but the evidence
now points to a much earlier date, at least before the first century A.D.

Care and Management of Horses Among the Greeks

Owning a horse in ancient Greece was an expensive enterprise. The
average horse cost from $180 – 720 while an ox was from $9 – 18, a
working class garment $1.80, and a cavalryman's cloak $2.16 (Morgan
in Xenophon, 77).

Horses were fed barley, spelt, oats, grass and hay. Homer mentions
wheat and "if we believe him, even wine to drink, and lotus (clover)
and marsh parsley" (Anderson, 94). According to Xenophon horses
were fed twice a day. Brood mares and foals grazed in meadows, and
working horses and cavalry chargers were stalled near the master's
home to prevent theft (Anderson, 89).

Horseshoeing was unknown in ancient Greece. To avoid sinking
into the snow Xenophon's forces fixed sacking on their horses' feet.
Later Greeks and Romans also knew the use of boots for draught

animals with injured feet (Anderson, 91). Xenophon mentions capturing Persian mules shod with fibre and Aristotle shortly afterwards (346 B.C.) describes horses shod in the same way.

While Xenophon recognized the importance of attending to horses' legs and feet, Trench points out, he "totally misunderstood the purpose of the frog. This hard, rubbery pad is designed by nature to absorb the shock of the horse's hoof striking the ground, thus saving it from concussion which can produce inflammation leading to navicular disease and other lameness in the foot. Xenophon thought that the frog was simply a weak spot in the sole of the foot, to be preserved so far as possible from contact with the ground. He therefore liked a horse to have 'high' or hollow hooves 'which ring on the ground like a cymbal.' One would expect his horses to suffer a great deal from lamenesses caused by concussion." Xenophon's view of the role of the frog was an error which persisted even into the twentieth century, and if Xenophon's horses kept good feet it was probably "because the hard, stony ground kept the walls of the hoof short and allowed the frog to do its job" (Trench, 300).

Roman Care and Management of Horses

Columella wrote that the horse requires painstaking care and plenty of fodder and a stud the most of all. Feeding grounds for horses were to be spacious, "marshy, mountainous, well-watered and never dry, empty rather than encumbered by many tree trunks and producing an abundance of soft rather than tall grass" (Columella, II, 191). In winter Palladius recommended that stallions have "rich and warm pastures, hard enough to strengthen their hoofs" and in summer they should be placed in the cool and shade. They should be kept apart "lest they hurt one another when furious" (Palladius, 134). Special care should be taken of stallions at breeding time and of mares when they are pregnant (Columella, II, 195). After breeding, mares should be worked in moderation, kept out of cold places, and neither overfed nor starved. Stable floors should be kept dry, windows and doors shut. The method of treatment and care of horses should vary according to whether they are for breeding, for racing, for cart, for carriage or military purposes (Varro, 244).

Stall feeding of hay, barley, oats, wheat and straw was most common. And some of those Romans who lived by the sea, like modern Icelanders, fed fish to their horses (Vigneron, 24). Columella believed a thin horse would be restored to health by a diet of wheat and barley with wine to drink (Columella, II, 203).

Romans, like the Greeks, were careful about grooming their horses.

Horses were bathed after working. Sweat was removed from a horse with a piece of wood in the form of a sword and instead of a curry comb they put a covering on their hands of a rough grain and composed of the bark of a palm tree. With this the coat was rubbed (Berenger, 77). Columella recommended that a horse have a daily rub down and like Varro was concerned that stable floors be kept dry to prevent the hooves from being wetted (Columella, II, 203).

The Romans were among the earliest to use devices like horseshoes. They first used detachable metal plates called hipposandals. Le Febvre des Noëttes' experiments with these shoes showed they were only good at a walk "and were therefore designed to protect injured feet". A first century B.C. Roman writer spoke of such metal shoes that draught animals wore "in a manner that suggests that they were too familiar to need explanation." They were not nailed, "but fitted to boots" to be "put on for difficult stretches of road and," then, removed. Iron shoes nailed to the hoof – that is, horseshoes as known in modern times – do not appear until post-Christian Roman times (Anderson, 91). White does not put them before the ninth century. Nailed horseshoes are referred to in the *Tactica* of the Byzantine Emperor Leo VI (886–911 A.D.) and about the same time are found in graves of the Yenisei region of Siberia (White, 58).

The Romans often branded their horses and they were named either for the part of the country from which they came, for their colour, or for a particular quality (Berenger, 85).

Breeding

Wealthy Greeks and Romans maintained breeding stables and applied systematic and selective breeding techniques to horses and to other domesticated animals as well.

Roman writers devoted more space to the discussion of breeding horses than to their general care and feeding. Recommendations varied from keeping one stallion for every ten mares (e.g., Varro, 237) to as many as twenty mares (e.g. Columella, II, 195). Stallions were believed good for breeding at the age of five while mares could be bred at two, but were not considered good after the age of ten; Palladius thought colts born of mares over ten years old were of little value (Palladius, 135). Stallions were good for greater age. "It is recorded that a stallion at Opus even continued to forty, only he needed assistance in lifting his fore quarters" (Pliny, 115).

Pliny appears given to repeating old wives' tales. He believed mares love their offspring more than any female animal "and in fact a love poison called horse frenzy is found in the forehead of horses at birth, the size of a dried fig, black in colour, which a brood mare as soon as she has dropped her foal eats up, or else she refuses to suckle the foal. If anybody takes it before she gets it, and keeps it, the scent drives him into madness of the kind specified" (Pliny, 115).

A well bred mare should be mated on alternate years so the foal produced will be stronger from the milk received (Columella, II, 197), a recommendation made earlier by Aristotle. Varro favoured breeding mares that are medium size: ". . . the quarters and belly should be broad." Stallions on the other hand should be large (Varro, 238). For breeding "the period of service is from the vernal equinox to the solstice so that the foal may come at a suitable season . . . ." A foal is supposed to be born "on the tenth day of the twelfth month after the mare" is bred and those "which are born after the time are usually defective and unfit for use. When the season has come the stallion should be admitted to the mare twice a day, in the morning and evening, under the direction of the [stud groom₆ for a mare held in hand is stinted more quickly, nor does the stallion waste his seed by excess of ardour. When a mare is stinted she makes it known by defending herself. If the stallion shows an aversion for a mare, her parts should be smeared when she is in heat with the marrow of a shrimp macerated in water to the consistency of honey, and the stallion allowed to smell of it" (Varro, 241). Varro tells us the highly unlikely story of a stallion who, brought to serve his dam was bred to her blindfolded and when the blind was removed, he had seen what he had done. Whereupon he killed the groom with his teeth! (Varro, 241).

Colts should be left to pasture with their dams ten days after birth so they will not burn their hooves standing in manure. At five months they may be fed "a ration of barley meal whole with its bran, or any other product of the earth which he will eat with appetite." This is done whenever the colt is brought to the stable (Varro, 242). Colts should not be weaned until the age of two years and they should be handled from time to time while with their dam "so that they may not be wild after they are separated" from her. Bridles should be hung in the stall so the colts "may become accustomed to the sight of them . . . . When a colt has learned to come to an outstretched hand you should put a boy on his back, for the first two or three times stretched out flat on his belly, but afterwards sitting upright" (Varro, 243).

According to Varro the best time for breaking is three years old, while Palladius not only favours two years of age but also opposes any handling of the foal until that time. Varro also recommends a special purgative procedure which should be administered at the time one is about to break the horse.

It is Vigneron's opinion that the techniques for horse maintenance used by the Greeks and Romans were excellent (Vigneron, 20).

Characteristics of a Good Horse

Roman ideas of what constitutes a good horse are not much different from those that prevail today. Such a steed, for Virgil, steps high, is nimble-legged, has its neck raised and tapered upward, possesses clean cut head and with short belly and quarters roundly proportioned, is muscular in the breast plate and is preferably coloured bay or blue grey (Virgil, 46). Oppian favoured a small head which rises high above the neck. "From the temples the hair should wave in dense curls about the forehead." The eyes are clear and fiery "under beetling brows", and ears small. A shaggy mane, arched chest, large breast, long broad back, abundant heavy tail, rounded cannons, straight long, sloping pasterns and rounded hoof are also stressed (Oppian, 23–5). Palladius in stressing qualities of form, beauty and colour, mentions three items not noted by the others: skin close to the bone, deep eyes, and wide nostrils. He believed bay, chestnut, liard or roan or light brown are particularly good colours. Blacks, and bays mixed with various colours as well as mousedun horses are less desirable. Stallions should be "one clear colour" and all others "excluded unless of singular merit" (Palladius, 133–4).

Telling the Age of a Horse by Its Teeth

Varro believed one can determine the age of a horse up to the seventh year when it finally acquires all its permanent teeth. In these early years age is established by noting the loss of milk teeth and the acquisition of permanent ones, as is done to day. But after the seventh year Varro was unable to ascertain age by this method except when "teeth project and the eye brows are white and have hollows under them, it is considered that the horse is sixteen years old" (Varro, 238). Varro is not quite correct in the specific ages he assigns to particular tooth conditions even in young horses. For example, he gives a horse a full mouth – a complete set of permanent teeth – at the age of seven, when it is invariably at the age of five. More significant is that the Romans were apparently unaware of the important changes which occur in horses' teeth after this age. Thus, they apparently did not know of the hook on the upper corner incisor which appears at about the age of seven and wears away at the age of eight. In addition, they did not know the relation of the development of Galvayne's groove to increasing age.[1]

Veterinary Treatment

Specialized horse doctors appeared in Greece and later in Rome. They often treated cattle as well and were associated with human medicine. Hippocrates, Aristotle and Xenophon among the Greeks all wrote on animal diseases and Vegetius among the Romans was especially noted for his veterinary treatises. The Roman army maintained special hospitals for sick and wounded horses in late Roman times and these were known as *veterinaria* (Vigneron, 40).

Greek and Roman contributions to horse husbandry and horsemanship rest largely in their making horsemanship an art and horse husbandry more systematic and rational. Both developed selective breeding techniques and within the realm of the Roman Empire different breeds were evolved. The Greeks certainly improved riding techniques and the role of cavalry in warfare. Neither, however, originated any fundamental changes in harnessing methods, although the Romans did make a limited use of shafts on carts and the pad saddle as a device to support the weight of the shafts on a cart.

[1] Galvayne's groove is a dark niche which appears in the upper corner incisors at about the age of ten. It extends down the middle of the tooth as the animal ages, so that it is about half way down the tooth at fifteen years old and is at the bottom at twenty.

IV

European Societies Marginal to the Graeco-Roman Civilization

VARIOUS European peoples dwelt on the peripheries of the Mediterranean centres of civilization. With the exception of the Iberians and Magyars they are Indo-Europeans and all but the Iberians have their antecedents in southern Russia and further eastward. Most were eventually heavily influenced by Graeco-Roman culture and became subservient to the Roman empire.

THE IBERIANS

First let us consider the ancient Iberians, who inhabited what is present-day Spain and Portugal during the second and first millenia B.C. The Iberians first appear as a Bronze Age people who, around 800 B.C., adopted the use of iron. Shortly thereafter they encountered the Celts as the latter moved westward across Europe. The Iron Age Iberians show strong influences from the Greeks and Phoenicians, but eventually became absorbed into the Roman empire and culture (Arribas).

Archaeological remains reveal that the Iberians were skilled horsemen as well as hunters of wild horses in the woods. "The profusion of horses in the Peninsula is attested by the vast numbers of riders in the battle contingents and by the exorbitant tributes levied by the Romans" (Arribas, 84).

The horse was highly prized and the most admired animal (Arribas, 121). It appears to have been used almost exclusively for riding. Horse burial is not common although at La Pedrera de Balaguer, Lerida Province, burials of horses were found, but Arribas mentions no other similar finds (Arribas, 141). Other graves show grave goods, including horse trappings and a chariot but no horses. Thus, it is likely that the Iberians eventually abandoned horse burial in favour of the similar Celtic practice of burying horse harness, gear, and wagons.

Instead of a saddle, Iberian horsemen used "a cover of leather, wool or vegetable material called the *ephippion*. Sometimes the padding was extended to cover the horse's neck in order to protect it from the friction of the reins and trappings." In some cases a "neck guard becomes a rein-control so as to enable the horseman to use both hands for his weapons," (Arribas, 84), although ordinarily one held the reins in the left hand and the weapon in the other. Stirrups were unknown, but spurs were used as were a halter and bridle with snaffle bit. The Iberians "adorned their horses to excess" with embroidered or painted patterns on leather and metal. On the crown of the animal's head they "placed a sort of parasol decorated with polychrome fibres and this is seen on the horse collars from Liria . . ." (Arribas, 85). Cheek pieces on bits took a variety of forms: rings, crescents and straight ones with S shaped extremities (Arribas, 86).

A sanctuary of El Cigarrelejo was "dedicated to the worship of a horse goddess very like the Epona of the Celts" (Arribas, 84).

INDO-EUROPEANS

The Scandinavians, Celts, Germans, Slavs and Balts represent closely related peoples derived from proto-Indo-European and Indo-European migrants into Europe from the southern parts of present day Russia between the fifth and third millenia B.C. They engaged in the cultivation of grains and root crops at first using the digging stick or hoe and later adopting the plough. They placed emphasis on stock breeding especially cattle which were also their primary beast of burden. Swine were next in importance; sheep and goats were uncommon. The horse was an animal of highest status used chiefly for the chariot by the Celts and early Germans and mainly for riding by the Slavs. For the most part sedentary village dwellers, there was some extensive practice of seasonal following of stock to new pastures accompanied by the setting up of temporary dwellings, later to return to one's permanent home at the end of the season.

In keeping with the general Indo-European pattern these societies were class structured, divided into tribes and patrilineally organized. A division of the tribe into exogamous clans in which members were obligated to fight in blood feud for the honour of the clan may have been a common feature of many of these peoples as well (Gimbutas, 1971, 141).

Ancient Scandinavians and Early Vikings

Horses were introduced into Scandinavia early in the second millenium B.C. Rock pictures, of about 1200 B.C. show the horse associated with the wagon. Riding as early as this is questioned by Davidson although a few carvings are thought to show men on horseback and may date from the close of the Bronze Age in Scandinavia. The Kivik grave, a Bronze Age site, contains stone slabs forming a grave chamber and one slab shows a man driving two horses from a chariot and also two horses facing "each other, as if for a horse fight". Both pictures suggest funeral games. Another slab "shows two pairs of horses, one pair facing right, and the other face to face, and between the pairs, lines of zigzag decoration suggesting water" (Davidson, 48ff). Some horses on Bronze Age stones have horns which leads certain investigators to suggest they were identified with stags and even others to hypothesize that this is proof that the reindeer preceded the horse. Davidson states it might indicate some merging of the stag and the horse and may have been an attempt to invest the horse with the ancient Northern symbol of power as represented by horned animals (Davidson, 57). Certainly the later horned horses depicted as, for example, on the Häggeby stone could be interpreted as having stag horns and, of course, even if they are stag horns we cannot tell whether they are intended to be deer, elk or reindeer if any of these. For that matter, that the horned horses may represent bulls makes sense when we consider the importance of the bull among Indo-Europeans and the possibility that the horse replaced the bull of an earlier cult. Further reason to suspect this is indicated in the horse fighting where horses are depicted with horns. Consequently, such fighting may have evolved out of bull fighting which was associated with ancient Greece and elsewhere in the Indo-European world.

Horse fighting was a common entertainment and sport in Scandinavia until Christian times. In it two horses, usually stallions, were picked out and goaded into attacking one another. Sometimes the owners as well as the horses were injured and the fights were often the basis for ill-feeling and feuds. A most notable account of the practice is recorded in the *Story of Burnt Njal*, probably the greatest of the Icelandic sagas, dealing with tenth century Iceland.

Horse sacrifice continued among Scandinavians until the end of the fifth century while the consumption of horse flesh carried on until Christian times or after (eleventh century). Horse meat is eaten by Icelanders even today. Horses were used for sacrifice to the sky god Vanir, indicating the animal's association with the heavens. Later, horses were offered to Freyr (Davidson, 121). In ancient Sweden the "[h]eads of horses and other sacrificial beasts, often the hides as well, were hung on trees as an offering to the gods" (Gummere, 459).

The Viking Age ship cemeteries contained horses placed on the starboard facing the prow. Cattle, dogs, swine, and sheep were buried in the ship as well. In the later Vendel graves (eighth century A.D.) in Sweden there was one grave containing a horse saddled for riding. This grave provides the first demonstration of the use of stirrups in

Western Europe. We may assume they were adopted by the Vikings from their contacts "in their eastward expeditions towards the Black Sea". The Vikings served an important role in the introduction of the stirrup into Medieval Europe (Jope, 557).

In later Viking graves two horses were placed face to face. At the Oseberg ship burial fifteen horses, an ox and four dogs were uncovered – "many of them beheaded" (Davidson, 115–6).

THE HORNED HORSES OF HÄGGEBY
From Davidson

Viking saddlery and harness were frequently elaborately decorated. Bridles were studded with pieces of silvered bronze while spurs and stirrups were often inlayed with silver. Norwegian saddles "seem to have been placed well forward on the horse, so that the rider's legs pointed forward." The form of the iron stirrups was derived from older ones made of leather and wood. Another item in the riding outfit, according to Norwegian evidence, was a kind of rattle, whose noise was probably intended to keep evil spirits at bay." (Brøndsted, 125).

Besides riding, the Vikings used horses on carts, including four-wheeled carts, and on sledges. Sometimes horses were employed to plough fields. Thus, the Viking chieftain, Oththere, told King Alfred about 880 that the little ploughing he did on his homeland in northern Norway was done with horses. Undoubtedly the ploughing with horses is related to the fact that the Norse by this time used a breast strap type harness and also did not engage in a great deal of ploughing anyway.

The Celts

Celtic peoples began moving into Europe between the ninth and seventh centuries B.C. Their antecedents were in the bronze and horse using (Battle Axe and Kurgan) peoples from South Russia and their immediate ancestors are likely to be found in the Bronze Age Urnfield people of the North Alpine area (Powell, 45). Halstatt burials of the seventh century B.C. found in the Upper Danube, Upper Austria, Bavaria and Bohemia are associated with the earliest Celtic people (Chadwick, 34).

Celtic society bore the general characteristics of the Indo-European. A warrior aristocracy comprised the upper class while a second class included priests, skilled craftsmen, and historians. A third class were the freeman-commoners and a fourth and lowest level, the serfs. The Celts lived in small sedentary villages, although from what we know of the early Irish there was a nomadic pattern to their lives as well. The Irish Celts, however, were more pastoral than other Celts (Powell, 88).

The Celts apparently kept large numbers of horses, but they were initially used primarily for chariots. Indeed, in the outlying Celtic areas such as Ireland and Britain they preserved the use of the horse and chariot longer than most other people. "Chariots were still found in the Caledonian host which opposed the army of Agricola in A.D. 84, somewhere in the Scottish highlands. They were still in use in Ireland in the time of St. Patrick" (Jankovich, transl. note, 29).

In Celtic Ireland cattle and horses were considered the stock of kings and higher nobility while pigs were the common stock of the poor. Cattle and horses were leased out by the nobility to their followers in return for annual payments.

While the horse played an important role in central and western Europe "its significance and its numerical proportion" among all livestock was much less than that of nomadic equestrian peoples (Bökönyi, 1968, 45). Bökönyi stresses the importance of ending once and for all the myth "that the Celts were the best horse-breeders of the Iron Age and their horses the best individuals of the period". J. Boessneck already (1958) "demonstrated that the Celtic horses were to be considered as the lowest link in a process of diminishing body-size; the smallest-bodied horses at the end of the chain" (Bökönyi, 1968, 46).[1]

It is not surprising then that they were not as commonly used for riding. Despite their size and the non-rational breeding technique, Bökönyi accepts the view that "a significant chapter of the European history of the horse began with the Celts' keeping horses: equestrian

---

[1] Bökönyi believes the Iron Age horses of central and eastern Europe comprised two separate "groups". The one was smaller, averaging about 12.2 hands, and found west of a north-south line drawn from Vienna to Venice and included the La Tene (Celtic) culture. The other was east of this line and included Scythian and other larger horses. The latter were bigger, averaging about 13.2 hands, because they were developed in the steppe where conditions were better for the horse than the wooded and mountainous zone to the west. Bökönyi suggests the difference is especially important under primitive stock breeding conditions where minimal rational breeding and selection means greater variation resulting from the natural environment (Bökönyi, 1968, 46).

traditions of western Europe originated with the Celts" (Bökönyi, 1968, 46). That is, Bökönyi suggests that the high esteem presently accorded the horse in western Europe derives from the ancient Celtic attitude (Bökönyi, 1974, 156). Certainly if we consider other aspects of the European equestrian tradition: rational horse breeding techniques, riding style, and riding gear, western Europe owes more to the Greeks, the Central Asiatic nomads and the Arabs.

After the Roman invasions of Britain the Celtic inhabitants began to accept the horse more for draught purposes and this led eventually to breeding heavier strains with infusions of Iberian and other horses, but the ox remained the favourite for heavy work (Hollis, 166).

The Celts worked the horse into their religious system although not as prominently as did the Germans. "[T]he cult of Epona, the goddess of fertility probably originated from the cult of a horse deity. The goddess herself was often represented mounted on horseback, surrounded by mares in foal, and by horses or asses. The horse may possibly have been a kind of totem-animal with the Celts . . ." (Bökönyi, 1968, 46).

Horses were apparently not buried with the aristocracy by even the early Celts since graves included burial of the dead in a four wheeled wagon along with harness, decorative fittings, including reins and bridles, but no horses (Chadwick, 34).

In Celtic Britain non-working horses were turned out into forests until they were required. Foals born in the woods received little attention (Hollis, 163).

Horseback riding eventually became prevalent among the Celts. Powell places the first true horse riding in temperate Europe in the seventh century B.C. on the basis of a burial of a single horse with a single warrior as well as the appearance of models and drawings of ridden horses. It was adopted by some of the Celts by the fifth century B.C., although the western Celts probably did not adopt or readopt riding much before Julius Caesar conquered Gaul and Britain (Powell, 1971). Cowen argues that the slashing swords associated with the Halstatt culture with which some of the Celts are identified were intended for a mounted warrior (Cowen, 1967). However, such a weapon employed by a rider without stirrups limited the mobility of the warrior and probably accounts for the fact that swords were not employed by mounted Scythian or Assyrian warriors and for the short period of their use by Halstatt people (Powell, 1971).

It has been suggested that the Celts learned to ride from the Scythians in eastern Europe although they never acquired the practice of eating horseflesh or drinking mare's milk. The Celts rode bareback without stirrups, riding "long". The ordinary bit employed was a two-link snaffle. However, in Britain and Ireland, snaffles with three links have been found and Powell believes "[t]his suggests the emergence of a finer breed, more sensitive to skilled control" since such a bit is a less severe device (Powell, 106). The Celts in central and eastern Europe developed a curb-like bit, possibly from Persian and Sarmatian models. Thracian-Hellenistic sites identified with the Celts between the third and first centuries B.C. yielded what are presumed to be curb bits (Vigneron, 73).

The Germanic Tribes

Early Germanic society differed slightly from that of the Celts. Tribes were ruled by warrior chieftains in conjunction with a tribal council composed of warriors. In the earliest time land was held as tribal property and distributed by the council among the various kin groups, being periodically redistributed. By the time of Tacitus (56 – 120 A.D.) these allotments were made to individuals rather than kin groups and in due course this tribal system disappeared altogether. In the early German society of the time of Caesar and before, there were no fixed social classes aside from a caste of slaves. Chieftains were men of great prestige who accordingly elevated their own families and kinsmen, but they were "men of influence" who could "rule" only with the cooperation of the warrior council. Centralized authority was weak and kin groups acted in many respects as autonomous units. In wartime war chiefs were elected.

By the first century A.D. a more rigid and formalized social structure had appeared including relatively fixed social classes of chiefs, commoners (including warriors and free cultivators), serfs, and slaves. Along with the class division there evolved among the freemen warriors a difference between horsemen and foot soldiers. In due course all the higher offices were filled by mounted men. Chieftains soon became petty "kings" of rudimentary nation-states. Throughout early German society the main measures of prestige remained ability as a warrior and the ownership of cattle, which, in contrast to land, was always individually owned.

Bökönyi claims neither the Germans nor Slavs ate horsemeat (Bökönyi, 1969, 228), although Gummere says the Germans did so until the eleventh century (Gummere, 41) and Smith indicates the Russians (Slavs) were eating it until after that time (Smith. 116). The development of a taboo against horsemeat consumption results from Christian influences. Eating horsemeat was identified by early Christian missionaries with pagan customs: the dedication of horses to pagan shrines, pagan feasts and the like. Thus, in 732 A.D. Gregory wrote Boniface in Germany: "Thou hast allowed a few to eat the flesh of wild horses, and many to eat the flesh of tame ones. From now on, holy brother, permit this on no account" (quoted in Gummere, 40). Later the religious taboo against horseflesh, which was not always carefully observed, was reinforced by prohibitions relating to the desire to conserve horses for war purposes.

According to Tacitus some Germanic tribes still fought from the chariot in the first century A.D. and gave up this technique in favour of cavalry organization on entering Roman employment as auxiliaries (Jankovich, 29). Before this time, however, some German tribes such as the Suevi, had developed a mounted infantry in which they rode to battle and dismounted to fight. They trained their horses to stand where dismounted and wait for their masters to return. To these Germans riding with any kind of saddle was considered disgraceful (Caesar, IV). Like the Romans, the Germans taught their horses an ambling pace, tying the legs on one side together with a cord so as to make the legs on each side move simultaneously.

The earlier Germans were known for the poor quality of their horses which were considered by the Romans to be small and ugly. But by the century before Christ the Tencteri became the first German tribe to discard these horses for a superior Greek breed (Ridgeway, 339) which in turn had been upgraded by the infusion of Eastern (Scythian) stock.

Tacitus singles out the Tencteri tribe as outstanding horsemen among the Germans. Their territory was on the banks of the Rhine and they were noted for their disciplined cavalry. "Horsemanship is the pride of the whole country, the pastime of their children, the emulation of their youth, and the habit of old age . . . horses pass as part of the succession, not however, by the general rule of inheritance, to the eldest son, but in a peculiar line, to that son who stands distinguished by his valour and his exploits in war" (Tacitus, 32).

The Goths, Germanic tribes of eastern Europe eventually absorbed the Alans, a major segment of the Sarmatians, and adopted by about 200 A.D. many of their horse practices. Important in this respect was the adoption of the Alan tactic for heavy cavalry – of "mailed horsemen charging home with couched lances. Indeed, they went further than the Allans, in discarding the bow altogether" (Trench, 59–60). Trench also claims the Goths acquired the saddle from the Alans. From them as well the Goths may have learned the use of the lasso (Ridgeway, 246). McGovern states that while the Goths adopted a goodly part of the Sarmatian horse culture they never totally embraced it. Their chieftains went to battle on horseback while the majority of the tribe fought on foot (McGovern, 359).

The horse was conceived as one of the noblest offerings which could be made to the gods. It had sacred associations with the oak and snow white horses were kept at public expense where they were relieved of all work except to draw the sacred chariot with either king or prince and a priest accompanying them. The priest was expected to observe the manner of their neighing and snorting for divining good and bad omens, their most trusted method of divination (Tacitus, 10).

Horses made the most prestigious of gifts and bride-wealth was often in terms of white horses. A bridegroom might bring such gifts as a caparisoned horse, a shield, a lance and a sword – full equipment for the horse soldier – to his bride's father (Tacitus, 27).

Among the Germans livestock were stabled, but horses were often cared for in droves watched over by a herdsman. "In the Old Saxon *Heliand*, a paraphrase of the gospels made early in the ninth century, the 'shepherds' of the original become in the Germanic rendering *ehuskalkos*, horse servants, who were not watching their flocks by night, but rather were guarding their horses" (Gummere, 41).

The Slavs

Like the Celts, the Slavs arose out of Kurgan people who had entered into Europe in the fourth millenium. Late Bronze Age sites (1200–750 B.C.) of Slav predecessors show horse meat was used in "funerary feasts as well as pork" and in "offerings to the dead" since "pots in cemeteries of Vysotskoe" contain "traces of fat and bone of horse and pig" (Gimbutas, 1971, 36). In the Early Iron Age the Chernoles site (750–500 B.C.) reveals a number of bronze bridle bits and cheek pieces of bone and antler. From this Gimbutas concludes they rode horses (Gimbutas, 1971, 42–3).

The earliest record of explicitly Slavic social organization comes from Jordanes in the sixth century indicating a "king" and "prominent men". Pomeranian and Polabian Slavs had a class of *vitiezi*, a kind of petty aristrocracy who performed "military service on horseback". *Vitiezi* may be derived from the Germanic word, "Viking" (Gimbutas, 1971, 141).

Later Sarmatian overlords introduced the Slavs to their technique of horsemanship. The riding horse and its Sarmatian style trappings became associated with the upper class of Slavic society. Among the early Slavs warrior graves containing both riders and horses are far less common than in Scythian, Sarmatian and Baltic graves. But after the sixth century, with the influence of the Avars, such burials occur more frequently among Slavs.

"Slavic royal tombs are as eloquent as other Indo-European royal tombs, be they Hittite, Phrygian, Thracian, Greek or Germanic." In tombs at the town of Chernigov, mid-tenth century, "three members of a royal family were interred in a timber mortuary house and equipped with everything – horses, weapons, sickles, buckets, pots – that was believed to be necessary for the after life" (Gimbutas, 1971, 159).

Russian sites from the sixth to the tenth centuries A.D. show from six to twenty-five per cent of all domestic animals were horses, and sites from the tenth to the fifteenth centuries, from six to thirty-three per cent. Of sixteen tenth to fifteenth century sites three contain seventeen, twenty-two and thirty-three per cent horse remains while the other thirteen are between six and fourteen per cent horse (Smith, 115).

Horses provided a small part of the early meat supply. It is likely that the consumption of horse meat declined after the ninth or tenth century with the appearance of field farming which replaced slash and burn techniques and increased the use of the horse for draught purposes (Smith, 116). Such use would have been facilitated by the horse collar which would have been introduced at this time. Smith believes at the same time the military demand for the horse was enlarged. Finally, Christianization (the Code of Yaroslav Vladimirovich, twelfth to the thirteenth century) forbade horse meat consumption as being identified with pagan practice.The continued use of horse for meat purposes in defiance of religious code is indicated by the number of horse bones apparently resulting from consumption of meat (Smith, 117). The enormous herds of 3000 mares and 1000 horses maintained by twelfth and thirteenth century princes, were not so much for draught and tillage as for pack and riding purposes. Mounted princes journeyed through their realms exacting tribute and engaging in warfare (Smith, 117).

In fifth century A.D. south Russia there appears a religious ideology presumably of Scythian derivation yet containing symbolism familiar to a more general Indo-European complex. It centred around sun worship and both the horse and the cock were solar symbols. By the sixth century horse symbols had become particularly important. Stables for sacred horses were constructed near solar temples and horses endowed with magical powers along with fire birds and cocks acquired a place in the local sagas (Rice, 181).

The Slavic war god, Svetovit, was also protector of fields. A white horse was dedicated to him and ridden only by the high priest. It might accompany an army. Before battle was joined it was walked through a line of crossed spears. The prospect of battle was good if the horse did not catch its feet on any of the spears. "Hence, the Russian phrase *veshchij kon'* – 'prophetic horse', which has an exact parallel in the

Avesta and among the Balts" (Gimbutas, 1971, 160). A horse oracle continued at Stettin until probably 1150 A.D. (Gimbutas, 1971, 154).

"The Common Slavic word for 'time', *verme*, interprets it as a wheel-track (old Indic *vartman*). This word was apparently connected with ritual chariot races" known from Mitanni (1380 B.C.). Both "Russians and Kirghizians imagined the Polar Star as a post around which an ox, reindeer or horse is forever walking. The horse draws the wheel of the seasons. When war or winter is approaching, that is the time for prophecy: for the cult of the horse and of Boundless Time" (Gimbutas, 1971, 161).

Reliefs of Dmitriev cathedral clearly are seen to depict a horse harness. "[T]he bits apparently consisted of two plates, narrowed towards the ends, but backwards and joined by a ring to the lightly twisted reins. The latter usually lay along one side of the neck." There are two forms of saddles – one, with a pommel and cantle and the other with neither. Saddle girths are shown in two reliefs and horseshoes in one. Stirrups of a single iron variety are comparable to other stirrups which first appear in Russia in late seventh or early eighth century (Smith, 45).

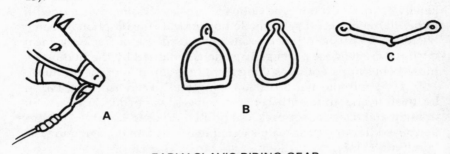

EARLY SLAVIC RIDING GEAR

A Bridle with rein to only one side of neck.
B Stirrups   **C** Snaffle.
From Smith

The Baltic People

Gimbutas remarks that nowhere else in Europe can one find such high esteem for the horse as among the early Balts, a fact still borne out by present-day folklore. The Lithuanians of the eleventh and twelfth centuries are the only Europeans to establish separate cemeteries for their horses. The riding horse accompanied his master to the grave

(Gimbatus, 1963, 164). During the first centuries of the Christian era Prussian[1] and Lithuanian horses were buried in a standing position and in full attire ready to be mounted. Among the Nostangians, a central Prussian tribe, the deceased was cremated on horseback. Deceased warriors and farmers were said to ride "their horses through the sky to the realm of the souls, and on horses they usually returned to earth to visit their families and to attend the feasts of the dead in October and on many other anniversaries". Even as late as the seventeenth century written records mention that "during the feast of the dead, the intestines and skin of a horse were brought to the grave in order to help the dead come on horseback to the host's house" (Gimbutas, 1963, 187).

The Old Prussian horse husbandry prior to the thirteenth century reveals numerous central Asiatic features, including breeding on the open range, the method of castration, the branding of livestock, milking mares, manufacture of koumiss and the restriction of its consumption to the upper class. In addition the Old Prussians rode small horses, waged war as mounted archers and used pack animals. They never adopted harnessed horses until the fifteenth century. Horse skulls were hung up in Prussian stables and the gable ends of houses in East Prussia were once decorated with wooden horse heads (Jankovich, 111–112).

Jankovich believes that central Asiatic horsemanship reached Scandinavia in particular, as well as other parts of Europe, via East Prussia and the Balts (Jankovich, 111–112). Certainly they were one source of diffusion, but there were others as well: The Scandinavians themselves travelled widely in what is now Russia and so beside their contacts with the Balts also encountered steppe nomads. Huns and Avars settled in central Europe, providing still another channel for the diffusion of the central Asiatic horse complex and, finally, the Byzantines had direct contact with the Avars and others of the Eurasian steppes, making a fourth avenue for the entrance of such a complex into Europe.

THE NON-INDO-EUROPEAN MAGYARS OR HUNGARIANS

These Finno-Ugric speaking peoples appear much later on the European scene than any of the above groups. They had dwelt on the steppes north of the Black Sea where they also mixed with Turkic

[1] These Prussians were Baltic people, not to be confused with the later use of the term Prussian as referring to Germans. The old Baltic Prussians were largely decimated by Germanic peoples.

peoples and gradually moved into Central Europe succeeding the Avars in that region around the ninth century A.D. The early Hungarians while having permanent settlements, had large numbers of herdsmen who spent most of their time tending extensive herds of cattle and horses, returning to their permanent homes for only a small part of the year. They made use of the lasso, branded their livestock and ate horsemeat; they also gelded and may have been among the earliest to practice this in Europe. Like other Eurasian pastoralists they, too, preferred riding geldings (Jankovich, 87ff).

At least until the time of St. Ladislas (1065–1095) the Magyars buried horses, although both in Avar graves of the sixth to ninth centuries and in Magyar graves of the ninth and tenth centuries most of the horses showed pathological lesions – generally lameness; some also possessed a superfluous incisor. Investigation of old Hungarian folklore showed that magical horses, animals imbued with extraordinary supernatural powers and probably owned by shamans, had two characteristics: superfluous teeth and lameness. Bökönyi believes therefore that these burials of deformed horses represent shamans' horses placed in the grave with their deceased masters (Bökönyi, 1974, 290–292).

In Magyar horse sacrifice the animals were beheaded – contrary to Avar and Turkic practice yet similar to early Viking custom. The skull and the feet were apparently interred. Probably the hide was left attached and this was stuffed with hay. These remains were then placed beside the corpse (Jankovich, 90).

Once Christianized, the Magyars gave up sacrifice, but later waves of invading Turkic peoples coming into Europe from the east kept up the practice until the fourteenth century. Turkic Kumans, although Muslims, buried a living horse and a living groom along with noted dead. The Hungarians, as Christians, replaced burial with bequests of horses and saddlery to churches (Jankovich, 117). And even in the eleventh century they fixed horse skulls to the walls of their living rooms as a protection against evil spirits, a custom of central Asiatic origin (Jankovich, 89).

The Hungarians perpetuated the central Asiatic technique of riding short with a bent knee and are among those responsible for the diffusion into Europe of eastern styles of harness as well (Jankovich, 110).

For the various marginal peoples discussed in this chapter the horse was retained as a noble animal identified with the warrior aristocracy. Only in isolated circumstances and at later dates does it appear employed in mundane workaday activity. The major role of cultural historical significance for most of these people regarding horsemanship and horse use is as perpetuators of ancient Indo-European practice or as conveyors of horse traditions associated with the equestrians of the Eurasion steppes.

V

Early Equestrian Nomadism of Eurasia

EQUESTRIAN nomadism as developed in the Eastern Hemisphere is characterized by a number of common cultural-ecological features which appear to have endured over an extremely wide area and from the first millenium B.C. down to modern times. We, of course, lack adequate data about the earliest of these people – the Cimmerians, Scythians, Sarmatians, and Huns – but may assume they at least conformed to the general pattern. The elements of this pattern are: 1) maintenance of extensive herds of sheep, goats, cattle and horses, including some herding from horseback and only the most incidental interest in cultivating crops; 2) a nomadic way of life involving seasonal movement between traditional grazing areas; 3) interaction and inter-dependence with settled cultivators and urban dwellers through trade and war; 4) the horse as a multi-purpose animal of general all round significance; 5) a segmentary patrilineal tribal organization and system of social stratification with a warrior nobility; 6) common elements of religious ideology in which the horse is important and 7) an emphasis upon warfare and raiding. The latter results from a combination of several factors inherent within the overall pattern. Thus, a motivation to maximize herd size creates constant pressures for grazing lands and conflicts over livestock. In addition, pastoralists invariably inhabit more marginal lands and are led to look upon oasis and city dwellers and their caravans as easy sources of loot. The mobility and social organization are also adapted to the pursuit of martial endeavours.

Origins of Equestrian Pastoralism

The background of equestrian pastoral nomadism lies in late Kurgan catacomb grave peoples, who ultimately produced the Cimmerians, and later, the Timber Grave-Andronovo people who, Gimbutas believes are proto-Scythians.[1]

Much of the earliest stock breeding of the eastern steppes is associated with enclosing animals and stall feeding. The Karasuk culture (13th – 8th century B.C.) which superseded the Andronovo in the Yenisei and Ob valleys provides evidence for a semi-nomadic way of

[1] Nomadic pastoralism appears earlier in the Near East, but there the horse has always been a comparative rarity.

life (Gryaznov, 103). Karasuk people moved between winter settlements and summer pastures much as was done until very recent times in the Altai region. Cattle and, secondarily, horses were important. Horse bones comprise "a third or a quarter of the quantity of cattle bones; but allowing for the slower reproduction of horses", Gryaznov believes the Karasuk people had a "fairly considerable stock of horses" and that they had become an important means of transportation.

"Bone cheek pieces from a primitive type of bridle" were found in the steppes of Eastern Europe and Kazakhstan and dated as early as the fifteenth and fourteenth centuries B.C. They are taken by Gryaznov as evidence for the use of the horse for riding (Gryaznov, 103). Cheek pieces from the Karasuk period were made from bone or bronze and had three holes for attachment to the bridle. These "early Scythian type" bridles lacked metal bits (Gryaznov, 103). Karasuk remains also suggest the use of the horse for drawing two wheeled carts with two shafts, according to Hancar (Hancar, 397).

Gryaznov believes that after 500 years of semi-nomadism such as that of the Karasuk there occurred a very rapid shift to full-blown nomadism. In a "few decades" steppe people of Europe and Asia took up nomadism wherever possible. On the general principle that if you cannot beat them, join them, sedentary peoples became nomadic so as to protect themselves from already existing nomads, who, as skilled horsemen, moved about in large parties carrying out swift raids on sedentary communities (Gryaznov, 131–2). People were rapidly forced to recognize that the acquisition of wealth and power in the steppes now depended upon "the ability to move with ease from a used pasture to a new pasture" and the "ability to control a wide range of alternative pastures" (Lattimore, 1962a, 63–64).

Full pastoral nomadism solves the problem of providing adequate grassland in lieu of dependence upon stall feeding. The nomad need only change locale when the feed supply is exhausted. Thus he is in a relatively constant state of movement to keep a steady supply of feed and water to satisfy the herd (Hancar, 556). Hancar concludes that the completion of a shift to herding nomadism in the steppes extending from the Northern and Southern Caucasus to southern Siberia and Eastern Turkestan probably occurred in the late second millenium and early first millenium B.C. However, he includes as nomadism the semi-nomadic transhumant pattern characteristic of Karasuk, Altaian and Caucasian peoples (Hancar, 557).

Stock specialization and nomadism resulted in the increase of the horse and of sheep in importance. The sheep provided many different products, were prolific, early maturing, as well as being mobile and easier to satisfy in regard to feed. For the nomad, horses had the advantage of a greater ability to fend for themselves, especially, to graze in winter and, of course, they were most useful for transportation. Further, horses were more valuable as riding animals because one was not dependent upon a vehicle. The variability of the terrain made riding, packing and dragging burdens far superior to dependence upon a cart (Hancar, 560). Improved breeding increased the size of horses so they became highly efficient as mounts – certainly a factor in the genesis of pastoral nomadism.

Horse breeding was greatly increased with the demand for horses from urbanized peoples of southwest Asia and China. Rudenko believes that the change to cavalry in the Near East, provoking even greater demand for horses, was a strong motivation for central Asiatic peoples to abandon agriculture and take up mounted horse nomadism (Rudenko, xxv).

Horse breeding also stimulated the exploitation of metal ores in the mountain regions of the Carpathians, Urals, Caucasus and Anti-Caucasus since these ores were important to the manufacture of harness parts and to the development of the mounted archer. As a result Hancar believes it is no accident that such mountain areas rich in metal ores also represent early areas of horse breeding (Hancar, 560).

To Lattimore the horse is formidable in war, but economically of minor importance. "The key to nomadic life was the herding of sheep and cattle, especially sheep, away from fixed habitations and without reliance on sheltered pens and stored forage" (Lattimore, 1962a, 466). "Even the military ascendancy of tribes with the best horse pastures was of no permanent use unless it was applied to the protection of sheep and sheep pasture" (Lattimore, 1962a, 75). While Lattimore is correct in thus countering others who may have been too enthusiastic in their emphasis on the significance of the horse to the central Asiatic nomads, it bears repeating that no people have ever produced a more versatile domestic animal – an animal with such multiple functions as riding, draught, sport, meat, milk, leather and hair supply, in addition to its religious-ideological role.

A major invention of the equestrian nomads was the mounted archer which may have been known to the "civilized" world in thirteenth century B.C. Babylonia, although the technique was not at that time adopted by them. The Assyrians in the time of Assurnasirpal II (883–859 B.C.) depicted nomadic riding archers in trousers, soft leather boots and belts, shooting backwards in the Parthian shot. Soon Assyria was abandoning the chariot for the mounted archer. Hancar observes that the mounted archer was undoubtedly a technique developed by equestrian nomads since it depends upon control of the horse and freedom of both hands for the bow. Riding without the use of one's hands would be "rooted in the basic needs of herding nomadism" and, thus, the mounted archer technique was undoubtedly developed by them, possibly first in the mountainous steppes somewhere in the Caucasus-Iran – eastern Turkestan region and more likely in the eastern Turkestan steppe. In the "centaur-like bond between archer and horse" and in riding without the use of the hands, Hancar finds the "keystone" to the second major "historical development of the horse as a history making domestic animal" (Hancar, 562). The first such development was in the horse and chariot.

THE CIMMERIANS

The first known historic people who seem to have been mounted nomads were the Cimmerians who developed out of the North Pontic Kurgan culture of the end of the second millenium B.C. and by 800 B.C. ruled north of the Caucasus and on the Pontic Steppes with an extension into Hungary. The Cimmerians were probably Iranians although they may have ruled also over Thracians and Caucasians (Phillips, 1965, 51). After a couple of centuries the Cimmerians seem to have settled around Cappadocia in central Anatolia and others around the Zagros Mountains where they were absorbed by the Medes (Phillips, 1965, 53). We know little or nothing of the Cimmerian way of life, only that it was likely mounted nomadism and probably followed to considerable extent the characteristics of Eurasian mounted nomadism noted above, though there is no evidence.

THE SCYTHIANS

Of the Scythians much more is known. Like the Cimmerians they were an Iranic people, and appeared as a distinct group about the eighth century B.C. (Rice, 19). As we have noted above they seem to be derived from the Timber Grave-Andronovo peoples of the Eurasian steppes. By the seventh century Scythians prevailed in southern Russia and the northern Caucasus. Another eastern and related group also lived in the Altai.

The Scythians are known to us primarily as a warlike people who were great horsemen. The earliest Scythians probably had a patrilineal, segmentary tribal system and were all pastoral nomads. However, it appears that the western Scythians – those of South Russia – by the fifth century B.C. at least, were partly sedentary agriculturalists. A branch of each tribe may have "lived in permanent or semi-permanent encampments which served the nomadic portions of the tribe as a base" (Rice, 21). This, of course, is a pattern not too dissimilar from modern practice among some Arab groups and among the Turkomen.

According to Rice the Scyths "formed well-organized communities, responding to their chiefs with ready discipline. But they were a turbulent lot, delighting in warfare, predatory raids and the scalping of their enemies" (Rice, 22). The Asiatic Scyths of the Altai elected their own chiefs but those of south Russia developed a system of hereditary kingship (Rice, 51). In other words the Altaic Scyths seem to have retained the traditions of the pastoral nomadic economy and more decentralized pattern of social structure whereas the western Scyths appear to have succumbed to south-west Asiatic and European influences becoming agricultural, sedentary and adopting hereditary kingship. Nevertheless, throughout, Scythian society was based on a military aristocracy.

The nomadic sections followed a seasonal movement in search of grass. In winter they encamped on the plains of lower elevation and in summer they moved to mountain slopes (Rice, 59). The order of march as they migrated put the armed cavalry in the front followed by mounted tribesmen driving the stock after which came the covered wagons carrying women, children and belongings. In the rear walked the slaves.

Wagons were four and six wheeled vehicles with roofs covered with felt and each with two or three compartments inside (Rice, 60). It is not known whether the Scythians made these wagons their homes or whether they were only used while on the move and, on encamping, actually set up tents in which to dwell. Another possibility is that the superstructure of the wagon could be removed from the wheels and chassis and used as a dwelling. Rice states that the decorations on the Pazyryk tombs were "clearly designed to transform the tomb into a tent" and therefore it is likely the Scythians when encamped dwelt in tents and not in the wagon (Rice, 61). The housing in any case was undoubtedly colourful. There were felt hangings and carpets and various fabrics employed as tapestries (Rice, 61). Their diet included koumiss as well as horseflesh, lamb and goat. Herodotus reports that if they lacked a cauldron they stuffed the meat in an animal stomach, added water and cooked the whole affair over burning "bones" (Herodotus, 261).

Aside from their own dairy products and domestic meat supplies, the Scythians hunted a considerable amount of game and those on the Caspian and Black Seas engaged in fishing, particularly tunny and sturgeon (Rice, 63).

The Scythians, who wore high soft leather boots, woollen or leather pants and belted tunics, are the first known people to have a proper riding habit, the design of tunic, pants and boots not only became the attire of all Eurasian horsemen but that of most Eurasians in general.

The Uses of the Horse

Scythian horses were probably of the same stock as the Mongolian pony, although from the Pazyryk graves it is evident that some of their horses were larger animals of the Ferghana type developed in Bactria. These horses were apparently only owned by Scythian leaders and were much prized by all Scythians, but even chiefs acquired only a few of them (Bökönyi, 1968, 43). Scythians employed horses primarily for riding in warfare, hunting, and in moving camp. Scythian women, however, never rode, but travelled in their wagons (Ridgeway, 254). To some extent horses were used for drawing carts as well, although this and other draught work seems to have been more commonly reserved for oxen, as it is among more recent Kalmucks and Nogais of central Asia. The far eastern Scythians of the Altai harnessed horses to their covered wagons and also to rough carts for carrying stone for topping burial mounds.

Carts were often drawn by four horses. In south Russia sometimes six were used and even eight. The cart had a central pole and the horses were yoked to cross pieces fitted to the pole. At the front of the vehicle there was a wooden platform upon which the driver sat. In the absence of a pivoting front axle turning necessitated moving in a wide circle (Rudenko, 190–191).

As we have noted another use for the horse was as a source of meat and milk, from which koumiss was made. To acquire mare's milk, Herodotus tells us, "they insert a tube made of bone and shaped like a flute into the mare's genitals, and blow; and while one blows, another milks. According to them, the object of this is to inflate the mare's veins with air and so cause the udder to be forced down. They make [slaves whom they blind] stand round in a circle, and then pour the milk into wooden casks and stir it; the part which rises to the top is skimmed off, and considered the best; what remains is not supposed to be so good" (Herodotus, 242). The technique of blowing into the vulva to make an animal give down its milk is, incidentally, still employed among East African cattle herders.

Much of what we know about the Scythians and their horses results from their elaborate burial mounds or kurgans in which they interred horses with a deceased chieftain or other important persons. The most renowned of these graves are those at Pazyryk in the Altai mountains and dated at the fifth to fourth centuries B.C. In each of these graves there was at least one horse of the Ferghana breed, the others were of the Mongolian variety. Except in one barrow where four draught horses were buried, all others were for riding (Rudenko, 42). If there was room in the grave, the horses were laid out in some order, but when space was limited "they were put on top of one another" and the heads usually faced to the east. They had apparently been dispatched "by a blow with a pole-axe in the forehead" (Rudenko, 40).

The stomachs of the Ferghana-type horses contained the remains of grain, not grass, suggesting they were "carefully stabled and fed" (Phillips, 79). However, Bökönyi has made the interesting observation that these horses all had pathological lesions of the teeth, vertebrae and extremities of the bones. "The horses must have been taxed to the utmost; they had to draw heavy loads or carry heavy riders, perhaps on very bad ground. These circumstances caused pathological lesions – sometimes such as resulted in disturbances of motion – on horses which grew old." It appears then "that weakened, diseased and lame individuals were chosen to be placed beside the dead" and this indicates "the growing obsolescence of a funeral rite, which still lived on in its form but had lost its content" (Bökönyi, 1968, 51). A similar situation was indicated for Avar and Magyar graves in Hungary between the sixth and tenth centuries A.D. Here, Bökönyi has offered another explanation, that the interred animals were shamans' horses.

Scythian Riding and Harness

Prior to their adoption of a snaffle bit it may be that the Scythians used some kind of jaw strap or nose band. As was noted above, "Karasuk" South Siberian nomads began using a bronze snaffle bit with a unique type of bridle which had cheek pieces with three holes. These holes were for the cheek straps which were split in three branches, the middle one going through a hole in the bit. This design spread rapidly over all the steppes as far as the Danube (Gryaznov, 134). In the sixth and fifth centuries B.C. they developed a new type of bridle with two holed cheek pieces, each one having a notch to secure the bit ring. This design also diffused rapidly over the same area (Gryaznov, 134).

Snaffle style bits were universally employed probably since they had more docile and patient ponies which were more readily managed by such devices. Bits were made from copper, bronze or wrought iron and cheek pieces of wood, antler, copper or bronze with "bronze shanks with decorative wooden terminals" (Rudenko, 123). Bridles often had no straps at the chin or across the forehead. "There were two longitudinal side-straps, starting from the cheek pieces and joining up at the horse's sinciput behind the ears on the left side." The noseband either attached to these side straps or was intertwined with them. A "throat lash consisted of two straps" (Rudenko, 120). Bridles from the Pazyryk

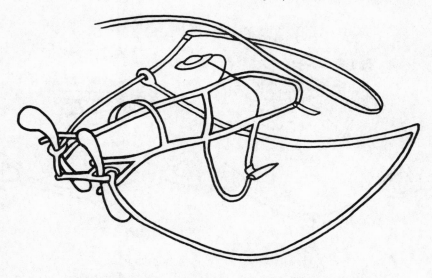

SCYTHIAN BRIDLE FROM PAZYRYK IN THE ALTAI
(Type for two Cheek Straps)
From Hancar, 531

graves were secured by bone buckles on the left side of the head. A "metal plate, held in position by a leather strand, was placed in the centre of the horse's forehead. This plate, the cheek and nose pieces, and every point at which a strap intersected another, indeed, even the straps themselves, were all lavishly decorated with geometric patterns and animal shapes" (Rice, 130). The straps were of excellent leather often adorned with gold plaques (Rice, 130; Rudenko, 123ff.).

The general style of Scythian bridles, with their snaffles, cheek pieces, nose, cheek and forehead straps parallels that of Assyria at the beginning of the first millenium B.C. and "was probably much the same as that invented by the world's earliest riders" (Rice, 130).

Saddle cloths of felt and woven materials were used. The Pazyryk saddles consisted of two felt cushions varying from twenty to twenty-four inches in length. They were secured by a girth band with two straps. A broad upper strap was laid on the cushions of the saddle and "held at some distance from its outer edges by special thongs passing through the thickness of the cushions, and a lower strap" went under the belly and was fixed to the upper one on the right. It was adjustable on the left side when the horse was saddled. A girth buckle made of horn and having a prong, but no return clip was found at Pazyryk in one barrow. "The buckles were pearshaped with double slits for the

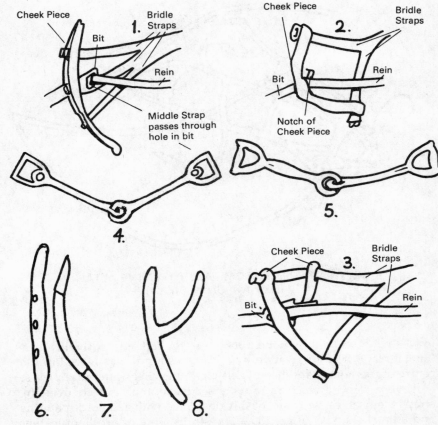

**SCYTHIAN CHEEK PIECE CONNECTIONS
FROM SEVENTH TO FIFTH CENTURY B.C.**
(from Jettmar, 1951, Plate III)

1. Reconstruction of three hole cheek piece attached to bit and three straps from bridle. The middle cheek strap goes through a hole in the bit and thence through the middle hole of the cheek piece.
2. A variant of the above in which the cheek piece has a notch through which the bit is placed rather than a middle cheek strap.
3. Another variant in which the cheek piece has an extended rod through which the bit is passed. At the end of the rod there is a hole through which the upper cheek strap goes.
4. Bit employed in first assemblage.
5. Bit employed in the two variants.
6, 7, 8 Cheek pieces of respective assemblages.

A second type of Scythian attachment using two cheek straps is shown on the Pazyryk bridle below.

girth-strap" (Rudenko, 131). The girth together with a breast band and crupper kept the saddle in place which was especially important in rough and steep country. "The cushions were stuffed with stag-hair, and they were often fitted with leather covers ornamented with stitching . . .". Some of the leather designs were almost like sculpture since the relief was so deep and further enhanced by adding leather cut-outs (Rice, 131; Rudenko, 129ff.).

Rudenko regards the Pazyryk pad saddles to be the oldest and most widely dispersed kind of saddle throughout most of the Eurasian steppe from the sixth to the fourth centuries B.C. (Rudenko, 137).

There were actually two types of "saddles" from the Pazyryk tombs. Those from two barrows are different from others since they had "wooden spacers between the cushions at front and back under the arches" of the cushions. These spacers were solid wood pieces "with projecting tongues at either end" embedded in the cushions. They were lashed to the middle of straps "fixed to the edge of the cushions by narrow thongs". Rudenko believes such spacers "may indeed be regarded as a first step towards the future frame, or tree, of the saddle" (Rudenko, 133).

From Chertomlyk on the Dniepr river in south Russia an important Scythian burial yielded a koumiss jug which has provided much data on Scythian horsemanship. It is presumed that the jug was made by a Greek and is dated at 380 B.C. Among other things are illustrated what appears to approach a true saddle complete with girth and breast straps and rather pronounced pommel and cantle. Of particular interest is at least one leather loop which hangs from the saddle. (There might well be two but this cannot be established for a certainty since the body of the horse hides the other side of the saddle.) It has been suggested that this loop may only be a loose girth attachment (Leshnik, 147). As was noted in the case of similar devices found in India from the second century B.C. such loops could also either be stirrups or aids for mounting, but as stirrups they would not have been very practicable.

The Scythians also made use of whips for riding and in the Pazyryk tombs, horses were decorated with heraldic crests upon their heads (Rudenko, 185–6).

The most valuable horses in the Pazyryk graves had their ears notched as marks of ownership and all of them were gelded. Apparently relying on a statement from Pliny the Elder, Vernam says the Scythians preferred to ride mares because they did not urinate so frequently as stallions and were less given to betraying their presence by neighing during surprise attacks on an enemy (Vernam, 12). Most scholars of the Scythians on the contrary believe they rode geldings, which while succumbing to the above military disadvantages more than mares are at least superior to stallions in these respects and less temperamental than mares. There are other reasons as well to suspect the Scythians mounted geldings. Thus, most contemporary pastoral peoples of central Asia show a distinct preference for them. What is more important, mares were and are used for milking for about half the year and it is necessary, especially given the limited feed, to conserve their energies for this end rather than riding.

The Pazyryk people are believed to have gelded their stallions at from two and a half to three years of age (Rudenko, 57). The Scythian technique in which the spermatic cord was crushed with a wooden mallet was a practice still utilized in sixteenth century Transylvania (Jankovich, 93).

Pazyryk riding horses, as well as horses represented on Scythian metalwork from the western regions, all had their manes trimmed and roached. They "were probably cut in order that they should not interfere with the aim of a rider loosing his arrow at full gallop, for the cart horses which appear on the metal work all have long free flowing manes. Most horses had their tails plaited but sometimes they were knotted at half-length instead" (Rice, 73; Rudenko, 119).

The Chertomlyk koumiss jug of the fourth century B.C. provides additional hints about Scythian horse management. From the illustrations it is apparent that they made use of the lasso in roping horses and also used hobbles on them. Other illustrations appear to show men breaking mounts.

Most "warriors owned a fair number of horses and the tribal chiefs generally possessed large herds of stallions and brood mares" (Rice, 71). The majority of horses received little or no supplementary feed in the winter, but were left to open grazing. Only the preferred Ferghana type received grain rations and they were, by comparison, pampered pets. Rudenko reports distinct indications of survival from periodic famines among most of the horses from the Pazyryk excavations; they are not present among those of Ferghana type (Rudenko, 58).

As we have already noted Bökönyi is of the opinion that the peoples of the Eurasian steppes were able to breed numbers of larger horses because the environment provided ideal horse rearing conditions which would be essential in primitive stock breeding where rational breeding programmes were absent. He further believes that central Asians may have developed a "high standard of horse keeping" (Bökönyi, 1968, 46–8).

The Scythians then were bearers of a horse tradition which formed an enduring pattern through time and was perpetuated long after all memory of the Scythians themselves disappeared. They were eventually defeated in warfare, especially by the Sarmatians. The western

Scythians became increasingly and, finally, totally sedentary, heavily influenced by Near Eastern and Greek cultures. By the beginning of the Christian era Scythian culture had disappeared. The legacy of the Scyths was carried on by the Sarmatians.

THE SARMATIANS

Sarmatians were another Iranic people, who lived between the river Don and the Urals on the lower Volga steppes between the sixth century B.C. and the third century B.C. By the second century B.C. they had displaced the Scythians on the Black Sea steppes and a century later they were on the Danube (Mongait, 163). Sulimirski says the Massagetae spoken of by Herodotus were among the early Sarmatians (Sulimirski, 1970b, 55). These Massagetae were a powerful Iranian equestrian nomadic tribe living in Archaemenid times between the Amu Darya and Syr Darya (rivers) east of the Sea of Azov. Apparently the Massagetae were divided into two sections: those who dwelt in the Delta of the Syr Darya and cultivated irrigated gardens in addition to herding livestock, and those who lived on the plains and lived exclusively on sheep herding and fishing. According to Herodotus the Massagetae diet was one of meat, fish and milk. When a man reached great age, all his kinsmen gathered and sacrificed him along with cattle of various kinds. The flesh was then boiled and eaten (Herodotus, 101).

The Sarmatians worshipped the sun to whom they offered horses. Herein, they betray close affinities with the ancient Persians who likewise associated the horse with sky divinities and were sun and fire worshippers.

Sarmatian women were quite distinct from their Scythian counterparts. Scythian women always lived in retirement, divorced from men's activity. The role of the Sarmatian woman may well have been the source for the view that Sarmatian society was once matrilineal, as it might well also have been the basis for the conception of the "Amazon". Young women rode, fought and hunted with their menfolk. The girls were even expected to kill a foe in battle before they were married, but after marriage they were required to confine themselves to domestic affairs (Rice, 48).[1]

In other respects, the Sarmatians were much like the Scythians. They too were great horsemen and pastoralists, living out of their ox

---

[1] Trench errs when he says the Sarmatians and Sauromatians are different peoples and that the role of women described here is to be associated with the Sauromatians, "a semi-legendary tribe . . ." (Trench, 53–4). Sarmatians and Sauromatians are the same people.

drawn wagons, which, during the winter they camped by the Sea of Azov and in the summer out on the plains.

Ammianus Marcellinus' description of the Alans, a late Sarmatian people of the fourth century A.D., is almost the same as Herodotus' description of the Sarmatians written 800 years before.[1] He says they put their carts in a circle on camping and give particular attention to horsebreeding, being especially careful of their horses above all other animals. From earliest childhood men are trained to use horses and they "think it beneath them to walk". Ammianus reported also that the Alans had no slaves and that all were nobles with the chiefs elected from among their noted warriors (Marcellinus, 581). If this was so it represents an unusual example of the equestrian pastoralist society, which is invariably class structured. Like the Scythians the Alans gelded stallions for riding purposes (Sulimirski, 1970b, 26). Pausanius, however, states that the Sarmatians bred many mares for war, sacrifice and meat, implying, it would seem, that geldings were not much used (Pausanius, I, xxi).

The Sarmatians are presumed to be the first people to use body and horse armour. Scales sliced from the hooves of horses were sewn on leather to produce a covering of scale armour for both horse and rider (Pausanius, I, xxi). Sarmatians are accredited as well, with developing something similar to the mounted phalanx, a cavalry attack in close ranks, a manner of fighting adopted by the Chinese, Mongols and Iranians in later times.

Sarmatian warriors held their lances with both hands in the charge so that they had minimum control over their mounts, having to rely on the use of voice and leg pressure. They also carried no shield. This cavalry was no doubt best suited against foot soldiers and not very effective against other cavalry (White, 8).

The Sarmatian harness differed somewhat from that of the Scythians. Thier iron bits had rings to hold the bridle leather and bridles were not so ornate. Early in their history they rode bareback or with saddlecloths. They are among the earliest to ride on frame saddles which they adorned with coloured glass and precious stones. The saddles had moderately high cantles appropriate for mounted cavalry attacks with a lance. The Sirace Sarmatians of the Kuban Valley of the north-west Caucasus left barrow graves which contained true stirrups. Sulimirski would give the Sarmatians a wood frame saddle about the beginning of the Christian era and true stirrups between 49 – 193 A.D. (Sulimirski, 1970b, 127). If this were so, it would make the Sarmatians the first to have both wood frame saddle and stirrups. Indeed, Rice

[1] Maenchen-Helfen, however, warns that Ammianus had a tendency to "embroider what he reads in old books" (Maenchen-Helfen, 14).

credits them with inventing metal stirrups (Rice, 150).

Others, however, have been much less eager to make any such claims. Thus, White believes efforts to "endow Sarmatians or Scythians with stirrups are groundless because of the extreme difficulty in dating nomadic tumuli" (White, 16). Miniature metal stirrups found in the Minussinsk area of Siberia possibly date to the first and third centuries A.D., but the date is controversial. Riders with stirrups are not portrayed on "the numerous representations of northern barbarians" in the Han Dynasty art of China (202 B.C. – 221 A.D.) (Maenchen-Helfen, 207) although some of other Han art might be interpreted as suggesting the use of a stirrup. What is more the earliest date for stirrups in the Altai ranges between 400 – 700 A.D. and for Iran is the eighth century, while they are indicated in Korea in the fifth century and Japan in the sixth (White, 16–17).

Concerning the wood-frame saddle we have already noted that the Chinese might have had this device in late Han times. In addition, finds dated as the beginning of the Christian era from the Minussinsk region and from the Karakol River *might* be from a true wooden saddle (Maenchen-Helfen, 208). In light of these factors it would seem that to attribute the saddle or stirrup to first century Sarmatians or Han Dynasty Chinese or any others in the first centuries of the Christian era is, at this time, somewhat premature.

The eastern dwelling Sarmatians were conquered and nearly annihilated by the Huns while the western branch persisted in Hungary and eastern Europe until the fifth century when they, too, were overwhelmed by the Huns. The Alans, a Sarmatian tribe we have encountered before, were absorbed by the German Goths. Thus, like the Scythians before them, the Sarmatians by about the sixth century A.D. ultimately disappeared by being mixed with other peoples; also like the Scythians they introduced lasting innovations in the use of the horse.

EARLY TURKIC AND MONGOL HORSEMEN

Horse mounted nomadism begins with Iranic peoples and was monopolized by them until the fifth century B.C. when Turkic and Mongol peoples adopted the complex and, in due course, themselves came to monopolize the tradition. The early inhabitants of Mongolia were primarily foot pastoralists and hunters and gatherers who practiced a limited form of agriculture (McGovern, 100–1). About the fourth or third century B.C. agriculture had spread from the Chinese heartland as far north as the area of diminishing returns. A semi-arid area – Inner Mongolia and Mongolia – produced a marginal people neither exclusively agricultural nor pastoral and these marginal people began to adopt pastoral steppe nomadism (Lattimore, 1962a, 63). "The use of horses, accordingly, became of paramount importance. Though it certainly was known before – the Chinese for centuries had used chariots and somewhat later had developed cavalry – what now occurred in the steppe was different. It was the rapid working out of a specialized technique of horse usage, which gave emphasis, range, and speed to the mobility that had become necessary in proportion to the decreasing practice of agriculture and increasing concentration on pastured livestock" (Lattimore, 1962a, 63).

Some Turkic-Mongol peoples adopted horse mounted nomadism by 400 B.C. or shortly thereafter since Wu Ling, king of Jao (approximately present day Shansi Province) (325–298 B.C.) borrowed the military technology of the nomads to the north in order to defeat the Chinese, who till that time used the short sword and war chariot and wore loose robes and slippers or sandals. The king of Jao changed to mounted cavalry, with compound reflex box, long sword, trousers and boots (McGovern, 101).

The Huns

About the same time a confederation of Turko-Mongol tribes arose, headed by one tribe known to the Chinese as the Hsiung-nu. Phillips says the Huns are likely some remnant element of the Hsiung-nu mixed with Iranic nomads and Mongoloids of the northern forests to form a single people (Phillips, 1965, 113). They spoke a Turkic language and racially were largely Caucasoid, but much intermixed, especially later in their history, with the Chinese and northern forest people, thus giving additional Mongoloid racial features.

Among the Huns each household and each tribe had an area of land reserved for its exclusive use in which no other group could pasture stock. They lived in dome shaped tents with felt walls. Their clothing was of skin and felt. Men wore trousers, leather boots with felt soles and a loose leather robe which reached to the knees (McGovern 103). As herders of sheep, cattle and horses they had little interest in agriculture, although as among Scythians and Massagetae, some of the tribes within the confederacy were farmers. Tribes and Chinese conquered by the Huns provided agricultural produce for them. The ancestors of the Huns may have been settled agriculturalists before abandoning it for pastoralism.

From the Chinese point of view, the Huns paid very special attention to the young and the strong while the elderly and weak were ignored. Horrified Chinese observers considered them to be lacking in etiquette and morality (McGovern, 106). Like the Scyths, the Huns were pat-rilineal and polygynists. A man was expected to marry a father's wives at the father's death. There was no priomogeniture and not infre-quently a younger brother succeeded to the chieftaincy of a tribe in the confederation since a chief often died before his own sons reached maturity (McGovern, 106). Lack of definite rules of succession led to chaotic interregnums after the death of a ruler as open conflicts arose over leadership.

Hun horses were of the shaggy, small Mongolian type, and as with other central Asian nomads, they had numerous functions, of which riding was the most prominent. Apparently having read Justin's description of the Parthians (cf. Maenchen-Helfen, 14), Ammianus Marcellinus prepared almost an identical statement about the Huns: "[they] are nearly always on horseback . . . and sometimes they even sit upon them like women if they want to do anything more conve-niently. There is not a person in the whole nation who cannot remain on his horse day and night. On horseback they buy and sell, they take their meat and drink, and there they recline on the narrow neck of their steed, and yield to sleep so deep as to indulge in every variety of dream . . . [T]hey all hold their common council on horseback" (Marcellinus, 578–9). A Chinese reported: "Their country is the back of a horse" (Krader, 1968, 83). And according to Chinese chronicles Hun children learned to ride at an age when other infants are learning to walk. The Hun diet was primarily one of dairy and meat products. Horseflesh was consumed fresh, dried or smoked and mare's milk was drunk either fresh or as koumiss. On occasion, the Huns may have drunk blood drawn from their mounts (Maenchen-Helfen, 220).

The Huns initially rode with only a pad on the horse's back but by the fourth or fifth century A.D. they clearly had wooden frame saddles with high pommels and cantles (Maenchen-Helfen, 209). It is not clear when the Huns acquired stirrups but the claim of Trench (64) and Epstein (1971a, 512) that the Huns invented the stirrup is not accept-able in light of the early role of Indians, Chinese and Sarmatians in the use of this device. And thus far the archaeological record has yielded no metal stirrups among the Huns. Of course, they could have had wooden ones which did not survive. One argument against the Huns having "stirrups is the fact that the Germanic horsemen rode without them for centuries after the fall of Attila's kingdom" (Maenchen-Helfen, 206).

The Huns had no spurs but used whips instead. Horses owned by kin groups and grazed on communal pastures were marked by cuts on the ears or by branding the hindquarters or shoulders. It may be surmised that the Huns like the other Central Asiatic nomads rode mostly geldings (Maenchen-Helfen, 210ff.).

The Huns spread and invaded China where they were eventually defeated, at which point they began a westward movement culminating in Attila's entry into the Roman Empire in the fifth century. Until their entry into Europe they had retained their nomadic pastoral patterns, but now they started to adopt settled ways, even establishing a fixed capital in what is now Hungary. At the death of Attila the Hunnish empire soon dissolved, in large part because of internal dissensions, and they as a people were ultimately absorbed by those whom they had originally conquered.

The Avars

The Avars are a slightly later group of Mongol – Turkic horsemen who followed on the heels of the Huns. They appear in the fifth century in Mongolia and eventually worked their way westward as well, to settle in Hungary around 570 A.D. After their defeat by Charlemagne in 791 – 796 they too disappeared from history. Remains of their graves in central Europe have been taken as clear evidence for the stirrup in Europe in the late sixth century – which would be the earliest this device would have occurred in that continent. The most important Avar grave containing stirrups also contained coins of Justin I (518 – 527) and Phocas (602–619). Thus, one might attribute a date of the beginning of the seventh century to such graves, but, then, the coins may have been old when they were placed in the grave. The stratification of these Avar materials is also unclear and as a result Hungarian archaeologists have rejected the suggestion that the evidence gives stirrups to the Avars in Hungary as early as the sixth century (White, 22).

It has also been suggested that the Avars introduced the breast strap into Europe as an improved harnessing method for draught horses (Needham, 311). Jankovich also points out that the Byzantines learned much about mounted military tactics from the Avars and were as a result enabled to defeat the Persians (Jankovich, 56).

The Early Mongols

The final great wave of equestrian nomads from Asia was carried forth by the Mongols. The T'ang Chinese mention the Mongols in the seventh century A.D. under the name of Meng-wu among a group of northern people called Shi-wei. "The Shi-wei shaved their heads, used cattle to draw their carts, and lived in huts covered with mats or in tents transported on carts" as among the Turkic peoples. They had saddles made "of grass and . . . bridles of cord". Their herds were composed primarily of cattle and swine. Horses were few in number and sheep were absent. This indicates that they were not at this time fully steppe pastoralists and nomads. It is more likely a description of forest tribes and it is even possible that other Shi-wei were Tungus.

The Meng-wu of Meng-ku appear later in association with the Tatars as nomads living on meat and sour milk, and as unsuccessful raiders of the Chinese in the tenth century. Phillips also points out that much of Mongol vocabulary pertaining to social organization and military command derives from the Turkic languages (Phillips, 1969, 24). It, therefore, seems likely that when the Mongols first appeared in history in the seventh century A.D. they had hardly begun to develop equestrian and pastoral nomadism, but with association with their linguistic relatives, the Turkic people, they soon adopted much of their way of life.

The basis of Mongol society is the *obok*, an exogamous, kin orientated group composed primarily of individuals who are partrilineally related, but it also includes slaves and servants who become attached to the group through defeat in war or other misfortune. Several *oboks* constitute a *yasun* or bone and these are grouped into tribes. Clans and tribes once had chiefs who regulated the grazing activities of their groups. Tribes defeated in warfare could be added to the victor's tribe as serfs. Like the Huns and other Turkic peoples, Mongol society was a stratified one with a khan at the head, a higher nobility of generals and army officers, and a minor nobility who were freed members of the lower class (Phillips, 1969, 27).

The Mongols dwelt in circular tents made of felt placed over a light wooden frame. They also had wheeled carts "with a chamber covered with felt for carrying valuables and especially small images of gods and spirits". The felt was greased to make it more resistant to cold, wind and rain and could be painted with lime or powdered bone. Birds, animals and trees were often painted on door flaps (Phillips, 1969, 28).

Horses were employed for the usual great variety of activities common to Central Asiatic nomads. Men milked the mares and beat mare's milk in great leather bags suspended from frames until the whey was separated from the curds. Marco Polo wrote: "In case of need, they will ride a good ten days' journey without provisions and without making a fire, living only on the blood of their horses; for every rider pierces a vein of his horse and drinks the blood. They also have their dried milk, which is solid like paste; and this is how they dry it. First they bring the milk to the boil. At the appropriate moment they skim off the cream that floats on the surface and put it in another vessel to be made into butter, because so long as it remained the milk could not be dried. Then they stand the milk in the sun and leave it to dry. When they are going on an expedition, they take out about half a pound of it and put it in a small leather flask, shaped like a gourd, with as much water as they please. Then, while they ride, the milk in the flask dissolves into a fluid, which they drink. And this is their breakfast" (Polo, 100). He does not state however, what kind of milk this was, more than likely it was cow's milk or ewe's milk.

Both men and women were expert riders and were trained to shoot the bow and arrow from the saddle. But wealthy women seldom rode because they became so fat (Phillips, 1969, 32). Horses were trained to be most obedient to their masters and if necessary a Mongol would stay all night on horseback under arms "while [his] mount goes on steadily cropping the grass" (Polo, 99). Falconry and mass hunting sports were carried out on horseback. Genghis Khan presumably had thousands of riders participating collectively in mass hunts, a practice which survived in Mongolia until recent time wherein great numbers of horsemen were used to surround the game (Polo, 142–3).

Horse racing was and remains one of the major sports of the Mongols. Under Kublai Khan an elaborate post system was developed in which posting stations were maintained at intervals of twenty-five miles and were equipped with horses in readiness for the Khan's messengers. Marco Polo claimed these stations, which numbered ten thousand, were lavish establishments and made use of 200,000 horses. In emergencies a rider might travel two hundred miles in a day obtaining a fresh horse every twenty-five miles at each post house (Polo, 151).

Many men had from eighteen to twenty horses to allow for an adequate number of remounts. Particularly on a long journey or a raid a man brought along three or four horses, each of which was ridden in turn. This system was needed because of the small size of their mounts (usually thirteen to fourteen hands), also because they were grass fed and so not at full strength.

Mongol nobles owned herds of thousands of horses. The Great Khan himself had ten thousand snow white mares alone and a stud of snow white stallions. The milk from the mares was reserved for the imperial lineage and for one other group known as the Horiat (Polo, 109). On New Year's Days it is said the Great Khan received gifts of 100,000 white horses.

Large numbers of Mongol horses were exported to India. Ibn Battuta said the total number at one time could be 6000 or more although the greater part would die or be stolen before arriving at their destination. For every fifty horses there was a drover with a stick which had a sliding rope loop at the end (known to modern Mongols as *uraga*). It was employed in lassoing livestock (Spuler, 183).

Horses were important in religious ceremony, especially in sacrifice. The Great Khan's astrologers and religious advisers recommended that he make libations of milk from his snow white mares every 28th of August, sprinkling the milk on the earth and in the air for all the spirits so they would protect his belongings and his people (Polo, 109). Before their conversion to Buddhism, the Mongols frequently sacrificed horses by cutting open the animals' breast cavity and opening the aorta (Birket-Smith, 1965, 144).

Plano Carpini the delegate of Innocent IV to the court of the Great Khan gave this report of a funeral, presumably of an important man: "The dead man is laid in the earth with his tent and provisions and mare's milk beside him. A mare with foal at foot and a saddled and bridled gelding are buried with him. Then they eat another horse, stuff the hide with straw and prop it up on two or four poles, so that in the next world the dead man shall have somewhere to live, a mare to provide milk, a foal to start another herd, and a horse to ride" (quoted in Jankovich, 90).

All livestock was turned out loose to graze freely with no herdsman except for sheep and goats which had shepherds. Livestock were also branded for ownership identification. Horses were not ridden until they were three years old and, then, usually for one day out of three or four.

Techniques of horse care and management are of course more well known for the Mongols of contemporary times. They are discussed later in greater detail and since they have likely not changed that much over the generations may be taken at least as an indication of the more ancient forms of Mongol horse husbandry.

VI

A Survey of the Evolution of Horse Technology and of the Origins of Riding

PERHAPS it is pertinent at this juncture to review the previous several millenia in terms of the evolution of specific devices to control and manage the horse as a means of transportation. At the same time we should also consider more directly the issue of the origins of horseback riding.

Bitting

Earliest indications of guidance devices on horses are from archaeological sites of the Kurgan culture of southern Ukraine going back to the middle of the fourth millenium B.C. Antler pieces from Dereivka could be cheek pieces from a bridle. Figurines of horses' heads from Kurgan sites of the end of the fourth millenium represent bridles according to Gimbutas (Gimbutas, 1970, 158).On the other hand an equally reasonable interpretation is that they represent halters or some kind of hackamore. Definite indications of bitting devices occur in the third millenium B.C. with bronze-copper cheek pieces from Transylvania (ca. 2250 B.C.) and a bronze cheek piece from Maikop in the Transcaucasus (ca. 2500 B.C.). Thereafter bits and especially cheek pieces occur with greater frequency in Europe. The oldest bronze snaffle bit, however, is from Egypt (1500 B.C.). That there is little indication of the early use of bits does not mean they were not employed, since it is almost certain that in lieu of metal bits, those of wood or bone were used and being less durable than metal have not survived to become part of the archaeological record. In addition, in all likelihood some kind of nose band or a jaw strap was employed and such material too would not be preserved.

Another ancient guidance device from Anatolia and Mesopotamia is the nose ring. The Kültepe seal, ca. 1950 B.C. from Cappadocia showing a god standing upon a horse directed by a nose ring, was until recently about the only clear demonstration of this practice. Lately, the Turkish archaeologist, Nimet Özguc, has stated that other cylinder seals from Kültepe in central Anatolia occasionally portray horses with nose rings (Moorey, 47). We have already noted the baked clay plaques from early second millennium Iraq which show this phenomenon.

The nose ring, adapted from the onager and the ox, certainly never had a wide distribution (probably central Anatolia and Mesopotamia), nor was it employed for very long. After three or four centuries at the very most it was replaced by the far more efficient snaffle. The wonder is that a nose ring was ever used at all. Downs has categorically denied that any horse would tolerate a nose ring (Downs, 1961, 1195). But the history of horsemanship is replete with examples of prolonged usage of sometimes incredible devices for control, such as nose bands emplanted with spikes and an immense variety of elaborately severe bits and curbs. If a horse will tolerate these it seems not unlikely that he could be trained to submit to a nose ring. This would be all the more probable if the ring were placed on the animal at an early age.

However, one may well wonder how efficiently such a device would control a riding horse. Indeed, the picture of the early Mesopotamian rider we derive from Moorey's analysis of the clay plaques suggests an outrageous riding style: sitting far back on the horse's bare back with severely bent knees and no stirrups, holding reins in one case very high, guiding via a nose ring and apparently grasping a girth with one hand. How one could sustain his balance in such a position is unclear. The horse's head would always be high and it would seem the animal would always be tossing it.

But the most unusual aspect of this entire nose ring issue is that the horse was most likely derived by the Anatolians and Mesopotamians from the east European steppes at least a thousand years after the steppe herdsmen had domesticated it and even after they had already developed some kind of bit (e.g., Maikop cheek piece, 2500 B.C. and Transylvania cheek pieces, 2250 B.C.). It seems downright unbelievable that in adopting the horse from the steppe folk the Mesopotamians would not also have taken along the trappings used to control it. It is impossible that some of the horses acquired by the Near Easterners from the steppe-Caucasus people would not have been broken to the bit. One would also expect that the clear superiority of a bit over a nose ring would be patently obvious. For these reasons one might question the extent to which horses ever were driven by a nose ring.

Alternatively, one could hypothesize that the horse in the Middle East was not originally derived from the Eurasiatic steppes, but was a product of local domestication. This would demand an already existing population of wild horses. Thus far, evidence for this has been extremely meagre. Recent finds of wild horse have been reported from a Chalcolithic – Bronze Age site of the fourth/third millenium B.C. near Elazig, Turkey. However, less than one per cent of the several thousand bones uncovered were horse, indicating that it was not a common animal (Boessneck and von den Driesch). True wild horses also may have inhabited ancient Iran. Here they could have been more numerous, although due to the nature of the remains it is difficult to distinguish between onagers and small horses (Firouz).

Hancar believes the evolution of the bit commences with a nose ring and is followed by the use of a muzzle. He holds that the first bit was a bridle strap mouthpiece or threaded bone bit (*Urtrense*). Yet as he recognizes there is no verification anywhere for this form of snaffle (Hancar, 533). There is also no evidence of a nose ring or muzzle in the Eurasion steppes where bits appear very early.

The second major development of the snaffle according to Hancar is the replacement of the strap mouthpiece either by a snaffle bar of bone with bone cheek pieces, or by a bronze snaffle with bronze cheek pieces which first take a wheel form (from 1600 B.C. onward), then a narrow rectangular form. Hancar states that the oldest bronze snaffles with wheel psalia (cheek pieces) belong to the Near East and are older than European bronze bits.

The third stage in the development of the snaffle is the replacement of the straight-piece snaffle by a two-piece mouthpiece, from 1500 B.C. on. The development of bridling from the muzzle to the bronze snaffle, Hancar believes, is to be located in the Syrian-Mesopotamian-Eastern Asia Minor mountain area – the rim which forms around the north end of the Fertile Crescent. This development represents as well the final link in the overall evolution of the war chariot (Hancar, 533).

Admitting that she is presenting "a model which remains to be proven," M.A. Littauer urges consideration of an alternate process of evolution of the snaffle and in so doing advocates a development which is internal to the ancient Near East. The muzzle which is employed, for example in conjunction with the nose ring on the onagers of the Standard of Ur might, according to Littauer, have served as a predecessor to the dropped noseband or cavesson and this in turn was modified in the Near East into the snaffle. Eliminating the ring and modifying the muzzle to produce a noseband with studs on the inner side of the band which is attached on either side by reins, would at least improve the directional control which would have been "impossible with a single line nose-ring" (Littauer, M.A., 296).

Following this, cheek pieces could be added, through the holes of which a solid straight bar could be passed to form a bit. Littauer questions the widely held view that the twisted, jointed snaffle had a rope prototype, because in the Oriental cheekpieces the rope would have passed through holes in the cheekpieces and thus in use would have been easily frayed and cut by the metal edge of the holes, making for a "highly impractical" device (Littauer, M.A., 297). The jointed snaffle would arise out of an attempt to relieve the excessive wear and tear on the cheekpieces and on the edges of the bit since a bit jointed in the centre would, when pulled, slant somewhat backward.

"This design of bit . . . may be seen as an attempt to separate directional control from braking, in a bridle on which the cheekpiece was still a part of, or was still connected to, the low noseband. The other possibility that it was designed so as to exert extra leverage on the jaw, would be eliminated so long as the noseband connexion was present, but would play a role when that was abandoned – as on the Assyrian and Luristan bits" (Littauer, M.A., 297). Littauer reminds us that the rope jawstrap of the American Indian passed around the lower jaw and did not function as a bit. Thus, she sees "the south-west Asian *mouthpiece* originating in a metal bar, the original role of which was to improve directional control" (Littauer, M.A., 298).

Whether the bit originates in the Near East or on the Eurasiatic steppe remains an unresolved issue. But, if we agree with those who attribute the use of bits to East Europeans in the fourth and third millenia B.C. it seems likely that the idea diffused into the Near East from the north. An independent invention of the bit in the Middle East even as early as the third millenium would seem improbable given the close proximity of the Eurasian steppe and the presumption that horsemen in that area already knew its use. In addition it appears likely that the first domesticated horses might have entered the Middle East from the steppes to the north, in which case the Near Easterners would hardly have been unaware of the riding gear of the steppe. Finally, it is clear that the Near East was the centre for major improvements in the bit.

Between 2000 B.C. and 1500 B.C. the combination of the horse with the spoked-wheeled chariot and metal snaffle bit provoked a revolution in warfare. This technology is undoubtedly a decisive factor in the rapid diffusion of the horse during these centuries throughout south-west Asia, into North Africa, Scandinavia and eastward into India and China.

To Hancar the chariot – a Near Eastern cultural creation – was the weapon par excellence of the second and early first millenium B.C. He agrees with Spengler's observation that the chariot is the first complex weapon of war "in which elements of chariot, horse and professional warrior unite organically and for the first time to introduce speed into world history as a tactical weapon. Rightly, he [Spengler] sees the war chariot as a key to world history of the second millenium B.C." (Hancar, 549). The horse and chariot were crucial to the expansion of centralized military-aggressive states in the second millenium. At the same time the formation of a noble class of professional warriors and the creation of a centralized military monarchic state were necessary prerequisites to the development of horse and chariot which required considerable financial investment to manufacture and maintain as well as to train charioteers, horses and shield bearers (Hancar, 549).

Metal snaffles were long employed as the only type of bit. Several centuries following the shift from chariot to cavalry, other modifications in the bit appeared for riding purposes. Presumably the Persians of the fifth century B.C. employed something similar to a curb bit, but other evidence of the curb does not appear until the third century B.C. in Thrace in conjunction with Celtic culture. Taylor suggests that curbs as we now know them really did not appear until after this and well into Roman times (Taylor, 75). Ring bits are definitely post-Christian while spade bits, developed by changing the port of the bit to a spade, originated much later, possible among the Arabs.[1] These more severe types of bits were developed to enhance capability in quick stopping and turning with a loose rein.

Improvements in Cart Harness

The throat band, originally employed on the onager, continued in use with the horse and with the same constraining results in compressing the wind pipe so as to inhibit efficiency. Some attempts had been made to ameliorate this style of harness in early times. Thus, in ancient Egypt the prancing horses at Karnak of the time of Ramses II (1290–1224 B.C.) show a martingale arrangement tying the throat strap to the girth through the horse's forelegs. The Assyrians of the eighth century B.C. and Persians of the fourth century B.C. both applied combinations of the breast and throat strap. Needham states that it is indeed remarkable that the throat and girth harness should have achieved such an enormous spread throughout the world and should have persisted essentially unchanged for such a long time. With the exceptions mentioned above, it was apparently the one method of harnessing horses all the way from western Europe to China for about two thousand years.

The Chinese are responsible for major fundamental changes in harnessing beginning with their invention of a breast strap possibly around 250 B.C. (Needham, 311–312). A breast strap with two traces suspended by a withers strap is "universal on all Han carvings, reliefs and stamped bricks" (Needham, 308). The idea of such a harness may have derived from the Chinese experience with human haulage, such as pulling boats upstream.

[1] The port is the raised and curved part in the middle of some bits, characteristic on curb bits. "Rings" and "spades" are elaborations on the port and are common on "Moorish", i.e. North African and Spanish style curbs.

TYPES OF HARNESSING

(Nos. 1, 4, 5 from Needham, IV, 305 and nos. 2, 3, and 6 from Needham, IV, 314)

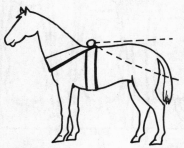

1. Throat and girth harness of occidental antiquity.

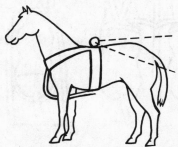

2. Martingale modification of ancient Egypt.

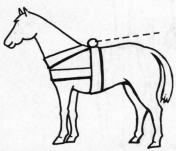

3. False breast strap of Assyria (8th century B.C.) and Persia (4th century B.C.).

4. Breast strap of ancient and medieval China.

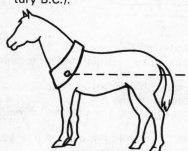

5. Collar harness of late Mediaeval China and the West.

6. Saddle Breast of Byzantium (10–13th century A.D.) and Cambodia (Khmer – 12th century).

TYPES OF HARNESSING (Needham, IV, 328)

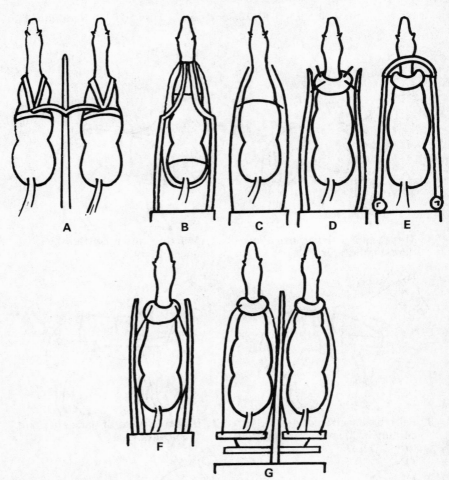

A	Pole cross bar, yokes and throat and girth harness.
B	Han breast strap harness with shafts, yoke vestigial, hip strap, and breeching present.
C	Postillion or later breast strap harness with trace attached to vehicle.
D	Traditional Chinese collar harness with the hard components, descendent of the yoke and ancestor of the hames, attached directly to the forward ends of the shafts.
E	A duga (Russian and Finnish hitch) retaining arched cross bar because shafts are not structurally part of the vehicle.
F	Modern collar harness with traces attached to vehicle directly.
G	Modern collar harness with central shaft and traces attached to whipple trees to receive pull of the collar.

Following the breast strap the Chinese invented breeching and after that the shoulder collar, possibly in the Han period. The common element in the Chinese collars of the fifth to tenth centuries is a collar piece attached at the lower part of the shoulder to a shaft. Some of them also show a curved piece of wood like a yoke passing over the collar and attached below at the lower part of the shoulder to the shaves. This wooden piece eventually, of course, became modified as the hames common to modern harness in the western world.

Le Febvre des Noëttes held that the dependence upon the throat band for the horse therefore limited its utility so that it was reserved as an aristocratic animal. He further maintained that the invention of the horse collar was the chief causal factor in the decline and disappearance of slavery. On the other hand, in the Mediterranean world it can equally be argued that no one bothered much about developing more efficient utilitarian harness for horses because of the prevalence of the belief that the horse was an aristocratic animal and should not be used for common labour. Further, in the Mediterranean world horses were always in such great demand for military purposes that they were too precious to use for common labour. And finally we note that once the throat band was abandoned in favour of breast bands and, later, collars, in Europe, the full use of the horse as a draught animal still depended upon the development of larger horses for such labour, as well as the ability to provide adequate feed to animals which were restricted in their use to draught purposes.

Concerning the extent to which the horse collar may be viewed as instrumental in the decline of slavery, Needham points out that slavery was not important in China, the original home of the horse collar, and that when it was introduced into Europe, mass slavery had already long since disappeared there. Furthermore, draught labour eventually assumed by collared horses was originally the work of oxen rather than slaves (Needham, 329–30).

In contrast to Mediterranean Europe and North Africa, it has been argued that horses were more readily available and not so rare to the Chinese, Huns and Mongols. The Chinese interest in developing efficient harness may have been encouraged because they had the available horses and did not have such an aristocratic view of them as the westerners (Needham, 330). Creel, however, clearly shows that throughout Chinese history horses have always been in short supply. Two examples will suffice to demonstrate this point. One Sung Ch'i (998–1061) reported that, "while China had a large number of cavalrymen, only one or two out of ten had a horse to ride" (Creel, 1965, 667). In "the Ming Dynasty (1368–1643) the need for horses was critical, and great efforts were made to import them". Because of the lack of horses

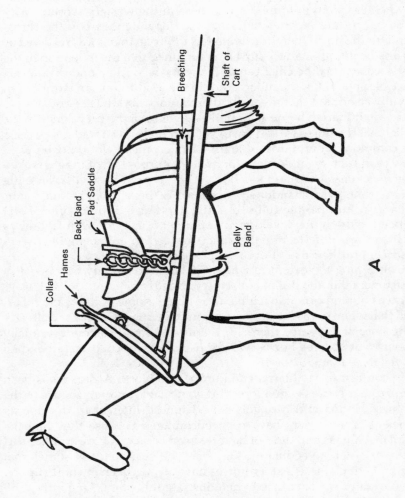

Breeching

Shaft of Cart

Back Band

Pad Saddle

Hames

Collar

Belly Band

A

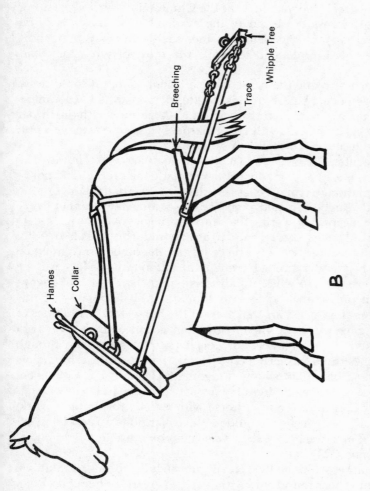

Hames

Collar

Breeching

Trace

Whipple Tree

B

MAIN FEATURES OF THE TWO PREVAILING
TECHNIQUES OF HORSE HARNESSING BY COLLAR

A.   Single horse, two shaft harness.
B.   Double harness with one shaft.

a great part of the Chinese silk and tea trade was aimed at acquiring them from neighbouring nomads.

Creel believes the Chinese were never able to solve their horse problem because of the immense pressures for land for intensive agricultural purposes and the consequent limitations of pasture and also because they did not pay as careful attention to proper breeding as they might (Creel, 1965, 669). That the Chinese interest in inventing good horse harness arose out of the availability of horses is to be doubted. Perhaps, on the contrary, since such animals were in short supply they were motivated to make the most of what they had available.

Collar harness made the horse more efficient so that it could draw much heavier loads. Le Febvre des Noëttes demonstrated experimentally that a team of horses can pull about 1,100 pounds with the throat band harness, "whereas with collar-harness the same team can pull four to five times that weight" (White, 60).

Tylden contests the claim that the horse collar was "one of the greatest inventions ever made." It never made the breast band obsolescent even though it may be less efficient in terms of traction, but the breast band "can be adjusted from one size of animal to another" very rapidly "by raising or lowering the strap which goes over the neck at its base." Not only does a breast band fit any shoulder but it is also readily made by any leather worker. The collar, on the other hand, must be made by a carefully trained craftsman. Although "collars can be changed and made to work on" different animals, this is not always easy and it can often lead to sore shoulders. "It is because of this necessity for altering collars that most of the horse drawn artilleries of the world gave up using them. Losses in action or from overwork might make it impossible to transfer collars to fresh animals, though with breast harness this gave no problems at all . . . in coaching days the horse and his collar belonged together" (Tylden, 10). Collars are also more suited to big draught horses with straight and heavy shoulders. It is difficult to fit a light horse with a collar for draught work, because with their sloping shoulders the collar rides up and hampers breathing. Thus, the breast strap was commonly used on light buggy horses (Haines, 23).

Breast harness ultimately spread from China through unknown peoples until it was found among the early Magyars, Bohemians, Poles and Russians. Central European burials from the seventh to the tenth centuries contained T-shaped bones or horn pieces which connected the breast and throat straps and the traces. After the tenth century these parts are no longer found; it is believed this is because breast straps had been replaced by collars (Needham, 311), which came into

Europe at the beginning of the tenth century and were found every-where in the continent by the twelfth century (Needham, 317). A Tunisian centre for the independent invention of a breast strap must also be considered as an ultimate source for the diffusion of such harness into Europe (Bulliet, 194ff.).

The Saddle

Cloths or skins placed over the horse's back appeared only in the first millenium B.C. The Assyrians used a horse cloth in the ninth century B.C. and the Greeks approximately three hundred years after. The Scythians may have used animal skins for this purpose as early as the Greeks.

There are essentially three different hypotheses regarding the evolution of the wooden frame riding saddle. Haudricourt and Daumas among others suggest the first wooden frame saddles probably arose out of the pack saddle (Daumas, 98). Even in modern times pack saddles are often ridden when not otherwise in use. Second, we might surmise that the true wood frame saddle developed from the Pazyryk model associated with the Altaian Scythians of the fifth and fourth centuries B.C. These oldest riding saddles with any wooden parts had wooden "spacers" in the front and back, but lacked a real tree frame. Finally, the camel saddle may have been the model for the horse saddle.

All wood frame saddles date from the post-Christian era, their earliest users being the Chinese, Sarmatians, and other as yet undesignated Central Asiatic peoples. Two basic saddle styles emerged very early. One was a light weight variety with a low fork and cantle and no horn, first appearing with the Romans in the fourth century A.D. and characteristic of west European and some African and Oriental saddles ever since. A second type has a high fork and a distinct horn. It is possibly of Central Asiatic origin. This heavier saddle became common in Mediaeval Europe and has been associated with most of those around the world who make their livelihood on horseback, from Central Asia to America.

Stirrups

There is a possibility that the evolution of the stirrup begins with leather loops presumably first associated with the Scythians of the fourth century B.C. We may surmise that loops were adapted by the Indians between 100–200 B.C. to barefoot riding as big-toe stirrups. From the third or second centuries B.C. until about the fifth century

A.D. the concept of a stirrup-like device seems to have been spreading around a vast area from the Black Sea to Central India and China, culminating at the end of this period in the metal foot stirrup. The stirrup idea appeared in China shortly after the beginning of the Christian era and, possibly by the second century A.D. or by the fifth century at the latest, the Chinese had developed a metal foot stirrup adapted to booted riding. Sarmatian metal stirrups might date to the first and second century A.D. but this is controversial. Between the fifth and seventh centuries the stirrup spread to Central Asia, southern Siberia, Korea, Japan, and Iran.

Shortly thereafter it became known to the Arabs, although there is a chance they had earlier become familiar with the foot loop as a result of direct contact with India. Such a loop was applied to camels (White, 18). The stirrup entered Europe at the close of the seventh century or beginning of the eighth at which time it was found in East Prussia, Lithuania and among the Germans (White, 22). Throughout the eighth and ninth centuries it spread to the remaining parts of Europe.

Spurs

Jope suggests that spurs imply booted riding (Jope, 557). This is not necessarily so since the Arab Bedouin and some Gauchos use spurs attached to straps and worn on bare or sandalled feet; the Carmargue of southern France used them in conjunction with wooden shoes. The earliest spurs were of the prick variety found first among the Greeks and shortly thereafter among La Tene Celts (400 – 250 B.C.). Prick spurs prevailed for well over a thousand years until in thirteenth century Europe they were superseded by rowells. Spurs "do not appear to have reached the Far East until recent times" (Jope, 557).

Horseshoes

True horseshoes which are metal plates nailed to the hoof, developed out of the hipposandal of pre-Christian Roman times. The earliest evidence for them is from the ninth century and from two widely separated places: Byzantium and the Yenisei River of Siberia. Bökönyi believes there is a connection between the appearance of the heavy horse and of shoeing in 9–10th century Europe. Because of their weaker hooves heavy horses need shoeing more than eastern ones (Bökönyi, 1974, 272). Horseshoes were an important factor in expanding the role of the horse as a draught animal.

In conclusion, the first four to five millenia (ca. 4000 B.C. – 600 A.D.) of the domesticated horse resulted in the development of all the basic patterns of horse use which we have today. In this time all the possible ways in which the horse could be exploited had been explored. The funamental patterns of draught harness and cart had evolved: the basic idea of the horseshoe, the bitted bridle, reins, shoulder collar with hames, or breast strap, traces, breeching, shaves, a two or four wheeled wagon with spoked wheels, and a pivotal front end. Only nailed horseshoes, the whipple tree, independent suspension and springs were yet to be added. In riding gear, the cavesson, snaffle and curb had been developed as well as the two forms of wood frame saddles, toe and foot stirrups, breast pieces, crupper and spurs. For the last millenium and a half no new basic patterns have been introduced with regard to riding – only modifications on ones long since in existence. For those who tend to see the last one or two hundred years as the time in which "everything" was invented, these are factors worth bearing in mind.

ON HORSEBACK RIDING AND ITS BEGINNINGS

The various data of archaeological sites which might pertain to horse riding are open to a diversity of interpretations. The best evidence is pictures, engravings and statues of men actually riding, but in most cases what is available is pieces of harness, especially cheek pieces from bitted bridles. To some, such as Bökönyi, the bridle is evidence of riding, since he believes the earliest use of horses on carts and chariots was with a muzzle strap (Bökönyi, 1968, 7). Others such as Hancar recognize that "every rider among us will decide without hesitation that riding is possible without bridles or reins, but that these means of communication with and direction of the horse are indispensable for driving. There is an enormous difference between the direct communication of the rider with the horse – through pressure of the thigh, weight shifting, touch by hand or with a whip – and the rather indirect communication of the driver with the horse while he is walking alongside it or sitting on the coachman's seat – with problems of the load, the road, the coupling of two horse temperaments.

"Riding without snaffle is proved by archaeological and historical evidence. The classical example for this are the Libyans . . . whose riding warriors did not use snaffles in spite of the fact that they were apparently familiar with the gag bit *(Knebeltrense)* of the Carthaginians, Romans and Gauls and in spite of the fact that they themselves used bits for mules in pulling carts" (Hancar, 552). Other similar examples abound in the use of alternatives to the bit for riding such as the use of a nose band (cavesson or hackamore). Le Febvre des Noëttes reports one of his friends, a French officer, who in 1885 mounted a vigorous pure blooded horse without saddle or bridle and galloped across a field, jumping over tent ropes, trenches, and other barriers, turned and stopped the animal at his bidding. The rider used a strap around the animal's neck to slow or stop it and to turn to the right or left he struck it on the neck with the flat of his hand. Le Febvre des Noëttes thus presumes this is the manner by which the ancient North Africans rode without a bridle (Vigneron, 104). These examples all demonstrate clearly that the presence of bridles, cheek pieces or bits or their absence in no way is a sure indication of riding or the absence of riding.

Furthermore, that bits and antler cheek pieces appear only after a certain date is no proof that jaw straps, such as were used by American Indians, made of raw hide or sinew or other non-durable material, were not used for some time before the appearance of more durable bits of bone or bronze.

Childe and others have noted the tendency for the bitted bridle to appear about the same time as the chariot and this would seem to lend credence to the hypothesis that the presence of bits in sites at least of the second millenium B.C. is more assuredly a sign of horse driving than of horse riding, not that the latter could not also be present as well.

Bearing these observations in mind let us then review the evidence for early horse riding.

Rudenko speculates that with the making of a simple halter, casual riding of horses probably took place from their initial domestication; he does not mention "serious" riding. He further assumes that "the widespread adoption of riding in Eurasia was not due to the spontaneous discovery of how to ride", but was stimulated by large scale horse breeding where it became essential. Such activity we associate with the equestrian pastoralists of central Asia who appeared towards the end of the second millenium B.C. (Rudenko, xxv). Gimbutas, however, apparently believes that horse breeding was sufficiently expanded in the fourth millenium B.C. Ukraine to demand use of the horse in the surveillance of herds (Gimbutas, 1970, 158). Certainly the thesis that the accumulation of large herds of horses or even of modest numbers in a half wild state demands mounted herding is one of the most convincing arguments for the origin of horse riding.

Downs had stressed the importance of the relation of bodily size of the horse to speed as an important factor in the development of early riding. The size of equines "explains why riding became an important technique so much later than driving . . ." (Downs, 1961, 1194). Both the tarpan and Przewalski's horse are about thirteen hands. Domesticated horses are all over fourteen hands; modern ones average fifteen hands. Domestic horses such as the mustang soon return to a smaller size when left to fend for themselves for a few generations. Down concludes ". . . that, in the early phases of domestication, the horse, ass, and onager were about the same size and could be employed interchangeably. None of these species was large enough to serve as a useful mount. At best they could serve as a sort of moving seat for a man, but sustained galloping would be out of the question. Like the ponies of Ireland, the Orkneys, and parts of Scandinavia, their value as mounts in war or hunting would have been negligible and their use restricted to simple transport" (Downs, 1961, 1195).

Downs does not mention the possible utility of the early horse for herding horses. But we know from the modern ethnographic records that pony-sized horses have been widely used for this end. Icelandic ponies, thirteen hands, have been ridden for a thousand years in rounding up other ponies. Many Mongolian and Central Asiatic ponies, especially those of the Yakut and Tibetans, are no bigger and are used for the same purpose. What is more, these ponies are further encumbered with the weight of saddles, a feature absent among the most ancient stockmen. Of course ponies mounted by full grown men will not gallop like an Arab or a Thoroughbred, but they will gallop when pressed. And in herding it is more often the short burst of speed rather than the sustained gallop which is more important. Further, the lack of speed resulting from being mounted can be counteracted by the cooperation of several mounted men, the use of trained dogs, or even letting the boys ride herd. With an abundance of available mounts, one can also frequently change from a tired horse to a fresh one.

Bökönyi among others has hypothesized that early horse husbandry was not much different from maintenance in the wild state. Horses would, therefore, graze in herds in open range, with no hand-feeding, under a stallion. Herds would comprise between twenty and fifty animals; nearly all would be unaccustomed to handling by humans. Some control of herd movement becomes a minimum essential so that even use of a "moving seat" under such conditions would be far superior to chasing around on foot. And Goodenough's view that perhaps men on chariots early guided herds is not very credible (Goodenough, 256) for herding demands the ability to make quick and sharp turns, to ride the rough ground as well as the smooth, and to ride among trees and other obstructions as well as on the open plain. It would also be more difficult to approach a half-wild herd with a formidable machine like a chariot.

It is not unlikely that far back in man's history boys or men started riding some tame or domesticated beast for a lark or a dare. There is little reason to doubt that plough or cart oxen were ridden on occasion and that the idea of riding was already conceived by the time horses were domesticated. Thus, both the impetus and the idea of riding must have existed among these early stockbreeders of the steppes. What was then necessary was a device to control the animal while riding. Evidence for some kind of head gear – bridle, halter or hackamore – is already present from the fourth, if not the fifth, millenium B.C. in the Ukraine. It seems therefore highly probable that horse riding is much more ancient that has previously been supposed. Dates of the mid fourth millenium B.C. are no longer outrageous. What is more, the generally held thesis that horse driving precedes horse riding must be questioned.

But the horse for riding did not become popular outside the Eurasian steppes until its military significance was perceived. This did not occur until we have both the development of adequate devices for control and guidance and the breeding of a horse large enough to bear a man on its back at a sustained gallop. Riding was stimulated by its application to a military role and at the same time riding induced a major change in methods of warfare. If the second millenium B.C. was the era of the chariot, the first millenium B.C. became the era of cavalry. Both the rapid adoption of the horse as a riding animal for warfare, for the nobility of Near Eastern nation-states and for equestrian nomads early in the first millenium B.C. is related to a specific configuration of developments around this time: the selective breeding for size of horses to produce more effective man-bearers; the techonological innovations in improvements in bits and saddlecloths; and the simultaneous improvement in knowledge of the mechanics of riding and of horse psychology.

VII

Europe from Mediaeval Times to the Seventeenth Century

The Mounted Knight

The primary developments in the role of the horse in Mediaeval Europe were the armoured knight and the great increase in the use of the horse for draught purposes for the farm, for cartage and as a carriage animal. Both of these developments are associated with the breeding of larger horses and the implementation of new types of harness.

The Mediaeval evolution of the mounted armoured knight represents the appearance of a fifth major pattern of horse use for warfare. First, there was the horse and chariot, secondly, the mounted javelin thrower, third, the mounted lancer and fourth, the mounted archer. The knight is basically an improvement on the mounted lancer, the foundation of which is in the breeding of large horses to bear the greater weight of armour for both horse and rider, and a heavier saddle. The armour, of course, provided more protection, but the saddle, with its high pommel and cantle and stirrups, was almost of equal importance in this respect in that it gave an extremely secure seat, considerably reducing the chances of being thrown off, an event particularly dangerous to a heavily armoured person who would be near helpless lying on the ground. A third necessary element in this complex was the employment of elaborate curb bits, since the rider, encumbered by armour, carrying weapons and shield, and required to hold the reins high due to the high pommel, had to have a device which would control the horse with a minimum of effort.

Such a machine of war involved considerable expense and therefore necessitated, as in the case of the horse and chariot warriors, an adequate system of support from those with accumulated wealth. Thus, kings and nobility were the patrons of the armoured horsemen. Ridgeway says the basis of chivalry is in the mounted soldier-landowner or the idea that land holding entailed being a warrior wearing "mail and mounted on a horse" – a pattern which evolved among the "Teutonic tribes at least a century . . . before . . . Charlemagne" (Ridgeway, 332). These features may have their basis in the Teutonic tribes, but the code associated with chivalry also owes much to certain parallel developments in the early Islamic world which penetrated Europe in the course of the Crusades.

While the Mediaeval knight is invariably identified with heavy armour and a large and heavy horse, this picture is in fact actually only true for the culmination of a pattern, after the thirteenth century. Neither armour nor saddlery of the period prior to the twelfth century was heavy and the horse resembled the light and medium hunter, not a massive cart horse. During the Third Crusade the favourite horses of Richard, the Lion Hearted, were a Turkmen and a Cypriot, both moderate-sized horses (Trench, 73).

Horses in the eleventh, twelfth, and thirteenth centuries carried somewhat over two hundred pounds: the knight weighing about 140 pounds, and some forty or more pounds of armour, lance, sword, shield and saddle. But there are today many cow ponies which carry this weight and work at the same time.

Heavier and more lethargic breeds – "cold-blooded" horses – had been bred in northern Europe from early times. They, however, were not large and massive creatures. The Romans also contributed to the breeding of heavier types, but it was in the Low Countries, especially in Flanders, from the eleventh century onward, that the breeding of "great horses" became important.

The invention of the cross-bow and the experiences of the Crusaders initiated a major development in heavy armour in Europe, and its employment was such that by the end of the twelfth century there arose a great demand for heavier horses to support the increased weight. Interwoven chain armour prevailed until about 1300 when metal plates gradually superseded the chain mail and "by the beginning of the 15th century the knight was sheathed from head to foot in a complete panoply of plate armour" (Ridgeway, 336).

A knight's charger about this time bore the following:

"Steel chamfron (or headpiece) for horse   5 lb
Bridle, bit and headstall   8 lb.
Remainder of horse armour, steel plate and leather   78 lb.
Saddle, girth and stirrups   24 lb.
Man's complete plate armour   80 lb.
Pair spurs   3 lb. 12 oz.
Sword, mounted pattern   7 lb.
Shield   5 lb. 8 oz.
Lance   10 lb.
Dagger   4 lb. 5 oz.
Man's clothing   10 lb.
Man's surcoat   5 lb.

Housing over horse armour	10 lb.
Helmet crest and pennant	5 lb.

	Total	255 lbs. 9 oz.
	Rider, say	175 lbs.
	All-up weight	436 lbs. 9 oz."

(Jankovich, 156).

Despite the fact that the estimated weight of the man may be over that of a normal Mediaeval knight, the horse would still bear well over four hundred pounds. By contrast Jankovich states that the standard English packhorse weight is about half of this amount and the Austro-Hungarian cavalry manual gives the total "all-up" weight for a troop horse as from 266 to 282 pounds (Jankovich, 156).

With this heavy load the Mediaeval knight's horse was expected to make periodic short distance charges at a gallop. Obviously these are accomplishments beyond the capabilities of a light saddle horse. At the same time the knight's charger was no plough horse. The Franks certainly "never rode anything like the ponderous cart-horses which popular history attributes to them" (Trench, 87). The knight's great horse which represents the culmination of Mediaeval horsemanship between the thirteenth and fifteenth centuries was larger than the earlier great horses, but also should not be confused with those which were bred in the sixteenth century nor the heavy draught breeds which began to appear about this time and thereafter. For example, the armour worn by a fifteenth century charger would not fit the smallest Shire horse of today.

Mediaeval knights employed two horses: One was the charger discussed above, a heavier horse caparisoned with armour and ridden by the knight for charging in close order over relatively short distances (Jankovich, 73). We speak of someone getting on his "high horse" and this is derived from the knight's practice of mounting his charger when he is about to do battle (Jankovich, 74). On the march this great horse, which was always a stallion, was led in hand by a groom while the knight rode a second horse, the palfrey, a light horse specifically bred for comfortable riding. The palfrey was a pacer (ambler) not a trotter.

A special technique of riding and type of saddlery was adopted to accommodate the style of fighting employed by the knight. The riding technique has parallels to the Greek and Roman styles of riding without stirrups. Greeks and Romans rode long with legs at a natural angle and slightly bent at the knee, not straight. Thus, they held on firmly with the upper leg while the lower part was free. The Mediaeval knight rode long in the stirrups, but also straight-legged with no bent knee, toes pointing down and feet well forward. His legs braced against the stirrup irons and his buttocks pressed against the cantle so that he was locked into position – a style preserved in a modified version by the American cowboy (Trench, 77).

"Part of the explanation" for Mediaeval riding style was "that the stirrup-leathers were then attached to the saddle as far forward as possible and thus well in front of the rider's centre of gravity, and this meant that he had to sit with his legs sticking out forward" (Trench, 77). Yet, more important is that the knight rode long and locked into position to prevent being toppled over the horse's head and so endangering himself on the high pommel if he was struck by an enemy. He rode stiff with feet well forward "so that his stirrups and legs absorbed the shock and kept him braced back against the cantle . . ." (Trench, 77). And the high cantle helped protect him from being pushed off the back of the horse.

"Field Punishment Number One in the severe disciplinary code of the Teutonic Order consisted of trotting in full armour by the hour" on the heavy horse or charger (Jankovich, 74).

In the course of the Mediaeval period saddle styles were modified to fit the general pattern of the riding knight. Cantles and pommels were made high and the seats were often padded. By the fourteenth century the pommel and cantle were carried "so far round the knight's person that they touch each other . . ." which must have created some interesting problems in mounting and dismounting. In addition saddles were made so high in the seat that the rider's knee was on a level with the horse's back (Hewitt, II, 320). Saddles were often elaborately decorated with scrolls, animals, monsters or heraldic figures. From early Mediaeval times they were secured to the horse with a single cinch and a breast piece, but in the later Middle Ages the crupper became common as well. The stirrups were of iron becoming more elaborately designed after the advent of horse armour. At the close of the twelfth century knights' chargers were attired in chain mail and later plate armour replaced the mail (Hewitt, *passim*).

The idea of chivalry, the heavily armoured knight on his great horse no sooner reached its peak in the fifteenth century when it began to decline rapidly in the face of gunpowder. By the beginning of the seventeenth century this cultural complex had become such a thing of the past that Don Quixote, in his singular attempt to revive it, was only viewed with derision.

The advantages of smaller, lighter more agile and swifter horses now began to be appreciated as the great horse came less in demand for military purposes. At the same time some of these great horses by Renaissance times were being selectively bred for dray and farm use. After 1400 the carriage was developed and eventually roads began to be improved in Europe. The invention of the Hungarian *koczi* in the seventeenth century gave impetus to the use of the coach for long distance transportation which became common and widespread in eighteenth century Europe. Thus, larger horses exchanged their heavy saddles, armour and knights for the traces of coaches and carriages.

The style and gear of riding also underwent considerable transformation. The traditional Mediaeval pattern as epitomized in the fourteenth and fifteenth century knights of Europe began to decline in favour of a new style which came from the Arab-Berber peoples of Morocco. The Spanish referred to the old Mediaeval style as *a la brida*. The Arab-Berber technique was called *a la jineta* after the Zenata-speaking Berbers who comprised a large segment of the Moroccan population and were largely responsible for its introduction into Spain. The *jineta* method involved riding with short stirrups and bent knee with a collected horse, using a light hand, but a severe bit and lighter weight saddlery. The Arab-Berbers had in turn adapted the riding seat from Central Asiatic nomads.

La jineta style of riding was introduced into Europe with the Muslim invasions of Spain. The Crusaders were also exposed to it in their adventures in Asia Minor, but the technique was ignored by the Europeans until gunpowder had begun to make the heavily armoured knight an anachronism. Earlier the Crusaders had seen how the light armour, saddlery and short-stirruped riding style had made the Arab-Muslim armies extremely mobile and made their horses less easily tired, but the short stirrups meant that the warrior was easily knocked out of his saddle on impact. The increasing use of gunpowder in warfare intensified the advantages of the Arab style and made the disadvantages irrelevant. Arab style prevailed in southern Spain by the fourteenth century and over both central and southern parts by the fifteenth, although in the north of Spain, and in Portugal as well, *la brida* style persisted until modern times and has apparently always been prevalent in Portugal. Graham claims that the Spaniards attached a great importance to mastering both methods of riding and it became the greatest praise to refer to a cavalier as "a man who could ride well in both the saddles". Occasionally, rather than the ordinary epitaph, this fact was written on a man's tombstone (Graham, 18). Both styles were therefore introduced into Spanish America at the time of the conquest. Eventually, *la jineta* riding diffused northward into the rest of Europe, but not until the seventeenth century.

The Horse in Sport

Apart from the use of the horse for warfare, Mediaeval Europe developed several war-related games or elaborated upon types of equestrian games having their origin in ancient Greece, Rome and Central Asia. As part of his training the knight practiced on the quintain. This was a post with a pivoted cross-arm at the top, hanging from which was a target at one end and a weight on the other. The rider charged the target with levelled lance being careful not to be struck down as the weight swung around behind him (Norman, 151).

When he had achieved some degree of success at the quintain the knight engaged in tournaments. These were expected to be mock battles engaging several knights, although not infrequently someone lost his temper and the melée was transformed into a serious encounter ending in participants being wounded or killed. Tournaments became extremely elaborate and costly affairs, often attended by kings, but they were also objects of suspicion by rulers as being potential centres for intrigues and plots of rebellion. Winners of events not only obtained prizes, but also the armour and horse of the defeated (Norman, 152 ff.; Hewitt, I, 362 ff.).

In time, the mass combat of the tournament was replaced by single combat, one knight charging at another, both with levelled lances. More and more precautions were taken to make these jousts as innocuous as possible. Thus, blunted weapons came into more common use and a special heavy tilting armour was made. In the early fifteenth century a wooden fence was erected to separate the opponents to reduce the likelihood of the horses colliding. By the sixteenth century the tournament was no longer a test of arms, but had become purely a pageant, in keeping with the overall demise of Mediaeval knighthood.

In Spain mounted fighting of wild bulls was a "gentleman's sport" pursued by Christians and Muslims alike before the eleventh century. In that century it had become an arena sport, although the wild bulls had by then become a rarity. Mounted bull-fighting reached its peak in Spain in the sixteenth and seventeenth centuries. Until about 1700 it remained a sport of gentlemen, but at that time a Frenchman, Philip of Anjou, ascended the Spanish throne. He despised this Spanish sport and directed his attention to drawing the aristocracy away from it. As a consequence bull-fighting became a spectator sport pursued by professionals and was modified into its present-day form (Trench, 201). The Portuguese, however, retained the old form, participated in by both professionals and amateurs. For it, horses are trained for as long as five to six years and bulls are trained to kill, although the object is not to kill the bull, but rather to implant darts in the bull's withers (Trench, 201).

Other Riding Uses of the Horse

The horse was not only ridden by the knight, but also by any who were sufficiently well-to-do to be able to maintain one. Travel during Mediaeval times was invariably by foot or on horseback since roads were generally in poor condition and the carriage did not become common until the sixteenth and seventeenth centuries. Non-military riders employed saddlery and gear similar to that of the knight but with their ambling-paced palfreys they preferred less severe bits. As Taylor suggests the type of bit employed was a symbol of one's social status. The aristocracy rode larger horses equipped with curb bits while the lesser folk made do with smaller horses and snaffles (Taylor, L., 85). In contrast to the knight whose charger was always a stallion, the lesser folk rode geldings. Mares were not approved as correct mounts for men; they were for carts and "ignoble purposes" (Berenger, I, 68).

With the development of the cattle industry in Mediaeval Spain, horses began to be employed for herding purposes, thus laying the basis for the later evolution of the Ibero-American horse and cattle ranching complex.

Mediaeval European clergy invariably rode mules, a practice which Dent derives from the ancient Jewish preference for mules and asses (Dent, 74). Throughout South-western Europe mules were frequently ridden as palfreys by laymen.

One of the equestrian developments of Mediaeval western Europe was the introduction of the side saddle specifically designed for women riders. In western European society riding seated sideways is identified with the horsewoman, but this style is still a traditional method of riding for both men and women in some of the rural areas of south-east Europe and the Middle East. Once, in eastern Mediterranean antiquity, horses might have at times been ridden bareback with the rider seated on the side. In the modern Arab world it is not uncommon to see donkeys ridden in this fashion, but they, like the horses of the Balkans, are more frequently ridden with a pack saddle. Farmers pack their goods to market on their horses and return home riding sideways on their pack saddles. The parent of the true sidesaddle is undoubtedly a pack saddle. Those which first appeared in Europe had their beginnings as pack saddles with a board suspended from one side so that a woman could ride and rest her feet on it for support. This device originated in Asia, possibly Central Asia, and appeared in Europe in Mediaeval times.

The vogue for the sidesaddle began in Italy, Spain and France in the twelfth century and soon spread north, although it did not become popular in England until after 1380. Before the end of Mediaeval times the sidesaddle was considered the proper riding mode for a woman throuthout western Europe, but sidesaddles as such disappeared from use in Asia (Vernam, 372–373).

Until the first part of the eighteenth century sidesaddles were equipped with a footrest rather than a stirrup and this forced the rider to be moved sideways with every motion of the horse. In the first half of the eighteenth century the footrest was replaced by a stirrup for the left foot to allow for more ease of riding in back and forth motion (Vernam, 377). The Western European custom of women riding sidesaddle did not start to decline in popularity until after the beginning of the twentieth century.

The Use of the Horse for Draught

In earliest Mediaeval times horses were not commonly employed for draught purposes, partly because adequate harness such as the breast strap or shoulder collar had not been introduced or was not yet widely accepted. Apparently in ninth century Norway they were, however, used in ploughing and other farm work, presumably with a breast strap type harness. Saxon records indicate no use of horses for these purposes. Known Saxon wills contain legacies of saddle horses, both broken and feral and of entire stud farms which were chiefly wooded places well supplied with feral horses. One farm, for example, contained one hundred wild horses and sixteen tame geldings. These were probably used for war mounts, peaceful travel or sport, but not for farm use (Trow-Smith, 63–4). The Domesday Survey shows that by the beginning of Norman times the horse was still not an important farm animal, although it was becoming so. Manors giving figures had from one to six riding horses, used for manorial officers on their rounds of the farm. The Domesday mentions a few horses for harrowing, but everywhere riding horses were in the majority on the manors. By the twelfth century harrow horses were in common use for dominial and villein cultivation in Great Britain (Trow-Smith, 84). Horses also hauled hay, grain, manure and other items.

In Mediaeval Europe two basic types of draught harness were employed for horses. One was the trace harness for ploughing and included padded shoulder collar, hames, back band and traces which were hitched to whipple trees.[1] The Bayeaux tapestry shows that collar harness was worn by horses and mules for agricultural work in this time. The other type of harness was for shafted carts. It dispensed with traces but required the addition of breeching strap and a pad saddle.

The breeching strap was discussed above in connection with developments of harness in the Han period of China. The pad saddle is a device aimed at distributing the weight of the shafts over a horse's back, by having a chain or strap passing from one shaft to another over the saddle. There is also a girth which goes under the horse to prevent the shafts from rising. These two types of harness have persisted down to modern times. A modification on these kinds of harness, the *duga*, has prevailed in Russia and been common in adjacent areas under Russian influence. The collar of the horse is hitched to shafts and to an arched bow which passes over his head. Other horses may be hitched to this centre horse with ropes or straps.[2]

There seems little question that horses performed widely in a light draught capacity – pulling carts and harrows – throughout northern Europe from the eleventh or twelfth century onward. As cart animals they were not only employed on farms but in mines as well. How extensively they were harnessed to ploughs remains however a question. White believes that by the end of the eleventh century the plough horse was common in northern continental Europe, and by the twelfth century it was becoming the normal plough animal in the drainage basins of the North Sea and the Baltic including Great Britain. In fact, he sees the abandonment of settlements, but not of cultivated land, which occurred between the eleventh and thirteenth centuries in Germany, as caused by the replacement of the ox by the horse. The latter was so much faster it permitted farmers to live much further from their fields, so they could live in larger villages and towns at some distance from the fields and, thus, abandon their small dispersed hamlets necessitated by the slowness of the ox (White, 68–69).

Others have some reservations about how widespread the horse became for ploughing in Mediaeval Europe. The earliest picture of a horse-drawn plough encountered by Fussell is from the thirteenth century. He doubts how much the horse ever replaced the ox in Mediaeval times in western Europe (Fussell, 69). Ploughing with horses appears to have been extensive, after the twelfth century, if not before, in Norway, central Sweden and central Finland, in northern France, the Low countries, and possibly Poland. Ukrainian peasants ploughed with horses in the twelfth century, as is shown by a report of a conversation near Kiev in 1103 (White, 63). But elsewhere in northern

---

[1] The whipple tree (also called whiffle tree or swingle tree) appears to be a European invention of early Mediaeval times. It equalizes the pull on a load especially when turning corners. In Ireland and to a lesser extent in England, ploughs and other farm implements were tied to horses' tails. This practice was not outlawed until the seventeenth century (Hollis, 172).

[2] For a detailed description of British types of draught harness see Keegan, 1974.

Europe, for example, in southern Sweden, south-western Finland, Estonia, Denmark and most parts of Great Britain, the ox prevailed as the plough animal, and even in those regions where horses were employed the ox was in no sense uncommon.

Ernle states that in England ploughing teams were seldom made up of horses alone and that as a rule oxen were preferred for ploughing (Ernle, 13). In mid-thirteenth century England, Walter of Henley recommended that "a horse be harnessed in front of a pair of oxen in plough in order to increase the speed" (Fussell, 69; Lamond, 11). Jope observes that the horse became common for draught purposes after the padded collar became more general, after the twelfth century, but that "even then oxen were preferred . . ." (Jope, II, 91).

In England, at least, controversy persisted from the thirteenth to the eighteenth century over the relative merits of horses as against oxen, suggesting that the horse was not all that popular, especially since most of the agricultural writers seem to be arguing for the ox. Many of the reasons given in favour of the ox would seem to suggest yet further why horses did not totally supplant the ox. It was widely held that oxen could be fed more economically, were subject to fewer infirmities and did not require constant grooming and attention. Harness for oxen was inexpensive and could be made on the farm, in contrast to that of a horse which was costly and had to be made by a harness maker. Oxen were only shod on the forefeet, horses on all fours. A worn-out ox could be fattened for market and sold for more than its original cost. Horses were more costly to purchase, more quickly worn out by farm work and depreciated more rapidly in value after their prime. (This argument would carry more weight in Great Britain where horsemeat was strictly taboo than on the continent where it was not). It was observed that the horse pulled less steadily and sudden strains greatly taxed the primitive plough (Ernle, 13).

That a horse worked more quickly and for longer hours during the day was not always a point viewed with favour. Agricultural labourers and peasants working on the nobleman's lands preferred the slow-moving oxen which worked shorter hours. Indeed, Lynn White sees Walter of Henley's support of oxen over horses as deriving from the fact that ploughmen would not permit a horse team to go any faster than oxen, thus, presumably defeating the advantage the horse might have over the ox (White, 65).[1]

[1] Walter of Henley states: ". . . a plough of oxen will go as far in the year as a plough of horses, because the malice of ploughmen will not allow the plough (of horses) to go beyond their pace, no more than the plough of oxen" (Lamond, 11). The argument over the relative merits of horses and oxen reflects the old social conflict between employers seeking to speed-up production, while workers desire to exert themselves no more than is necessary.

White raises the question that if modern harness as well as horse-shoeing were known in Europe in 800 A.D., why did it take three hundred years before the horse was used in agriculture, particularly for ploughing. He believes the answer lies in the fact that the three fields system of cultivation involving triennial rotation was not adopted until the twelfth century. This system allowed for expanded production and, especially important in terms of the issue under discussion, was the spring planting of oats, barley, and various pulses. The oats provided additional horse feed and the pulses improved the European's diet. Thus, the new system of agriculture expanded the possibilities of the horse in draught (White, 68–69).

Slicher van Bath states that it is almost impossible to keep a horse under the old system of a two course rotation unless oats is imported. On the other hand, oxen can be used with either a two or three course system because they require less feed "and can be grazed on the common pasture". Oxen were given at most half as much oats as horses. Thus, with the changeover to the new three course system a farmer now had a choice of continuing with oxen or adopting horses (Slicher van Bath, 60–61). The association of a transfer from oxen to horses with the change from two to three fields system is clearly shown in a late example from Poitou in France in 1790 (Slicher van Bath, 60–61).

There is a distinct increase in the employment of horses in European farming from the inception of the three fields system, but the ox continued to be the preferred animal for ploughing over extensive areas of western Europe until the sixteenth century (Jope, II, 91–92) and was not completely replaced by the horse until the nineteenth century.

There must therefore be additional reasons for the tardiness of a universal adoption of the horse as a plough animal. It must be remembered that horses in Europe had been for centuries closely identified with aristocracies, sport and pleasure, and for millenia the ox had been identified with the plough. Peasants, noted for a tenacious conservatism, can be expected to be reluctant to abandon the ox, particularly when the superiority of the alternative is not exactly clear and straightforward. Nor is the association of the horse with war and sport readily displaced when horses are not that numerous and remain comparatively small in size.

That the horse was early used for ploughing in Norway and Russia, one suspects, is related to the greater abundance of horses in those countries. For Norway, also, in contrast to most other parts of Europe there was not that much arable land and the soils were light and so more easily tilled by horses. For Russia there was always a closer affinity to Central Asiatic tradition and the multiple use of the horse.

That the horse became more commonly used for ploughing in northern France and the Low Countries, appears related not only to the adoption of the three fields system, but also to the breeding of larger heavier horses, a speciality in this area after the eleventh century. Such breeding was directed not to the demand for farm animals, but rather for mounts for armoured knights. By the sixteenth century this demand no longer existed, and it is interesting that it is at this time that Jope reports horses becoming important for farm ploughing in western Europe. They could now be obtained more cheaply for farm work. The intensification of the use of the horse for heavy draught work in western Europe also concided with increased demands for cartage as trade throughout the continent became more extended. Horses supplied the power.

Of some significance too is the type of soil that is cultivated. With the ancient type of heavy plough, oxen were preferred in ploughing heavy soils, whereas horses and oxen both worked satisfactorily in light soils. Perhaps some areas which had already adopted the three field system persisted in the use of oxen because of the heavy soil.

The transfer from oxen to horse, Slicher van Bath associates with increasing agricultural prosperity. Oxen die out in favour of horses where there is an expansion of farming land, as occurred in post-Reformation Europe. The horse becomes favoured because of its faster pace. "The ox saves food, the horse saves man-hours" (quoted in Slicher van Bath, 290). In one day, it is claimed, a horse can do the work of three or four oxen. White reports the Slavs as giving the horse a slightly lesser advantage over the ox. In Slavic territory east of Germany ploughland was measured as the amount of land which could be tilled by a yoke of oxen or by one horse (White, 63). Demands for horses under expanding agricultural conditions would also be increased since reclaimed lands are usually poorer quality, and lighter and so more easily worked.

For Hollis, the horse was not more quickly applied to farm work because of the lack of technological developments producing implements which would be better suited to it. As he says, little attention was paid to improving crop production until the eighteenth century (Hollis, 170).

Finally, we must consider the role of cultural values. Horses do not become favoured purely because they are faster or more enduring than oxen, or because of the appearance of suitable technology, or because of the introduction of an agricultural system which will provide more feed. They come into common use when the proper techno-economic-geographical conditions exist which allow for the full expression of already long-existing values which prize the horse among all animals. The prestige attached to the aristocrat's riding horse is transferred by the peasant to the draught horse so that having a team of draught horses becomes more prestigious than having a team of oxen. In the seventeenth century a combination of conditions was arising which now more than ever before allowed the peasant to fulfil one of his desired goals – the acquisition of horses – but his economic condition was such that he could not have a stable full of pleasure horses, but must satisfy himself with a good team of draught horses and a wagon.

In southern Europe (the Iberian Peninsula, southern France, Italy and the Balkans) the horse never attained the position as a draught animal it had in the north. During Mediaeval times, as in the north, the ox was common for heavy draught, but in Spain and Portugal and to a lesser extent in Italy, the mule came into more extensive use, while the horse continued to be reserved for the special status it had had since Classical times. There are several reasons why Mediterranean Europe did not adopt horses for heavy draught, but retained the ox and to some extent resorted to the mule. First, this region did not adopt the three course rotation system, but continued with the two course system because winter grain was their chief cereal crop and rainfall was insufficient to produce a satisfactory spring grain crop. (In Andalusia a modification of the two course rotation was adopted with one year cultivation and two years fallow) (Slicher van Bath, 58–9). This would mean that there could be no adequate provision of horse feed. As a result oxen remained in favour because they would work on less feed and on poorer quality feed than horses.

The adoption of the mule as a draught animal in Mediterranean Europe was probably motivated by the same reasons which led Southern plantation and farm operators in the United States to adopt mules in place of horses and oxen. They are faster and at least as strong as oxen, yet probably not much more expensive to keep. It is commonly believed that mules require less feed and certainly less choice feed than do horses, so that they would be easier to maintain in the traditional agricultural system of south-western Europe. It is also believed that mules require less attention and care than horses and that they work better in warmer climate than do horses – especially the heavy breeds of northern Europe. South-western Europe had a large donkey population lacking in the north, and, thus, had a solid base for mule production. Except in Ireland donkeys were never common in the north because they do not adapt well to colder climate.

Furthermore, both south-western Europe and the southern United States were more heavily under the influence of the tradition which identified the horse with riding, pleasure and war. It should not be forgotten that Spain was greatly affected by Arab-Berber culture where both donkey and mule were important for riding and for draught.

Mules never became common in the Balkans for farm draught as they did in Spain. In most of Yugoslavia, Greece, and Albania, in general, oxen continued to prevail until recent times. Buffalo were gradually diffused in Bulgaria and Rumania to supplement oxen, and horses were used in conjunction with oxen in Rumania.

We may summarize, then, the development of the horse for ploughing in Europe. Before 1100 the ox was the dominant type of plough animal throughout the continent, with the exception of Russia and Norway where horses were probably more readily available and where, for Norway, not a great deal of ploughing was done anyway. These would also represent important regions of the earliest European adoption of collar harness. After 1100 the horse came into more common use for the plough in northern Europe in conjunction with the adoption of the three fields system, the breeding of bigger horses in northern France and the Low Countries, and the spread of collar harness. In southern Europe the ox prevailed, but mules, rather than horses were often employed on ploughs especially in Iberia. This condition persisted in southern Europe to modern times. In northern Europe, the horse, especially after 1500, became increasingly more common, until by the eighteenth century it was more frequent on the plough than the ox over the entire area, ultimately completely supplanting the ox in the following century.

With the obsolescence of the heavily armoured knight before the sixteenth century, the great horses were turned to alternate uses and bred in directions with these uses in mind. Some, as we have seen, were for farm labour, others were employed in drawing heavy carts on highways; and still others, of a lighter frame, drew carriages. The appearance of the true carriage or coach with an adequate suspension system is an accomplishment of the fourteenth century Hungarians (Tarr, L, 184).[1] By the sixteenth century the coach was spread widely over Europe wherever highways were in a condition to bear them. Certainly the spread of coach travel provoked increased concern for improved highways, but at the same time some efforts had already been initiated in western Europe as early as the thirteenth century to improve them (Tarr, L., 169–170). Relatively good roads had been maintained by the Roman Empire, but with its demise they soon deteriorated in quality. Until the seventeenth century they remained in such a state that most traffic was by foot, horseback or litter.

[1] The evolution of the coach is adequately covered by Laszlo Tarr and will not be recapitulated here (Tarr, Laszlo, 1969).

Consumption of Horsemeat and Other Horse By-Products

As we noted before, the Pope had early decreed against the consumption of horsemeat as a sign of the continuation of pagan practice. Later the Eastern Orthodox patriarchs followed suit in prohibiting it to horse-eating Russians. These prohibitions seem to have had only a minimal effect. For example, in 1000 A.D. monks had a special blessing in the Roman Church for the flesh of the wild horse (Vesey-Fitzgerald, 80). The Poles continued hunting wild horses down to the seventeenth century and poor peasants throughout the continent were not about to permit the flesh of a dying or broken down horse to go to waste. But additional prohibitions were imposed by several European rulers, not because of religious scruple, but because horses were in such great demand for military purposes. Once this demand declined and, possibly also because of the various crop failures which occurred in Europe between 1400 and 1870, these rules against horsemeat were relaxed.

Horsemeat may be considered a normal part of the diet of continental western and northern Europe, but it probably was not as common as pork, mutton or beef. Its consumption also does not appear to have been as frequent in the southern extremities of Europe, and of course, the taboo was most rigidly observed by the British who later transplanted it to North America and Australia.

From horsehide was developed the high quality cordovan leather. Much of the Mediaeval knight's attire was manufactured from horsehides, including parts of shields and bucklers and the leather coat worn under the chain armour. Most harness as well came from horsehide. An unusual application of horsehair was made by some of the Mediaeval religious penitents who fashioned horsehair shirts to be worn, the better to enjoy their suffering.

Horse Management and Breeding

In most of Europe, horses were certainly not a common form of livestock in early Mediaeval times. Some idea of their prevalence in England is given in the Domesday Survey for 1066. In the county of Norfolk 767 horses were reported, slightly more than one for every village. For the county of Suffolk, there were 527, or five for every six villages, while the County of Essex yielded 790, or nearly two per village. These were chiefly mounts owned by the lords of the manor; few villagers except "the largest sub-manorial fiefholders and the clergy had riding horses" (Trow-Smith, 84). In Somerset, the Bishop of Coutances owned at least 130 feral horses; the Count of Moretain possessed seventy-two and William de Moiun kept sixty-eight. A considerable portion of the horse population comprised feral animals and unbroken mares (Trow-Smith, 85).

A variety of sites from Mediaeval central and eastern Europe provide a very general idea of horse frequency. As we noted earlier horses ranged between six and thirty-three per cent of the animals in several sites in tenth to fifteenth century Russia. In Poland they appear to have comprised only one per cent, in Slovakia, ten per cent, Bulgaria 7.7 per cent and Wurtemberg less than three per cent (Bökönyi, 1974, 79–83).

English horsebreeding at this time centred in the woodlands and was perhaps a side-line of some lords, particularly those who were obliged to provide mounts for their personal servants, manorial officers, and knights. Forest clearances between 1066 and 1086 undoubtedly account for a decline in horses during this time. Thus, in Norfolk there were only forty per cent "of the number of wild brood mares in 1086" as in 1066 (Trow-Smith, 85). After this they gradually increased in numbers.

As early as Saxon times regulations were established in Britain concerning the buying and selling of horses, aimed at protecting the less suspicious purchaser. Animals "for sale had to be warranted against staggers, black stangles, farcy and restiveness" (Hollis, 163). A person who sold a horse had to answer for its being free from "giddiness for three days before the time of sale, a broken wind for three months, and a dropfly for a year" (Berenger, I, 313–4). A seller also had to guarantee the horse for a year against tiring when on a journey and "to warrant that he neither loathed water nor food." If the horse was found wanting in any of these respects it could be returned or one third of the price recovered (Berenger, I, 313–4).

Throughout northern and western Europe common husbandry practices for horses existent in Mediaeval times have in general outline been preserved to the present. Horses were stabled, especially in winter, and fed oats and hay. Other feeds included beans, malt, wheat and barley, peas and vetch. When no fodder was available they were fed bread. Horses were carefully groomed and tended to with greater attention than any other farm animals. In late summer particularly they were pastured on cutover hayfields.

Walter of Henley's records provide some idea of horse husbandry in Mediaeval Britain. The carter or waggoner was to sleep beside his horses, repair rope harness, keep the carts in order and do the harrowing. Henley advised the plough horse be kept in a stall from 18th October to 3rd May and fed every night "at least the sixth part of a bushel of oats," and chaff. In summer he thought it would consume "at least twelve pennyworth of grass" (Lamond, 13). This ration was increased in farm practice to one bushel of oats a night between 29th

November and 1st April for work horses at the Westminster Manor of Stevenage (1273–4) and for the month of April three quarters of a bushel was given. Trow-Smith states that "a modern ration for a fifteen cwt. horse in average work is about one fifth bushel of oats plus hay" and, thus, "the advice of Henley for a smaller horse may be considered sound and "the Stevenage bailiff indicted of waste or dishonesty" (Trow-Smith, 116).

In sixteenth century western Europe, stallions were employed for stud purposes between ages three and twenty, while mares were considered available for breeding between ages two and ten. Better farmers bred their mares every two years. It was believed that a stallion could serve up to twenty mares, and when being prepared for service it was fattened on barley, vetches and chick peas. Mares were not to be too fat before breeding or while pregnant, nor should they travel or be exposed to extremes in weather during pregnancy (Fussell, 100).

Most of the British horses were small; large numbers descended from Celtic ponies or blends of Celtic ponies and Roman, Saxon and Scandinavian horses. They were not strong enough for the demands of agriculture nor for the armoured knight. Thus, some heavy Danish, Polish and Swedish horses, as well as Spanish and French hunters began to be imported to improve the British stock. In 1535 Henry VIII, one of the last to be concerned about breeding heavy riding horses, required all "substantial" landowners to maintain at least two "entire" mares of thirteen hands or over. In 1541 he forbad pasturing of stallions of less than fifteen hands "on common grazing lands in the midlands and southern counties of England" (Trow-Smith, 254). Laws were enacted obliging every archbishop and duke to keep "seven trottynge stone horses[1] for saddle – each fourteen hands high at three years." "Each person having benefices to the amount of 100 pounds a year or a layman, whose wife shall wear any French hood, or bonnet of velvet, are obliged, under the penalty of twenty pounds, to keep one such trottynge stone-horse for the saddle" (quoted in Berenger, I, 176–7). These regulations were repealed under James I.

The list of horses required for the household of a sixteenth century English earl is provided in "The Regulations and Establishment of the Household of Algernon Percy, the Fifth Earl of Northumberland. Begun anno 1512. London, printed 1768.

"this is the ordre of the chequir roul of the nombre of al the horsys of my lordes and my ladys, that are apoynted to be in the charge of the hous yerely, as to say: gentill hors, palfreys, hobys, nagges, clothsek hors, male-hors. First, gentill hors, to stand in my lordis stable, six.

---

[1] Stone horse = stallion

Item, palfreys of my ladys, to wit, one for my lady, and two for her gentill women, and oone for her chamberer. Four hobys and nagges for my lordis oone saddell, viz., oone for my lorde to ride, oone to lede for my lorde, and oone to stay at home for my lorde.

"*Item*, chariott hors to stand in my lordis stable yerely. Seven great trottynge hors to draw in the chariott, and a nagg for the chariott man to ride; eight. Again, hors for lorde Percy, his lordships son and heir. A grete doble trottynge horse for my lorde Percy to travel on in winter. *Item*, a great doble trottynge horse, called Curtal, for his lordship to ride on out of tounes. Another trottynge gambaldynge hors for his lordship to ride upon when he comes into tounes. An amblynge horse for his lordship to journey on dayly. A proper amblynge little nagg for his lordship when he gaeth on hunting or hawking. A gut amblynge gelding, a trottynge gelding, to carry his male" (quoted in Berenger, I, 178).

Slicher van Bath believes that from the sixteenth to the eighteenth centuries there was actually an "over abundance" of horses in western Europe. Particularly in the Netherlands there seems to have been a great number. In one district in 1602 there were 61 – 69 for every one hundred hectares of arable land and Dutch farmers with less than five hectares of arable land had three and four horses. By contrast, in fourteenth century Bruges there were between sixteen and thirty horses per hundred hectares and at an abbey in northern Brabant in the thirteenth century 233 hectares were worked by seventy horses. In fourteenth century England on the Merton College estates there was about one horse for every ten hectares, although it is not clear if oxen were used as well (Slicher van Bath, 181). These estates had a ratio of one horse to 2.8 and 3.3 cattle which is near to that of the Domesday Book of the earlier period, one horse to 3.4 cattle (Slicher van Bath, 180).

Elsewhere in Europe as well, horses appear in some abundance in the post-Reformation period and after. In the bishopric of Ratzeburg (east of Lübeck) horses were the most common form of livestock in 1630: 4254 horses, 3859 hogs, 3116 cattle, and 2525 sheep. In the west Finnish countryside in 1719 almost fifteen thousand households owned 9918 horses, more than seven per cent of all livestock (Slicher van Bath, 291).

Figures for livestock in Lincolnshire between 1530 –1600 show there were 235 owners of between one and five horses, 163 having from six to ten and 58 had eleven or more, but all had forty or less; three had from thirty-one to forty head (Thirsk, *passim*). As a very broad guess this would seem to suggest about one horse to twenty or thirty persons – a considerable increase from the time of William the Conqueror when there was far less than one horse per hundred persons. Part of the reason for the increased number of horses may be the poor road conditions which required more horses for cartage in an expanding trade. Also the great extension of cultivated areas from the sixteenth century onward meant that manure had to be hauled greater distances and, thus, more cart horses were required (Slicher van Bath, 293).

Obviously, the horse was of crucial significance to the Mediaeval knight as it was also to the seventeenth century cavalier who followed after him. However, it is easy to overstress the horse in these roles and forget its equally important albeit less glamourous place in agricultural traction. Much of the horse husbandry and horse-related farm activities developed in Europe in Mediaeval and post-Mediaeval times served as the horsekeeping model up to modern times. Similarly, the principles of a systematic or "scientific" horsemanship evolved during this period continue to serve as a lasting guide to the contemporary rider.

VIII

The Horse in Europe and North-eastern America from the Seventeenth to the Early Twentieth Centuries

TWO basic patterns initiated in Mediaeval times were greatly extended and intensified after the beginning of the seventeenth century. In riding, *a la jineta* style, originating with the Arabs and spread into Spain, now became popular in more northern Europe. Related to this were associated changes in saddlery and the rise to prominence of the cavalier, replacing the Mediaeval knight. At the same time heavier horses were becoming more widely employed in north European agriculture.

These phenomena are associated with the concomitant settlement of America and the growth of capitalism – an international market economy based on accumulation of profits by entrepreneurs employing labour for wages. With this type of economy appeared the yeoman farmer, whose development helps to clarify the role of the horse in northern Europe and its overseas satellites from the seventeenth century to the first part of the present century.

Let us first consider the rise of the yeoman capitalist farmer and the role of the horse. In Britain in Elizabeth's time there were four main classes of tenant farmers. In the best position were freeholders who were virtually owners of land in return for a specific payment to the manor lord. Among the freeholders were "gentlemen" or the "high" born, and prosperous yeomen – freemen not of gentle birth. Both had parliamentary franchise. Less fortunate than the freeholders were the leaseholders who were mostly yeoman farmers holding lands from a lord or a freeholder for a fixed rent. Through craftiness, diligence and thrift some of these yeomen were able to buy up lands, particularly from overly extravagant gentlemen, and eventually work their way into the class of gentlemen themselves (Byrne, 139).

In Britain the yeomen "made up the solid middle rank of rural society, from which the ranks of the gentry were constantly being recruited" (Byrne, 139). Yeomen are the independent landed proprietors of "common" origin aspiring to the ways of the gentlemanly class and achieving them primarily through the capitalist-style operation of their farms. The crucial economic elements of the system become acuumulation of property in land and livestock and employment of tenant and wage labour to produce goods for sale on the market at a profit.

On the continent as well the appearance of such a class may be noted. Thus, in France, peasants became rich enough to buy their freedom en masse; whole villages paid a heavy lump sum and received general emancipation. In Flanders and northern Germany, the pioneer-peasant had great influence. Draining marshes and clearing forests under some great lay or ecclesiastical lord, he received land for himself on terms which practically made a yeoman out of him; and his prosperity naturally reacted upon others. The lords found less and less profit in enforcing feudal dues, and more profit in selling them; the princes passed laws definitely in favour of the peasants, and at last the little that remained of bondage was not worth the lord's while to enforce (Coulton, 365–6).

The Black Death helped further to break down the old system. It made labour scarce and so encouraged working for wages as "free" labour since a villein would flee to a town or to another manor and each lord tried to make his land available at a cheap rate. Thus there arose a system of money leases with fixed rents. This inevitably declined as in Flanders, north Germany and France, peasants were able to buy their lands. So Mediaeval feudalism died, and out of it began an agrarian capitalism.

This system was readily transported by the British and French to their North American colonies. Particularly in the American colonies which eventually became the United States, the combination of the settlement by Non-Conformists and poorer classes on pioneer land created a situation in which the ideal aim was to make everyone (Whites at any rate) yeomen farmers.

The increase in the number of yeomen farmers and the growing prosperity of agriculture from the seventeenth century onward also meant the more general use of horses and the increase in the number of those who owned them. In Britain proper yeomen aspired to gentlemanly ways. A major symbol of such ways was the cavalier; thus, a yeoman should be mounted on horseback, or at least ride in some kind of horse-drawn "buggy". The riding horse became more divorced from its association with aristocracy and military organization. The proliferation of moderately well-to-do and independent farmers meant a proliferation of horse ownership. More modest peasantry, also imbued with a high regard for the horse, but at the same time imbued by the poverty of peasant life with a certain pragmatism and thriftiness were, thus, obliged in their acquisition of horses to put them to practical use. The adoption of the three course rotation in Mediaeval times, the eventual freeing of the peasantry and their increasing prosperity all allowed for a limited satisfaction of the desire of the peasant to acquire prestige through ownership of horses.

Coupled with these processes was the rise of egalitarian, pragmatic and libertarian doctrines espoused or stimulated by the Protestant Reformation and its more radical elements. The "Protestant" world view which frowned upon frivolous pleasure, extravagance, and unproductiveness, would help turn the horse from a plaything of cavalier dandies into the common means of transportation and cultivation of the soil.

All of these forces were in differing degrees influential on the continent, but they came particularly to bear in the northern American colonies where the necessity of swift transportation in an area of isolated homesteads and communities tended to make the horse more of a practical necessity. As well, the colonies had the grazing and arable land available for producing horses inexpensively.

In line with the expanding role of the horse, new styles of saddlery arose. If the riding horse was no longer for the armoured knight, but rather, in war the bearer of a lightly armed rider and in peace an instrument of pleasure for the aristorcracy and a means of transportation for all of any means, the saddles could become smaller and lighter. Actually such saddles had begun to appear in Europe after 1200, including "pad saddles, hornless saddles, light frame saddles, padded seats, padded pommels and cantles, and saddles without any cantles" (Vernam, 156).

These lighter styles arising in the Mediaeval period gradually become the fashion in northern and western Europe ultimately reaching a climax in what we today know as the "English" saddle which appeared in the early nineteenth century. This is the epitome of the pure pleasure principle in riding, obviously designed to expedite the speed of the horse and make for ease in jumping. It has been adopted throughout modern Europe and much of the rest of the world. Possibly today it is the most popular single form of saddlery.

Trends to lightness had less effect in Spain where saddles remained large and well-fitted and so, best adapted to the mounted herding which became from the seventeenth century onward so important an enterprise in Hispanic America.

Sixteenth and seventeenth century western Europe produced an immense variety of stirrups. "And it was Europe that went on to develop the weird array of sixteenth century bits which no other age has ever duplicated" (Vernam, 169). Curb bits had prevailed in Europe since the beginning of the days of chivalry, but after about 1700 there was a major shift in north-western Europe to snaffles and other easier kinds of bits.

In post-Reformation times elaborate and enormous spurs appeared as did all kinds of fancy boots and gauntlets. Such manifestations must be seen as in keeping with the cultural milieu of the times – the age of the gay cavalier of Louis XIV and Charles II. Also consistent with the tone of those times, was the appearance of the first organized flat racing. In Britain riding to hounds in the fox hunt and horse jumping began to become popular. James II was an early fox hunter and keeper of hounds. Trench believes that jumping was common in England by 1688 (Trench, 149), but it did not appear on the continent until much later since there were no hedges, but mostly trails through forests.

While ambling was still a favourite gait, the trot gradually became more prominent, especially in England with the spread of the idea of posting or rising to the trot which finally prevailed there by the beginning of the nineteenth century. What is today recognized as English-style riding is actually a relatively new pattern evolving in the seventeenth and eighteenth centuries in good part in response to the increase in the activity as a sport.

This suggests another significant development, namely, the beginnings of European scientific equitation from the sixteenth century onward. The first riding school was established in Naples by Fererico Grisone who also published a book on equitation in 1550. His teaching spread rapidly over Europe and many others followed him in publishing guides to a scientific approach to riding and in establishing schools for teaching specific methods. All were, of course, initially oriented exclusively to the narrow confines of European aristocracy, but later were expanded to independent men of wealth.[1]

The Horse as a Farm Animal in Western Europe

The introduction and development of adequate harness and horseshoes after the eighth century and the intensive breeding of large heavy horses after the eleventh century as well as the introduction of the three crop rotation for improving the supply of feed all laid the groundwork for ultimately producing an efficient heavy draught horse. As we have seen, horses came more and more into common use for these purposes in the course of the Mediaeval period, but it was not until the eighteenth century that they supplanted the ox. During this and the following century further agricultural developments favoured the use of the horse. These included the increasing of yields of oats, the introduction and spread of carrots, turnips and clover. At the same time the seed drill and cultivator were invented and both operated

[1] Trench presents a good summary of the history of western European scientific equitation, (pp. 101–153).

more efficiently when pulled by the faster, more even pace of the horse. A lighter plough was also introduced which provoked a further shift to the horse, especially in those areas where there were heavy soils which with the lighter implement could now be easily worked by horses (Slicher van Bath, 295).

By the nineteenth century in western Europe perhaps fewer horses were necessary to do the same amount of work because of the spread of heavier and stronger types, the introduction of better implements and the improvement in road conditions. Nevertheless, small farms appear to have continued to be overstocked; this problem we will note remained characteristic of the farming of eastern European peasants down to the present time.

One of the effects of the spread of the use of the horse for farm draught purposes was to reduce its exclusive, prestigious status and make it a more plebian animal; at the same time the ownership of horse teams elevated the status of peasants and farmers. Thus with the diffusion of agrarian capitalism, with innovations in agriculture and the resultant increasing prominence of the horse as the farm draught animal, goes also an increasing democratization or "vulgarization" of the horse. Such a process is made more intense when we recall that the saddle and carriage horses were also becoming less associated with aristocracy as the number of yeomen farmers increased, especially in the American colonies.

The two basic styles of harness for traction continued to prevail with minor modifications. The first of these styles, it will be recalled, included the use of collar, hames, and traces attached to a whipple tree used in double or multiple harnessing particularly. The second employed the collar, hames, traces, breeching, and a pad saddle for supporting a back band used in single harness in two-shaft carts.

An ancient cultural contrast between north-eastern and south-western Eurasia, wherein animal traction in the north-eastern part was a two-shaft one-animal vehicle and in the south-western a one-shaft two-animal conveyance, still holds to some extent. But since the Mediaeval period and more so in recent times the two-shaft, one-animal vehicle has become familiar to portions of the south-western zone especially the British Isles, France, the Low Countries and Germany.

The general character of western European horse management continued the Mediaeval traditions: horses were stabled, particularly in winter; they were fed primarily on oats and hay and in general draught horses were shown preferential treatment by farmers at the expense of their other livestock. Breeding and rearing of horses were left to the more well-to-do and only the wealthy estate owners possessed stallions for stud. A farmer owned from one to five horses on an average; ordinarily a good pair of plough horses was a basic essential.

Horse management, at least in Britain, apparently experienced little change from the Mediaeval period until the end of the eighteenth century. Two major innovations of that period were the introduction of turnip and legume (clover and alfalfa) feeding for livestock (Trow-Smith, 222).

Rees gives some picture of the horse in rural Wales which may be taken as in most respects exemplary of western Europe for the late nineteenth century.[1]

Old Welsh laws stated that "Neither horses, mares nor cows are to be put to the plough" (quoted in Rees, 58). Nevertheless, horses ultimately replaced oxen by the early nineteenth century and their number increased considerably until World War I.

Welsh farmers of this period liked to have the stables near to the house since horses, being regarded as the most valuable livestock, could be heard in the night if they broke loose or got hurt. For these reasons wagoners and other farm workers once slept in the stable loft (Rees, 57). Since horses lent their owners esteem it was only appropriate that stables be close by the house. The best food was reserved for the horses and a wagoner who stole grain for his horses was considered a positive asset. The wagoner was the aristocrat among the farm-labourers; he presided at the servants' table and sometimes assumed a managerial role in farm work. The prestige lent by the horse persists to modern times where the eldest brother on a farm takes care of the horses, the second, the cattle and the third, the sheep (Rees, 59). Before the days of mechanization, farmers placed their horses in competitions at shows and vied with one another for the honour "of taking the Sunday School for an outing or the choir to an *eisteddfod*" (Rees, 59).

The Welsh rural attitude towards the horse, Rees believes, is derived from the English "horse culture". In the community he studied Welsh words were used for almost everything relating to cattle, but for horses a great many English words are employed. Cattle are given Welsh names such as Cochen, Penwen and Frochwen, but horses have aristocratic English names such as Prince, Captain or Duke. Cows are spoken to in Welsh while horses are treated as if they did not understand that language, but only English (Rees, 58).

From the statistics on a Welsh community provided by Rees, the horse population seems to have peaked about 1918 when there were over three horses on an average per farm; by 1939 this had fallen to slightly more than two per farm and horses constituted only two per

[1] See also Keegan's study (1974) especially pp. 109–122.

cent of all livestock (Rees, 175). Today there is undoubtedly less than an average of one horse per farm.

The horse has had equal prestige and is afforded preferential treatment among livestock in England and on the continent as well. Farmers throughout northern Europe not only took pride in an elegant team of horses, but also in well-kept harness and wagons.

In south-western Europe, that is, Spain, Portugal, Italy and the south of France, for reasons we have discussed in the foregoing chapter, the horse was not often employed for heavy draught purposes. Here the ox was retained; mules were widely used for the plough as well as for carts and carriages and, less frequently for riding. The ass, too, was an important means of transportation.

With the colonization of the Americas, Iberian reliance on ox- and mule-drawn ploughs and the peasant's "horse", the donkey, were transferred there.

Eastern Europe

In north-western Europe and the American colonies it is possible to suggest that the spread of an agrarian capitalism and a "Protestant" ethic are among the factors which tended to break the close association of the horse with the aristocracy. No such statement however can be made in considering the role of the horse in eastern Europe or in the north-western margins of the continent. Let us first consider eastern Europe including Russia.

Mediaeval economic structure dominated this area much later than the rest of Europe so that it was not until well into the nineteenth century that one finds anything like the yeoman farmer. Indeed up to contemporary times a major segment of east European peasantry remained "non-capitalist". Peasant proprietors produced primarily for their own subsistence requirements rather than for a market and the farm labour force was made up of family members; there was little or no wage labour. The twentieth century brought some increase in agrarian capitalism, but as is well known what existed of this system was soon replaced throughout this area by various degrees of collectivization.

The horse had been a primary source of labour power employed for ploughing and all other types of farm work in Russia since the eleventh century. In Poland, Hungary, Czechoslovakia and the Baltic it had been used for lighter draught work and during the eighteenth and nineteenth centuries gradually came to replace the ox. These dates are well before any burgeoning of agrarian capitalism in these areas. The influence of any "Protestant" ethic was also not introduced until the sixteenth and seventeenth centuries and, then it only affected the Baltic, and some segments of Hungary and Czechoslovakia.

Further south, in the Balkans, the ox always maintained its primacy as a plough animal, and in Rumania and Bulgaria the buffalo came into some prominence for farm draught purposes. Horses were reserved more for pulling wagons, for threshing out grain, or for harrowing. In some parts of Rumania double teams of horses and oxen were used for ploughing in which a team of horses was hitched ahead of a team of oxen, thus following the old Mediaeval European recommendation that horses ploughing in the company of oxen speeded up the operation. In parts of Greece, as well, horses came into more common use as plough animals.

Except in Albania where there were few wagon roads, peasants used horses and carts and rarely indulged in horseback riding. In the mountainous zones where roads were absent, such as Greece, Albania, and southern Yugoslavia, they had an important role as pack animals. Rather than carting their goods to market the peasants packed them on mule or horseback and, generally, on the return journey home rode the animals. In Greece at least, this meant, for both men and women, riding sidesaddle on top of the pack saddle. For central and northern Europe the peasant was identified with horse and wagon, as in Iberia and southern Italy he was identified with donkey riding. The landed gentry on the other hand were identified with horse riding.

The evidence therefore suggests that the specific uses of the horse in eastern Europe were related to the particular type of agricultural system, whether a three course or two course rotation, to the type of terrain and the road conditions. However we must again stress the fact that a cultural pattern pervasive throughout Europe has been the high regard for the horse and this, given the proper physical conditions, must be viewed as crucial to an understanding of the widespread ownership and use of horses by east European peasantry and the manner in which they were employed.

Much of eastern Europe is noted for its horse breeding. Thus, Poland for a long time was prominent as one of the world's major horse breeding countries. Rumanian horses are mentioned in the Nibelungen Saga and were prized by the Germans who acquired them as remounts for their cavalry. Breaking with the old Mediaeval custom of stallion riding, the Germans in the sixteenth century began adopting the Wallachian (Rumanian) geldings. From this use of the Wallachian gelding is derived the German word for gelding, *Wallach*. The Turks also appreciated Rumanian horses and part of Moldavia's tribute to the Sublime Porte was "forty good Moldavian horses". The Turks had a proverb: "There is nothing to beat a Persian peasant and a Moldavian horse'' (Mitrany, 358).

Hungarian and Russian horses were equally notable. As in other parts of Europe horse breeding was chiefly an activity for the well-to-do. In Hungary it seems that some people identified the prosperous farmer as one who raises foals. He "drives a relay horse (a colt or a filly harnessed to the team of horses) or a four in hand team with colts" (Fel and Hofer, 234). In pre-revolutionary Russia studs were kept by private owners of large estates and, as in other parts of Europe there were also state stud farms. In 1907 European Russia reported 6138 private studs with an estimated 17000 stallions; the Government kept 5420 stallions at its breeding stations (Antsiferov, et al., 87).

Nearly all horses were of the "light" or more "hot-blooded" type, but this did not prevent them from being put to heavy tasks. Eastern Europeans never adopted the heavy draught horses found in western Europe because of their high fodder requirements. In addition, they desired a draught animal which could not only be used in the fields, but also for pulling wagons to villages and towns and making visits to neighbours. Heavy draught horses were too slow for these purposes. In a word, they tried to develop a multipurpose horse, ideally of medium size, so that they could afford to satisfy their desire to own horses and at the same time be able to put them to a maximum number of practical uses.

In the early twentieth century, prior to the Revolution, Russia had the highest number of horses per one hundred inhabitants of any European country except for Iceland. Of more than thirty million Russian at this time 86 per cent were peasant-owned and the remaining fourteen per cent belonged to nomads and estate owners (Antsiferov et al., 87). About sixty per cent were reported as "farm horses" and between thirty and thirty-five per cent as "saddle horses" with the remainder "racing breeds" (Pavlovsky, 301).

Hourwich in a Pre-Revolution investigation of the province of Ryazan, in middle Russia south of Moscow, reports an average of 1.4 horses per household. He observes that a household with no horse can do no farming and one with one horse is "liable to go down in the long run" (Hourwich, 99). Peasants from such farms tended to become a rural proletariat; they were people who have stopped working their farms altogether or have given up cultivating part of their fields. In two districts in Ryazan province about a third of the peasant households were horseless (Hourwich, 72) and in one district in Voronezh province the figure was over forty per cent while another forty-five per cent had only one horse (Hourwich, 125). Fel and Hofer in their study of a Hungarian rural community find as well that the distinction between families with teams and those without was an important index of socio-economic standing. And as in Russia it appears that two horses for a family was deemed necessary as a reasonable sign of prosperity (Fel and Hofer, 253).

Despite the necessity for a minimum number of horses under pre-mechanized peasant agricultural conditions in eastern Europe, there was still considered to be an excess of horses in much of the area in the first half of this century, particularly when compared to other livestock which yield protein consumption goods. In the vine growing region in south-eastern Bulgaria one village reported 195 oxen, 25 working cows, 657 horses and 330 mules and donkeys, a total of 1207 work animals for 2816 hectares of arable land or 44 animals per 100 hectares. This is compared to "producing" livestock: 13 cows, 1916 sheep, 4002 poultry (Warriner, 121–2). In Rumania larger farms of five or more hectares had one horse or a couple of oxen and only four or five sheep and a pig (Warriner, 117).

Dumont claims the general characteristic of the poor farm from Slovakia to Greece is the excessive number of draught animals. While a man required two horses to make a successful farming operation they were used for only a small part of the year, in some cases not more than one hundred days of farm work. In addition, horses not only demand more by way of fodder, but are in fact favoured by most peasants. Thus, in a Slovak village the yields of milk from cattle herds suffered because the best feed went to the horses (Dumont, 493).

In the village of Atany, north-eastern Hungary, in the mid-nineteenth century forty-two per cent of the lands associated with the village were still grasslands. Animals were grazed from early spring until late autumn on these ranges and were winter fed on meadow hay, straw and chaff. Horses and cattle were kept in stables. In summer, working animals were driven to pasture at night after their day's work (Fel and Hofer, 45). Horses have replaced oxen for draught work since the end of the eighteenth century so that by 1828 Atany reported 435 horses against 267 oxen (Fel and Hofer, 44).

In Feudal times the pastures of Atany were common lands controlled by manors and the state. But with the end of the feudal power the pastures came under the control of peasant landowners, each of whom had grazing rights which could be bought, sold or inherited (Fel and Hofer, 51–52). Those who had grazing rights in the village pastures formed a Pasture Association which regulated the grazing of animals and selected herdsmen. The Association kept stallions, bulls and boars in separate stables, where the appointed herdsmen tended them in winter. The Pasture Association also looked after watering wells and their equipment. It built herdsmen's huts and animal enclosures. Until the close of the nineteenth century the common pastures of the village maintained from one to two hundred horses, but in 1901 the herding of horses was abandoned (Fel and Hofer, 314 ff.).

Hungary has long been noted for its extensive pastures which have been reserved for vast herds of cattle, horses, sheep and swine. Two enormous livestock ranges (*puszta*) survived down to mid-twentieth century – one at Hortobagy and the other at Bergacs. The Hortobagy *puszta* at least has been much altered by the extension of irrigation farming and the raising of rice, lucerne, barley and oats (Dumont, 482).

When horses were herded in Atany the chief horseherdsman as well as the cattleherder were elected by members of the Pasture Association. The horseherdsman was the highest ranking of the herdsmen followed by the cattleherder who tended those livestock left on the open range. In third rank was the cowherd charged with those cattle which were driven out to pasture daily; finally, there was the swineherd. Except for the latter each head herdsman was required to be a property owner as an insurance for livestock in his care (Fel and Hofer, 316). Vuorela has noted that in old Hungarian tradition the herdsmen constituted an internally graded guild which placed the horseherdsman in the highest status and the shepherd in the lowest position (Vuorela, 347). Such granting of the highest status to the man who handles the horses reminds one of the primacy of the rank of wagoner and horse teamster among farm workers in western Europe.

Atany herdsmen remained out in the pasture all season with the stock, returning to the village only occasionally for food and clean clothes. They were paid in kind for their services and allowed to recruit boys to assist them in their duties for which the herdsman paid the wages (Fel and Hofer, 316). Vuorela states, regarding Hungarian practice in general, that the chief herder might also be paid in money, and that employers were responsible for providing weekly supplies of food or else the herdsmen had the right to slaughter animals from the herd for their own consumption (Vuorela, 347).

In Atany an important focus of farm activity was the stable. Here the horses and cattle were kept, especially during the winter months. Here also the men gathered and usually made their sleeping quarters. The end of the stable which quartered the horses was the most distinguished part of the building and the owner slept a good part of the year on a bed behind the horses. Presumably the reason for sleeping with the animals was to protect them and be able to care for them, but the stable served as a kind of men's clubhouse where especially in winter men sat around a fire and talked. On leaving school at the age of twelve a boy was awarded a sleeping place in the stable, which thus gave him considerably more freedom than he ever had while in the house. During summer if the animals happened to be "in the stable the farmer

slept in the open door way to protect them". Even so thieves sometimes stole horses by leading them "out of the stable right over the
head of the sleeping [farmer], by covering the floor with straw to
muffle the noise" (Fel and Hofer, footnote 93). If animals were outside
in summer, the men slept near them often in a pile of straw in a cart (Fel
and Hofer, 89–92).

Horses were important symbols and measures of one's standing in
the village. Fel and Hofer however believe the " 'equicentred' husbandry was no heritage from the distant past; it developed probably
around 1800" (Fel and Hofer, 45). Wealthy farmers could be identified
as those who "in summer . . . take the horses out of the stall only when
it is cool; 'they protected them even from the rays of the sun' " (Fel and
Hofer, 234). As we have mentioned above, the prosperous farmer was
identified especially by elderly people as one who raises foals. Beside
owning a wagon for everyday use, the wealthy farmer had "parade
harness" and "a 'light carriage' with fine mountings and paint for
festive occasions. It is said that in the 1930's, 'Mankind competed
fiercely one against the other in the matter of horse trappings.' The
[landowning peasants] followed new fashions every year, trying to
surpass each other." It was considered foolish to be a miser accumulat-
ing and saving one's earnings. "'No one sees it, no one esteems you for
it'" one informant said, "'but if I drive through the village or into the
market everyone stares at me'" (quoted in Fel and Hofer, 275).

Another villager is recorded making this remark about another:
"What a store of books he had – two bookcases full of books with
golden covers, but his horses could hardly pull an empty cart." Fel and
Hofer add: "Therefore he was not esteemed at all". Horses brought
status to the individual, but they must be well kept; mean and scrawny
ones were a disgrace to the owner (Fel and Hofer, 275).

Before 1945 the basic social division of "people of the soil" was
between team owners and teamless farmers. The latter represented the
poorer segment. Yet many smallholders who owned horses found it
necessary to engage in other activities to augment their income. Thus
they became horse dealers or carters or hired out to cultivate land. A
man who owned about twenty-one acres of land could "drive two
good horses; he has his bread and butter too; there is peace in his
family" (Fel and Hofer, 253).

A somewhat more well-to-do farmer with fifty-seven to about
seventy acres could engage in some extensive horse breeding (Fel and
Hofer, 234).

When horses were stabled they were fed and cared for by the
farmer's eldest son or by a servant if there was one. Apart from
feeding, horses were always wiped clean in the morning and, in

summer only, given a good brushing on Sunday. The man responsible for the care of the horses also worked with them in the fields. One servant remarked: "In the service of the landlord one always had to go out, but in that of the [farmer-proprietor] the horses were taken out only in good weather" (quoted in Fel and Hofer, 242). Horses raised by a farmer were given his own brand, but the animals of the poorer people frequently had two or three different brands since raising none themselves they had no brand of their own and bought stock at the fairs (Fel and Hofer, 281). Military service resulted in those returning to the village introducing "new methods of tending, care, and grooming horses" and cures for horse diseases learned in the army (Fel and Hofer, 368).

Hungarian traditional culture has a strong pastoral element. Yet the practice of sending village herds out under the supervision of herdsmen either daily or for prolonged seasonal stays has been widespread throughout Europe. Seasonal grazing some distance from the homestead is particularly common in transhumant mountain areas such as Norway, Switzerland, Spain and Rumania. What distinguishes Hungarian practice from the rest of Europe is the use of the stable as a kind of men's club and residence, although even this finds its parallels in the old British customs of having the teamster or wagoner sleep in the stable by his team and making the stable the centre for farm management (Cf., Keegan, 109).

While most Hungarian horses were of the light variety, about a fifth are reported to be heavy draught animals mostly found in western Hungary (Dumont, 471). Despite the prevalence of light horses, Hungarians like other east Europeans did not ride horseback as much as they used horses for drawing wagons. Indeed, as we have already seen the Hungarians made some important contributions to the development of wagonry.

According to Jankovich, with the spread of light cavalry in Europe, the Hungarian practices of using geldings and the Hungarian wooden frame saddle along with the bent knee technique of riding were adopted in most of Europe's cavalries (Jankovich, 122–5). It is possible that this writer's bias might be exaggerating the role of Hungarian equestrian customs in European affairs.

Even up to modern times some Magyars used an interesting type of riding gear in which the stirrups were attached by narrow leather straps to a piece of heavy woollen rug: no girth was used, the "saddle" merely being "thrown over the horse and held in place by the rider's weight". (Vernam, 62). Such cinchless "saddles" are also reported for some early American Indians (Vernam, 62) and for eighteenth century Arabs. Today, donkey saddles in the Sudan often consist of a wooden frame with neither stirrups nor cinch. These saddles obviously enhance the difficulties of mounting and dismounting and demand additional skill in maintaining the seat.

Hungarian horsemen also developed a distinctive dress, wearing high boots, broad-brimmed hats and elaborately embroidered heavy woollen capes, and carrying braided quirts or whips.

As in the other east European countries there has been a considerable decline in the once colourful and important horse industry of Hungary. World War II greatly reduced the number of horses and collectivization afterwards replaced horses with tractors. Of the village of Atany, for example, Fel and Hofer say "[T]here are hardly any horses in the village now" (Fel and Hofer, 382).

North-western Margins of Europe

The islands of the North Atlantic, the Scottish Highlands and Norway may be said to constitute still another distinct area of horse use in Europe.

Until modern times the pony was the prevailing form of horse and was used by all classes for riding and packing, to a less extent for the wagon and plough. As this is an ancient pattern it means that the general use of the horse which characterized the area is not related to the spread of agrarian capitalism or a "Protestant" ethic. Rather, it was explainable in terms of the absence of roads, the greater ease of travel by horseback and pack and the prevalence of abundant pasture combined with the practice of open range grazing. Thus horse keeping is relatively cheap and easy and so readily available for all. As is typical of other parts of Europe, here, as well, the horse has always been highly regarded.

From a cultural-historical point of view Iceland should be included within this area. However, this country has developed an agriculture which is clearly a form of livestock ranching. Therefore, it will be discussed in that context in chapter X.

In the Scottish Highlands, including the Hebridean islands, the traditional horse was a sturdy, sure-footed pony, called a garron. It was once used for a wide variety of enterprises and was left to fend for itself on the moorlands. As in Iceland, its chief uses were as a riding and pack animal. It carried peat and seaweed on its back and in the Hebrides the harrow was once attached to the pony's tail (Grant, 85–6). Sledges similar to the travois and drags were drawn by these ponies at least as late as the eighteenth century. By that time more sophisticated districts in the Highlands acquired simple two wheeled carts (Grant, 281).

In the following century major changes commenced as the garron was replaced by larger Clydesdale types and a new agricultural technology was introduced including rakes, tedders, iron ploughs, reapers, and binders (Grant, 85–6). Today the old Highlands horse complex has disappeared and even that which appeared in the nineteenth century based on the heavy draught breed is rapidly succumbing to the tractor. In the counties of Argyll, Ross and Cromarty, and Sutherland there were 882 tractors and 11,001 horses in 1944 but fifteen years later there were 4887 tractors and 1897 horses (Grant, 87). At the present time the main economic use of horses, as it is becoming in Iceland as well, is for pony trekking for visiting tourists.

The use and maintenance of horses in the islands north of Scotland parallels that of the Highlands.

In the Shetlands ponies have been used to carry in the peat for a few weeks of the year, but other than this are left pretty much to themselves to graze on the open moors (Cluness, 254). Occasionally they have been used for riding, but in these smaller islands there is not the distance to travel one encounters, for example, in Iceland. Nor are horses much used for farm draught purposes. In the Shetlands crofters have traditionally used a spade for tilling their gardens; few ever ploughed (Livingstone, 96). In modern times the primary demand for Shetland ponies comes from an export trade for children's mounts particularly to Great Britain and the United States.

In Norway horses have for centuries functioned as general purpose draught animals for ploughing, carting, packing and riding. In contrast to the northern islands horse management, they have commonly been stabled in winter and fed on hay and oats. But in summer any horses not in use are driven to uplands moors along with other stock under the care of herdsmen to return to the lower elevations in early fall. In the latter half of the nineteenth century the Norwegian Government undertook to improve horse breeding by controlling summer pasturing of horses in these highlands. Prize winning stallions were distributed by the government to grazing lands of from three to seven thousand feet elevation. Each stallion had his territory and a harem of mares taken from private farmers who paid a small fee for the service. In the early fall the mares were returned to their owners and the stallions put out to stable with individual farmers (Hayward, 78).

In passing we may note that Norway has made one contribution to equestrian sports in the invention of *skijoring* in which a skier drives a horse on long reins and is thus pulled around on his skis. A modification of this appears in the United States where a horse rider hitches his lasso to a skier and rides off at a gallop.

Norway, the Scottish Highlands, the Shetlands, Orkneys and Faroe

Islands along with parts of Ireland may be viewed as a single cultural-geographical province in terms of the domesticated horse. Until the introduction of the agricultural technology of the nineteenth century and, to a lesser extent improved breeds during that century as well, this region was characterized by the prevalence of ponies of hardy, sure-footed type who sustained themselves primarily on open range with minimal care and attention. They were employed largely as pack and riding animals, but also for all farm draught work. Harness and gear were of similar type.

Gypsies

While the bulk of Europe falls into one of the five areas of horse use delineated above, the Gypsies represent a marginal group worthy of separate mention. They are, or were, a nomadic, primarily nonpastoral people with their roots probably in northern India. Particularly with their movement into Europe in late Mediaeval times they are identified with various service-type occupations such as tinkering, fortune telling and horse trading.

Gypsies are however deemed "very poor" horsemen. For them the horse is mainly a draught and pack animal and their note derives from trading in horses rather than their ability on a horse's back. "Their greatest art and their reputation consists in 'putting right' the beasts which they show at fairs." That is they have acquired a reputation for being adept at disguising and covering over any defects on the horses they put up for sale. According to Clebert, at any rate, before showing a horse in the market they have been known to excite it by pricking it with a hedgehog. They shake pebbles in a pail under the animal's nose until he "is almost crazy". Then at the market place they show the horse the pail and it will "begin to prance like a spirited cavalry charger". A Hungarian Gypsy trick was to put a piece of ginger in the horse's anus in order to made the horse hold his tail nicely and "look mettlesome". "To rejuvenate a sorry old nag" a Gypsy formula was "to bore holes in its teeth and fill them with rosemary". How effective this method is is not indicated. "To make a horse's breathing good for a short time, he is fed (henbane) mixed with (elder?) berries" (Clebert, 137). It is no wonder that Gypsies would rarely, according to Clebert, buy horses from one another or sell them to other Gypsies (Clebert, 138).

Since the Gypsies have been sometimes maligned and frequently stereotyped by outsiders it is perhaps naïve to accept all such reports of their presumed behaviour without some reservation.

Some have claimed that Gypsies became horse traders after entering

Hungary. Clebert feels this may be possible but seems unlikely since the Gypsies, who had lived on the borders of Sind, certainly must have known of capturing wild horses and breeding them (Clebert, 136–7). However, this does not necessarily mean they would have practiced these arts. Clebert himself notes that for drawing the Gypsy wagon the horse only replaced the ox when the Gypsies arrived on the Danubian plains in the fourteenth century, a fact which would seem to indicate horses were a good deal less common, to say the least, among Gypsies before entering Europe (Clebert, 223).

The Gypsies' chief use of the horse was in hauling their four wheeled covered caravans, which bear a similarity to the ancient Scythian vehicle. It probably has its origin among the central Eurasian pastoral nomads, particularly since it is known that at first the Gypsies travelled on foot and only later adopted the wagon (Clebert, 223).

Other Asiatic horse customs are associated with the Gypsies in their values and ideology. Gypsies never say "I hope that you will live happily", but "May your horses live long". The horse to the Gypsy is pre-eminently a funerary and psychoceremonial animal (Clebert, 135). Until recent times Gypsies perpetuated horse-oriented funerary rites reminiscent of Central Asia. Thus, "Alexandre Bertrand, who associated with them in the Caucasus in 1885, ends the account of a funeral ceremony thus:

'After the burial of the corpse, for several days at the dinner hour the deceased man's horse was saddled and the order given to the servant to lead it to the new grave, and there to call the deceased three times by his name, to invite him to dinner' " (Clebert, 136).

While Gypsies in general observe a strict taboo against eating horse-flesh, the Gitanos in southern France ignore this regulation or do not consider it part of their behavioural code (Clebert, 136).

A Gypsy considers the horse his best friend, while he has no great affection for the dog. These also are south Asiatic traits.

In western Europe and North America Gypsies have largely given up their traditional use of the horse drawn caravan in favour of automobiles and trailers if no more permanent apartment and house dwellings. In so doing they have modified their old trades of tinkering and horse trading to become auto body workers and used car dealers, where they can 'put right' old cars which they buy up and resell as in the past they had 'put right' horses.

The Horse in the American Colonies and Early Eastern United States

The history of the horse in the Americas has been described in some detail by Denhardt (1947), Howard (1965) and Haines (1971) and it is only my intention here to present a brief summary of major events.

The earliest Puritan settlers in Massachusetts were not horsemen. At Plymouth Colony in 1632 there was but one mare, a saddle horse for Governor Bradford (Howard, 31). Between 1640 and 1660 horsemen from Ireland emigrated to the Colony and Irish horses were imported. These circumstances transformed the Puritans more into horsemen. A crew of "cowboys" made the first cattle trail drive in what was to become the United States, from Springfield to Boston Common in 1655. Branding, periodic sorting and "rounding up" of commoned cattle were likewise an early part of Massachusetts' agricultural tradition. By mid-seventeenth century, Massachusetts horses were being shipped to the West Indies as mounts and also for work to drive "the brass and iron rollers" which "crushed the juice from the sugar cane". "The death rate of these animals was appalling; any plug-ugly freebred on the commons could be used on these millsweeps. Prime prices were also being offered, especially in Barbados and Jamaica, for lively pacers who would carry the plantation overseers on inspection trips" (Howard, 40).

Horse trade with the West Indies became so important that sailing vessels were equipped with built-in deck pens to hold 150–200 horses. Such ships were called "jockeys" after the Scottish nickname for small Jack. They made two round trips a year between New England and the islands of the West Indies. Other vessels also sometimes carried two or three dozen horses on their decks. As late as 1774 jockey ships carried four thousand horses a year from New England to the West Indies. The demand for horses resulted in the establishment of stud farms throughout southern New England and the Connecticut Valley. On the salt hay pastures of Narragansett Bay, Rhode Island, the Narragansett Pacer was developed (Howard, 14). But the American Revolution resulted in a British blockade and the industry consequently declined. A "moderately prosperous" Connecticut farmer in the 1750's owned "four negro servants, 50 head of cattle, 800 sheep and 30 to 40 horses" (Howard, 44).

The creation and development of the horse trade during the seventeenth and eighteenth centuries was instrumental in changing the Puritan view of the horse from the "gentleman's mount" to a mundane creature from which one could make money and which could be used by "everyman". As we have indicated above the American colonies became a major centre for the yeoman farmer. It was a land predominantly composed of independent landed proprietor-farmers who indulged in horse breeding and made extensive use of horses for riding and carting. There was however some Puritan influence which tended to prefer the trotting horse attached to a buggy rather than a riding horse which was more a symbol of pure and sinful pleasure. At the same time colonists preferred oxen to horses for heavy draught work. The Dutch, however, had very early introduced heavy draught horses into their New Amsterdam colony and these eventually spread elsewhere. By the end of the eighteenth century draught horses were coming to prevail in Great Britain and they were also supplanting oxen in North America.

In the American South a different cultural tradition evolved. Here Puritan values were less in evidence; the development of the cotton and plantation system and the great reliance upon slave labour fostered the role of the gentleman farmer and a lack of emphasis on the Calvinist glorification of hard work – a phenomenon which also occurred among the Boers. As the North-east tended more to industrialization and urbanization and became the home of growing immigrant populations, the South preserved and reinforced its agrarian and British or "Old American" roots. The Southern White farmer aspired to become a country gentleman and a cavalier protecting an agrarian tradition which incorporated ideas reminiscent of chivalry. While in the North farmers shifted from working with oxen to draught horses, in the South the shift was more and more in the direction of the mule, while the horse, as a result, became increasingly identified with riding, with pleasure and with the gentleman.

At the risk of oversimplifying the situation we might propose that the Southerner came to dichotomize his world: Within his Southern context on the one hand was the complex of the Black slave – hard work – vulgarity – the mule, and, on the other the White freeman – yeoman gentleman – civilization – the saddle horse. Between North and South, the Southerner viewed the North as representing modern industrialization, the city, the decay of traditional values by them, and by "foreign" immigration. The South, in contrast was seen as the perpetuator of the Jeffersonian ideal of the yeoman-agrarian community based upon British-American traditions.

The different orientation of Southern Whites had, among other things, the effect of making them more horsemen than were the Northerners. This was demonstrated in the Civil War with the superiority of the Confederate cavalry. It was primarily Southerners who moved into Texas to become the first Anglo-American cattle ranchers. These Texas cowboys later taught the Northerners the mainly Hispanic techniques of handling cattle on the open range. Texans and other Southerners also filled the ranks of the ranches on the Northern Plains. Today the Montana and Alberta cowboy, is for the most part, a copy of the Texas original (Frantz and Choate, 35).

It was in the South as well that such activities as fox hunting and race-track betting were more widely patronized. The "Border" state of Kentucky especially became a major breeding area for Thoroughbred racing stock and Standard Breds for sulky racing. Even today in the vicinity of Lexington, Kentucky, there are several large breeding farms, some of which keep up to three hundred mares. Many Southerners carried on the old English tradition of riding. Although they used the light English type saddle, they rode with long stirrups and many preserved the ambling gait. Others also developed the 'rack' gait.

In the American South, with the exception of Florida the mule gradually came to prevail in agricultural activity. In our discussion of mule use in south-western Europe several reasons for the preference for mules for farm labour were given. Parallel reasons pertain as well for the adoption of the mule in the American South. Lamb concludes there is no irrefutable proof that in the Lower South the mule is superior to the horse, but the advantage seems to be a matter of personal preference buttressed by the fact that "a mule's hardiness, longevity, cheapness to feed, and ability to withstand heat may have been more impressive than those of the horse . . ." (Lamb, 83).

We may note finally that while mule use was concentrated in the cotton South, most mules were reared in the "Border" states where there was extensive grassland and no cotton. In the 1840's the "'great nurseries of the mule' were clearly in Kentucky" (Lamb, 8); by 1860 there was a shift to Tennessee and by 1890 Missouri had become the leading producer (Lamb, 11–15). Now, with both the dramatic increase in agricultural mechanization and the equally dramatic decline of Negro farming in the South, the mule has all but disappeared from the American scene.[1]

In the Northern states horses became increasingly associated with farm work from the beginning of the nineteenth century. The invention of the reaper, the mowing machine and the threshing machine all favoured adoption of horses rather than the ox. Both mower and reaper required the steady rapid pace characteristic of the horse. In addition to the invention of more implements, more horses were attached to farm machinery as agriculture extended westward. "The limit on a set of harrows and drills was reached [in the American West] with one man driving thirty-six horses. The very large combined harvester-separator [thresher] with forty-two horses needed a crew of

---

[1] In 1850 there were 559,000 mules in the United States. They reached their peak in 1920 with 5,432,000 (three quarters of them in ten Southern states). Estimates for 1976 are about 65,000.

about six men, one to drive and the others to handle the grain as it spewed forth. Such large hitches were not uncommon. On most field teams four to eight horses were the custom" (Haines, 171). By 1920 the average wheat farm had ten horses and twenty-six acres cultivated for each horse used. "The Bureau of Animal Husbandry figured that each horse worked about six hundred hours a year" mostly in Spring and Fall (Haines, 171). In this regard it would appear that the American wheat farmer was similar to the east European peasant in maintaining a number of draught animals who are at their leisure for most of the year.

Prairie farmers however did not raise many horses. There was a very low ratio of colts to horses especially when compared to the Western range where there was a high colt crop. The West supplied much of the Central States market, particularly the light-weight horses of which one to two were kept on each prairie farm for buggies, light wagons, or, occasionally the saddle. Some farmers "used saddle horses to ride behind the harrows, guiding the teams with extra long lines, instead of plodding along in the dust" (Haines, 173).

According to Haines horses and horse drawn implements on farms were most numerous about 1900 (Haines, 173), although from the statistics, I would say the date is more correctly 1910. Certainly by 1940 they had been supplanted by gasoline motors. As the horse proved faster than the ox so the tractor was faster than the horse. Thus, to plough two and a half acres with two horses and an early nineteenth century walking plough required thirteen hours forty-two minutes; using four horses and two ploughs cut the time to five hours and fifty-seven minutes which actually was not much slower than an early tractor with two ploughs: four hours and nineteen minutes. A modern large tractor with an eight plough attachment requires only forty minutes for the job (Russell, 193–4). In addition, the tractor has caused a shift in the nature of the resources exploited. In the United States alone, by putting eighteen to twenty million farm horses out of work, the tractor has permitted seventy to eighty million acres of farmland to revert to uses other than feeding horses. But at the same time it has added to the strain on reserves of oil and has made farming the biggest single user of oil products in America.

Freight Wagons and Stage Coaches

One of the major developments of the post-Mediaeval period of Europe was the immense increase in transportation spurred as it was by growth in trade and improvement in roads. Freight haulage on land until the invention of the railway was almost exclusively accomplished by horse and wagon; oxen declined in importance, but were used for long hauls over trails and bad roads, where speed was not important. The railway expansion from 1830 to 1890 drew most of the freight away from horse-drawn vehicles and left the latter with carrying materials on short haul, particularly in intra-city traffic. The horse and wagon managed for a few decades – until the end of World War I – to maintain its position in this realm, but by that time the auto-truck had reached a stage of development, and roads were sufficiently good, that it started to assume an increasing percentage of freight business. During the nineteen twenties the use of the horse and wagon was confined to an ever decreasing orbit even in intra-city traffic. In the United States it survived with the aid of World War II until about the end of 1946 by which time the last remaining refuge of the horse cart – the milk and bakery wagons – were motorized and the old horse-drawn ice wagons disappeared with electric refrigeration. In more conservative western Europe the horse and wagon may still to be found in a few isolated instances.

The horse competed longest with the truck on regular delivery routes in heavy city traffic since it did not, overall, travel at a much slower speed and there was the particular advantage that the horse learned the route so that the amount of actual driving or guidance required was minimal.

Ponies were introduced into coal mining in early seventeenth-century Britain. Their use in hauling the coal out of the mines spread and they became indispensible for the operation. Hundreds of thousands of ponies gave their lives to the industry and not a few spent their entire existence underground, never seeing the light of day. In this century they were replaced by electric power and the last ponies were retired from the British mines in 1971.

The earliest public passenger coaches may have begun in England in 1500 with wagons which carried both goods and passengers. But serious development of passenger service commences in about 1640 at which time in England and Germany scheduled stage coach services were initiated. These coaches were lighter than those which had been in previous use and were provided with a suspension system, but they had only simple wooden bench seats. They were drawn by from four to six horses and carried up to eight passengers. Invariably crowded, hot and dusty in summer and bitter cold in winter, highly accident prone, covering an average of only four miles an hour and invariably far behind schedule, they were a trial and tribulation for every traveller. Macaulay referred to travellers of a much improved system in the early nineteenth century as the "martyrs of the highway" (Tarr, L., 261).

Improvements made in the course of the eighteenth century were the addition of steel springs and of more comfortable seats. The mail coach was introduced in 1784 into England which since the seventeenth century had been the leader in the stage coach enterprise. Mail coaches greatly hastened the pace and improved the schedule, even making up to eleven miles an hour on an average in some cases (Tarr, L., 256). By the early nineteenth century they had been adopted throughout most of Europe. It is interesting that the Spanish mail coaches were not drawn by horses but by mules (Tarr, L., 282).

The period from 1700 to ca., 1840 represents the peak of the horse drawn stage coach for public transportation. As in the case of carrying freight, here, too, between 1830 and 1890 the railway rapidly whittled away at the coach trade, so that by the end of that period, for most places horses were used for intra-city traffic and the few remaining short runs unserviced by rail. Electric railways introduced into cities after 1880 further cut into the horse drawn traffic, but the automobile and the omnibus annihilated all horse drawn passenger services shortly after World War I.

Mail service in Britain was conducted by boy postmen riding horseback until the introduction of the mail coach. Similar mail service arose for a short, but noted period in the United States between 1860–61 in the Pony Express which carried mail between St. Joseph, Missouri and Sacramento, California, a distance of 1838 miles, in approximately ten days. Along this route were 157 stations between seven and twenty miles apart. Each rider changed horses seven or eight times on his scheduled run of 75 to 100 miles. The mail was fitted in to one of four leather boxes that were attached to the four corners of the *mochila*, a square leather piece which was thrown over the saddle and had a hole for the horn and a slit for the cantle (Settle and Settle, *passim*).

Pollution has been a major popular discovery of the last two decades sometimes reaching fad proportions. It is not surprising that some horse fanciers half jokingly sought to exploit this to encourage the sale of horses and promulgate horsemanship with slogans such as "Fight pollution! Buy horses!" Certainly horses do not exude the noxious fumes of the cleanest of motor vehicles nor do they travel at such terrific speeds or make the noise of cars, snowmobiles, and other machines. Nor do they require so much valuable land turned into elegant and costly paved highways.

However, as nineteenth century cities testify horses create their own pollution problems. In 1900 American cities had between three and five million horses. Milwaukee with 350,000 people in the early part of this century had 12,500 horses which produced 133 tons of manure a day. New York City had 150–175,000 horses in 1880, but with the introduction of the electric cars or trams they were reduced to 120,000 in 1908. Rochester, New York with 15,000 horses around the end of the century, in one year, it was calculated "produced enough manure . . . to make a pile 175 feet high covering an acre of ground and breeding sixteen billion flies" (Tarr, J., 66).

In American cities and towns "during dry spells any little puff of wind filled the air with powdered horse manure that settled on the passerby and had to be wiped from eyes and lips" (Haines, 85). In wet weather streets were often turned into cesspools with accumulated manure and urine. Animals which fell and broke a leg were shot. Others fell from overwork and the remains eventually had to be collected from the streets. As late as 1912 Chicago removed 12,000 dead horses from the streets. "Small wonder" says a *Newsweek* article, "that turn of the century scientists hailed the development of the auto as a clean and efficient means of transportation" (*Newsweek*, 57).

Besides the pollution problem there was a safety problem in those days as well. The fatality rate on travel by horse and horsedrawn vehicles was estimated by the National Safety Council at 25.5 fatalities per 100 million miles travelled, but that by auto is only one tenth of this figure, at 2.1 fatalities per 100 million miles. Early motorists who saw the automobile as a safer means of travel were then quite correct, even if they were less correct about its polluting effects (*Newsweek*, 57).

Horsemeat, Hides and Hair

Attempts to stamp out consumption of horsemeat by Christian enthusiasts and later by rulers interested in maintaining a supply of horses for military use were never totally successful in Europe. Some consumption of horseflesh was common particularly on the continent in western Europe – France, the Low Countries, Germany and Scandinavia. Only in Britain was the taboo faithfully adhered to, and the avoidance of such flesh was carried by British settlers to America and Australia. Horse and mule meat were, however, common food for soldiers, especially during the Civil War. In the course of the twentieth century a demand arose for horsemeat for feeding zoo animals and a particularly lucrative trade developed in the pet food industry.

Horse hides and hair have been in demand for furniture, the manufacture of harness, saddlery, baggage, belts, gloves, shoes and other garments. Glue and gelatin are also derived in part from the horse. Throughout the United States, Canada and other countries there are several horse farms which are maintained for the purpose of producing serums and other medicinal materials. The Province of Ontario alone has one hundred pregnant mare's urine farms, which together keep between three and four thousand head to produce estrogen from the urine for manufacturing birth control pills and medicine for the treatment of the side effects of the menopause.

Conclusion

Following the decline of the Mediaeval system north-western Europe developed a yeoman agriculture and transported it to its overseas colonies. Two different types of agriculture arose out of the European background: one emphasized the cultivation of the soil with stock breeding as an important secondary operation; the other specialized in stock breeding. In this chapter we have been concerned with the European cultivators and have suggested that there are at least five major horse using areas among them:

1. North-western margins of Europe where the pony prevails and is employed for pack and riding and to a less extent for heavier farm draught. They are maintained chiefly on open range with minimal care.

2. North-western European Heartland which is the realm of the heavy draught horse employed for all types of farm labour and of light breeds reserved for riding and for carriages. The latter are identified more with the well-to-do, with pleasure and leisure. Where ponies exist they are of little economic importance. Animals are stabled and horses are given preferential treatment. They are chiefly fed oats and hay. Breeding is limited to the larger wealthy farmers and estate owners.

3. Eastern Europe where horses are of light breeds employed in farm draught and carting. As in western Europe horses are stabled, fed oats and accorded preferential treatment over other animals. In most parts the peasant is associated with the horse and wagon; the aristocracy with riding.

4. The Balkans where horses are also of light breeds. They are employed for light draught and carting and in mountainous zones as pack animals, but their use on the plough is much less common than in the north, although it does occur in parts of Greece and Rumania. Heavy draught in the Balkans is more associated with oxen and in Bulgaria and sections of Rumania with buffalo as well.

5. South-west Mediterranean Europe where the horse has retained more of its pre-Mediaeval specialization as a riding and light draught animal, only rarely engaged in heavy draught. This, also is a region for light horses, but one where the mule has taken on considerable importance as a work animal, in addition to the ox.

Due to the expansion of western European cultures into the Americas, Australia and South Africa there arose extensions of the North-west European Heartland area into central and eastern Canada, central and north-eastern United States and the farming, non-ranching sections of Australia and European South Africa. Earlier, Iberian tradition was introduced into gcentral and South America. Here, however, almost from the start there were two different kinds of agriculture entailing different roles for the horse. One was based upon the cultivation of crops on large plantations and small peasant holdings, while the other involved the raising of cattle and sheep on even larger ranches. We shall consider the latter in a subsequent chapter.

In the Latin American plantation and peasant system horses were, as in Spain, reserved primarily for riding by the gentry and estate managers for surveillance purposes. There is a similarity between the nineteenth century south-eastern part of the United States to this Mediterranean pattern, but the two differ in that the latter makes extensive use of the donkey as a riding animal for the rural lower classes. In the Old American South the lower classes were either slaves who were usually not permitted to ride anything or small farmers who were rarely so poor that they could not at least own a mule.

The special characteristics of these areas result from a combination of several factors: the perpetuation of ancient tradition and values concerning the horse; the development of new agricultural systems and forms of social organization, particularly the alteration of the nature and character of the social classes; the introduction of different breeds of horses; and the availability of alternative forms of draught power. Of primary motivating significance is the high regard for the horse, an ancient and pervasive European value, which from early Mediaeval times gradually achieved increasingly wide expression and realisation, especially in northern Europe, as a result of technological and economic changes. Modest peasants in great numbers came to enhance their status by owning horses, even if they were work animals. The enlargement of the number of yeomen farmers, particularly in the context of British America, afforded opportunity for wider ownership of carriage and riding horses.

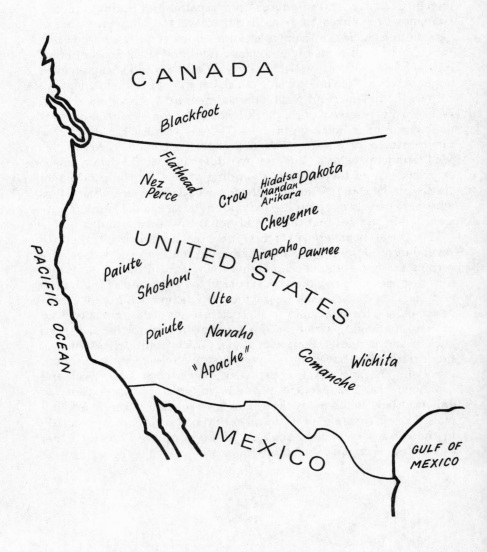

INDIANS OF THE NORTH AMERICAN PLAINS

IX

The Reinvention of Equestrian Nomadism: The Indians of Plains and Pampas

THE adoption and particular adaptation of the horse by Plains and Pampas Indians represents a reinvention of equestrian nomadism in the New World, but several features distinguish it from the Old World pattern. First, the horse and the dog were the only domesticated animals kept by these Indians. The horse was a hunting aid, especially in North America, for the search for buffalo. Among other things this meant that the total Indian herd wealth was in horses while that of the Central Asiatic nomads was in sheep, goats, cattle and occasionally, yaks or camels besides horses.

Whether the Plains Indians can be considered pastoral nomads or not is a question. Most acquired so many horses they were forced to learn and practice equine husbandry and spend considerable time engaged in their care and management. Horses compelled the Indians to locate their camps where there was good pasture and water. They demanded protection from raiders and, in the north, had to be provided with supplementary feed for at least part of the winter. At the same time the Indians of the Plains depended for their food supply upon wild herding animals shot from horseback. Sahlins calls them "Equestrian Hunters" (Sahlins, 41). The Plains way of life was a unique and quite new mode of socio-cultural adaptation to hunting wild game and as such is not the same kind of mounted nomadism that one encounters in Eurasia.

Eurasian and American mounted nomadism diverged also in the mode of social organization. The Eurasians were an immensely greater population. One "people" – Kazakh or Kirghiz, etc. – in the seventeenth or eighteenth centuries included several hundred thousand people and each divided into several tribes of many thousands. The total number of Plains Indians was by comparison only a handful, and Plains peoples – Dakota, Cheyenne or what have you – composed populations of from one to ten thousand individuals. Eurasian nomads were able to amass large forces and organize true aggressive-imperialist oriental nation-states – an undertaking which no Plains Indian tribe ever attempted.

Plains Indians no sooner developed their unique mode of life than it was destroyed by invading European settlers and pioneers. We will never know, if left to their own devices, in what direction their mounted hunting activity might have taken them. We will not know if with their enhanced efficiency of rifle and horse, they would eventually have reduced the buffalo numbers to the point where they would have had to adopt other sources for food or starve. Dependent on wild game they could not artificially breed and rear stock and control their number. Hence it is highly unlikely they could ever have approached the Turkic-Mongol nomads in numbers and ability to organize large resources and facilities without abandoning this dependence upon wild game.

Another social organizational difference is that the Eurasian nomads had a patrilineal form of tribal structure coupled with a system of aristocratic and commoner tribal sections. Equestrian hunters of the West had hardly more than a band organization which involved bilateral or, sometimes, matrilineal forms of kinship. Divisions existed based upon wealth, but were not formalized into specific social classes. There was no hereditary aristocracy and no hereditary lower class.

The role of the horse in changing the way of life of a large segment of American Indians is a fairly well documented development which was unfolded in recent times and over a relatively short period.

The horse eventually found its way into most American Indian societies outside the far north, taking on a minor and limited role, except among the Plains Indians, the Indians in the southern part of South America on the Pampas and in Patagonia, and isolated examples of other Indians who in adopting the horse took over the general pattern of Spanish stock breeding. Such "ranching" Indians, being stockmen and not hunters are therefore discussed in the chapter on ranching.

Horses as a species originated in America, but they had disappeared from the American continents well before the beginning of the Christian era and were not reintroduced until the Spaniards came in 1492. Within a remarkably short space of time their numbers proliferated, especially as feral animals. By the end of the seventeenth century they were running wild from Tucuman to the Canadian border (Denhardt, 33). It has been claimed that the source for horses in the Americas dates back to those lost or abandoned by the De Soto and Coronado expeditions. This is to be doubted since an occasional abandoned or lost horse is unlikely to find mates to reproduce in sufficient numbers for survival. J. Frank Dobie remarked: "If another fable had placed Adam in Asia and Eve in Africa the chances of mating would have been about as high" as the chances of a stray stallion from Coronado's expedition mating with a stray mare from De Soto's (Dobie, 35). Besides, horses, which in Spain had been well cared for and stable-fed would not be likely to breed in enough numbers to survive under such new and strange conditions. Finally, if the leaders or the better horses did stray they would have been searched out and returned (Roe, 35).

Horses were first introduced on the Pampas in 1535 by Pedro Mendoza and when he was "forced to abandon the early settlement where Buenos Aires now stands, he reportedly turned loose five mares and seven horses, although it seems more probable they would have been salted down for provisions" (Denhardt, 34). Nichols has pointed out that these Spaniards had by this time been reduced to eating shoe leather, in which case they would hardly turn their horses loose (Nichols, 1939). The wild horses which in due course covered the Pampas obviously originated from later settlement.

In western North America it is more probable that the early development of wild and other herds of horses resulted from horses being handed over to, and later, being stolen by American Indians. The stealing did not commence until the Indians began to appreciate the value of the horse and started trading with other Indian tribes. The first official record of giving horses to Indians was in 1542 when the Viceroy Mendoza mounted alllied Aztec chieftans to lead their tribesmen in the Mixton war in Mexico. By 1567 Indians in Sonora, Mexico were reported to be eating and riding horses. The early Spaniards however were not eager to have Indians mounted or knowledgeable about horses. By keeping them pedestrians, they hoped more readily to subordinate and subdue them. But they were very early forced to employ Indians as their grooms.

The introduction of missions and the gathering of converted natives into *rancherias* in the vicinity of missions impelled a need for food and, thus, cattle and gardens. This led to a need for *vaqueros* to care for the cattle. Consequently the missions mounted some of their Indians. With a few now acquainted with horses as grooms and others as *vaqueros*, a core of Indians was created with a good knowledge of horsemanship. Some of these eventually left the missions and *rancherias*, to return later to steal horses and cattle. At the same time they spread their knowledge of the horse to other Indians. Forbes claims Indians also might have learned horsemanship by watching Spaniards and learning by trial and error. Some Indians were taught by anti-Spanish Mexicans and Tarascans who joined them and, possibly also, by runaway Negroes and Mulattos (Forbes, 191).

A knowledge of horsemanship by at least a few Indians seems a necessary prerequisite to the spread of the horse among them. This is because it is unlikely that a people totally unfamiliar with any livestock, and especially with horses, will independently seek to subjugate and use them for riding purposes. This is particularly so in the case of the American Indians who were exposed to highly spirited, often unbroken horses and who, on initial acquaintance with them, were deathly afraid of them. "The native fear of horses was the most effective weapon the Spaniards possessed, and they encouraged the Indians to believe that the horses were gods" (Denhardt, 57). And in fact, Cortez' horse, El Morzillo, was made into a god by the Mayan Itzas.[1] "The Zempoaltecas said that the horses were so ferocious that the Spaniards had to put bridles on them to keep them from devouring humans. It was commonly believed that they ate the metal bits. The Indian allies of Spaniards told how the animals could run as fast as deer, nothing being able to escape them. Whenever the horses would neigh, the natives "quaked with fear (Denhardt, 57).

"Once mounted, the Indian with his quiver of arrows was superior to the Spaniard with his single-shot arquebus" (Denhardt, 103). Thus the mounted Indian bowman may have been an important factor in inhibiting the expansion of the Spanish Empire into the Plains.

In the east, colonies attempted by Ponce de Leon, Luis Vasquez de Ayllon and Jacques Cartier were abandoned and the horses are presumed to "have been killed and eaten by the Indians, wolves or wildcats" (Howard, 25).

Spanish sources indicate that by the last decade of the sixteenth century horses were reaching what is now the United States. Certainly by 1600 they were on the border areas of Texas. By 1579 wild horses in north central Mexico were so abundant the Indians did not need to resort to stealing and they were becoming common among the Indians of this area. It is possible that some of the Pueblo Indians in New Mexico had horses as early as 1582, but they certainly had acquired them by 1606–7. In Arizona they were not introduced until at least two decades later (Forbes, 192–202). The Apache were riding by 1659. Lowie claims it was certainly after 1630 "for in that year a group of nomad Apache are known to have travelled exclusively with dog travois and to have hunted buffalo unmounted" (Lowie, 1963, 43). In 1690 the Hasinai in Texas possessed four to five horses for every household, but along the Red River the Caddo could only muster about thirty head in all (Lowie, 1963, 43).

The Kiowa had horses by 1682 and the Paiute and Utes by 1700 at the very latest. The Comanche arrived in New Mexico in 1705 and it is assumed that by that time they were horsemen. The Wichita had

---

[1] Briefly the story is that Cortez was forced to leave his horse with the Mayan Itza because it was lame. The horse soon died, but when the missionaries visited the Indians about a century later, as the first European visitors since Cortez, they discovered a temple in the centre of which was a great statue of a horse which, of course, was duly destroyed by the mission padres (Denhardt, 70–71).

horses by 1717 and Pawnee about the same time. "In 1719 two Pawnee villages on the Arkansas owned a total of 300 – less than one horse to a man – while by 1800 probably every Pawnee village on the Platte and Loup rivers had several thousand. In 1724 a body of 1,100 Kansa travelled with dogs exclusively, and another group of the same tribe had only a few horses. Prior to 1735 there were no horses north and east of the Missouri; in 1766 the Dakota of central Minnesota were still travelling in canoes rather than on horseback, but by 1772 horses had become common, and by 1796 their canoes had been replaced by horses. Farther west the Shoshone, Flathead, and Nez Perce preceded the Blackfoot and Crow as equestrians and may be taken as the source of supply for them" (Lowie, 1963, 43).

By the second quarter of the eighteenth century, horsemanship had spread into the northern Plains; to the Plains Cree by 1738, Assiniboine, 1742, and Blackfoot by 1754. The Cheyenne acquired horses about the same time as the Dakota.

Uses of the Horse

Buffalo hunting was economically the most important use of the horse. The horse turned the Plains Indians into masters of the buffalo and provided a means by which an abundance of food and materials for clothing and shelter were acquired.

A specially trained mount for buffalo hunting was a major asset to any Indian. The buffalo horse had to have enduring speed as well as intelligence and agility, surefootedness and courage. He could not fear the buffalo (Ewers, 153). He had to ride close by the buffalo and "as soon as he heard the twang of the bow string, a good buffalo running horse swerved away from its victim in order to be well out of harm's way when the wounded beast turned and charged" (Wallace and Hoebel, 58). Sometimes the horse was not quick enough and got gored or stepped in a prairie dog hole and broke his leg. For the Commanche all these risks were taken with joy (Wallace and Hoebel, 58). Buffalo horses learned to stop quickly, to bear two riders, and to remain near their riders when they dismounted (Ewers, 196–7). Among the Blackfoot, training for this service started at four years of age, and all buffalo horses received special preferential treatment.

The hunting technique involved either a surround or open chase. In the surround a "considerable number of horsemen" encircled a herd and started it "milling in a circle", shooting down animals as they rode amongst them. "The chase was a straightaway rush by mounted men, each hunter singling out an animal" to shoot, riding alongside for the kill (Ewers, 154).

A hunter often rode a common horse leading his buffalo horse until he came upon a herd at which time he changed mounts (Ewers, 156). Comanches and Blackfoot normally rode bareback on the hunt, although some used a pad saddle. The Cheyenne preferred a dark coloured horse for hunting, believing white horses scared the buffalo, but as Grinnell points out the dark horses were not as noticeable as white horses (Grinnell, II, 204).

Buffalo hunts were surrounded by strict regulations which were enforced in most tribes by soldier societies. There were, for example penalties for premature hunting in tribal buffalo hunts. Among the Wind River Shoshone one who broke the rules of the hunt was punished by whipping his horse over the head. And the Kiowa shot an offender's horse. The Ponca destroyed a man's dogs and horses and then proceeded to give him presents to help restore his losses (Ewers, 164). For the Cheyenne there were three crimes only: homicide, disobeying the rules of the buffalo hunt, and repeated horse theft. The punishment often entailed a severe beating of the culprit and destruction of his horses, tipi, bow and other personal possessions (Driver, 342).

A skilled hunter mounted on a buffalo horse could kill enough buffalo in a morning's run to feed a family group of twenty or so for several days with plenty of meat for the drying racks and scraps for the dogs as well. Thus a successful hunter had considerable leisure for visiting, caring for his horses, making weapons and raiding (Haines, 71). Most hunters among the Blackfoot "rarely killed more than one or two buffalo at a chase" (Ewers, 159). A poor family with no buffalo horse and unable to borrow one, or lacking an able rider, was forced to seek charity (Ewers, 162).

Horses were also employed on other types of hunts as well. The Shoshoni used them for the antelope chase. Ten mounted men with five or six assisting them on foot surrounded the antelope running them around until they were tired, at which time they moved in at a fast pace to shoot them (Steward, 36). Some men owned winter hunting horses which were valued for the ability to move around readily in winter snow and storms.

Raiding and Warfare

It is questionable whether one can rightfully call the intertribal hostilities of Plains Indians warfare. They were not aimed at territorial expansion and political subjugation of a defeated foe, nor were they organized on a large scale basis with chain of command and "armies". Plains hostilities are more correctly seen as raiding and feuding carried out in a highly individualized manner, but according to rules. There is some controversy over the fundamental cause of these engagements. Ewers argues that "[n]eed, not greed or glory, was the major stimulus" and the need was primarily for horses (Ewers, 311).

Lowie, writing of the Crow, admits their desire for horses was an economic motive for fighting, but states that a Crow achieved greater status if he took a single picketed horse rather than several on the open range. He also points to those who possessed large herds of horses, such as Greybull who owned seventy to ninety, and suggests they actually needed only a few fleet buffalo horses and some pack animals, while the remainder were sheer ostentatious display. An "owner could offer twenty horses for a wife instead of five" and make "frequent presents to his father's clanfolk if he liked to hear himself eulogized" (Lowie, 1935, 228). The acquisition of horses was a major motive for raiding parties, but the motive arose out of both "need" and "glory".

In some years the three Blackfoot tribes went out on over fifty raiding parties. The Blackfoot were "deficient in planned and coordinated cavalry tactics under fire" (Ewers, 198). They were capable of initial charge in force but if unsuccessful their fighting "disintegrated into a large number of contests between individual Indians at close range. If the first charge was repulsed the Blackfoot rarely regrouped for another assault on horseback" (Ewers, 198).

"Upon overtaking a mounted enemy the Blackfoot tried to unhorse him with his shock weapon. Then, if the enemy were still active, the Blackfoot dismounted" to dispatch him on foot (Ewers, 199). In charges horses were often shields to riders who placed their left heel over the horse's hip bone, grasped the mane with one hand and fired a rifle under the horse's neck. Blackfoot knew of this feat and presumably learned it but did not commonly rely upon it (Ewers, 205).

Many Indians went off on a raid on foot with the expectation that they would be able to ride back home. Otherwise they rode out on a pack horse leading a buffalo horse until the battle at which time, like a Mediaeval knight, they mounted the better horse (Roe, 231). A man took his winter hunting horse along when snow was on the ground (Ewers, 196).

The central idea of horse raiding was to capture the enemy's picketed horses by stealth without the owner's knowledge and without bloodshed. This was always viewed as an aggressive act requiring retaliation, so that raiding had the qualities of feuds as well. Captured horses were distributed among members of the war party under the supervision of the party's leader (Ewers, 188). "A horse retaken from the enemy was considered the property of the man who recaptured it," since he had risked his life for it, although he might out of generosity "return the animal to its former owner, but he was not obliged to do that" (Ewers, 211).

Sport and Recreation

Horse racing and betting on horses was a much loved and popular sport. Among the Comanche in one type of race the contestants ran at full tilt to a tree and the one touching it first won. In another they rushed to a pole dangling about six feet off the ground. If one stopped too soon he was unable to touch it and if too late he was knocked off his horse. Relay races were also common. Before a race most Comanche racers were administered a special potion by the medicine man who spit it into the horse's ear and mouth. This was "power" and women were prohibited from approaching a racer, so treated. After the race the rider and horse went to a creek to wash off the medicine effects (Wallace and Hoebel, 49–50).

The Comanche were not above trying to fleece others in a race. "Colonel Dodge has left a story of a race which the officers at Ft. Chadburne, Texas, to their regret arranged with some Comanche. After the first bets had been laid, the Comanches innocently brought forth a miserable-looking pony with a three inch coat of thick hair and a general appearance of neglect and suffering. Its rider 'looked big enough to carry the poor beast on his shoulders' and was armed with a club with which he belaboured the animal from starting line to the finish. Yet, to the surprise of the Whites the Indian pony managed to win by a neck. Within an hour the officers bit again and lost by a nose. Then they suggested a third race and brought out a magnificent Kentucky racing mare. In a frenzy of excitement the Indians bet everything that the whites would take. With the starting signal the Indian rider threw away his club, gave a whoop, and his little mount 'went away like the wind'. That Kentucky mare was soon so far behind that for the last fifty yards the Comanche sat backwards on his pony beckoning to the white rider to come on. The whites afterwards learned that the shaggy pony was a celebrated racer, and that the Comanches had just come back from fleecing the Kickapoos to the tune of six hundred ponies with that same little horse" (Wallace and Hoebel, 50).

The Blackfoot, too, enjoyed horse racing and a winning race horse was the most valued animal a man could own. There were races between men's soldier societies and betting was a common feature of such events. Guns, robes, blankets, food and horses were all common stakes. Horses were stakes in other sporting competitions as well, such as foot races, and hoop and pole games. Sometimes, especially when distinguished Indian or White visitors were present, there were displays of sham battles.

Draught and Pack Horses

Before the days of the horse the Indian's worldly goods were packed on a travois drawn by a dog or were placed upon the backs of women. With the horse the travois was adapted to the larger animal and, as a result, it could be made of heavier and longer poles and to bear much larger burdens. In this way the introduction of the horse was a force for women's "liberation" among Plains Indians, since on the march they no longer carried heavy burdens on their backs, but invariably rode horseback like their men. The greater carrying capacity had further repercussions as well. The size of the lodge became bigger as the horse could pull more and larger lodge poles and more buffalo hides. The Indians were likewise enabled to transport greater quantities of food, particularly dried provisions for winter camps as insurance against famine. In the hunt the horse not only allowed for closer following of buffalo, but also more saving of meat since it all could more readily be packed back to the camp.

Riding and Riding Gear

Indians, of course, acquired most of their horsemanship ultimately from the Spanish, but because the early Indians had no saddles or bridles certain modifications were introduced. They first learned to mount and handle horses from the right side – a legacy from the Moorish Arabs via the Spaniards (Roe, 63–4). A rider took a strong grip on the mane and "placed his left hand on the center of the horse's back as he jumped on . . ." (Ewers, 68). The Pima Indians in mid-nineteenth century were reported to mount on the right side "having one girth loose, which is used as a stirrup, one foot in it at a time" (Ezell, 65). At a walk or a trot the Indian "sat bolt upright, riding down to the crotch, not quite straight legged but with a forward slant to his thighs which rested on the pony's barrel, his lower leg vertical". To gallop he leaned forward as his thighs gripped tightly while his lower extremities were "slightly behind the vertical" (Trench, 220).

On adopting stirrups the Indians took to riding with bent knee and short leathers. The rider thus acquired "the necessary leverage to move from side to side and to rise and turn in the saddle" according to his need. He could better employ the lance and bow and it was easier "to weave his body from side to side when under fire in battle" (Ewers, 70). By partially adopting *la jineta* style of the Spanish, the Indian learned the advantages of the short stirrup technique for shooting with the bow just as the horsemen of the steppes of central Asia had done long before.

When the Indians acquired European type saddlery they also shifted from right to left hand mounting and handling of horses.

Among the Blackfoot, horses were not given verbal commands for turning, but the best trained of Indian ponies turned with knee pressure or the shifting of the weight of the rider and could be ridden without a bridle much as the Numidian riders of North Africa in Roman times used to do. But the great majority of Blackfoot horses were not so well trained and had to be handled by a two rein bridle (Ewers, 70). Whips were also invariably used by Indian riders, but spurs were not.

Geldings were preferred for riding. A Comanche warrior was strongly averse to riding mares and certainly never rode one to battle (Wallace and Hoebel, 46).

Blackfoot children were early trained to ride and were good riders at the age of six or seven (Ewers, 67). Riding was one of the first things taught a Comanche child. He started out riding on his mother's back pack before he could walk. Later he was strapped to a gentle mare. By four or five a boy would have a pony of his own. Girls were almost as good equestrians as boys. Boys learned such tricks as picking up things from the ground while riding at full gallop. They learned to gallop in pairs to a fallen person and simultaneously pick him up at full speed, one rider swinging him in front of him onto the horse (Wallace and Hoebel, 48). This was in preparation for assisting fallen comrades in battle.

Among the Cheyenne as well, boys learned to ride almost as soon as they could walk. They did not fear horses or dread falling since they began by riding gentle old pack horses and by five or six they rode young colts bareback. Soon after they learned to ride to the hills herding ponies and early became experts in roping (Grinnell, I, 109). Girls were good riders as well.

The Comanche often rode bareback, but sometimes a small pad was used or a rope around the horse's body into which the knees were thrust to keep a firm seat (Wallace ahd Hoebel, 58).

Indian saddles were chiefly skin pads stuffed with hair. On some, these pads were attached to wooden sidebars imitating Spanish saddles. J. Frank Dobie considered the Indian saddle "notoriously cruel on a horse's back" (Dobie, 51). The pad saddle had a girth and stirrups and weighed no more than the modern American racing saddle. It may have been nearly universal among Plains Indians in the eighteenth century, spreading from tribe to tribe along with the horse, while the wooden frame saddle diffused more slowly. It is likely that the model for the pad saddle could be the Spanish-Mexican pack saddle.

An Indian style wood frame saddle was normally a woman's saddle, consisting of a frame of cottonwood covered with rawhide and having a high cantle and pommel, with girth and stirrups (Ewers, 85). "[T]he design of the Indian 'wood saddle' was not copied directly from Whites, but was a remodelled adaptation of the white man's wooden frame saddle in the construction of which the Indians exercised considerable ingenuity" (Ewers, 91).

Making saddles was somewhat specialized women's work, at least among the Blackfoot (Ewers, 81).

Bridles were most often simple jaw straps. A war bridle used for buffalo hunting and general riding consisted of a "two-rein bridle formed of a single length of rope with a honda (fixed loop at the end of one rein through which the other rein passes). The end with the honda served as one rein, at the forward part of which two half hitches were taken, placed in the horse's mouth, and tightened around his lower jaw . . . . The rope continued around the other side of the horse's neck (serving as a second rein), passed through the honda, and the long end remaining was carefully folded or coiled and placed under the rider's belt at one side" (Ewers, 76). There was sixteen to thirty foot of rope so that if a rider was thrown he could catch hold of the end of the rope and hold the horse, but, of course, there was always danger of injury by becoming entangled in such a long rope (Ewers, 76).

In the northern Plains and the Plateau areas hair bridles were common, as were also halters and hackamores of this material. The Indians also made these, as well as reins, from rawhide and leather. Haines reports that a "few specimens of Spanish halters, bits, and saddles found their way as far north as Alberta by 1790" (Haines, 74). From the nineteenth century on Spanish style saddlery and curb bits became increasingly more common among the Indians and by the early twentieth century they had become prevalent among them. Before this time, as well, the Plains Indians had become adept in the use of a rawhide lasso forty feet long (Haines, 75).

Trading of Horses and Gifts of Horses

Trading of horses among Indians went along two major routes. One led from the upper Yellowstone eastward to the Hidatsa and Mandan villages on the Missouri River and a second led from the Spanish villages of New Mexico and Texas to the vicinity of the Black Hills in South Dakota via the western High Plains, thence westward and north-eastward to the Arikara, Hidatsa and Mandan. Thus, although they were not as outstanding horsemen as some other Plains tribes, the village-dwelling horticultural Hidatsa, Mandan and Arikara became major horse dealers and traders. The Crow also were outstanding in this respect and the Kiowa, Kiowa-Apache, Comanche, Arapaho and Cheyenne were important middle men in this trade in the early nineteenth century (Ewers, 7–8). Oregon Indians sold slaves at The Dalles for horses and some of them received their first horses in this manner (Driver, 391). But for every horse acquired by trading it is estimated a hundred were acquired by stealing (Driver, 374).

Horses were most prestigious gifts. They were sometimes presented by one tribe to another at treaty making ceremonies. Thus, at a peace treaty in 1840 amongst the Cheyenne, Kiowa and Comanche gifts were exchanged among the various parties and a Kiowa chief presented the Cheyenne with 250 horses (Dobie, 77). More customary was the offering of horses by a man to his bride's father. One also enhanced his position by making a gift of a horse to the brother of the girl one was courting. A most gracious gesture for a Comanche was to make a gift of a horse to a friend (Wallace and Hoebel, 40).

Horses also served as a medium of exchange and as a device for paying damages. Thus, among the Comanche, a cuckolded husband could demand the favourite horse of the defendant as damages (Wallace and Hoebel, 226). To kill another man's horse was a most serious offence and the most common form of revenge against an adulterer among many Plains Indians was for the husband to kill, if he did not take, the adulterer's horse, besides beating his wife (Roe, 272).

Horse in Religion

Most of the tribes in the United States killed a horse or a dog at the death of the owner as a sacrifice to the supernatural (Driver, 448). An owner might request a favourite horse be sacrificed at his death. But the Comanche had some qualms about such sacrifices. Among them a man sometimes asked that his favourite horse be given to his best friend instead. Rather than slaughtering a number of horses, they resorted to the sacrifice of a single favourite horse and distributed any others among the survivors (Lowie, 1963, 91). The slaughter of a single favourite horse was likewise common practice among the Crow and Arikara as well, but the Blackfoot sometimes killed as many as twenty horses. The number of horses slaughtered at a funeral varied considerably from tribe to tribe and depended upon the wealth and importance of the deceased. Unlike the Central Asiatic nomads such sacrifice did not entail a feast of horseflesh.

The Horse Medicine cult was common among most Plains tribes.

This comprised the horse medicine men who attended cult ceremonies and exchanged their secrets. Associated with it were special songs and dances. Horse medicine power could be transferred from one person to another by request and the offering of appropriate gifts to those already invested with the power (Ewers, 257–62).

Cheyenne horse doctors, some of whom were women, were paid for their services with one or more horses. No doctor would strike a horse on the head for fear he would never receive any more patients if he did. In his lodge all lassos, bridles and whips could not be left on the ground, but had to be hung up. Taboo to him as well, was the eating of horseflesh and the killing of any horse, wild or domesticated. On their war parties the Cheyenne invariably took along one or more horse doctors (Grinnell, II, 140–2). While much of Indian veterinary care was in a magico-religious context, it is an error to interpret all of it as so much superstitious quackery. As in the case of the Indian techniques for curing human ailments there was a mixture of what we today call the magical and the empirical.

The Use of Horse Flesh, Hair and Hides

Only a very few Indian tribes made a common practice of consuming horseflesh; as a general rule it was not considered desirable food. It was eaten with some regularity by the Apache groups and the Comanche and, on occasion, such as during famine, by some others. In the Great Basin area where life was particularly hard because of the paucity of resources, there was a general reversal of common Plains customs. The Shoshoni on the Humboldt River hunted and ate horses, but did not ride them and the Southern Paiutes ate them more often than they rode them. For both, horses were too expensive to maintain as mounts since their territory harboured no buffalo to hunt (Steward, 152 and 181).

Horsehides were used for a variety of products and were favoured for drumheads among the Blackfoot. Horsehair was made into decorative fringes on clothing, for rope, bridles and reins. Horsetails made tipi decorations, but among the Blackfoot, "only if the owner 'dreamed' of them as part of the" lodge ornamentation (Ewers, 223). The Blackfoot also cut away horse callosities for manufacturing perfumes and several tribes made necklaces from horse teeth and neck pendants of horses' hooves.

Horse Management

Horses were greatly esteemed by the Indians. Yet some authors have charged Indians with negligence or cruelty towards them. There is undoubtedly some universal or absolute definition of cruelty, but certainly a considerable flexibility in the meaning of the term inevitably arises as a result of varying cultural contexts. The harder, somewhat more rough and tumble life of a Plains Indian would produce different interpretations of cruelty to those of a well insulated, apartment-dwelling New York dowager. Secondly, the difference between tribes and between individuals within tribes must be taken into account. Not all Plains tribes were the same, nor were members within a tribe carbon copies of each other.

Many Indians apparently paid little or no attention to sores on their horses' backs. Presumably riding on raw backs was not uncommon, especially in Mexico and South America. Dobie, however, points out that Indians and cowboys believed a sore did not hurt after it "warmed up" (Dobie, 51). Most Indians seem to have been particularly concerned about their favourite mount or mounts. A Comanche warrior took great care of his favourite horse, tending it, keeping it picketed by his lodge and petting it. "'Some men loved their horses more than they loved their wives' said Post Oak Jim. To this, others added, 'or child or any other human being'" (quoted in Wallace and Hoebel, 36).

Open range grazing was universally observed by Plains Indians. However, a case of hand feeding of grain is reported among Texas Indians in 1683 (Roe, 248). In the northern Plains, horses were provided with special treatment during winter. The Pawnee, Arikara, and Blackfoot among others cut cottonwood trees and the horses subsisted on their bark and tender twigs (Roe, 248ff.). The Mandan put horses in lodges in a particular compartment in winter and fed them maize. The Sioux built sheds against the winter lodge to protect selected horses from severe weather and from thieves. The women provided a limited amount of hay and cottonwood bark and branches for the horses (Roe, 252). The Hidatsa used dried grass for their horses in winter (Roe, 253). Cheyenne drove horses into protected groves in bad winter weather.

The Blackfoot did not put up wild hay for winter, but when the snow was too deep for the horses to paw away, people tried to clear areas and collect grass. "[T]he most common supplemental feed was the inner bark of the round-leafed cottonwood". In winter horses were not hobbled, so as to permit them to paw away the snow for grass. On very cold nights they were driven among trees and thickets of river bottoms to protect them from the wind. By spring all horses were thin and weak from their winter ordeal (Ewers, 43–46).

Among the Blackfoot daily care of horses was in the hands of boys between ages eight and twelve, except in the worst weather in winter when the men took over the task. The boys were expected to get up early to go after the horses in the pasture and drive them to a watering place after which they were driven to good pastures near the camp. The owner generally went out and selected what animals he wanted for the day. At noon the horses were watered again and at evening a third time, after which they were turned onto night pasture, hobbling the lead mare to prevent the herd from straying (Ewers, 37). A coulee or valley served as night pasture where the animals would not be seen by raiders. There was normally no night herding except where trouble was anticipated (Ewers, 38).

Blackfoot hobbled their horses on the forelegs with soft tanned buffalo skin or rawhide fastened so it could not chafe yet tight enough to prevent slipping (Ewers, 38). The best horses were picketed at night near the lodge. A mild mannered horse was tied on the foreleg while a more lively one was fastened around the neck with a short line (Ewers, 39). Among the Blackfoot corrals for horses were sometimes constructed especially in winter and during other seasons when the chief thought there was danger from raiders (Ewers, 209).

Stallions were gelded, the Blackfoot believing this made them "more tractable and fleeter of foot". Ordinarily many stallions were gelded at one time and specialists were employed for the task (Ewers, 56–8). The Comanche gelded all their riding horses at about two years of age but left a few choice stallions for breeding (Wallace and Hoebel, 46).

Among the Comanche favourite horses, war horses and race horses would be given personal names but others in the herd usually did not have names (Wallace and Hoebel, 46).

Peter Pond reports that the Dakota slit the nostrils of their horses so that they would breathe more freely. Dobie adds that this practice was "widespread" (Dobie, 50). However, if it were one might expect mention of it by ethnographers. Yet I have seen none. At any rate, where the operation did occur it was probably, as among the ancient Egyptians, in connection with the employment of a low noseband.

The ear tips of one's favourite horse were trimmed for style, but also for the practical end of facilitating "identification by feel in darkness". For warfare and ceremonial display, horses were painted and decorated, sometimes with necklaces of bear claws (Dobie, 50).

Horseshoeing was not an Indian practice, but J. Frank Dobie reported the Comanche used to harden tender feet by applying the smoke and heat of burning rosemary. They also made rawhide boots for the sore hooves of their favourite animals (Wallace and Hoebel, 47). Roe states that the necessity for shoeing depended to some extent on the kind of country traversed, but he gives no examples of Indians actually shoeing horses (Roe, 253).

Breaking for Riding

Blackfoot adolescent boys broke yearling colts for their own use, but most horses were trained at the age of two or three. A halter or hackamore was applied before training to ride. The Blackfoot had four methods for breaking: One man on a broken horse led the horse to be broken into a stream or pond where it was mounted. Here it would be easier to subdue a bucking, thrashing horse because it would tire more quickly; the water was also a softer spot to fall when thrown. A similar technique was to mount an unbroken horse in boggy ground.

With dry-ground breaking a surcingle was used. The front legs were often lassoed and the horse thrown. As the rider mounted the thrown horse a band of rawhide was passed "around the horse's belly, enclosing [the rider's] knees and shanks, and quickly tied . . . in front of him". The rope around the legs was loosened and the rider then attempted to stay on the horse. This method often required three days before the horse was broken and each time one was expected to ride until the horse was played out. Another technique was to apply a pad saddle and girth while using the surcingle as well in the above fashion (Ewers, 61–4).

Denhardt, describing "Indian" horse breaking, portrays a firm, yet "slow and easy" technique. A man ropes his horse and while several others hold the rope another slowly works his way towards the horse "talking" to it until he can touch its nose, then its head. The hackamore is shown to the horse and cautiously applied. The breaker continues to "talk" to the horse, also hissing while he proceeds to handle it all over. Eventually he presses his hands on the animal's back and, finally, he raises a leg over and mounts (Denhardt, 245–7).

In the seventeenth and eighteenth centuries Indians raised few horses themselves, but, instead, depended upon what they could acquire by raiding Europeans and other Indians, as well as by trading. The multitude of wild horses provided a ready source of mustangs. Wild horse hunts were an important feature of Plains life until the feral stock fell into an abrupt decline in the latter part of the nineteenth century.

The Comanche built a corral with diverging wings near or around a water hole and horses were driven into it – a practice derived from their early hunting techniques. Wild horses were also caught by use of firearms. The horse was creased "through the muscular part of the neck above the vertebrae" and the animal dropped paralysed to the ground long enough to rope and tie it. This was not an easy method since it required expert marksmanship. A third method of capturing wild horses was by lassoing them and this was common in winter and early spring when the horses were especially weak; in fact at that time of year they could even be run down on a good horse.

The Comanche also ambushed wild horses at water holes. A mustang ate grass until thirsty and then went to the water hole by running the whole distance, arriving there hot and thirsty. Thus, he drank until he became water-logged, easy prey to the Indians. A team of cooperating hunters also stalked horses. This was the best technique for capturing wild stallions. A wild herd tended to move in a limited area and, "when flushed, it was likely to travel in a circle" round to near where it was first found. The idea was to keep the herd running round and round until it was exhausted (Wallace and Hoebel, 41–43).

A Cheyenne method for catching wild horses was to ride out and run one down. As the rider approached along side his prey he dropped a lasso loop over the animal's head, choked it and threw it and tied its feet. Some Cheyenne could place a hackamore on a wild horse while running alongside it. A wild horse was often tied to a gentle mare with a rope attached to the tame one's tail and, then, around its neck. Thus, the mare tamed the wild horse. The owner went out frequently to handle and pat the mare and then proceed to pet the wild horse. When it became accustomed to handling it was mounted and set free, at which time it proceeded to follow the mare around (Grinnell, I, 291–295).

Stealing horses was a better way to acquire them as far as the Comanche and many other Plains Indians were concerned. There were instances "of Comanches stealing hobbled and guarded mounts of soldiers" and of entering army stables and stealing the best horses when both the enclosed yard and the stable were guarded (Wallace and Hoebel, 44). A report of Crow accomplishments in horse thieving made by Jim Beckwourth, "mulatto chief of the Crows and authentic liar of magnificent proportions," claimed the Crow stole 5000 horses from the Comanche and 2700 from the Kootenays. Later the Blackfoot took 1200 from the Crow but the Crow recovered 2000 after this. The Blackfoot reciprocated, taking off with 3000 from the Crow and the latter then recovered 2500 plus 3500 from other sources (Dobie, 81).

Ewers summarizes the influence of European riding and horse handling upon Plains Indians. He lists as traits of "probable" European origin: the use of rawhide covered, wooden frame saddle, short stirrups, cruppers, martingale, double saddlebag, horse armour, lariat, horse corrals, and the practice of gelding (Ewers, 328). To this I would add the hackamore. Traits which "may" be of European origin include: colour names for horses, one or more Spanish horse commands, the surcingle method of breaking a horse, mules primarily used as pack animals, and the pad saddle (Ewers, 329). Traits of Indian invention are: boys responsible for daily care, cottonwood bark in winter feed, picketing choice horses near the lodge at night, children taught to ride by tying them on the saddle,[1] the right side mount for a right handed rider, and the war bridle (Ewers, 330). To these one might add some of the techniques developed to hunt wild horses and break them.

Some European traits were rejected by Indians: branding as means of identification, use of spurs, bitted bridle, left side mounting, use of sidesaddle for women, Spanish method of use of lance by horsemen, Spanish men's preference for stallions for riding (Ewers, 329). Yet branding, bitted bridles, and left side mounting did eventually prevail among the Indians.

Number of Horses Owned

Among the Blackfoot a man was considered rich who owned forty horses. This invariably meant he also had good saddlery and many possessions of other kinds. The majority of the Blackfoot were of more modest means having between five and forty horses while the poor were deemed those who had under five horses and these constituted about a quarter of the population; they were dependent upon the wealthier, often having to borrow horses (Ewers, 243).

An average Blackfoot family required about twelve horses: one "to carry the lodge cover and its accessories; 2 horses to drag the lodge-poles; 2 horses for packing meat, . . . food and equipment; 3 horses to carry the women and infants (at least 2 of which would pull travois); 2 common riding horses for the men; and 2 trained buffalo runners for the men" (Ewers, 138). A well balanced herd required four or five additional animals for replacements (Ewers, 139).

Ewers reports figures for tribes in 1874 ranging from 11.7 horses per person among Cayuse, Walla Walla and Umatilla down to 0.7 horses per person among Fox, Iowa, Jicarilla Apache, Omaha and Brule and Yankton Sioux. The Arikara, Hidatsa and Mandan, well known as horse traders, had only 0.1 (Ewers, 28). In terms of absolute numbers some tribes had several thousand horses (e.g. Nez Perce and Osage each had about 12,000 and the Navaho about 10,000). In total perhaps 160,000 horses were owned by the 120,000 odd Plains Indians in 1874. Such proportions are, of course readily comparable to the numbers of horses among Central Asiatic Mongols and Turks, but among the Indians it was a short-lived affair. The full glory of this horse complex was no sooner reached than it was ended as the Indians were herded onto reserves and the buffalo brought near to extinction. In general the

[1] A practice also once common among the Kazakh.

separate and distinct American Indian equestrian hunting pattern was diverted and absorbed into the Hispano-American ranching complex.

On the Effect of the Horse on the Plains Indians

Roe has stated that the horse was not an unmixed blessing to the Indian and reviews some of its presumed disadvantages. It has been claimed, he states, that the horse promoted large scale hunting and waste and, thus, by implication, that the practice of mounted hunting was a contributory factor to the decimation of the buffalo. Further, it is claimed the horse fostered long migrations so that it made nomads out of sedentaries (Roe, 190).

Roe takes issue with the view that when the Indian acquired the horse he began to contribute to the extinction of the buffalo. He believes there is abundant evidence to show that with the horse the Indians killed less buffalo individually at least before the initiation of intensive fur trading. ". . . [F]or the first time in their age long history, in all probability, they were under no compulsion to take an entire small herd, good and bad alike, but could kill, as I have said, qualitatively. They were able at last to pick their beasts" (Roe, 356). Not only could they be more selective in their slaughter, they were more readily enabled to remove all the meat from a kill site and to carry larger quantities of meat from one camp site to another. The buffalo hunt was also conducted in a regulated fashion under the command of soldier societies with strict rules of participation. Rather than contributing to buffalo extinction the use of the horse, on the contrary, appears to have ended an era of mass slaughter and made for more conservatory use of the buffalo by the Indian.

Whether the fact that the horse made nomads out of sedentaries is a disadvantage or not seems to depend more on one's value judgement. But the horse did allow for several families to move together to the various sources of food and it did facilitate food procurement. Thus, in a sense a conservation policy was followed which encouraged movement out of one area to another so that specific places would not be overhunted and others underhunted. Although there is no question that the horse did encourage nomadism, it also fostered a congregation of families into large communities since large quantities of food could be transported to central locations (Steward, 232). For the Shoshoni Steward says the horse actually allowed them to become less nomadic in being able to settle in more permanent groups because of the greater yields of food (Steward, 201).

It is true that in some localities, as we have already indicated, the horse was of little economic importance and indeed competed for the very scarce resources with the human and game population. Steward, referring to the Western Shoshoni, says that scarcity of grass made the horse difficult to keep, eating the very plants upon which the people depended. In lieu of game herds the horse could have no significant role in hunting and was too costly to keep purely for transportation. Thus, in much of the Great Basin, horses if available were eaten (Steward, 235). Dimitri Shimkin has questioned the economic value of horses in Wyoming where "[t]he density of population in the Wind River area was no greater" after the equestrian era than before, indicating there was no advantage to mounted hunting for the provision of greater supplies for more people (Lowie, 1963, 46).

That a profound change occurred in the shift from pedestrian to equestrian hunting life has often been claimed. Ewers argues that this change was of basic importance and of a qualitative character. The horse "not only enriched the material culture of the tribes . . . but it altered their habits of daily life, served to develop new manual and motor skills, changed their concepts of their physical environment and the social relationships of individuals" (Ewers, 338). The most significant repercussions were social rather than material, particularly in the development of status differences into what Ewers calls a class system (Ewers, 339). Steward believes the horse revolutionized the Shoshoni economy by making new methods of hunting possible, providing greater greater wealth and making for larger and more permanent social groupings (Steward, 201).

Wissler and, later Lowie and Roe, argued on the other hand that no fundamental change occurred in Plains culture, but rather what occurred was an intensification of already existing cultural traits (Wissler, 1914). Roe believes the portrayal of the pre-equestrian hunter of the Plains as a mean, half-starved, barely surviving savage is a gross exaggeration and the differences between the pedestrian and equestrian hunter of the Plains have, therefore, been overstated (Roe, 175). Lowie writes: "Though the horse became integrated with daily life, it did not evoke much originality except in a minor way. Without creating new forms the Indians did make their own riding gear – saddles, bridles, stirrups, quirts, ropes, cruppers – in this way they made their horse culture independent, whereas guns, axes, knives, cloth always had to be acquired from Whites" (Lowie, 1963, 44).

The introduction of the horse did provide for greater wealth and accumulation of property. These enhanced the possibilities for displaying one's status and, in an individualist socio-economic system, of intensifying social differences – a point stressed by Ewers. However, the emphasis on individual achievement of status and prestige already existed in Plains culture before the horse. The horse only provided a device for intensifying this emphasis and for further elaborating the individualist theme.

Ewer's interpretation of the Blackfoot social structure as involving the development of social classes is to be questioned. The Plains system – following the traditional pre-equestrian emphasis upon individual achievement of status – was such that a man could be reduced to poverty as a result of a raid, winter storm, or an epidemic and another poor boy made rich by successful raiding or by being adopted by a wealthy man. It was a relatively fluid system. Further, members of the same family or kin group might have very distinct status and wealth differences. In any case, the differences in style of life between the top and the bottom were not that outstanding and no sense of class identification or the existence of classes is indicated for Plains Indians. Ewers, I believe, has as an anthropological observer looked at the Blackfoot data and categorized the population according to certain culturally significant factors, such as the ownership of horses, and derived from this "social classes" which in fact had no functional or meaningful place in the Blackfoot society. All that can legitimately be said is that the acquisition of the horse enhanced status differences; it did not create social classes.

To assume that the Indian desire for war was a new reaction following the advent of the horse also has little warrant (Roe, 219). "Certainly it is an error to assume that the desire for horses was responsible for the warlike spirit characteristic of the Plains. Apart from the overwhelming evidence of the craving for glory, it is clear that precisely the same eagerness for distinction prompted the tribes of the South-east and of the western Woodlands from which the majority of the historic Plains Indians emigrated into their subsequent habitat" (Lowie, 1963, 121). In other words, the Plains Indian war complex was most important to the pre-equestrian culture; it was not produced by the adoption of the horse. "That the craving for horses or other economic values was required to evoke warlike undertaking is preposterous in the light of the evidence" (Lowie, 1963, 231).

It is as ridiculous to argue that the horse made the Indian martial as it is to make this claim for people in general. A warlike and martial people on the adoption of the horse will invariably make their warfare more effective and lethal, but the horse alone cannot create the warlike orientation, any more than it creates aristocracies or social classes.

In general the addition of the horse to Plains Indian cultures produced significant change in that it allowed for the elaboration of already existing cultural patterns. The creativity and ingenuity of the Indian was in seeing the application and adaptability of the horse to these several patterns. Whether this resulted in a major "qualitative" change remains a question and, likely, not an answerable one at that.

Equestrian Hunters of South America

Horses were introduced into the Pampas and Patagonian regions of southern South America by the sixteenth century Spanish colonists and in due course became incorporated into the culture of the surrounding Indian peoples in a manner remarkably similar to that of the Plains Indians of North America – and with notably similar effects. Steward and Faron noted how several tribes, such as those of the Chaco, had been horticulturalists and on adopting the horse virtually gave up their small scale cultivating for a nomadic life dependent upon hunting game and raiding Spanish settlements for livestock (Steward and Faron, 378, 386). This parallels the history of several tribes in the North American Plains such as Cheyenne. The horse in the South American plains likewise provided greater mobility and the opportunity to move more and larger pieces of personal property. With the horse the Indians covered greater territory and improved their hunting efficiency. "Rheas, guanaco, deer, and peccaries were no longer stealthily approached on foot but deftly surrounded on horseback, killed in larger numbers, and driven more efficiently" (Steward and Faron, 421). Techniques for gathering wild plants were altered because women could ride out to more distant places.

Various changes in social organization arose as a consequence of the introduction of the horse. The size of bands increased. A Tehuelche band in 1849 was observed to have 1000 persons. "Each band consisted of several lineages, but their size and composition fluctuated as one or another chief attracted or lost followers." Thus, the band became an amalgam of often unrelated kin groups functioning as a collective hunting and warring unit – a composite band, to use Steward's terminology (Steward and Faron, 384) "Band solidarity was enhanced by warfare, for population movements and amalgamations caused by expansion and confusion of band territories brought Indian groups into conflict with one another" (Steward and Faron, 384). This creation of "composite" bands seems to have been more common in the South American Plains than among Indians in the North American Plains.

Among the Mbaya class stratification was "incipient" in pre-Spanish times. Steward and Faron believe the introduction of the horse and the consequent intensification of warfare "solidified class distinctions" into nobles, warriors, serfs and slaves. Peoples defeated by the Mbaya in warfare were incorporated into Mbaya society as serfs and slaves. Elsewhere status differences were enhanced as mounted warriors and successful hunters and raiders accumulated wealth, power and prestige. The ancient kinship basis for leadership founded on the seniority of elders declined as authority based on persuasiveness and especially military capability increased.

Gregson has warned against an overemphasis upon the role of the horse as an agent of change among South American Indians. He insists more attention should be paid to the nature of the incipient culture as well as to innovations aside from the horse. "Thus the sheep, cattle and agricultural products (as well as horses) formed a resource complex the benefits of which were transferred to the Chaco Indians not only because of their ability to raid on horseback, but also because they had been warlike aboriginally and most important, because the Spanish settlements were able to suffer these attacks yet continue to support themselves" (Gregson, 1969).

The Indians met their needs for horses by theft since they did not breed any themselves. "It is said that in a single raid a man might return with four hundred horses, easily escaping the armor-encumbered Spanish cavalry, which bogged down in crossing the Paraguay River and the marshes of the eastern Chaco" (Steward and Faron, 421). Raids against Spanish garrisons and settlements provided the Indians with livestock as a source of meat and there was continual raiding and "warfare" between tribes themselves – all stimulated by the more effective weapon, the horse.

Steward and Faron consider the equestrian Indians of South America to have been "magnificent cavalry men". "They attacked on horseback, deployed into several striking forces, hung from their horses in such a way as to avoid missiles, and sometimes concealed themselves entirely by hanging under their horses' bellies" (Stewart and Faron, 423).

Pampas Indians are reputed to have had more of a taste for horse-flesh, especially mare's flesh, than the Indians of the North American Plains. The Mapuche, at least, continue to regard mare's meat as a supreme delicacy. So plentiful were the wild horses on the Pampas in the seventeenth and eighteenth centuries that the Indians burned their bones and grease for fuel (Dobie, 27).

Horse sacrifice became common among these Indians especially in connection with funerary rites and sometimes with the birth of a child. Patagonian Indians sacrificed four horses at the death of a chief; the skins were stuffed and these propped up on sticks at the four corners of the grave. The flesh was then eaten (Howey, 201). On the death of an ordinary man his favourite horse was slaughtered and set up in the same fashion with the head facing towards the master's grave (Howey, 201).

At the birth of a child a cow or a mare was often killed and the child was laid in the stomach once it had been removed from the carcass, the remainder of which was eaten. H. Heskith Pritchard goes on to describe another form of horse sacrifice:

"If a boy is born, his tribe catch a mare or a colt – if the father be rich and a great man among his people, the former; if not, the latter – a lasso is placed round each leg, a couple round the neck, and a couple round the body. The tribe distribute themselves at the various ends of these lassos and take hold. The animal being thus supported cannot fall. The father of the child now advances and cuts the mare or colt open from the neck downwards, the heart, etc., is torn out, and the baby placed in the cavity. The desire is to keep the animal quivering until the child is put inside. By this means they believe that they ensure the child's becoming a fine horseman in the future" (quoted in Howey, 189–190).

The Indians of the Pampas and Patagonia copied and modified somewhat the Spanish riding gear. Most eventually acquired Spanish bridles and saddles. They made use of the lasso as well as their own *bolas*. According to Steward and Faron, the Pampas Indians devised their own toe stirrups (Steward and Faron, 413). On the other hand toe stirrups are found in various parts of Argentina and Brazil, most likely introduced by the Portuguese, and it would therefore appear that the Pampas Indians made their toe stirrups from these models, possibly as a kind of stimulus diffusion.

Like the equestrian nomadism of the North American Plains, that of South America is today completely a way of the past, finding its nearest contemporary expression in the largely Spanish style livestock ranching complex. Perhaps the Gaucho is the nearest one might come to a legatee of the old Indian horse tradition of South America, but even he can hardly be said to survive today.

X

Livestock Ranching

THE livestock rancher is a particular kind of yeoman farmer, specializing primarily in cattle production and to a lesser extent sheep and horses for sale on a competitive market. A major source of this type of industry is Mediaeval Spain. There, sheep were originally of primary importance. They grazed on extensive plantations and were driven to high pastures in the north of Spain in summer and returned to central Spain for winter pasture. Some cattle also were involved in this transhuman movement and by the thirteenth century cattle ranches existed in Castile and in Portuguese Alentejo. This industry thrived on the sale of hides and beef, so that beef became more important than sheep in many parts of Iberia.

In contrast to most of the rest of Europe, in Spain cattle were driven by mounted herdsmen. They grazed on enormous estates (*latifundia*) on unfenced ranges; there were annual roundups for branding, sorting of livestock for market and for breeding, and large scale cattle drives. Cattlemen's associations (*mestas*) for the protection of sheep, cattle and horses and the general welfare of the producers were organized. Even the rodeo is recognizable and the dress of the twelfth century cattlemen of Salamanca and Old Castile would not be unfamiliar to anyone who knows modern cowboy attire: "the broadbrimmed hat, bolero jacket, tight fitting trousers, sash, boots and spurs" (Dusenberry, 21, Bishko, 498 ff.).

Spain was a land in which the conflict between shepherd and cultivator persisted for more than seven centuries, and in which the shepherd remained in the favour of government from the thirteenth to the end of the eighteenth century. Only at that time did any enclosure or arable lands begin and the office of *alcalde entregador*, the official charged with protecting the interests of the *mesta* or the shepherd's protective organization, was abolished (Vives, 528, 644). Of course, once the Spanish livestock system was introduced into America, its development there soon eclipsed its parent industry. Livestock ranching, primarily sheep, survives in parts of northern Spain, and the Camargue area of the south coast of France preserved the ancient techniques of mounted cattle herding.

The full flowering of livestock ranching as a specialization occurs primarily in conjunction with the post-Mediaeval development of colonialism and agrarian capitalism – the settlement and exploitation of areas remote from Europe by European settlers. In some cases these areas have always been marginal for any other agricultural purposes, but the exploitation of good farming land for cattle grazing has been too common to associate livestock ranching purely with the utilization of marginal land. Thus, in the nineteenth century western United States cattle ranching was soon replaced by farming when it became apparent that farming brought in higher income in these areas. Remote Argentina perpetuates a cattle industry in areas which are perfectly good for commercial farming. As a general rule livestock ranching appears, then, to start in those regions which, regardless of their fertility, are most distant from major centres of population. Eventually it is recognized that greater incomes can be derived from the more fertile areas by cultivating them; as a result the stockmen remove to still more isolated areas or are left to pockets of less productive land.

Apart from the Iberian source for this type of specialization, later adaptations of livestock ranching arose with the Dutch settlement in South Africa and the British settlement of Australia. Yet another isolated independent development was in Iceland which dates back to Mediaeval times. Since the Icelandic case is ancient and did not spread beyond the confines of the island, let us first consider it.

EUROPEAN LIVESTOCK RANCHING

Iceland

Iceland is a cultural extension of Scandinavia, but because of its particular geographical situation differences from the rest of Scandinavia have arisen. For most of its history the country has comprised a population primarily resident on isolated farmsteads and engaged in sheep breeding, with cattle, especially of the dairy type, as a minor enterprise. Stock are grazed on open range and farms are of considerable size, often several thousand acres. Wool, hides and meat are produced for an export market. The cultivation of the soil is minimal with hay being the chief crop; there is no grain production. Thus, largely because of circumstances of climate, terrain and isolation, Iceland developed an agriculture which conforms to the ranching complex.

The Vikings brought their hardy ponies along with them when they settled Iceland in the ninth century and for the past eight hundred years no horses have been imported (Löwe and Saenger, 189). Consequently, a special Icelandic breed developed.

The lack of roads, and the prevalence of damp and rough country discouraged the use of carts, carriages or other wheeled vehicles and, as pastoralists, sea travel was never developed despite the Viking tradition. Rural Icelanders came to depend upon riding and packing ponies as the main means for travelling. This mode of transportation was standard until the last few decades during which time road improvements have been made and automobiles have come to prevail.

Ponies were and continue to be employed in the periodic sheep round-ups and in rounding up other ponies; thus, much of the herding activity, like that of the Iberian world is mounted, although it is less completely so than that of the Americas. The traditional European method of sheep herding on foot with the aid of dogs is inadequate in Iceland where the sheep are fast runners and do not graze in herds, but tend to scatter in the open range. Icelanders also believe the best meat is from sheep which feed on the distant high pastures. Mounted herding is therefore a necessity.

Particularly with the adoption of the hay rake, tedder and mowing machine, horses were more extensively applied to hay-making, the major farming operation. Hay had always been carried on ponies' backs to the stacks. Today as elsewhere in the Western world, this draught work has been taken over by trucks and tractors.

In the nineteenth century a trade developed for exporting Icelandic ponies to Great Britain, for use in the coal mines. This demand has since disappeared. In recent years some ponies have been exported to other countries as pleasure animals, but on the whole the horse industry in Iceland is in serious decline. Most of the animals kept on farms today are rarely worked, being left by farmers to run at will. In the mid-nineteen-fifties sixty per cent of the horses were in a half-wild state (Löwe and Saenger, 189). Despite Iceland's high level of mechanization and economic development, it continues to have the highest proportion of horses to persons of any European country and to be among the highest in the entire world in this respect. The retention of such a horse population is in part a result of a combination of sentiment and tradition with the availability of abundant pasture land. Apparently, many of Iceland's city dwellers have, like Americans, taken to keeping a horse or two for pleasure. Of equal if not greater importance is the fact that Icelanders have always supplemented their diet with horseflesh. Horses fare better over the winter than do cattle.

The Icelandic pony is the only five gaited saddle horse. Besides the walk, trot and gallop, it is also capable of the amble and the rack (tølt). The latter is characteristic of some horses in the United States and requires a "four beat motion, in which the feet are set down in the series left hind, left fore, right hind, right fore, not in pairs but one after the other; and it can take place at any speed from that of a walk (which it much resembles) to the equivalent in m.p.h. of a fast gallop" (Jank-ovich, 75). Some Icelandic ponies, as some Scandinavian ponies, are, according to Jankovich, native born rackers. W.H. Auden reports a further accomplishment of the Icelandic pony: "The Icelandic pony is of course an amphibian. He can even swim a river with someone in the saddle but it has to be the right someone. There is a legend of an Icelander who in the early days of tobacco used to swim his horse two miles out to sea to meet the tobacco boat" (Auden and McNiece, 184). Icelanders do not consider a pony good for work until it is five years old and after that time it presumably can be used until it is twenty.

As with other pony riders throughout the world, Icelanders, when embarking upon a trip take two or more ponies along and change off periodically. This use of small horses for long trips, coupled with the employment of pack animals rather than carts, was one of the main factors for the large number of horses in traditional Iceland, as it was also in central Turkestan and Mongolia.

There has been some specialization of ponies in terms of their work so that they are divided between riding, pack and draught animals, although if necessary any can be ridden (Summerhays, 1968, 135). Some herds are also kept purely for slaughter for meat consumption. Besides their reputation for endurance, and multiple gaits, the Icelandic pony is particularly famous for its highly developed homing instinct (Campbell, 81).

Riding gear in contemporary Iceland is not very different from the English equipment. The saddles are light weight with a low pommel and cantle and uncovered stirrup leathers with simple iron stirrups. Bridles ordinarily are provided with snaffle type bits. Ponies are taught to stand when the reins or head rope is trailing. Rope hobbles are sometimes put on them. Icelanders shoe those horses they intend to put to work.

Most animals are left all year round on open range except for those which are required for riding or packing and these are kept in stalls where they are fed hay. One of the unusual features of Icelandic feeding practice, probably much more common in the past than at present, is the use of fish heads as horse feed. Since all grain must be imported into the country it would be a rare horse indeed that received this as feed. Because of the dependence upon open range, a severe winter can result in as high as fifty per cent mortality of horse herds (Löwe and Saenger, 189).

Horse husbandry in other north-western extremities of Europe bears marked resemblances to the Icelandic complex in part because of similarities in geography, but primarily because of shared cultural-historical roots in ancient Scandinavian and, to a lesser extent, Celtic tradition.

The Camargue

The Camargue district is located on the south coast of France on the Gulf of Lions. It is a marshy region where cattle and horses have been raised since ancient times in a fashion closely parallel to old Spanish and Western American style. Here ranchers reside in fixed households but spend a great deal of time in the pastures herding their horses and black cattle. Each family usually also has an apprentice herdsman and other cowboys, known as *gardiens*.

Cattle are herded with the aid of a thirty-six foot long horsehair lariat and a trident. The rope is never thrown from horseback since it is very light and does not carry well in the air. Rather it is used from the ground in corrals (Vialles, 15). The trident is employed for handling cattle outside the corral in the marshes. It is an aid in helping to throw calves for branding or to control unruly bulls or half wild cattle, to stop stampedes and protect one's self from attack (Vialles, 15). The close similarity of the Camargue trident to the lance used by earlier Spanish and Mexican cowherds and by some Brazilian *vaqueros* until very recent times should be noted.

Cattle are branded with the initial or heraldic emblem which distinguishes the owner's stock. Most branding is accomplished in a spring round-up which, in modern times, has come to be more of a holiday during which races, riding and roping contests and other sports, interspersed with dances and games, are performed.

The Camargue wild horses, according to tradition, descend from horses of the Numidian cavalry introduced in southern France by Flavius Flaccus early in the Christian era. They also may have been added to by Moors who occupied Provence in 732 A.D. (Sidney, 242–3). They were too small to bear the heavily armoured knights of the twelfth to fifteenth centuries. This and other factors resulted in their taking refuge in the marsh areas. While most of the horses remain feral, some are broken to ride and others were employed until recent times in treading out the sheaves of wheat. The horses were forced to go round and round on the sheaves at a fast trot from early morning to evening with breaks for water and rest. They were given to eat only the straw they could pick up under their feet as they worked under the watchful eye of their driver with his whip. After a month their work was completed and they were turned out on the marshes again until the next harvest (Sidney, 243). Today they have been replaced by the threshing machine.

For riding, the Camargue people use "curb bits with long curved sidebars", but unbroken horses are trained with a hackamore. Riders wear rowelled spurs and most "use only a single spur, doubtless figuring that the other side of the horse will keep up without any special attention" (Vernam, 109; Vialles, 19). The saddles are equipped with high, heavily padded cantles and a "wide, curved, hornless pommel" which is also padded. Both are trimmed with brass nails. There are two cinches and long fenderless stirrup leathers bear large wrought-iron stirrups which "have curved bars across the front to keep the rider's heelless wooden shoes from slipping forward" (Vernam, 111; Vialles, 19). Saddle bags, cruppers and breast pieces are common, but horses are seldom shod. Women once took part in the range work and rode behind the men on blankets which were fastened to the crupper. Now they have adopted modern style, "dressing and riding astride like the men" (Vernam, 111).

The Camargue people indulge in various equestrian games. In one, six to eight riders on each of two contesting sides wear three scarfs bearing the colour of his side. The object is to tear the scarfs from the opponents' arms before they take yours. They also play a kind of "puss in the corner" on horseback (Vialles, 22). While they have a form of bullfighting it does not involve horses or bloodshed. Its object is to remove a cockade from between the bull's horns. However if a bull can manage to keep it on for fiteen minutes the band strikes up the toreador song from Carmen and the owner of the animal takes a bow (Kammerman, 679). This seems to be one form of bullfighting which recognizes that the bull, too, can win.

In most respects the Camargue represents a kind of refuge of old Iberian cattle and horse keeping and as such has very close similarities to that system as it has been perpetuated in the Americas. Its chief deviation is the tendency for riders to wear wooden shoes rather than boots, representing an adaptation to the damp, marshy surroundings.

The pastoral way of life of the Camargue is now rapidly disappearing as irrigation and modern agriculture have spread.

NORTH AMERICAN RANCHING

Cattle ranching in North America has been described in a multitude of sources readily available to any interested reader and probably a high proportion of readers will be in some respects more acquainted with this cultural complex than with any of those hitherto mentioned. Therefore, in the following presentation I propose to deal with a few basic characteristics of the complex and to concern myself with specifics only where it is necessary to fill out the general picture for adequate contrast with the foregoing discussions.

The earliest ranching in Mexico, Argentina and other Spanish domains developed first as a market for hides for the Spanish leather industry. Hooves and horn were of secondary importance, while beef was purely for domestic use. Eventually, the Argentine beef market grew to supply the demands for salt beef for Brazilian slave plantations. Increasing densities of population and growth of industrialization in western Europe and the eastern United States sparked heightened demands for beef in the nineteenth century. As a response, cattle ranching spread rapidly in the western United States. With the first refrigerator ships in 1879 Argentina soon became the abattoir of Great Britain in addition to supplying other parts of western Europe as well. In Australia beef production was likewise of little significance until the introduction of canning and refrigeration and there was no large scale cattle ranching there until after the middle of the nineteenth century (Strickon, 1965).

Livestock ranching, then, is, in general, a response to a demand for a limited range of commodities. As such it is a highly specialized industry – a one crop economy, either beef or sheep. Moreover, a large number of Anglo-American ranches were so highly specialized that little or no attempt was made to produce or process subsistence requirements for the ranch or to make it self-sufficient. It was much more like a beef factory than a peasant homestead.

The Spanish system of cattle management was brought to America and adapted to the new habitat. The first Spanish cattle were large, rather wild beef types with big horns. In Spain they had been tended on horseback and prods were used in handling stock. Whether or not roping was a method of controlling cattle seems to be unclear, although the early diffusion of "complex techniques and vocabulary throughout the New World cattle industry . . . points to an Iberian origin" (Bishko, 508). Also the fact that the snubbing post placed in the middle of a corral was a very early device in America would indicate its likely importation from Spain as well. But in the New World this snubbing post was soon abandoned. Cattle were grazed in open range so that one could not always be set up. Thus, the saddle horn was developed as a substitute (Rodriquez, 1974).

Each range for cattle had a watering place. "Every few days a *vaquero*, or cowboy, rode out to look at the herd, turn it back if it tended to stray off the range, and search for predators and thieves" (Haines, 44). A cowboy's work consisted mostly of "branding young animals, periodic sorting out of those belonging to other *estancias* and separating and killing those destined for the market" (Chevalier, 110). Under this system of limited handling and, then, only from horseback, "cattle became rather wild, but they required very little supervision through most of the year and were still accustomed to being handled by mounted men, although they could be dangerous to men on foot" (Haines, 44).

In Mexico "cattle and horses lived and multiplied in a half wild state . . . . Contemporary accounts tell of fierce bulls emerging from the tropical forest on moonless nights . . ." and of "splendid mares with flying manes and silky coats, almost impossible to tame even when by a stroke of luck they were taken alive. Only ten leagues from Mexico City, bands of wild horses roamed the swampy meadows of the Rio Lerma, on the road to Toluca, as late as the seventeenth century" (Chevalier, 110).

The early *vaqùeros* continued the use of the double edged knife which had been part of the gear of the Mediaeval Spanish cowherd. With the knife he cut the tendons above the hoof of the right and left hind legs of the desired cow, then, dismounted and killed the animal by driving the knife behind the horns, severing the spinal column. He skinned out the steer and took with him the hide and tallow. The meat was left behind unless he happened to want some for his own use. In Mexico the *mesta* or cattlemen's association outlawed the use of the knife in 1574 and it was replaced by the lasso, but the knife continued to be used for some time thereafter in the north of Mexico, not only against cattle but against one's fellows as well (Chevalier, 112). The lasso at least allowed one to look at the brand before slaughtering an animal and was also an important tool in branding.

Especially in its earlier form, Anglo-American livestock ranching is a kind of compromise between sedentariness and nomadism. Head-quarters were established by a stream with an ample supply of water. Here the ranch owner maintained his homestead along with houses for hired hands, barns, stables, corrals and implements. While the ranch owner passed much of his time here, sleeping and eating in his house, he was frequently on the range overseeing stock and hired hands. The latter devoted even more time on the range stationed at temporary camps. The range, it must be remembered, invariably covered thousands of acres and in the days before any extensive fencing, ranches maintained a human fence of line riders who continually patrolled the ranch boundaries (Frantz and Choate, 56).

In addition, cowboys tended to change jobs rather frequently, moving from one ranch to another or on occasion moving off to establish their own ranches. The "drifter" became frequent in Mexico and the American West. In fact, Bennett says most of the early cowboys were of this type. Some were "crooked", working until they got too old and then opened a livery stable or worked in a saloon (Bennett, 100ff.). These semi-nomadic workers had their predecessors in Mexico as drovers of sheep who had no claim to any range and no particular destination (Dusenberry, 71). Cowboys throughout Mexico lived a vagabond's life and were "called saddle tree lads because", as an

inspecting magistrate in New Galicia wrote in 1607, "their sole possessions were a 'wretched old saddle, or lightly stepping mare (stolen),
and their harquebus or short lance'" (quoted in Chevalier, 112). They
banded together roving the country and terrifying the local population. Ranchers were compelled to employ them for lack of anyone else,
but not all the early cowboys of the West were vagabonds. For example, in Mexico there were stable populations and small *estancias* operated with a few Indian herders (Chevalier, 113).

Early Anglo-American ranches often had a temporary character. A
man located on a range and water holes, staying there as long as he
could until, because of pressure from homesteaders or Indians, it
became more profitable for him to move on. Although the rancher
might at first, with his body of armed herdsmen, be superior to the
homesteader, the latter in the end had the support of the law. Therefore, a stockman did not expect permanent tenure and among other
things never paid much attention to the construction of buildings.
Bennett believes that the lack of concern for the appearance of one's
buildings which persists in the ranching country of the American West
is a tradition derived from this early more transient condition (Bennett,
78–9).

In many ranching areas a transhumant pattern is observable in the
grazing of cattle. This is particularly true of the more northerly and
mountain ranches. Before the commencement of winter, cattle are
brought in close to the ranch homestead to graze on adjacent pastures
where hay had been harvested in the summer and left in stacks. As the
winter progresses and snow piles up, grass becomes less accessible so
that hay is fed out from the stacks. Such feeding constitutes the bulk of
the rancher's winter work and means that he is "at home" during this
season. Early spring, particularly if it is a stormy one, engages the
stockman in overseeing and caring for newborn calves. Following a
late spring round-up for castrating, branding, and, in modern times,
innoculating and ear marking new calves, the herds are driven to
summer pastures, moving as the season permits to those at higher and
higher elevations – all at some distance from the ranch homestead. In
early fall, the herds have to be brought to continually lower ranges as
winter again closes in. Moving cattle between these two ranges as well
as fence mending and building carry the hands furthest from the
ranch. A large part of summer time is occupied with hay-making in the
vicinity of the ranch headquarters.

As a general rule the nomadic qualities of cattle ranching were more
prevalent in earlier times, more characteristic of the largest establishments, and more associated with the hired hands. But, ranching had
distinct sedentary features as well – a permanence which contrasted

with, say, the Central Asiatic nomadic pastoralism. The ranch homestead was a relatively fixed settlement. Only the working men moved from place to place and, then, only during certain seasons; they were not accompanied by whole families. These remained behind at the ranch headquarters.

Today on most ranches one rarely is required to spend a night away from the home ranch out on the range. Of course, the fact that branding and similar operations are today conducted in corrals near the homestead helps account for this.

Another feature of the ranching enterprise is the manner in which it combines "feudal" and agrarian capitalist characteristics. The ranch is dependent on sales of a highly specialized crop on a competitive market and operates for a profit for the owner. It is also dependent upon hired wage labour. In these respects it is a commercial, "rational", capitalist enterprise. It has also been classed as a modified form of the "plantation" system, different because of its horse complex, its "exclusion of female labourers", and the "small number of workers" required (Wagley and Harris, 436). In Anglo-America with the large number of smaller operations, most ranches could no more be classed as a sub-type of plantation than a North Dakota wheat farm or any other "family" farm. Another difference between the "plantation" and the livestock ranch is that the latter never depended upon slave labour. Presumably this is because slavery and ranching do not mix (Strickon, 1965). The diffuse nature of ranching in grazing over wide areas makes it difficult to keep workers under surveillance. Herders are also mounted and, invariably, armed. Thus there is a need for a type of labour which does not require continual supervision by a boss, but rather necessitates the "inner directed" man. Consequently, one relies on the cowboy, *vaquero* or gaucho, each of whom works because he wants to work.

Cowboy life has, of course, been grossly romanticized starting with the novelists and pulp writers (*The Virginian* is the first great cowboy novel). Then, the motion pictures took up the theme. About twenty per cent of Hollywood movies have been Westerns and the *Book Review* digest lists about a thousand Western fiction titles (Frantz and Choate, 4–6). Thanks in large part to novelists and Hollywood movie producers the American cowboy was made a folk hero, composite "of all the frontiersmen who inhabited the . . . Great Plains in the latter half of the nineteenth century . . .. Only the cowboy has captured and held the imagination of the American people with an interest undiminished by time" (Frantz and Choate, 8).

The cowboy was the last of the frontiersmen, the last representative of the Westward movement (Atherton, 249). The "Western" movie incorporates this nostalgic figure into the old morality play with its emphasis on the victory of good as symbolized in the masculine individualist mounted on a faithful steed. He is hard living, the rugged outdoor type, agile, honest, faithful, self-reliant and mobile.

To dispel the romantic notion of the cowboy, other writers have attempted to provide more realistic portraits most based on their own experience.[1] Thus, for example, Stewart Edward White illustrates the boredom often associated with the life of the cowboy, in telling "how he spent his time looking at the bunkhouse ceiling and counting bullet holes – 3620 of them – put there by bored cowboys shooting at flies overhead" (Frantz and Choate, 64–5).

Atherton writes: "In reality, the cowboy's life involved so much drudgery and loneliness and so little in the way of satisfaction that he drank and caroused to excess on his infrequent visits to the shoddy little cowtowns that dotted the West. A drifter, whose work and economic status made it difficult for him to marry and rear a family, he sought female companionship among prostitutes. Most of his physical dangers scarcely bordered on the heroic, necessary as they were in caring for other men's cattle, and they served primarily to retire him from cowpunching, not to glorify his career. Older men could not endure the rigours of such a life, the major reason for the youthfulness of the group. In the true economic sense, rank-and-file cowboys were hired hands on horseback, and very unromantic ones at that. Realistic observers during the cowboy era agreed with Bruce Siberts' evaluation. While living in the Dakotas in the 1890's as a cowhand and small rancher, Siberts concluded that most of the old-time cowhands were a scrubby lot, and that many of them suffered with a dose of the clap or pox: 'Only the few good ones got into the cow business and made good'" (Altherton, 243).

Strickon in referring to the cowboy as a rural proletariat, thus concurs with Atherton's description. Yet the cowboy was a peculiar kind of proletariat, the peculiarity of which is illustrated by Frank Gipson's picture of a cowboy friend, ca. 1950: He never shot a man, "never chased a rustler across the Rio Grande . . . never rescued a beautiful girl from ruthless bandits and rode off into the sunset with his arm about her waist . . . [But] [h]e can rope a cow out of a brush patch so thick that a Hollywood cowboy couldn't crawl into it on his hands and

---

[1] Besides Frantz and Choate (1955) and Atherton (1962) earlier titles include: Charles Goodnight, *Cowman and Plainsman*; J. Ebetts Haley, *The XIT Ranch of Texas*; Joseph G. McCoy, *Historic Sketches of the Cattle Trade of the West and Southwest*; Ernest S. Osgood, *Days of the Cattlemen*; Louis Palzer, *The Cattlemen's Frontier*; Charles A. Siringo, *A Texas Cowboy: Fifteen Years on the Hurricane Deck of a Spanish Cow Pony*; Patrick T. Tucker, *Riding the High Country*; Philip Ashton Rollins, *The Cowboy*.

knees. He can break a horse for riding, doctor a wormy sheep, make a balky gasoline engine pump water for thirsty cattle, tail up a winter-poor cow, or punch a string of post holes across a rocky ridge." He can work under all kinds of weather conditions with any "patched gear, sorry mounts and skimpy grub, and still get the job done . . . he works with the thorough understanding that it's the livestock that counts, not the cowhand" (quoted in Frantz and Choate, 59).

Rollins refuses to put the cowboy into a fixed mould or type. "In reality, there were no species, there was no type. Cowboys, as Bart Smith, one of them, said, were 'Merely folks, just plain, every-day, bow-legged humans.' Cowboys, like the rest of the ranchmen, were simply the men of a particular trade . . .. Fictitionists to the contrary, the ranks of the cowboys, of all ranchmen, contained but few swash-bucklers, particularly such as wore long hair. Those ranks were com-posed largely of men with character and heart, of men of whom future generations well may regard with pride" (Rollins, 37–8).

Both cowboy and ranch owner share an individualist egalitarian ideology in which each one likes to think he is his own man. The ideology involves an intense pride in one's work and seems to be an extended and "intensified version of masculine values which are widespread in the Euro-American culture area" (Strickon, 1965, 243–4). The rodeo, stampede, or Argentine *domada* are extensions of the common daily work of the cowman. "I rather doubt whether a sugar plantation worker has ever lived who spent his free time cutting cane just for the fun of it" (Strickon, 1965, 244). One might add that the Hottentot and Bantu workers on a Boer ranch also never developed anything comparable to the rodeo, for probably the same reasons the sugar workers never evolved parallel modes of entertainment. The cowboy may be a hired hand, but he thought of himself as a profes-sional, equal to any man, better than some.

Atherton observes that "[r]omanticists were glorifying the Wild West at the very time when the ranching industry was expanding and in need of more workers. Many rank-and-file cowboys looked on their occupation as an opportunity to participate in a colourful era, not as a means of earning a living" (Atherton, 181).

Particularly in the days of the open range and when the West was more of a frontier, in other words before 1880, there was a definite tendency for the cowboy to identify his interests with those of the "outfit" for which he worked. His status as a "professional" cowman rested on his responsible care of cattle. So he had some loyalty to the herd and at the same time this entailed a solidarity with the other men engaged in the same task. The "bunk house" bears many of the attributes of a men's club house and the camaraderie of the ranch hands is reinforced by the isolation of ranches from each other and from towns. Cattle barons themselves often did not live at or display signs of a much higher standard of living than their hired hands. They, or their managers, had sometimes been cowboys themselves or at least of much more modest means. Such equalizing factors operate to reinforce loyalty to the ranch. An owner might also solidify relations with him men by being in frequent contact with them and working with them.

Atherton suggests two important developments in the United States which tended to jeopardize a cowboy's identification with the "outfit". Of major importance was the growing number of ranches operated as impersonal corporations and extensive partnerships, which then removed any and all contact with the owners, who were now absentees, often not cowmen at all. A second development was the organization of ranch owners into exclusive associations which served to separate further owner from employee (Atherton, 181).

On occasion cowboys did become aware of their class position *vis à vis* the ranch owners. Many Texas cowboys belonged to the Knights of Labour between 1884–1887 and there are even cases of cowboy strikes for higher wages (Atherton, 182). Yet these appear to be exceptions rather than the rule. Farm labour, in general is more difficult to organize because it is scattered and because it has generally been all too easy for the farmer or rancher to employ more tractable hands as replacements for strikers and "trouble-makers". Moreover, the individualist orientation, more particularly of the cowboy, is not conducive to joining in organized groups, nor is their professional pride and loyalty to the herd and "outfit" conducive to collective "walk-outs". Changes in ranching in the 1880s toward the establishment of corporation ranches, and stockmen's associations as well as the existence of a caste system discriminating against Mexicans, Negroes and Indians in the Southwestern United States did not completely prevent the cowboy from retaining a sense of loyalty to and identification with the "outfit". In this respect he is distinguished from most other wage workers.

Part of this retention derives from yet another facet of the individualist-egalitarian ideology shared by cowhands and stockmen. This is the fact that the American West as a new frontier was a land of great hopes and of high mobility, both vertically, in terms of status, and horizontally, in terms of movement from place to place. The great American dream of "rags to riches" had more reality here than elsewhere; also the reverse, the nightmare of "riches to rags", was not uncommon. There were many stockmen who had very modest beginnings and some who were able to carve for themselves a small livestock empire out of animals lifted from time to time from herds of the big barons. Yet few cowboys ever made it to the ranks of the cattle kings. Nevertheless, the existence of "self-made" men, the insecurity of the top position once attained and the possibility of moving on to greener pastures all tended to reinforce dreams of the "big chance" and the ideas of equality and individualism. In other words, it encouraged one to overlook the raw fact that one was at the moment only a hired hand, and even to see working conscientiously in such a status as not only enhancing one's self respect, but as a means to ultimate personal success.

That the cowboy was mounted and often armed fostered the sense of his significance and equality with others. The cowboy was not a pedestrian worker – a peon – like some plantation worker. The estate manager did not ride up to him giving orders from atop a horse as the cowboy stood, hat in hand, on the ground below. The cowboy received his instructions on horseback – equal to the manager. Not only did the ranchman provide mounts for his workers but the astute rancher provided good horses for them.

That horses were so readily available also meant great mobility for all. The cowboy invariably had a horse of his own and could therefore easily move from a job he did not like. This was possible as well because the cowboy was commonly young and unmarried, without family obligations.

The great equalizer of the West, of course, was the six shooter, which in the earlier days was viewed to some extent as necessary for the herder's job. It is probably unnecessary to repeat here that the Hollywood portrayals of gunfights and the solution of problems of conflict via the "draw" have only a remote similarity to the traditional American West. Nevertheless, especially in the days before the 1880's – before the end of the open range – a cattle rancher could engage his wage labourers as a body of mounted and armed "knights" or yeomen assigned to protect and extend the manorial domains against losses of livestock and land from other barons, small farmers or rustlers, and to engage in their own rustling or vengeance raids. Threats, real or imagined, from other ranchers or farmers sometimes served as a solidifying force among employees of a ranch. But, the combination of the horse and the revolver in the cultural context of the times lent dignity to the cowboy's task and gave him the pride he shares with mounted men through the ages.

To summarize, the structure of cattle ranching was in keeping with the landed estate or plantation where the boss was the owner of vast amounts of land, and large herds worked by a dependent class of wage hands, but the frontier conditions, the mounting and arming of the working force, the fluidity of social mobility, all operating in a context which prized equality, individual achievement and masculinity, tempered this structure immensely. Spanish and Portuguese-American ranches, however, contrasted with the Anglo-American in the extent to which they much more closely followed a well-defined class structure as a legacy from Mediaeval times. This is to be expected in the light of the contrast between Iberian and British traditions and the fact that there was never much true frontier in Latin American due to the manner in which lands were distributed. Nevertheless, if in the Middle East and much of Medieval Europe the horse was an implement to impose inequality and the authority of the few, in the cattle ranching world of the Americas it became a device for encouraging egalitarianism even if it was not fully successful in achieving it.

Having discussed some of the salient characteristics of livestock ranching in the Americas, I now propose to present a brief chronology of the spread of the complex especially through North America.

Ranching, particularly the raising of horses, was an early developed and widespread enterprise in Hispaniola. Cuba was rapidly settled in the sixteenth century and the chief occupations became ranching and mining (Denhardt, 38). ''The ranchers on the islands built up an aristocracy that was envied by all Europeans'' (Denhardt, 40). They raised fine horses and cattle, and originated a forerunner of the Mexican saddle ''covered with silver, inlaid with gold and studded with jewels'' (Denhardt, 40).

Stock raising spread from Hispaniola to the northern coast of South America, to Jamaica, Cuba, and thence to Mexico. In the sixteenth century it is reported that 50,000 cattle, 200,000 sheep, 4000 mules and 4000 ''horses were driven to and sold in Mexico each year.'' Honduras and Nicaragua also became important cattle and horse rearing areas; Nicaragua was probably the greatest horse rearing area in the mainland during this time (Denhardt, 42).

The introduction of missions and the gathering of Indians in their vicinities led to a demand for food and, hence, cattle and gardens. To answer the need for cowherders the missionaries turned to and trained Indians. Some mission heads became cattle barons, such as Padre Kino in Pimeria Alta who supported the missions of Baja California with his cattle (Denhardt, 105).

The early settlement of Mexico was based on the old Spanish idea that grass was a gift of nature so that ''pastures and untilled fields were free and open to all, in the same way as stubble was after the harvest.'' Thus, Spaniards set up great areas of open range grazing land and rapidly built up huge herds of cattle. The rapid increase in cattle created some pressure on land so that owners claimed squatters' rights on pasture. In lieu of royal approval local authorities in Mexico sanctioned these claims of the early cattle barons. Thus arose the *estancia*, land "granted by local authorities as so many paces around or in a square" (Chevalier, 80ff.). Less than twenty years after its settlement, the Toluca Valley, near Mexico City, contained about 150,000 cattle and horses on more than sixty *estancias*. Some stockmen had ten to eleven thousand head (Chevalier, 93). The rapid increase in cattle in Mexico was followed by a speedy growth of horse and sheep populations. "By the middle of the sixteenth century, mounts could be had for not much more than the trouble it took to break them . . .. The humblest mestizo and the poorest Spaniard always possessed his own horse" (Chevalier, 94).

The multiplication of stock in Mexico however did not continue forever. About 1580 herds appear to be reproducing poorly. Jeronimo Lopez the Younger had 4000 mares on one *estancia* and from these branded 600 colts and sold 300. There were many years in which thousands of livestock died in droughts (Chevalier, 103).

While cattle ranching spread rapidly throughout what is present-day Mexico it move only slowly into those parts of Mexico later appropriated by the United States – California and Texas particularly. It was in Texas that Anglo-Americans first encountered Spanish methods of herding and horse handling. When the Americans entered Texas a high proportion of the cattle was wild. The only thing a cowboy "feared as much as a decent woman" was to be put on foot on the prairie since with no horse he was prey to wild beasts and especially the wild long-horns who could readily trample him in a stampede. "But a man on horseback was a superior being who could rule elemental Nature and could triumph over an adverse environment. The affection between man and mount, cemented through months of sharing privation and danger and adventure, was therefore an almost human thing; and many a cowboy, as Paul Horgan points out, would gladly share the last of his water canteen with his horse rather than see his equine friend go thirsty" (Frantz and Choate, 23).

By 1850 when both California and Texas had been annexed to the United States the cattle industry had come under the control of the Anglo-Americans. It is clear that their ranching techniques were largely adopted from their Hispanic neighbours, although one must not overlook the fact that the Anglo-Americans also carried with them their own tradition of cattle husbandry. Taking cattle on long drives, "round-ups", and open range grazing were also part of the Anglo-American culture. And Southerners, especially, wore broad brimmed hats and rode with long stirrups before any contact with the *vaqueros*.

In 1860 there were ten times as many cattle in Texas as in 1850 and during the same time, ranching began to develop north of that state. It had already existed to a limited degree in connection with missions and garrisons in New Mexico and Arizona, but these regions remained longer as Indian territories, so were not opened to extensive ranching until well after the Civil War. This conflict arrested the growth of cattle ranching, but immediately thereafter it spread rapidly into the northern Plains. The first cattle drive to Montana occurred in 1866 and by 1876 southern Alberta was cattle country. Shortly thereafter southwestern Saskatchewan was similarly transformed. Cattle had been earlier introduced into western Canada to supply beef to the gold miners in the Cariboo district of central British Columbia in 1859, and this date actually marks the inception of the industry in that country.

Cattle ranching from about 1835–1840 to 1885–1890 was characterized by several interrelated traits. It was based on open range feeding, reliance upon natural sources of surface water in water holes and streams, absence of pure-bred stock and any rational breeding programme, periodic annual round-ups involving the collective work of neighbouring ranchers and the necessity of branding for identification, and trail driving of stock over long distances to markets in lieu of adequate railroad facilities. Such a system had no sooner reached its maximum geographical limits stretching from Texas to southern Alberta when it collapsed and was transformed into modern-style ranching, or the ranching was superseded altogether by farming.

Barbed wire was invented in 1874 and large ranchers were fencing their ranges within ten years thereafter so that after the mid-eighties barbed wire had become so common that the great round-ups were disappearing. Those who had formerly been line riders now became fence riders. Branding and round-ups continued, but they were more to prevent rustling and affirm a legal ownership than devices for establishing ownership (Frantz and Choate, 59). Branding, except for the biggest ranches, gradually came to be accomplished within a corral rather than on the open range where mounted men roped cattle out of the assembled herd (Bennett, 53).

Fencing facilitated the spread of homesteading farmers within the cattle country, but it also allowed a rancher to deal more independently with his own stock without having to consult neighbours. Enclosures meant a man could introduce improved stock and embark upon a more rational breeding programme since animals no longer had to mix indiscriminately. While intruding farmers and government homestead laws are sometimes blamed for the spread of fencing and the ending of the open range, part of the reason for the collapse of that system was the overgrazing by stockmen themselves (Atherton, 165).

Fencing necessitated modifications in water supply and about the time that barbed wire was invented, the large scale manufacture of windmills began in the United States (1873).

Trailing cattle to market, which occurred mostly between 1870 and 1885, rapidly declined after that period as railroads were extended to the most remote parts of the West before 1890.

Ranchers of the northern Plains had not resorted to supplementary feeding in winter to any extent until after the severe winter of 1886–1887. Previously they had faithfully relied on the proposition that any snow would within a few days blow off the prairie baring the feed grass beneath and, therefore, there was no need for hay. The winter of 1886–1887, however, converted ranchers to winter hay feeding, a practice, of course, which demanded fencing as well. In sum, old-style ranching based more upon chance and free movement hardly lasted half a century when it was rapidly modified with the adoption of more rational management techniques, all of which curtailed freedom of movement and forced the cowboy to become for the most part a farm hand who spent more of his time with a pitch fork or post hole digger in his hands than with reins.

Not only was the ranching complex itself modified internally, but the area it encompassed was from the 1870's onward gradually whittled away in favour of farming operations. Major segments of Texas, Kansas, Nebraska, the Dakotas, and Montana were transferred from cattle ranching to agriculture. Frantz and Choate write: "If the western part of the United States had been as wooded and well watered as the country east of the Mississippi it is unlikely that such a person as the cowboy would have emerged. But the Great Plains presented a problem unlike anything hitherto challenging the American in his westward questing. [In encountering the Great Plains₆ the Anglo-American saw a region beyond his personal or ancestral experience." He saw the "Great American Desert," a place useful for cattle and nothing else. But, in due course, after the Civil War, he came to appreciate that it was not a great desert, but had immense agricultural potential, at which point he saw fit to push the cattle rancher off into still more remote and marginal zones (Frantz and Choate, 49). Webb outlines the evolution of the western range in four stages: first, open range cattle ranching; secondly, fenced range with no windmills; thirdly, fenced ranges with windmills, and finally, ranches are superseded by farms (Webb, 238).

Since World War II cattle ranching has experienced additional major changes such that the old gap between "farmers" and "ranchers" has been considerably reduced and in some places obliterated. Much of the work once involving the horse is now accomplished by the truck, the jeep or even the aeroplane. Horse riders no longer even drive cattle herds to the rail heads, a task now undertaken with trucks. Most market cattle are sold as yearlings to feed lot operators so that far fewer animals have to be wintered on the ranch than was the case a few decades ago. This practice results from improvement of the quality of stock, the development of faster maturing animals and more sophisticated pasture management. In the northern regions fewer cows bear their young in the open range as the use of large maternity barns spreads among ranchers. More ranches are diversified today, especially as they engage more in feed grain production. In the course of this century the number of extremely small ranches like the number of extremely small farms has declined. So also have the enormous ranches encompassing tens of thousands of acres, although it must be remembered that contemporary ranches make much use of lands leased from the federal government. There are still several hundred in the United States which are over 20,000 acres.

The southern Interior Plateau of British Columbia is a Canadian example of a ranching district with extensive federally owned grazing lands and a high ratio of grazing land to livestock. The Forest Service administers some eight million acres of range land. At the same time nearly three million acres are in private ownership (Weir, 53). Thus, an area more than twice the size of Massachusetts sustained, in 1961, only 150,000 cattle, 30,000 sheep and less than 8,000 horses (Weir, 77). Ranges are divided for seasonal use: upland meadows for summer and fall and lowlands for winter and spring (Weir, 54ff.). The famous Gang ranch, largest in the province and among the largest in the continent, is located in this plateau and makes use of about two million acres, mostly in lease, for its six thousand odd cattle. A permanent crew of forty men is maintained and an additional dozen are hired seasonally (Weir, 103). The other ranches in the vicinity are considerably smaller: sixty-eight per cent of 567 ranches in 1948 had between 25 and 499 head of cattle. Another quarter of the ranches were non-commercial units with fewer than twenty-five head (Weir, 70).

The Role of the Horse in Ranching

Throughout the history of the American West the primary role of the horse has been as an aid in herding livestock. A few were kept for pulling wagons or light buggies and in early Spanish America they were employed in a variety of tasks such as pack trains, mining and grain threshing often with no concern for their well-being (Cf., Haines, 42). After 1880 in the United States they were used on hay mowers, rakes and tedders, but most were for range riding.

Horses are here not pleasure animals, but respected workers. While they are often of a general utility sort, some are trained as cutting horses to single out a steer in a herd and separate him from it. These are the most highly trained, if not the most intelligent horses, in a ranch herd. They are required to make sharp and fast turns, to stop and start quickly and in general have many of the attributes desired by the Arab Bedouin for his raiding horse. Some men even claim their cutting horses could work without any guidance from the rider whatsoever.

Another important specialist is the roping horse which is trained to assist the rider in roping steers. It learns to follow fast after a desired animal and the moment it feels the tug of the rope as it engages the steer and the rider dismounting from the saddle, the horse is trained to pull back and hold his place firm. Like the Arab horse any good cowpony should be trained to stand still when the reins are dropped over its head onto the ground. This is important not only for emergencies, but because there are few trees or readily available hitching posts on the range. Some Canadian horsemen, however, carried with them long stakes to drive into the ground to hold horses on needed occasions.

Horses were important in hunting activities both as an aid in and as an object of the chase. Hunting prong horned antelope on horseback was considered a great sport, while hunting the wild (feral) horses was sometimes sport, but more often a serious business enterprise, if conducted on a sufficiently grand scale. The decimation of the approximately two million wild horses who roamed the western plains did not really get under way until the beginning of the twentieth century, starting with the sale of large numbers for use in the Boer War and later in World War I. Following this, the application of the most modern and sophisticated technology to capturing feral horses in order to fill the demands of pet and chicken feed producers ultimately brought the wild horses to the brink of extinction (Ryden, *passim*).

Prior to the Civil War, horse thieving was a common problem. John Chisum, ranching in southern New Mexico, lost 1200 horses "in one swoop to a small party of Mexican bandits from south of the border. He and his men gave chase and had to shoot three of the thieves before they could reclaim their herd". Horse rustling was also a major occupation in the North-west where rustlers could run animals across the border into Canada (Haines, 169).

The Spanish introduced many equestrian games and contests into America. One "game" which is now, happily, no longer performed involved the capture of wild bears on horseback. A team of two men roped a bear. As soon as one man roped one leg, the second roped the other. If he missed, the first roper had to make a mad dash to safety. With both ropes in place they stretched the bear and forced him into submission. Obviously, only the bravest – or most foolhardy – horses could be used for such ventures. The bear was dragged to a bull ring where it was tied to a wild bull by a thirty foot rope and the two animals were left to fight to the death. Spanish Americans also engaged in various forms of bull fighting where the horse was more frequently a secondary aid.

But the most popular and lasting sport was and remains the rodeo. Originally the rodeo was not a sport but referred to the cattle round-up. The early Mexican rodeo which appeared in the mid-sixteenth century was a technique to facilitate the sorting of herds, inspired both by the original Spanish procedure and by the Indian hunts. Cowboys fanned out in a circle and drove the cattle towards the *estancias* or made the herds converge on a fixed point and sorted them with the aid of their lances. Eventually these round-ups involved one hundred or more cowboys spread out in an immense circle. Unbranded animals were divided up among stockmen; strays and unfamiliar brands were handed over to the king's representatives. Originally rodeos were held between midsummer day and mid-November (the first day of the rainy season). They soon became a necessity if only to acquaint the cattle with men so they would not become too wild (Chevalier, 111). In the process of the work of sorting and branding, informal contests arose between individual cowboys as demonstrations of skill and daring. These were at first casual and localized competitions which were incorporated into local fiestas. The practice spread among the Anglo-American ranching population in the United States and into Canada where the term "stampede" was applied to the more formal-ized contests which began to appear there in the beginning of the twentieth century.

Non-professional rodeo contests and "shows" appeared as early as 1869 at Deer Trail, Colorado, but the first professional affairs date from 1882. Haines attributes the organization of the first professional rodeo to Buffalo Bill Cody who managed Fourth of July celebrations at North Platte, Nebraska in that year, putting on contests in shooting, riding and bronco-busting, with prizes donated by local merchants. A year later Cody organized these events as Cody's Wild West Show (Haines, 183). Vernam, on the other hand, reports that in 1882 also Col. George Miller of the 101 Ranch produced his first Wild West Show as an "impromptu cowboy contest at Winfield, Kansas" (Vernam, 397).

Eventually, various western towns began giving shows each sum-mer featuring bronco riding, steer and calf roping, bulldogging and a band of Indians dressed in their elaborate Plains costumes (Haines, 183–4). Today rodeos occur in the middle of haying season suggesting the origins of the activity in warm Mexico and its incompatibility with northern style hay-based ranching. This timing has helped to make rodeoing more tourist orientated and more an activity for professionals. However, the general trend of any competitive sporting activity in America is for it to become professionalized. Rodeo is nevertheless not yet associated with the exhorbitant and grandiose incomes, the unprincipled competition, or the unethical practices so characteristic of other professional sports. Part of the explanation for this is that it has never become "big business". There is no betting, no heavy financial investment; there are no "big" professional promoters or coaches, and no enormous "gate" receipts. Furthermore, rodeo may entail competition between participants, but built into it is a heavy dependence upon mutual aid among the competitors as, for example, in such necessary activities as the mounting and recovery of riders from bucking animals.

Riding Style and Gear

The Spanish conquerors introduced both *a la jineta* and *a la brida* riding style into America. The Inca Garcilaso de la Vega says in his chronicle on the Conquest of Peru: "'My country was won *a la gineta*', that is, by men riding in the fashion of the Moors" (quoted in Graham, 18). But this style was early modified in the New World to suit riding half-wild horses. Longer stirrups and riding with a straighter leg provided a more secure position in the saddle for knee grip on a bucking horse and it was also easier to mount with a long stirrup. In addition it is useful in roping in that it provides additional support to the shock of a 300–500 pound steer suddenly caught in a rope the other end of which is looped around one's saddle horn – a parallel to the Mediaeval knight's need to protect himself against the shock of a strike from an enemy lance.

In the West, when mounting, the rider turned his back to the horse's head, held the horn, reins and a bit of the mane with the left hand as he slipped his foot into the stirrup. A good horse on feeling the rider's foot in the stirrup would start to walk in a slight circle towards the mounting rider to help him swing aboard. Dismounting contrasted with the English practice since one invariably got out of the saddle while still keeping one's left foot in the stirrup until off the horse. Nineteenth century cowboys tended to ride with extremely long stirrups, but in more recent times there has been a trend toward shorter stirrups, so that modern cowboys have adopted a style which is more acceptable to the "proper guardians" of "scientific" equestrianism although it still is not approved by them.

Western riding relies primarily upon the walking gait and a slow canter (lope). The jog-trot is also employed, but the rider does not post or rise in the stirrups, rather he grips with his knees and pushes against the stirrups with his feet. Riders less often resort to the full trot

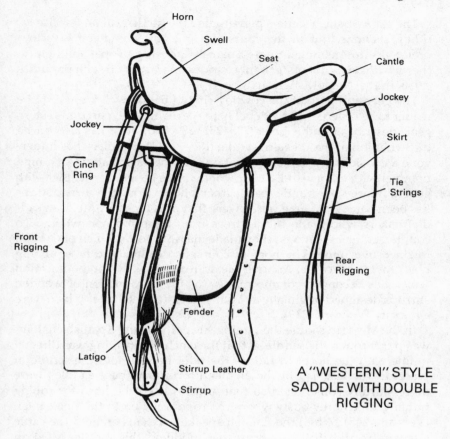

Horn
Swell
Seat
Cantle
Jockey
Jockey
Skirt
Cinch Ring
Tie Strings
Front Rigging
Rear Rigging
Fender
Latigo
Stirrup Leather
Stirrup

A "WESTERN" STYLE
SADDLE WITH DOUBLE
RIGGING

particularly since on rough and uneven ground it becomes a more jarring and uncomfortable gait. Ambling is characteristic of some Central American horses, especially in Guatemala, Nicaragua, Costa Rica and Honduras. Although Mexican horses as a rule do not know this gait some of them owned by gentry are trained in it. In Nicaragua, Squier in the last century observed that horses have three important gaits: *paso-trote*, a gait between a trot and an amble, *paso-llano*, a very rapid gentle gait which will permit a rider to carry a cup of water without spilling a drop while travelling at six miles an hour, and the *paso-portante*, the amble (Squier, 156). Since amblers do not often gallop well and can rarely jump from a walk directly into a gallop, an essential for the cow horse, they are not much desired by stockmen. Presumably those used in Central America are for travellers and are not an important part of the stock on cattle ranches in those countries.

The early Spanish settlers perpetuated the Mediaeval preference for riding stallions, but in the course of time this has given way to a preference for geldings. Some Spanish speaking people still hold to the view that it is not quite manly to ride a mare; but no such prejudice exists in the Anglo-American area.

The gear and garb of the cowboy should be too well known to the reader to be covered in any detail here. Vernam, an expert on Western gear, describes it in his book (238–252; 289–370). Rice has also traced the evolution of the Western saddle (Rice, 1974). Saddlery has undergone a considerable stylistic variation, but the basic pattern of a high pommel with a horn and a high wooden tree covered in leather with generally large skirts and broad leather fenders along the stirrup straps has been constant. Large horns were first developed by Mexican saddle makers who made saddle trees from light and soft woods. To counteract their weakness they made massive horns which have been retained over time. The horn of course is eventually the "snubbing post" for roping cattle. Another Mexican development or modification which has become a commonplace was the introduction of wooden stirrups designed originially as a substitute for metal ones which were a scarcity (Vernam, 239).

In the Mexican saddle the rigging strap, following Spanish custom, was put through the saddle so that the cinch or girth ring was directly in line with the horn. In riding, the rider helped hold the saddle in place. In the last half of the eighteenth century these saddles were more sturdily constructed so that *vaqueros* used the horn for roping rather than as previously where the rope was tied to the horse's tail (Vernam, 245). When the English speaking Texans entered the cattle business in the 1830's, they further modified this saddle. Mexican *vaqueros* were strict "dally" ropers who roped their stock, took a few turns of the *reata* around the horn, and left the ground work to pedestrian peons. The Texan cowboys worked both from horseback and on the ground, continually mounting and dismounting. This necessitated a well secured rope tied to the horn as well as a saddle which would remain in place while a cow was roped. Consequently, they introduced a double cinch; at the same time they reduced the size of the horn and raised the cantle (Rice, 1974).

Early Mexican and Texan saddles, following an Arab prototype, were made by placing over the saddle tree a removable large square piece of leather with a hole for the horn and one for the cantle. This *mochila* was about 1870, modified so as to become an integral part of the saddle (Vernam, 321). Soon thereafter appeared what is known as the "half-seat": a leather seat extending from the cantle to the stirrup slots and having wide fenders which were first hung high so as to serve as seat jockeys, but these, too, were soon further modified by the addition of seat jockeys[1] (Rice, 1974). Iron horns replaced the old wooden ones which had been easily broken off. Indeed, Texas cowboys had come to tie their ropes to the saddle fork rather than the horn because of this weakness (Rice, 1974).

Between 1885 and 1900 further modifications resulted in the creation of a full seat with the seat leather extending from the cantle to the base of the fork, originally with slots for the stirrup leathers but these slots, which let rain and snow in under the saddle, were later discarded (Rice, 1974). Quilted saddles although introduced as early as 1880 were originally not very popular since when they got wet they were difficult to dry out. Today, Rice says eight out of ten saddles are quilted (Rice, 1974). Swell forks, cushioning devices made by enlarging the fork on the forepart of the saddle, evolved out of bucking rolls, and first were employed around the beginning of this century by riders of difficult horses as an aid to staying in the saddle. They soon became common parts of the saddle, reaching, by 1920, such enormous size that in an emergency a rider could scarcely dismount without exposing himself to injury. Today swell forks have been considerably reduced in size (Rice, 1974).

In the North-west another major modification in saddlery occurred when the cattle industry was introduced into Wyoming and Montana. The men of the North-west had been involved in buffalo hunting and the fur trade. In entering the cattle business they did not rely on the heavy roping techniques of the Texans. Instead, they followed the "dally" method prevalent in California and Mexico. For these reasons, they preferred not only a lighter saddle, but one unencumbered with a double cinch (girth) and, so invented a "three-quarter" rig in which a single cinch was placed in a position which would be midway between the centre-style cinch and the Mexican forward cinch, in other words, in a three-quarter position (Rice, 1974). This meant that Western American saddlery by the late nineteenth century had four different types of rigging, largely associated with specific regions: the Spanish-Mexican front style in Mexico and to some extent California and the south-west; the double rig of Texas and immediately adjacent areas; the three-quarter rig found from Oregon to Montana and Wyoming as well as adjacent Canada in the north. The centre rig appeared on some California saddles and some of those of the north-west.

Western bridles have commonly been of the curb or more severe type. Ring bits were most popular in Old California and in Mexico, and

---

[1] A seat jockey is a leather piece or cover immediately beneath the saddle seat and directly on top of the larger leather cover known as the skirt.

spade mouthpieces as well as ring bits were common elsewhere. Bit chains were also frequent – a heritage from Mediaeval days when chains were used rather than leather to prevent the reins being cut by an enemy. With the severe bits went a style of holding a loose rein and of light reining. Like the archer or Mediaeval knight, the cowboy often had his hands full with work aside from guiding a horse and, therefore, required some device which would control the mount with the greatest of ease with one hand (indirect reining) and a horse that was well trained to respond to leg pressures and bodily shifts in the saddle. To facilitate handling, spurs are a common part of cowboy riding gear.

Management

The horses on a ranch are collectively referrred to as the *remuda*. On large ranches the horses are kept in a herd – the *remuda* – under the supervision of, often, younger or more elderly ranch hands. For the heavy work of a major annual round-up from eight to fourteen horses are allowed per cowboy, so that he can change off frequently, and always have a fresh horse available. The number of horses varies depending upon what sort of a task the man is doing and also the general condition of the horses. Horses are ordinarily assigned to the cowhand so that each one becomes acquainted with and identifies with his "own" horses. Large ranches often kept three to five hundred horses, although such numbers are today no longer common.

Aside from the horse wrangler, one or more ranch hands might specialize as horse breakers, training the wild or unbroken animals.

Non-working horses are turned out to pasture to fend for themselves and in the Northern Plains are given supplementary feeding of hay during the severest part of the winter. Horses in continual use are kept in corrals, barns or small pastures near the homestead and must therefore be handfed hay and oats. Shoeing is today common for horses which are working, especially on rough ground. In the early days of ranching, horses were more often left unshod. Every horse is branded with the mark of ownership.

Breaking Horses

Horses are usually broken with a hackamore instead of a bit and bridle. This has the advantage of protecting a young horse's mouth from the more severe type bits which are normally used. An unbroken horse is apt to rear and fall backwards in response to a bit, which he will not do with a hackamore (Denhardt, 123). There must be proper timing in converting from a hackamore to the bit. A horse left too long on the hackamore may come to hang on it so that it is "heavy on the hand" while one fitted with a bit prior to learning to obey the touch of the reins often acquires a "hard mouth" (Trench, 229).

One common technique for breaking involves running the horse into a breaking pen where it is roped to a snubbing post. Then, the hackamore is applied and the animal is allowed to get accustomed to this. Once this has been accomplished the "sacking out" or second stage begins. Here, while the horse is held by the lead rein, a blanket or rain slicker is run over the back, rump, neck, head and under the belly and waved in front of the animal so that it will become used to such handling. When tired out, and with one leg tied up, the green horse may be pushed over on its side. The breaker kneels beside it and rubs his hands over its body, legs and feet. When accustomed to this treatment the horse is shown a saddle which is placed on its back and removed. When this has been done on several different occasions, the saddle is left on and the breaker starts mounting and dismounting, again many times. Finally, he rides, training the horse not merely to accept him on its back, but to abide by the commands of rein, foot and bodily movements.

A considerable number of horses reared on smaller ranches are "green broke". That is, they are continually handled from infancy, gradually becoming used to being led or ridden so that training is not really a "breaking" process in any radical sense.

Horses are regularly named among European and European-derived peoples. Throughout Spanish America and its areas of influence naming horses after their colour has been customary. Sometimes horses receive their names from the "bronc buster" or horse breaker who first trains them.

Breeding

Herders of large bands of horses on open range in the Eastern Hemisphere (such as the Central Asiatic people and Ethiopians) tend to permit stallions to breed pretty much at will. Horse breeding practice in American ranching has been different. The *remuda* is comprised of geldings and mares and is essentially a work, rather than a breeding, force. Not all ranches keep studs and those that do, segregate them from the other horses. Mares to be bred are brought to the stallion and are removed after being served. Breeding is therefore controlled and not a free and casual affair. One reason for this is that American ranching, like European horse husbandry in general, has been given more to rational breeding procedures and an emphasis on pedigree and pure breeding. Until one or two centuries ago there was greater interest in controlled breeding of the horse than of other types of livestock.

A stallion may be allowed to cover from 25 to 100 or more mares a year; pure bred and older studs breed fewer mares while grade stallions and those in their prime cover larger numbers. Stallions not to be used for breeding are invariably gelded at an early age – by the age of two or before. Their use for breeding begins at about the age of two and for mares at about three.

Modern American Indians

The present day American Indians of the western United States and Canadian Prairies have long since abandoned much of their old horse complex in favour of the Spanish American style of riding and gear. To a limited extent they have become involved in the ranching complex, but it is invariably on a very small scale, more of a subsistence nature.

The Navaho Indians of Arizona are not only the largest Indian group numerically, but the major pastoral tribe as well. They, however, keep far more sheep than they do cattle and engage in some gardening, particularly the raising of corn. In their matrilineal society – most atypical for a pastoral people – lands and houses pass through females. Before the eighteenth century the Navaho were largely hunters and gatherers, but they have since adopted a Spanish style pastoralism.

Any livestock owned by an individual at the time of his death remains within the extended family where the deceased was resident (Kluckhohn and Leighton).

Among Navaho where perhaps a third or half of the families have pick-up trucks, every homestead has at least one horse and more often two or more. The riding horse and even the wagon is still important (Downs, 1972, 50). One horse is usually left tethered by the house and is used to pick up horses which have been turned out to graze. If a man does not have many horses he can borrow one from a neighbour to round up his own when needed. Most homesteads have a horse corral but it is not used longer than is necessary since feed is too expensive (Downs, 1972, 51).

Because horses are highly prized and have habits different from other livestock, horse husbandry is not "simply a facet of the other herding activities". Horses seldom if ever graze near sheep and while they may be pastured with cattle, they rarely graze with them. When confronted with a storm horses and cattle have different reactions: horses move into it and cattle move with it. Because horses are allowed to graze freely and thus frequently intrude upon neighbour's pasture, conflicts arising "out of the grazing of horses are the most frequent livestock disputes encountered in the" area of Nez Chi'i where Downs did his research (Downs, 1972, 52).

Both cattle and horses are herded on horseback and at branding time are driven into corrals for roping; they are never roped on the open range. When corraled, horses are conditioned to mill about in the corral until they feel the touch of the rope and, whether roped or not, they stop (Downs, 1972, 73).

The Navaho ride *a la jineta*, as Indians did when they learned the use of horses from the Europeans. "In the vernacular of the West, 'Indians ride like Chinamen' and in fact they do" (Downs, 75). For rodeo performances however they lengthen the stirrups. Many Navaho horses do not "respond to any leg or knee signal save for a vigorous kick in the ribs", but all quickly react to the quirt which the Navaho rider constantly employs. The most common gait is a lope (Downs, 1972, 77).

Spanish style saddles and riding gear are used, but often a blanket with a surcingle or a surcingle alone is applied at which time the surcingle serves as something to grab ahold of in case of emergency (Downs, 76). Women ride as well as men and as a concession to them a blanket is thrown over the saddle which helps protect "the woman's legs and inner thighs from chafing" (Downs, 1972, 78).

Downs says Navaho are nonchalant about falling. "If you haven't been pitched off a few time, you're not a rider." Falling off is not, to the Navaho, a sign of inexpertness in riding and is not taken very seriously (Downs, 1972, 79).

Horses are work animals needed to maintain life in an isolated and virtually roadless area. Navaho are very considerate of their horses less out of kindness than out of practical concerns. Thus, an old horse is never expected to do a job it cannot do. Because Navaho do not rope on the open range their horses are not used as hard as those of some White men. After a tiring ride Navaho horses "are turned out to graze and allowed to rest for several days" (Downs, 1972, 77).

While horses are individually owned they are used by anyone in the homestead. Precedence for riding goes to the owner first, then his brothers and sisters, then the spouses and to other more distant kin and, finally, to young children who have access to horses according to relative age without concern for nearness of kinship (Downs, 88). Navaho curers who constitute "a loosely organized association of horse doctors sharing esoteric and ritual knowledge" of the treatment of horses are resorted to in cases of serious ailments of horses. Most Navaho men however know "a traditional form of treatment for 'knocked' shoulders that demands a certain degree of surgical skill, in as much as it requires incisions to drain off surplus fluid that collects between the flesh and the hide." Also, most claim to know how to deal with removing 'lampers' – horny growths in the roof of the mouth acquired by eating large amounts of rough and thorny material; all can also deal with common ailments of the feet and legs, chiefly by that most common of all horse cures – rest (Downs, 1972, 80).

Horses are trained in a casual and gradual fashion. The young follow their mothers until weaned and run after them when the older horses are being driven or ridden. Thus colts become accustomed to human presence. Small children begin to climb on a colt's back so that after a while it is "green broke". "Training beyond the elementary stages is not generally undertaken except by young men interested in rodeo competition". Rodeo participants require well-schooled horses for roping and bull dogging. On the whole, Navaho horses do not appear to be "particularly well trained" for roping. Apart from exceptionally good riding horses most are driven as well as ridden (Downs, 1972, 78).

Navaho particularly enjoy horse racing. On rabbit hunts a good horse has a "talent for spotting rabbits and following them closely without direction from the rider" (Downs, 1972, 78). Both racing and rabbit hunting have declined in importance and have been replaced by an interest in rodeo which among Navaho includes a horse race, gymkhana events including barrel racing, and also a demonstration of the Navaho hoop dance. Rodeo is an important political vehicle in Navaho society; anyone or any group seeking self-advancement politically must become involved in the planning and execution of such events (Downs, 1972, 127).

SOUTH AMERICAN RANCHING

South American ranching is in broad outlines similar to that of North America (especially that of Central America). In contrast to the Anglo-American ranching, social classes are sharply drawn; social mobility is more restricted. The *estancia* approximates the model of the plantation, although for reasons we have already discussed it, like its Anglo-American counterpart, remains distinct from the plantation in notable respects.

The major cattle areas of South America are north-eastern Colombia, central Venezuela, east central Bolivia, and the great grassy plains extending from southern Brazil through Paraguay, Uruguay and covering nearly all Argentina. There are also substantial pockets of beef raising in northern Brazil, in Guyana and Chile. It is not proposed here to deal with all of these areas, but to describe selected regions in order to indicate the variation in South American cattle ranching.

First let us consider two examples which, like the Navaho and other

American Indians of the North, tend to be less market-oriented forms of ranching. One of these is the Guajira Indian adaptation of the Spanish horse-cattle complex in northern Colombia. The other is an example of Portuguese-Brazilian ranching in northern Brazil. Finally we may consider ranching in Argentina.

Guajira Indians

The Guajira Indians, like the Navaho, represent in many respects an unusual cultural complex involving ranching and matrilineal social organization. Like their Arawak neighbours, the Guajira were once horticulturalists who hunted and fished and gathered wild plants for subsistence. As a result of their contact with the Europeans they adopted cattle, goats and horses just as the Navaho also changed their mode of life from an early seventeenth century pattern of hunting and gathering to one of sheep herding with incidental numbers of cattle and horses. The Guajira still do some fishing and raise corn as a staple crop (Bolinder, *passim*). Only a few Guajira own large herds of cattle yet most of them consider pastoral activities their principal employment.

The Guajira area, a peninsula in North-western Colombia, is sometimes called the Arabia of South America because it is an arid peninsula which has largely been inhabited by semi-nomadic herdsmen. The Guajira live in *ranchos* which are collections of small huts from which they herd their stock. Boys tend the cattle and milk them, keeping an eye particularly on calves, kids and lambs (Bolinder, 71). At least in earlier times lands were owned by the matrilineal clan, each having a specific territory, but a man had a right to graze his stock and collect wood in the land of his wife's clan as well. Gardens were planted along water courses. A semi-nomadic pattern arose with rather temporary houses and a movement for grazing purposes within a clan territory as well as one's wife's clan territory. Class distinctions appeared with the growth of differences in the size of herds; slavery was also once a feature of the social order. Nowadays the old matrilineal clan structure has declined in importance (Bolinder, *passim*).

Guajira have many horses and donkeys, the latter being mostly ridden by women. The horse saddle is very light "chiefly of two boards placed at an angle to each other, across which sheepskins are laid".[1] Several sheepskins are required. Stirrrups are simple metal ones similar to those of an English saddle and they are ridden long. Men also have a habit of riding naked (Bolingder, 179). Unlike their

---

[1] This brief description suggests a close similarity to the old style Gaucho saddle discussed in more detail below.

Creole neighbours, the Guajira never feed their horses corn but leave them on open range to graze (Bolinder, 148). The Guajira use a long hide rope fitted with a heavy weight on the end. "It is thrown so that the weighted end entangles the feet of the animal to be caught, in bola fashion. The long rope, however, allows the thrower to hold onto his victim. This is a decided advantage to the Guajiras, who do their roping on foot" (Vernam, 198).

Ranching in Northern Brazil

We have said that most American ranching arose in remote areas in response to the demands of a market economy. Yet we have also presented examples of American Indian forays into ranching activity which are more on a subsistence level. Riviere describes an area in northern Brazil, the Territory of Roraima, formerly called Rio Branco, where ranching activity, because it has been so remote from the markets, has also been more oriented to subsistence. Although these ranchers have many peasant characteristics such as little interest in the money economy and an adherence to the "image of the limited good"[1], they each have assets of thousands of dollars – some of a half a million – so that it makes little sense to call them peasants (Riviere, *passim*).

The extreme northern part of Brazil is a grassland to which cattle were first brought in 1787 (Riviere, 13). The population has always been sparse: in 1960 there were 30,000 people and over 200,000 cattle in the area. Of over five hundred ranches almost half are in excess of one thousand hectares and 22 are over five thousand hectares (Riviere, 25). Isolation results from the fact that the region has no land connection with the rest, and the most populous parts, of Brazil. Thus cattle must largely be shipped by cattle boat down the river if they are going to be sold.

Ranch layouts are similar to those in North America with a ranch house of most modest dimensions, bunkhouses and corrals. But they usually have pigs, chickens, and often sheep as well (Riviere, 25). *Vaqueiros* are often hired at a pay of one calf in four plus full board and lodging. Like the Hungarian herdsman, the *vaqueiro* if he wishes to have help must hire and pay for it himself. He runs his own stock with that of the rancher and in this way may eventually build up his own herd (Riviere, 42). This contributes to a lack of stratification since every cowboy aspires to be a rancher and there is no cultural or socio-

---

[1] The "image of the limited good" is the view that there is only a fixed amount of "good" available; it is not expandable so that as a result one can only improve one's own standing at the expense of others (Foster, 1965, 293ff.). It is presumably a view characteristic of many peasants.

economic break between the two (Riviere, *passim*).

Ranching is of the open range type and therefore periodic round-ups are an important part of the work routine. Round-ups are often collective affairs involving a number of ranchers working together. Cattle are driven into corrals which is a hard job since many are half wild and run at the sight of a mounted man. In the corrals work, including the roping, is done on foot. Horses are branded, like the cattle, only on the right leg rather than on the quarter. Castration is usually by professionals. Particularly the castration of stallions should not be undertaken by a nervous person, since this influences "the character of the gelding". Also in all castrations one takes into consideration the phases of the moon. Thus, horses should only be castrated during the week after new moon. It is believed horses have large amounts "of blood, which becomes increasingly turbulent during the waxing of the moon and reaches its most active point at full moon" so castration at this time would lead to dangerous bleeding. The moon is believed to influence blood and growth; a waxing moon is associated with growth and a waning moon with death (Riviere, 68).

Cattle trail drives are made to embarkation points on the Rio Branco where cattle are shipped to market. Horses are a general necessity for any travel in the area because of the poor roads. They are also used as pack animals and for races at fiestas, but their primary use is ranch work.

By the time a boy is twelve or fourteen he should be a good rider. He moves to the bunkhouse and takes up cowboy duties (Riviere, 75).

Horses are "a small, sturdy nondescript" variety which spend most of their time "running free in herds on the open savannah" – some are wild, but the majority are cow ponies. "The cycle of work is such that a horse will spend months" in pasture and be brought in for a short period of intensive hard work of about a month's duration. In one week, Riviere recorded two horses doing over forty hours of work each under the blazing sun, rarely at a walk and over rough ground (Riviere, 48).

Mares are rarely ridden being held to be too temperamental to be good cow ponies. A young horse is ordinarily broken at one to two years, normally by a young man or an Indian worker. At the same time the horse may be given a name although many horses never have one.

Horses are treated for worms; they are groomed; their trails are pulled and manes are cut. "When working they are watered and washed."

Riding itself is not considered a prestigious endeavour. It is expected of everyone, but the important thing is the ability to ride herd on a good horse. Horses, however, receive no special training (Riviere, 48).

Despite the large herds there is a shortage of horses due to the fact that half are mares and are not ridden, others are old or not considered good cow ponies because of lack of speed and stamina. Still others are wild, and there is some loss from natural causes (Riviere, 49).

Most horses that are ridden have scars from saddle sores and some wounds are so bad they never really heal. The saddle is a local product, very light compared to the North American one. Riviere states it is comfortable for the rider if not for the horse; it has a double cinch and the seat is well back. The stirrup leathers are long. Some ride with toe stirrups usually for the big toe; others have small foot stirrups. Horses carry "goat skin or other hide coverings, on which" to put saddlebags and other goods. The saddle has numerous thongs used to attach loads. A lasso when not in use is tied on top of the saddle bags by a thong. "When in use, the lasso is fixed to a metal ring just in front of the rider's right leg."

Bridles are rarely used; instead a nose band is most common with double reins which meet in a metal ring where the rider holds them. The horse also wears a halter to which is attached a rein used for holding it in leading or tying it up. When riding, this lead "rein is coiled and placed around the pommel". If a man is thrown from the horse he holds it so the horse will not run away. Reins are held loosely in the left hand near the ring and relatively high, "slightly to one side". This style is kept at any speed and the horse is usually allowed to make its own

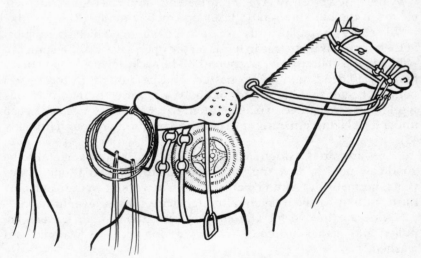

A SADDLED HORSE, RORAIMA TERRITORY,
NORTH BRAZIL
From Riviere

way. For stopping or changing direction the right hand collects the reins lower down. For quick stops the rider at the same time pulls his body back and his legs forward. Hobbles are invariably employed and are kept with the rider (Riviere, 50).

In general one notes here and in other parts of northern and central Brazil the prevalence of a complex combining old Mediaeval-Portuguese techniques with those the Portuguese carried to the New World from India: The saddle, with high pommel, long stirrup leathers, toe ring stirrups, barefoot riding, riding with light sandals, the nose band, and the ring holding the reins.

South American Pampas

The immense grassy plains of Southern South America extending from Southern Brazil, through Paraguay, Uruguay and Argentina is one of the major cattle and horse producing areas of the world. Large scale grazing in Argentina began in the seventeenth century, but cattle had been introduced there in 1536 expanding rapidly in number to constitute gigantic herds of wild and semi-wild animals which were hunted down as game. In fifty years (from 1536 to 1586) horses increased from a few dozen to an estimated 100,000 (Sears, 131). Apparently the Spanish government prohibited the catching and taming of horses by colonists, believing they all belonged to the Crown, but by the end of the sixteenth century this view no longer prevailed. Wild horses seem to have been a menace in eating up grass and in being able to charge into herds of tamed horses and lead them off. Travellers soon learned to stop on seeing wild horses approaching and ride round their own horses towards the wild ones to scare them away (Graham, 114).

The Gaucho and his Tradition

The first Gauchos appeared in the seventeenth century as vagabond horsemen living in isolated huts on the Pampas and at first subsisting on hunting wild cattle and horses. They also engaged in not infrequent forays with Indians. Their lonely life bred a strong individualism and emphasis on manliness and, according to Nichols, a combative nature (Nichols, 16). She also considers them highly competitive and concerned about gaining acclaim. So they sought valour and were great actors (Nichols, 16). Graham portrays them as extremely hospitable and great lovers of music and gambling (Graham, 1968, 295). Thus, they seem to have most of the traits one identifies with the mounted herdsmen of Ibero-America.

Gaucho living was modest; in the early days particularly they dwelt in straw roofed huts usually without windows or doors and constructed of wattle and daub. There was no furniture; a cowskull was the nearest thing to a chair and a skin was often used for a bed. Bullock tallow and mare's grease were used for light. Roast meat was almost the only food consumed and parts "not eaten were thrown out, where their odour attracted carrion birds and infinite flies and beetles". Meat was more often than not eaten without salt; *mate* was the main drink while tobacco and white rum were luxuries (Nichols, 12; Graham, 1968, 295).

Traditional dress contrasted somewhat with the northern *vaquero*, the Brazilian *vaqueiro*, or the American cowboy. The Gaucho wore a poncho and *chiripa* – a coarse cloth extending to the knees and "tied at the waist by a broad sash" which might be adorned by silver coins if one were sufficiently wealthy. Boots which extended half way up his legs were sometimes worn, although he often went barefoot. On his head he wore a headband under a narrow brimmed hat and around his neck he tied a handkerchief. A fourteen inch knife carried in a sheath was his most essential tool. A bola and lance were also carried on occasion (Nichols, 14).

According to Thomas Falkner in the early eighteenth century, tame and wild horses roamed the Pampas in immense numbers. Both wild horses and cattle grazed on the plains with no owners (Graham, 1968, 289). Through the seventeenth century Gauchos were the main group exploiting these herds and, then it was only by hunting them down for their use. It is said that cattle were so common that a man might slaughter one for the bit of meat he required for his meal. Apparently soliders also shot a cow so that in the absence of trees they could tie their horses to its horns (Simpich, 466).

An important aspect of eighteenth century Pampas life was the *vaqueria*, an organized large scale cattle chase. At first this was a hunt for lost cattle. Then it expanded into a device for restocking *estancias* with wild cattle. Initially no permits were necessary for one who only wanted a few thousand head, but by the eighteenth century the *vaquerias* had expanded into immense hunting operations for the acquisition of hides and one was expected to obtain a government permit. *Vaquerias* were organized only by the wealthy since they required considerable expense to outfit and hire the necessary men for such an undertaking. The organizer hired between thirty and fifty Gauchos and gathered and outfitted dozens of carts and thousands of horses for the hunt which often lasted six months (Nichols, 22–3). The wagons, carrying the supplies had great wheeels ten feet high and were drawn by oxen (Simpich, 461). The *vaqueria* was viewed as a gentlemen's sport despite the fact that the hired participants were often "disreputable" and the hunt itself a brutal affair (Nichols, 23). When they came upon cattle the hunters formed in a half moon and those on the sides drove the animals towards the centre while another with "a long pole tipped with a very sharp curved blade" hamstrung as many as were necessary. Then he rode out and stabbed them all to death. The others dismounted to remove the hides and the meat was left to the jaguars, carrion birds, and wild dogs (Nichols, 23). This follows a similar procedure used in Mexico slightly earlier, especially the employment of the "spear".

Hides frequently took the place of money. As a result of the Treaty of Utrecht, England gained a monopoly on slave importation into the River Plata country and she required that slaves be exchanged for hides and tallow (Simpich, 466).

After the eighteenth century *vaquerias* declined sharply as Argentina embarked upon a more rational approach to livestock keeping much in response to demands for salt meat from Brazilian slave plantations and, then, with the invention of the refrigerator ship, the European demand for fresh meat.

Aside from their employment in cow hunts and their own individual cattle slaughter, Gauchos sometimes engaged in an outlaw life. They collected Uruguayan cattle and drove them to purchasers on the Brazilian border, which because of Spain's merchantilist policy in claiming a monopoly on the trade in her colonies meant that the Gauchos engaged in smuggling activities.

According to Nichols the Gauchos were primarily responsible for winning Argentine independence and in the struggles which followed were a major force in the success of caudillism (the rule of the military strong man) with its civil wars and tyranny. They were important as well in the victory of the federalist principle for organizing the new republic as against the centralist principle (Nichols, 4). The role of the Gauchos in securing independence and in forming early traditions of the republic is the main reason for the building of the romantic picture of the Gaucho in Argentina as a symbol of independence and manhood. This is, of course, broadly parallel to the role of the cowboy in the United States, yet, there, the romanticization arises in conjunction with the disappearance of the frontier and unlike the Gauchos, American cowboys are not associated with political activity.

In Argentina, too, the frontier and the old style of ranching disappeared in the nineteenth century and along with it went the Gaucho. Sheep raising was greatly expanded and *estancias* with tame cattle became of prime importance. Barbed wire, introduced shortly after it appeared in the American West, ended the open range. Windmills and improved stock from Great Britain were introduced. Greatly expanded immigration which helped increase the Argentine population between 1850 and 1900 from about a million to almost five million, along with the rapid spread of the railway, curtailed the Gaucho's freedom and traditional life. Increasingly Gauchos hired out to *estancias* to break horses and herd cattle, living the life of the *vaquero* or cowboy. The adoption of this way of life spells the end of the traditional Gaucho, since the latter was different from the cowboy in that he was not a mere wage labourer on horseback, although he sometimes supplemented his income as we have seen with work on a cow hunt. The Gaucho was primarily a free roaming, mounted cattle hunter. Argentine cattle herders or *vaqueros* are still referred to as Gauchos because they preserved many Gaucho traditions, especially those related to horsemanship, but they are not to be confused with the old free roving types. The Gaucho who condescended to become a *vaquero* on a ranch at first, like his North American counterpart, only considered work on horseback worthy of his time and energy, but with the changes and diversification in the modern Argentine *estancia* this view as well is breaking down.

At present Argentine *estancias* are generally owned by absentee landlords and operated by professional managers. They range between one thousand and 90,000 acres in size and those owners who possess over 5000 acres are part of the country's national elite. The bulk of an *estancia*'s employees are *criollos*, the true legatees of the Gaucho way of life. They include cowboys, sheepherders, artisans such as blacksmiths, cooks, fence and gate makers, and the bulk of the unskilled labourers (Strickon, 1962). On the present day *estancia* about 2.5 men are required per 1000 cattle, 1.5 per 1000 sheep and goats (Strickon, 1965, 245). Large *estancias* provide "every facility from harness shop to hospital" (Simpich, 482), but smaller ones are more dependent upon the neighbouring towns which are commercial centres and homes for retired *criollos*. On the ranches some *criollos* own a few horses, chickens, pigs and sheep "which are raised to be sold" but none owns either house or land. Ordinarily a house is provided for them by the employer along with a few acres (Strickon, 1962).

Gaucho Horsemanship

The Gauchos used horses for a variety of activities. They churned butter on horseback by putting sour milk into a hide bag and fastening it to a long strip of hide rope attached to the girth. Then the horse was mounted and ridden hard over the camp to churn the butter. Horses were used on *estancias* for threshing corn and mixing clay for bricks

(Nichols, 19). Gauchos even fished on horseback, and they bathed by riding into the water and swimming round the horse.

In 1800 there were so many horses they were valued at about two dollars each. Buenos Aires Province and the Pampas at that time were full of wild horses. "To illustrate how numerous horses became there was a common saying 'In Montevideo the beggars ride'" (Denhardt, 35).

Horse racing and gambling were important pastimes. The vertebrae of the horses' spine were used as knuckle bones for gambling. One Gaucho game involved permitting a friend to throw a bola at his horse while it was going at a full gallop and "when an animal turned turtle its master had to light on his feet like a cat or lose his reputation." Another game was *El Pato* which has vague similarities to *buzkashi*, the famous Central Asian horse game. In the Argentine a duck was sewn up with four handles and several Gauchos tried to grab it and gallop away to a previously agreed upon ranch. The man successful in carrying it to the ranch then held a dance and party (Tinker, 1964).

At present day fiestas horsemen engage in several different kinds of contests which have Spanish origins. A rider going at a fast gallop and with a small Y-shaped spear in hand seeks to remove a ring hanging from a post. One who succeeds is awarded a red handkerchief which he ties to his horse's bridle. In another contest a bottle or kerchief is buried in the sand with a part showing. Riders take turns attempting to remove it as they lean from the saddle at a gallop. If one gets the object the other contestants seek to take it from him (Service, 211).

Of course the main use of the horse is for riding herd. Modern "Gauchos" – the *vaqueros* – have replaced the bola and lance with a hand braided raw hide lariat which is longer than that used in North America (seventy-two feet as against sixty feet). It is claimed that because of the longer rope the Gauchos are better ropers (Barbour, 432). The bolas originally used were adopted from the indigenous Indians and were sets of two or three heavy balls fastened to the ends of connected thongs. Properly thrown they entangled the legs of a victim and held it firm. Thus, they required no horn on a saddle to hold the animal.

Gauchos, like the Colombian and Venezuelan *llaneros*, the *guazos* of Chile, and the Mexican and American cowboys adopted a modified form of *la jineta* style riding with slightly lengthened stirrups. They rode with a high hand so as to neck rein and used a "Moorish" curb bit. The bit often had a high port to effect quick turns. Many Gauchos ride with no bit, but use a dropped noseband which acts on the soft part of the nose like those of the ancient Egyptians and modern Arabs.

The typical Gaucho saddle is rather a complex device developed for a minimum use of wood in an area where trees are scarce. It is composed of three basic parts. First, there is a rudimentary "tree" without horn or cantle, but merely two wooden sidebars joined together by a wide leather piece, attached to which is one cinch strap. Secondly, another wide leather piece having a second cinch strap passes over the tree. Attached to this segment are the stirrup leathers and there are also two rounded projections on either side of the forward part to which the two cinches are finally tied. Thirdly, a sheepskin is strapped onto this piece and the second cinch is made to encompass the entire rig before being secured on the above mentioned forward knob. This second cinch is a "modern version of the old surcingle roping cinch" added to the early Gaucho saddles when they took up roping, as a place to tie the rope as well as to further secure the saddle. Plain fenderless straps hold the leather covered iron stirrups which are ordinarily disc shaped to accommodate the rider's toes (Vernam, 198).

Toe ring stirrups were common among barefoot Gauchos and Indians over most of South America. "In Chile, Argentina, Uruguay and Paraguay the ring was commonly made to accommodate only the big toe. A slightly larger type for two or three toes predominated in the north. The latter kind is still in vogue in the Amazon Delta country. The idea behind such stirrups was chiefly to save weight. They were also convenient for men who habitually rode barefoot." Patagonian horsemen used toe stirrups which are merely leather straps (Vernam, 199).

Among the Gauchos big leather flaps were "fastened to the saddle fork, much like the early Mexican leather shields which evolved into North American chaps" (Vernam, 198).

Fifty years ago "if a man came to a house with a tired horse", he would be granted the loan of a fresh one. The lender always said: "When you have arrived at home (ten, fifteen, twenty leagues away) let loose my horse at night, so that he is not seen by anyone, and he will soon be back" (Graham, 1949, 119). Many a Gaucho would not steal a horse feeding around a house or one which looks like it is in its own country, but would take one on the "home trail" (Graham, 1949, 119).

Because they were often too numerous, Gauchos did not name their horses but referred to them by colour: his *Bayo* (cream coloured), his *Overo Azuleja* (slate and white piebald) or *Lobuno* (wolf-coloured).

The main paces of Argentine horsemen are a slow gallop of about six miles an hour and for longer distances a jog trot of four and a half miles to five miles an hour (called *el trotecito* in Argentina and Mexico and the stockman's jog in Australia). At these gaits sixty miles a day is considered a good trip, eighty miles a long journey (Graham, 1949, 126). Natural amblers occur, but they are more often trained. The Peruvians developed a famous natural ambler, the Paso, but like other amblers it is not for working cattle, but more specialized for long journeys. Other special gaits employed in South America include the "overpace", galloping front legs, trotting with the hind, and the gait known in Arabia as *siar*, in Turkey as *rakhwan*, or *marcha* in Brazil. On hard ground it sounds like the rhythm 1, 2, 3, 4 – 4, 3, 2, 1 (Graham, 1949, 125). Apparently Graham is referring to what is also known as the 'rack'.

Geldings are generally preferred for riding. Mares are not considered to be proper mounts for a man and, in Paraguay at least, it seems that a man who rides one feels ashamed (Service and Service, 79). Sears reports that Gauchos look on a mare as only good for a squaw (Sears, 132). Stallions are ordinarily not ridden.

Horses are broken at the age of two to three and in Paraguay in a "literal sense", "most violently" (Service and Service, 79). A horse selected for breaking is roped and tied very short to a solid post where it is left to kick and pull until worn out. Then a severe curb bit is applied wih which it is again left to struggle. Finally, a saddle is put on. Not long afterwards the Gaucho has a mount under his control and can now proceed to training it to become a cutting or roping horse or both (Trench, 243).

It is general practice for horses to be left on pasture and possibly worked a couple of hours every two or three days, but an animal which is worked very hard or one that is being trained for a race is given a special diet. Maize and alfalfa are in South America the usual special horse feeds. As a general rule horses are left unshod, but branding is, as in North America, universal.

Perhaps we should not leave South America without mention of the Falkland Islands since they represent an enclave with one of the highest horse to man ratios of any political-geographic unit in the world, second only to Outer Mongolia. With a present population of about two thousand, there is an equal number of horses and maybe a few over.

The islands were settled by the British in the early nineteenth century and have been primarily devoted to sheep rearing ever since. At the time of British settlement there were some 60,000 wild cattle and 3,000 wild horses which had been introduced earlier by the Spanish and French, but after mid-century these numbers dwindled rapidly as the animals were exterminated to make way for sheep, domestic cattle and horses.

Falkland horses are mostly imported from Argentina and Chile and are a necessity in the roadless islands for travel in the "camp" or countryside and for getting around the large sheep "stations".

While the population is British, the riding style and gear is entirely Spanish and characteristic of the Argentine Pampas with the typical "Gaucho" type saddle covered with a big sheepskin and having a girth which goes around the horse and saddle alike. Similarly in care, horses are left on the open range to forage for themselves.

Where British islanders have entered into range type livestock breeding they have, on encountering Spanish type riding and gear, found that type superior and more appropriate, since in western Canada, western United States and in the Falklands they abandoned the British style in favour of the Spanish. Only in Australia, where the British had no alternative, was the British style adapted to the context of mounted herding.

American cattle ranching and its attendant horsemanship has been distinctly Iberian in its character. Yet cattle ranching has also been an important industry in two other areas marginal to the main world centres: South Africa and Australia.

SOUTH AFRICA

Settlements of southern Africa by Dutch Calvinist farmers began in the latter part of the seventeenth century. Two main groups of Afrikaaners arose: the first were farmers and townsmen around Cape Town and the second, Trekboers, who were semi-nomadic to nomadic pastoralists exploiting the remote grasslands of the Colony. Events of the nineteenth century finally put an end to Boer pastoralism in favour of permanent farm settlements. But while it existed it bore similarities to the Old American West: a frontier community, sparse population, immense herds of livestock, law and order more commonly in the hands of armed mounted stockmen with vigilante type organizations – the Boers called it a "commando" system –, a hostile indigenous population, a democratic, egalitarian and individualist organization of the European population and a gradual retreating pastoralism in favour of more settled agricultural activity.

But there were some distinct contrasts as well: the Boers were a highly homogeneous population sharing a rural, Dutch, conservative Calvinist way of life; the American West was much more heterogeneous in composition. The Boer culture should not be confused with a New England Puritanism. It, like Puritanism, frowned on frivolity and pleasure and favoured a stolid moralistic view of the world. However, the Boers had fewer qualms about drinking intoxicants and were not particularly dedicated to the gospel of hard work. A further contrast with the American situation was in the nature of the indigenous populations encountered. The Boers were confronted with a population – the Bantu – who were in very considerable numbers and were themselves cattle pastoralists and iron tool using cultivators with a sophisticated culture. The hostile relations with the Bantu from the north and with the British from the south, combined with the Boer biblicism and pastoralist orientation, made fertile ground for breeding a doctrine of the Chosen People trekking in search of the Promised Land. Probably the closest parallel in America was the Mormon phenomenon.

The extent to which Boer society relied upon slave and serf-like indigenous labour also contrasts with American Western ranching and makes it more similar to the plantation. Traditional Black African pastoralism is pedestrian rather than equestrian. The Boers drew most of their labour force from the Black population which continued to herd Boer cattle in the usual pedestrian pattern with which the Boers themselves were already well familiar since it was customary practice in Holland. Traditional Trekboer stock raising depended not only on unlimited sources of free land, but also upon cheap labour and security for each man to live at peace on his own farm at some distance from a neighbour (Walker, 68).

Because of the reliance on cheap, pedestrian labour, the horse did not become a central part of the ranching system in South Africa. One could not risk mounting a number of poorly paid subservient labourers to herd livestock. Furthermore, mounted herding was not part of the cultural traditions of either Boer or Bantu anyway and the interest, as well, in keeping a herd of docile animals would not be conducive to seeing any merit in mounted herding which has the effect of making cattle less tractable. Horses, however, were employed to reinforce the caste-like power structure, since they were reserved for managers and owners to oversee the hired labour. From horseback they directed activities and gave orders to servants standing in the dust or muck below. As we have seen, American stockbreeding was based on a mounted labour force drawn largely from the European settler population. There was no real source of "native" labour readily available, although in parts of Spanish America such as Mexico there were closer parallels to the Boer system in that owners of *estancias* were "Spanish" while *vaqueros* tended to be more "Indian". In other words the Boer system, like that of the cotton and sugar plantations of America, was more distinctly a caste-like arrangement; the Anglo-American ranching system was more of an open class arrangement, while the Spanish American was ambiguous, fitting somewhere between the two extremes.

Because of the features of Boer pastoralism, the stockman wanted a docile horse for riding around his farm, for going to the village and visiting friends and relatives, for "commando" service and for hunting. The horse ranked with the cattle and wagons and guns as the chief possessions of the Boer. The earliest horses in South Africa were imported from the East Indies and later this stock was improved by importation of stallions from the Netherlands, Iran and South America, as well as Arab, Barb and English Thoroughbred stock (Trench, 172–3). On the whole the Boers used stock they bred themselves. "These were thicker set and uglier than European horses and could not draw such heavy loads; but they could go without shoeing, climb better, and do with much less fodder. They could cover sixty miles a day if they were not pushed too fast, going a good half of it at the *tripple*, an easy canter, and be none the worse for it after a good roll" (Walker, 35). The *tripple*, according to Trench, is actually an amble (Trench, 174).

Such colonial-bred horses were good for hunting and for Boer-style warfare which was similar to hunting. They were trained to stand like the Western cowpony when the reins were dropped over their heads on the ground. They followed steadily and stopped at a touch of the rein. If a rider dismounted to shoot, the horse permitted him to place his heavy rifle across its back or neck. The horse likewise stood still if the rider wished to fire or reload while mounted. Many horses were trained in lion hunting. African servants and "the big fierce mongrels that swarmed on every farm" first located a victim. The farmers then rode out and, linking their bridles, they backed their horses to within thirty yards of the lion. Half the hunters fired at the lion and if that failed the other half fired as the animal sprang. "If that failed . . . *dan moet jy'n plan maak*. (Then you must make a plan)" (Walker, 36).

Today South African equestrian sport reflects Boer use of the horse as it does also the preservation of more Mediaeval customs. Here there are no rodeos, since there is no tradition of roping cattle or handling wild steers or horses, but at gymkhanas and fairs there are contests in "tent-pegging, beheading a dummy 'Turk' with a sabre, shooting balloons with a pistol from the saddle at speed" or wagon races where the draught animals are either black Friesian horses or mules (Dent, 123–4).

Some observers have felt the Cape horse is too subdued and have criticized it as being lifeless and even stubborn (Trench, 173). Presumably it is good in harness. "To drive a four horse waggon at a smart trot, knocking down small birds with the long whip as he went, was one of the accomplishments of the Afrikander" (Walker, 36).

Boer horses were once largely range fed and kept in *remudas* or large herds, on the range. Any supplementary feed was usually maize and oat hay. The main technique for breaking was similar to one used by some American Indians. The horse was ridden while tied by the head to an old horse. This has the disadvantage that one has to have a good break horse and, also it often is difficult to induce the green horse to ride off alone (Trench, 173). The Boer technique of riding is with a loose rein, long stirrrups, and the right hand free to hold a rifle. The gaits include the walk, a lope or slow canter, gallop, and amble. The latter apparently comes naturally to many South African horses (Trench, 174). They are not much given to galloping.

Afrikaaner saddles follow a north-west European or English design with extremely low pommel and cantle. They are "wide towards the cantle and have a good dip in them" (Trench, 174). Curb bits are standard, which conforms to their light one-handed reining. English immigrants employ English style riding and gear.

Modern livestock farms in South Africa continue the traditional system of Black servants, now mostly Bantus, acting as herdboys working on foot as the managerial-owner class move about the estate on horseback. British managed stock farms in Rhodesia present more the picture of the manorial estate of the American south or of Mediaeval England than they do the Western American ranch (Cf., Sears, 127–30).

AUSTRALIAN RANCHING

As in the case of South Africa so with Australia there are numerous parallels as well as important contrasts to American stock rearing and cultural-historical patterns in general. Australia was not settled until the nineteenth century and, then, it originated as a penal colony. It was therefore somewhat late in opening up its frontier and, as a colony, became noted for the greater dependence of its people on the state. The immigrant settlers included a great number of working-class British in contrast to the Americans and South Africans whose frontier settlers were largely derived from pre-industrual Europe. Further, Australian land policy was aimed at providing land at a price to those who had wealth to begin with. As a result there developed in rural Australia a small body of large estate holders, derived from the more well-to-do of the British homeland and a large class of farm wage labourers: sheep shearers, cattle drovers, etc. drawn from British lower classes.

The Australian Aboriginal population, did not pose anywhere near the problem created for settlers in frontier America by Indians or in frontier South Africa by Bantu. Unlike the Plains Indians, Australian Aboriginals showed little inclination towards becoming horsemen. They had been hunter-gatherers with only a meagre technology and a small population scattered in groups of only fifty to one hundred individuals. They were, thus, easier prey to incoming European settlers. Ultimately many Aboriginals came to work on cattle stations where they became good horsemen and many were horsebreakers as well. A major portion of riders on Australian stations today are Aboriginals no doubt in large part because they can be hired most cheaply.

Sears sees the Australian cattlemen as guided more by English and Scottish concerns for frugality, practicality and money-making in contrast to the more easy-going temperamental Spanish style in America; yet Atherton makes it clear that the character of many Anglo-American ranchers was not very different from an American businessman imbued with the "Protestant ethic" (Sears, 79; Atherton, esp. 171 ff.).

The Australians adopted their own pastoral terminology reflecting more the British tradition. Thus, a mob of bullocks is a herd of steers; a stockade is a corral; a station, a ranch; a muster, a roundup; and a pad is a cow trail (Sears, 79–80).

Australian ranching is on a far grander scale than that of the Americas or South Africa, particularly in Queensland, the Northern Territories and Western Australia. In the northern part of the latter state a small, hardly profitable station has twenty thousand acres which can support only a few hundred head of cattle. The smallest successful stations are over 300,000 acres and a majority of all cattle stations in the northern parts of Western Australia are over one million acres in size, running about 10,000 head, about one thousand of which are marketed annually. All of the "outback" area of Australia is open range country, with a few fenced "paddocks" ranging from five to 200 square miles in size. Even the largest stations are managed by only two or three Whites and twenty or so Aboriginals (Treloar, 53–66).

Because of the immense size of these establishments a considerable amount of time must be spent in cattle round-ups. In addition, due to the distance to centres of modern transportation there continue to be long trail drives of one or two months' duration. When the wet season ends "teams" of ten to fifteen men and seventy or more horses set out from each station for a month's roundup. While horses are frequently alternated in the work, many are not used more than once "and mortality is often high due to accident, poison plants and over work" (Treloar, 55).

The Australian "stockman rode exactly like nineteenth century fox hunters, rather straight in the leg, holding his well-bred, spirited horse hard by the head and driving him into the snaffle-bit. His saddle was an ordinary English hunting-saddle, with an enlarged weight-bearing surface and sometimes fitted with knee-rollers to help with a buck-jumper" (Trench, 175). The Australian cattleman also sometimes straps a blanket roll in front of the saddle and this aids in keeping the seat with a difficult horse (Sears, 297). Saddles are equipped with plain iron stirrups and simple leather straps. Neither Australians nor Boers attempted to make any elaborate stamped design or silver mountings on saddles and bridles as is characteristic of Spanish American saddlery.

Cattle are not roped on the range, but are driven, with the aid of long stock whips, to a corral where they are sorted, branded and ear marked. "Practiced Bushmen can cut the ashes off a cigarette or crack a blue-fly on a 'drags' horn, with his sixteen foot bullwhip, or use it as a substitute for firecrackers on a holiday" (Sears, 83). In his use then of the stock whip he resembles the Boers and the American Southerners. Trench believes there are other similarities between the latter and the Australians in terms of ranching methods (Trench, 176). Presumably these would primarily reflect the common British antecedents.

The Australian has no horn to which to attach his rope; in its place a roping horse wears a collar for tying the lariat and a snubbing post is used as further aid in roping. By these means sixty calves may be branded an hour. This snubbing post is not as Sears has maintained "an exclusive Australian institution" since as we have noted it was earlier used in Mexico (Sears, 82).

The Australian cowboy is called a bushman or ringer and once lived a quasi-nomadic life like his American counterpart. Now his way of life is as much modified from the old as is the American cowboy's. "Seventy years have seen the rise and the decline of the Bushman's paradise. Like the *vaquero*, cowboy and gaucho he will soon be but a memory. His ever-present enemies – sheep and man's greed – have crowded him to the semi-tropical northern eighth of the vast continent" (Sears, 84). Nowadays the chances are he belongs to a labour union and works a forty hour week with extra for overtime.

A favourite pastime of Australians is flat racing. Also steeplechasing and riding to hounds after kangaroos are common in some circles. "Since in the early settlements timber was plentiful, (the Australian) was accustomed to jump his horse over deadfalls, stout post-and-rail fences, and even wire" (Trench, 175–6).

The yeoman agrarian capitalism which developed out of the Mediaeval background of Western Europe is associated with two major kinds of horse complexes. The one involves farming and the cultivation of the soil, entails the greatest development of the heavy draught horse found in any agricultural system and, until the advent of the automobile, employed lighter horses for buggies more than it did for riding. This complex is now on the way to extinction. Another complex developed in relation to the specialization in cattle and sheep raising under range conditions. Here that which evolved under heavy Iberian influence and the British form which appeared in Australia made full use of the horse for herding purposes so that it became a crucial element of the ranching system. However in South Africa and a limited development in isolated other parts of Africa, such as the Kenya Highlands and Rhodesia, pedestrian herding by subject classes of servants was the rule and the horse was limited to being a means of transportation, of sport, and pleasure.

Riding styles in the cattle ranching area were adapted to their peculiar situations. From Hispanic America to Boer South Africa and British Australia there was a preference for riding with rather long stirrups and for having bigger, more padded saddles. Yet prominent pommels and cantles occur only in the American area. Where herdsmen do not rope from the saddle as in Australia, Iceland, South Africa or Southern South America among the old Gaucho riders, there is no need for a horn on the pommel.

XI

The Horse in the Modern Middle East

THE ARABS

THE Middle East may be defined as the area of North Africa from Morocco across to the Red Sea, and south-west Asia including Afghanistan and the Pashto inhabited regions of Pakistan. This definition is roughly appropriate for the period from Mediaeval times to the present. It incorporates a number of different ethnic groups who share a considerable number of cultural features. Two of the more important of these are the prevalence of Islam and the tripartite division of the population into urban town dwellers, rural village farmers, and pastoral nomads, each of which is involved in an interdependent relation with the other two. Despite the popular notion of the Arab as a nomad in a night shirt riding across the sandy wastes on a camel, the fact is that the great majority of all Middle Eastern peoples, Arabs included, are settled village and town dwellers engaged in trade and agriculture. And more than anything else they have been until modern times donkey riders.

Slightly over half of Middle Eastern peoples are culturally definable as Arabs. This means, among other things, they speak one or another of several dialects of the Arabic language; they have a patrilineal, patriarchal family system which in many places and, especially among nomadic Arabs, is further characterized by a segmentary tribal structure; they share particular types of cuisine and dress that distinguish them from their neighbours. Like the other Middle Eastern people most Arabs are peasants, largely engaging in irrigation agriculture along water courses and in oases. Not much more than ten percent are pastoral nomads and of these probably a third are primarily cattle herders (Baggara) living in the central part of the Republic of Sudan and in Chad. The remainder (Bedouin) herd camels, sheep and goats in the most arid sections of the Arab world. It is among these latter that the famous Arabian breed of horses was developed.

Perhaps, at this point, it should be made clear why the Arab nomads as well as other nomads of the Middle East whether Berber, Tuareg, Iranian, Kurdish, or Pashto have not been included in the discussion of equestrian pastoral nomads. First, among the majority of Middle Eastern nomads the camel is most frequently ridden, and among the others there is more of a pedestrian emphasis. Secondly, the horse, relative to other livestock and relative to the Central Asian case, is a rarity and is kept by the more well-to-do and for highly restricted purposes. If Central Asia represents an area of maximum versatility of horse use, the Middle East is one of singular specialization for riding in war, sport, and display.

Among all Arabs, villager and nomad alike, the horse is held in high esteem. Umar, the second caliph and companion of Muhammad, is reputed to have said: "Love horses and look after them; for they deserve your tenderness; treat them as you do your children; nourish them as you do friends of the family, and blanket them with care. For the love of God, do not be negligent for you will regret it in this life and the next" (quoted in Daumas, E., 32). A marabout (holy man) in conversation with Daumas remarked: "Horses are our riches, joys, life, and religion. Has not the Prophet said: 'The blessings of this world until Judgement Day shall hang from the forelocks between your horses' eyes?'" (Daumas, E. 29).

The status of the horse and particularly of horse riding was at one time affirmed in the Middle East and in other Muslim realms as well by a prohibition against non-Muslims riding horseback, and a mounted Muslim was expected to dismount when confronting a pedestrian who was his superior. In Mediaeval Egypt the ruling elite reserved horse riding for itself alone. Particularly among the Mamluks (1250–1517) the equestrian arts were developed to a high degree. The Mamluk knight was exposed to a training programme which began with practice on models of horses. Later, he graduated to riding an unsaddled horse, learning first the canter, then the trot, gallop and jumping. Finally, he rode on a saddled horse, learning correct reining and seat as well as the amble. Once his teachers recognized that he had mastered the horse along with the use of the lance, the Mamluk went to the hippodrome for cavalry training. Still he was not considered correctly trained unless he could treat his sick horse (Rabie, 154–157). He was also expected to know the breeding of horses and have a knowledge of horse pedigrees (Staffa, 211).

A further indication of the development of equestrian science during the Mediaeval Islamic period was the appearance of several treatises on horsemanship which described various methods of jumping, riding and the like. In addition there were works providing information on equine veterinary subjects.

But, Fisher has suggested that perhaps the conception of the horse in Islamic society has been over-romanticized. At least – there appear to be some ambivalent notions about the animal among Muslims. For example, Fisher has stated that Umar himself rode a donkey and forbade his administrators to ride horseback. In the early centuries of Islamic North Africa, it appears that the donkey was considered the proper mount for a judge (Fisher 1973: 373). Objections have sometimes been raised to riding horses in towns because riders might see over the compound walls and, thus, the secluded women (Fisher 1973: 374).

Between the sedentary and nomadic Arab population there is a difference not only in the role of the horse, but in riding gear and care as well. Arabs of the agricultural villages keep very few horses. Thus, in an Egyptian village of several thousand inhabitants there may be only a half dozen or so. Their most notable use is for purposes of display on festive occasions when they are gaily caparisoned and induced by their riders to dance to accompanying music. Such horses may also be used for racing contests. Others still are kept for the wealthy landlord and his farm manager for overseeing the operations of the estate as well as for their pleasure, but this is an aspect that, with the loss of power by the aristocracy and the acquisition of mechanized vehicles, has all but disappeared.

Apart from their employment on taxi carriages and occasionally on carts in towns, the use of horses for draught among Arabs has a limited distribution. As a result of French influence coupled with the introduction of a light iron plough, horses are not infrequently involved in field work on farms in Tunisia, Algeria and Morocco. In southern Iraqi villages they are apparently kept primarily for ploughing. How long this practice has existed is not clear. It, too, could be a consequence of European or Turkish influence. In Iraq horse maintenance is so costly that only the wealthy own entire horses; most peasants have as little as one eighth interest in a single animal. Owners are by no means necessarily groups of neighbours or close kin, but may in fact live miles apart. Since horses like other livestock "are offered for sale at public markets", joint ownership agreements are made at the time of sale by any who are interested. Use of the horse for riding is the privilege of the man who stables the animal. Other part-owners may have its use for a limited number of days each year and a share of any profits which might be derived from the sale of a colt. One who owns a fourth interest "may, during his period of use, also plough his non-horse owning brother's land in return for cash or, more commonly, for a substantial meal. Thus, use of the horse extends even beyond its multiple owners" (Fernea, 111).

Multiple ownership spreads the risks attendant with horse ownership and also the burden of capital investment amongst a number of individuals as well as a number of different kin groups so that they can better bear the loss of an animal and afford the purchase of one. Fernea notes that "[the horse] is the most familiar object of non-lineage partnership" (Fernea, 112).

It is among the sedentary Arabs that one finds the most elaborate riding harness with the use of severe curb bits, decorated headstalls, often provided with blinders in North Africa, and equally decorated saddles with high pommels and cantles and shovel shaped stirrups the sharp corners of which double as spurs. Many of these saddles resemble the Mediaeval tilting saddle with their chair backs and the square iron stirrups. It is more common to enumerate the items the Crusaders carried back to Europe from the Middle East and to overlook the European contributions to this area during that time. It may be that the distinct chair back cantle of the saddle and the square stirrups are derived by the Arabs from this contact, just as the cross handled swords still used by the Beja and Arabs of the Sudan most clearly have their origin in the Crusader sword (Murray, 5., 101). The high forked saddle with pronounced pommel and cantle possibly spread to Iran from Central Asia and was adopted by the Arabs and Europeans alike from Byzantine-Turkish-Iranian sources.

Village Arab horses are kept within the house compound; on occasion they are turned out in fields – particularly stubble fields – to graze at which time they are invariably hobbled.

Most of the remainder of this discussion will focus on the nomadic population since it is here that the horse has its greatest importance and horsebreeding and horsemanship its most sophisticated development. Among the nomadic population as well the highest proportion of horses per man are kept, although the actual number is extremely small; everywhere horses represent one percent or less of all livestock owned. The best and most famous horsebreeding tribes of north Arabia have at most four to five thousand head and many other Arabian tribes can muster only a few hundred. Estimates indicate there are only between forty and fifty thousand horses in all of Saudi Arabia (Simpson, 48).

The Horse in Raiding

Among the nomads the horse's primary economic value is as a weapon for obtaining booty and influence; other than this its economic importance is negligible (Musil, 371). The more horses a tribe has the greater it is feared by its neighbours. In mid-nineteenth century Algeria a man could not expect to accumulate a camel herd until he had a horse with which to protect himself against raiders (Daumas, E., 38).

Raiding an enemy camp to see how many of the livestock one can drive off has been endemic among nomad Arabs. In preparation for a raid one half of the horses should be left at home to repel any possible attack. Extra horseshoes are taken along on the raid. Among the Rwala of North Arabia, at least, the vaginas of pregnant mares great with young are sewn up in the belief that this will prevent miscarriage (Musil, 508). Horses are rarely ridden to the raiding place, but are led, while the warrior proceeds on camel back, up to the point where a charge can be made on the enemy; then, he changes mounts. The camels are also important since they haul skins of water for the horses. One rode bareback into battle if the enemy was also mounted since in the fray the girths fequently loosened and the pad saddle slipped under the horse (Wentworth, 106).

Among the Rwala, a boy on his first raid cuts a lock of hair from the tail of a captured mare and hangs it up in his tent. This is done for every horse captured so that all will know how many animals he has acquired (Musil, 539). A horse is encouraged to participate in the fight itself so that when riders encounter each other the mounts, too, attack and rear trying to strike each other down with their forelegs. This is a matter of training and a practice not uncommon amongst people who use their horses mainly for raiding and warfare.

Hunting and Sport on Horseback

A common form of sportive riding is the fantasia in which Bedouin ride in circling exercises and throw their spears. This has been modified in some areas to a performance in which the riders gallop down a strip and at a given moment rise up in their stirrups and, balancing on the galloping horse, fire matchlocks into the air. This kind of fantasia is especially common throughout Morocco, Algeria and Tunisia where it is shared by Berbers and Arabs alike. It is also found as far east as Turkmenstan. Related to the fantasia is the game of *el jerid* where riders form teams and attempt to throw bamboo canes at one another either to dodge them or catch them in mid air and throw them back.

To a limited extent Arabs engage in acrobatics on horseback, including standing on the saddle at a fast gallop, then throwing a lance, or standing on one's head (Berenger, I, 124). Aside from hawking which is a favourite sport of Bedouin, horses are employed in other types of hunts as well. Among the Baggara, or cattle nomadic Arabs of the Sudan, giraffe and elephant hunts are conducted on horseback.

Riding Style

Arabs prefer mares for riding and general use since they produce offspring, do not whinny in combat, and in Arab belief ride more easily, are less sensitive to hunger and thirst and demand less attention and feed (Daumas, E., 56). Muhammad said: "Prefer mares: Their bellies are a treasure and their backs seats of honour. The greatest of all blessings is an intelligent woman or a prolific mare" (quoted in Daumas, E., 56).

At the time of Muhammad (570–632 A.D.) Arabs were reported riding bareback and without a bridle. Like the ancient Numidians of North Africa they guided their horses with a neck rope and short stick (Brown, 45). Berenger reports Arabs in 1749 as riding a girthless saddle.

Stirrups were not adopted in the Arab world until after the time of Muhammad – possibly the end of the seventh century. White believes the Arabs might have acquired them from the Persians (White, 18–19). Horsemen in North Africa and Spain at first continued to ride long as they had done without stirrups. Trench claims, however, that as a result of the contact between North Africans and Turks from the east during the Meccan pilgrimages, the former adopted the riding seat of the steppes with short stirrups and bent knees (Trench, 146).

Dodge compared the Arab riding style with that of the American Indian: the rider was "apt to lean forward; from hip down to knee the leg is almost perpendicular; and from knee down it is thrust back at . . . a most unhorsemanlike angle" (Dodge, 233). The Arab attempts to ride as close to the withers as possible and so achieve something of the order of the "forward seat".

The major gaits of the Arab horse are the walk, canter and gallop. Occasionally, a horse is trained to the rack or the amble (Dodge, 303). The trot is definitely not cultivated, especially since it is not a comfortable gait for a stirrupless rider. Furthermore, the Arab horse is a fast walker with a light long pace. A large number of Arab horses are trained in a prancing gait which is employed on festive occasions or in times of danger. This gait is induced by the rider holding his mare up short so that she leaps forward, rises slightly on her hind legs, backs and leaps forward again (Musil, 378).

Saddlery

A considerable amount of horse riding is accomplished without saddle, stirrups, or bridle. Especially those commoners who have horses, ride bareback with a nose band (Dickson, 390). Sheikhs and others who can afford them have a pad saddle which is simply a leather or quilted cushion stuffed with wool or cotton and sewn to a cloth cover. It is fastened on the horse's back with a surcingle. Tweedie states that during some seasons the saddle is never removed from the horse's back except when swimming a river (Tweedie, 142). Stirrups, if used, are of iron and not so massive as the shovel shaped type known to sedentary Arabs. They are used with short leathers. Bedouin in the Arabian Desert do not commonly ride with stirrups. Tweedie says without stirrups a rider can, should the occasion require it, more readily roll off the horse and sometimes keep his arms around the animal's neck so that he can swing on again in a moment (Tweedie, 144). Among Algerian Bedouin thick callouses develop from the constant rubbing of the bare foot against the eye of the stirrup, as a result of standing in them. Daumas claimed one can therefore tell who the riders are in a group – at least the ones who ride with stirrups. A certain bey is reported to have punished a tribe which had revolted against him by executing all those men with these particular callouses on the foot since they were assumed to be the warrior horsemen (Daumas, E., 139).

Except occasionally in warfare, Bedouin never ride with a bit, although the town and village Arabs all do so. In any case, where bits are employed they are of a severe curb type; snaffles are not used. Dickson describes a ring bit used in Iraq of "Persian and Syrian" style as having ". . . in place of a curb chain . . . a thin circular metal band which is attached to the cross-piece of the bit itself. This latter usually has an unpleasant-looking metal spike, which as the bit is pulled, engages the roof of the mouth and causes pain. All Arab horses ridden on these bits continually throw their heads up, to the great discomfort of the rider" (Dickson, 390). Such ring bits and other similar harsh devices were introduced into Spain and thence to the Americas where they became part of the harness of many *vaqueros* and cowboys.

The Bedouin horse is chiefly ridden with an ornamental headstall of coloured wool ending in a loose nose band made of coarse metal chain which passes over the nostrils and under the chin. To this chain a round woollen head-rope is attached under the chin and passes on the left side of the horse to the rider as his rein which he holds in the left hand (Dickson, 388–90). This type of nose band arrangement is the source of the hackamore so common in Spanish influenced areas. A throat lash may be applied to the horse on special occasions and it has a tassel, and often an amulet of Koranic verse (Brown, 20). A blue bead as protection against the evil eye is sometimes attached to the headstall.

A staff, which is also a symbol of honour carried by a sheikh, may be an aid in guiding the horse, but never to strike it. The stick which "has a reverse crotch at the thick end" is used to catch the halter on a horse or the ring in a camel's nose (Brown, 88). This is the nearest the Arabs

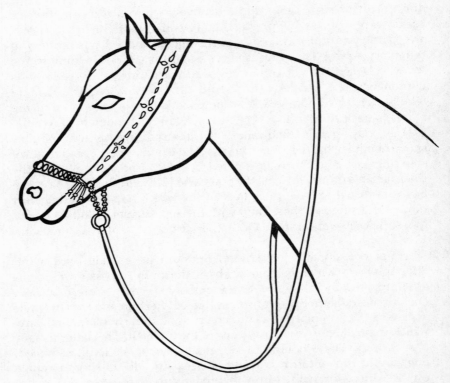

ARAB BEDOUIN CHAIN NOSE BAND BRIDLE
From Tweedie, 140

come to the lasso. Spurs are also widely employed as riding aids.

That the Bedouin can ride with such ease on a simple padded saddle without stirrups and control his mount by a rope attached to a nose band is only partly because they are accomplished riders. Careful training, intimate care, and continual handling all make for a docile or more obedient horse. Furthermore, in the proper hands, the Bedouin nose band is a most effective device for control.

Horse Sacrifice

In contrast to the Turks and Indo-Europeans the horse was hardly incorporated into the religious life and belief of Hamitic or Semitic people. Tweedie mentions an example of horse sacrifice in connection with a death among "ancient" Bedouin. Supposedly a mare or a she-camel was tied beside a dead man's grave where it slowly died. Tweedie attempted to find evidence of the practice in his time (late nineteenth century) and says that every Arab townsman and desert dweller had heard of it and several said they had seen it done "but such statements are not to be trusted" (Tweedie, 336). In other cases, apparently, the horse was led to the cemetery and then back to its stable (Tweedie, 130, footnote 5). Such observances while now extinct suggest some occurrence in the past of horse sacrifice in connection with funerary rites among nomad Arabs. There is no evidence for it among other Arabs, or for Berbers for that matter.

To all Arabs horseflesh is highly taboo, as is the drinking of mare's milk. Hides are processed into leather and hair from the mane is sometimes braided for harness pieces.

Horse Management

"The nomad rider loves his horse, but it is a fierce, brutal love, a stern admiration which knows no mercy for failure, no sympathy for weakness, no kindness for age or wounds" (Wentworth, 107). A mount may be given preference over wives or daughters especially when there is a question about the distribution of a meagre food supply. The family mare "is literally loved and cared for as if she were a daughter of the house" (Dickson, 380). However, such presumed careful attention must be viewed in its proper context – that of a difficult often onerous life in the harsh desert which caters least of all to the daughters of the house. The Bedouin do not groom their horses except that Saharan Arabs are reported to occasionally rub their animals down with wollen cloths and sometimes bathe them in summer (Daumas, E., 108). Consequently, they are often dirty and unkempt looking, but the lack of grooming again should be viewed in the context of a people who themselves are rarely able to wash except in the performance of the mandatory ablutions which precede Muslim prayer (Dickson, 380).

Horses are often left to wander about the vicinity of the camp, usually wearing iron hobbles on their forefeet, returning home when thirsty. Among the Rwala certain pastures are reserved exclusively for horses, usually those which are "shut in by steep slopes" so that they can be easily guarded (Musil, 309). Grain, invariably barley, is fed only when it is necessary to prepare a horse for a raid or if as in summer, the grazing is so poor it is necessary to supplement with grain to prevent starvation (Dickson, 380). Brown has reported that horses are commonly fed twice a day "not more than three or four pounds of barley or chopped straw, and a handful of beans" (Brown, 74). In the Algerian oases when grain is scarce horses are fed dates and as they eat they spit out the pits. In other areas the pits are ground and fed mixed with dates (Daumas, E., 100–1). Brown found that horses were trained not to accept food from strange hands or after undergoing a tiring ride (Brown, 74).

In cold weather woollen blankets are placed on horses and in inclement weather they may be brought into the tent or, not infrequently, they invite themselves into the tent for shelter on cold nights and during the heat of the day. Here they are given dates and water by the women of the household. This and other attentions they receive from women and children contribute to their docility. Dickson has noted their apparent gentleness in relation to children and the women who attend them (Dickson, 381).

Throughout the desert, horses must become accustomed to thirst.[1] They may sometimes go for three or four days without water. Of course, in winter when there is ample moisture in the grass they have less demands for water. From the first of March to the end of April a horse must drink every day, and beginning in May and for the balance of the summer, it must be watered three times a day (Dickson, 381). In time of water scarcities camel's milk may be given instead. Indeed, camel's milk is almost the foal's only food. Foals run beside the she-camel, nursing from her and being treated by her as one of her own (Brown, 74).

It goes almost without saying that the horse of the desert is in its peak condition in spring and early summer when there is adequate grazing and water supply and its condition gradually deteriorates as the summer advances. The horse learns to wait patiently long hours for both food and drink.

Bedouin horses are ordinarily shod, some on the forefeet only, others on all fours depending on the terrain in which they live. St John Philby said of Ibn Saud's horses that they were shod "with a nearly heart-shaped piece of metal, pierced in the centre by a hole (for ventilation) and fastened by two nails at the side" (Wentworth, 104). According to Dickson, horses are always kept well shod with flat saucer-shaped shoes covering the whole sole of the foot so as to keep out stones and prevent bruising the bottom of the foot. They are reshod only when an old shoe falls off and as a result many animals have very long hooves (Dickson, 388). In nineteenth century Saharan Algeria shoes were removed from the horses when they were turned out to spring pastures (Daumas, E., 132).

The farrier constitutes a special caste in the traditional Bedouin society. The shoeing of horses is their exclusive speciality and one who is not a farrier does not handle farrier's tools or marry his daughter to a farrier (Tweedie, 176). In the Algerian Sahara each tribe has its special

---

[1] The resistance of the camel to thirst is proverbial, but it also appears that goats, sheep and donkeys are all more thirst resistant than are horses.

group of smiths and their families. These smiths are an endogamous group and the craft is inherited from father to son. They do not pay taxes and are exempt from tribal obligations including those of hospitality and military defence. At the same time they are considered neutrals in warfare, having a protected status similar to women and children. The caste position of the blacksmith has a long history and widespread distribution. It probably originates with the appearance of a highly skilled trade which is known only to a few and at the same time is of central importance to the perpetuation of important traditions. In the case of the blacksmith we note the dependence of the practice of raiding and inter-tribal warfare upon well shod horses and, once at least, upon having good swords.

Gelding, and castration as a general practice, is prohibited by Islamic law, and thus throughout the Middle East it is less common than in Europe. The Bedouin of the Arabian Peninsula consider it an unthinkable practice – "a disgrace and a brutality" – to geld a stallion (Wentworth, 105). On the other hand this prohibition may apply only to the *kushlani* or pure-bred Arab horses and not to the *kadishi*, the less pure, as is suggested by Brown (Brown, 98). Castration of both horses and camels is apparently common in the Western Sahara where stallions are gelded between the ages of two and eight (Daumas, E., 171–2).

For various disorders a hot iron may be applied to individuals as well as to animals, including horses. If a horse does not show great suppleness in the shoulders at fifteen to eighteen months a hot iron is applied to the scapulohumeral joint in "the form of a cross whose four extremities are joined by a circle". Firing may also be applied to the knees if these are badly shaped or have a tendency to bony tumours (Daumas, E., 74). Horses are fired on the chest as well (Tweedie, 184).

Horses are all given names, but these should not be those that are applied to free men. Thus, many have names appropriate to slaves (Daumas, E., 89–90).

The Arabs classify horses according to their colour for which there are a great variety of names; they are also referred to by their particular age, there being a term for each year up to the age of eight after which all are referred by the same age term (Dickson, 393). Carl Raswan catalogued a 1050 word "vocabulary of Arabic hippology" used by Bedouin, but he did not attempt any systematic analysis (Raswan, 1945). Judith Wentworth, on the other hand, categorized much of the Bedouin terminology in a meaningful fashion. She lists words for fleet, swift running, galloping or rushing horses, thirteen for herds of horses, one hundred for colours, thirty-eight of which are for greys and whites. There are twenty terms for noble, high bred horse or mare; eighteen for fiery horse; fifteen words for starting a horse; fourteen words for trotting; twelve for prancing; five for ambling; twenty-one for different kinds of walk. There are terms pertaining to a mare just foaled, a mare seven days after foaling, and a great number associated with breeding, fighting on horseback, and breaking horses in (Wentworth, 157), all of which clearly demonstrate the abiding importance and value of the horse to the Bedouin.

Breeding and Selection of Horses

Arab horses are divided in the Peninsula and adjacent areas into three classes:

Attashi: with no pretence to pure Arab blood; these include all foreign breeds.

Kadishi: are more or less of Arab blood and include the largest number of Arabian horses; these may be gelded.

Kushlani: are pure Arabs which are never gelded. The *kushlani* are also called *hudúd* (approved) or *asíl* (of noble origin) and are sometimes referred to as *kuhaylan*. According to tradition the five mares of Salaman, a descendent of Ismail, are the ancestors of the five strains (*al Khamsa*) into which the *kushlani* are divided. This terminology becomes somewhat confusing since *kuhaylan* designates both the first of these strains as well as all five strains together. The term is derived from *kuhl* (kohl) and Brown supposes that this is to impart the meaning of one anointed with *kuhl*, or the black eyes (Brown, 98). In other words, a beauty. On the other hand, Tweedie believes the association with *kuhl* or blackness is because of the colour of the skin which is a dark blue especially in the white and grey haired horses (Tweedie, 233).

A second strain is called *saqlawi*, "the swift one or large of flank"; a third *ubayan*, "cloak carrying, perhaps after high tail carriage"; a fourth the *hamdani* and a fifth the *hadban*, "one with shaggy hair, or dense long eye lashes". In addition there are several approved offshoots from the above (Brown, 98). Wentworth points out that the *khamsa* classification is a "post-Islamic invention" and a romantic myth. The Arab horse is derived from many strains and all strain names used at present are relatively modern (Wentworth, 35).

Line breeding has long been common among Bedouin while close in breeding is less common, sometimes being necessitated because of the scarcity of pure stock or because of hostilities with neighbours (Brown, 113). Here there are parallels to the Arabs' own customary practice of preferred marriages within the patrilineage and marriage to one's father's brother's daughter. Simpson observes that "[p]urity of line is so fanatically regarded by the desert Arabs that if a mare has once mated with a *kudsh* (kadishi) stallion, her progeny ever after are *kudsh*, even though their own sires be *asil* of the best. This idea that foals may inherit not only from their actual sires but also from previous mates of their dams is completely false, but it has been traditional not only among the Arabs but also among many European and American breeders. The desert Arabs' ideas of purity in breeding are so rigid that many horses that are, in fact, excellent Arabians and that would be accepted as purebred by our standards are by them despised as *kudsh*" (Simpson, 49).

Brown says Bedouin are very "fastidious about pedigrees". Since the mare is held to be most important – more so than the stallion – pedigrees are traced through her, an interesting contrast with the usual patrilineal emphasis in the Arab's own kinship system. But the mare as the producer of progeny is a source of wealth; it is considered "superior in heat, hunger and thirst" and can be turned out to graze unattended (Brown, 113).

It is "a matter of honour among the tribes to receive inviolate an emissary from a neighbouring tribe with whom they have been at war, and give him a complete pedigree of the horses captured by the enemy, and vouchsafe him a safe return." Each tribe believes the tables may some day be turned and eventually one might be able to recover offspring of lost horses (Brown, 112).

Arab horses have been used for centuries in inter-breeding with other breeds all over the world in order to upgrade stock. Brown describes a number of breeds which are closely related to the Arab: Syrian, Barb, Persian, Turkmen, Tazec (the horse of India said to be descended from Persian stock bought by Timur), the Java pony, Andalusian, Abyssinian, Libyan, Thoroughbred, Morgan, Percheron, Hackney, Standardbred, Connemara, Highland, Shetland, Welsh ponies, Orloff, Austrian, French and Tarbaise (Brown, *passim*).

The best breeding area in Arabia is in the Nejd. The Hijaz is poor horse country and Yemen has today no horse breeding people. In the early Islamic period and as late as the seventeenth century the Yemenis and their rulers bred high quality horses and oxen for export. With the Ottoman conquests and the decline of trade to India, horse production dwindled. Except for a small section of north-eastern Uman, Uman and the Hadramaut are not horse producing areas. The Umanis especially are camel breeders. The Island of Bahrain has been famous in the past for its horse breeding among a settled population (Wentworth, 100).

Among the Saharan Arabs studding between equals "is paid for, according to the custom of the tribe, with a large nose bag of barley, a sheep, or a large jug of milk. It would be a shameful thing to offer or accept money, for then they would be called pimps in a stallion's love affairs" (Daumas, E., 59). It is apparently not uncommon for a stallion owner to refuse to mate his stud with an inferior mare because of the possibility of offspring which would reflect adversely on the stallion (Daumas, E., 59). Neither does one give his mare to a jack (Daumas, E., 60). A common belief in the Arabian Peninsula is that a foal is supposed to get his "bone, tendons, nerves, and disposition and speed from his sire" and colour, form, and size from his dam (Brown, 110).

Every sheikh of importance in Arabia keeps one or more mares from which he breeds a particular strain and so acquires notability (Dickson, 384). Breeding stallions are owned by the sheikhs of a tribe and among the Rwala there is about one for every large clan. They are kept separated from the mares. Dickson says they are well kept and fat and have a tendency to develop fierce tempers. A stallion is usually placed in the care "of a favoured slave, who is allowed to take a small regular fee from every person bringing a mare to be served", having first received permission from the sheikh (Dickson, 387). On the surface this practice may appear inconsistent with the Saharan Arab conception that it is shameful to accept payment for such service, a view also affirmed for the Arabian Bedouin by Brown. But the payment to the slave is on the same level as a guest leaving a small gratuity for a household servant belonging to one's host.

Witnesses are present at the time of breeding of a mare who often is taken long distances to secure proper mating. Daumas claims that among Saharan Arabs supervised mating is preferred because they are afraid the stallion may injure himself in attempting entry or may wear himself out (Daumas, E., 62). Suitable breeding age is from four to twelve years of age for a mare and six to fourteen for a stallion, although only the wealthy follow this rule; the poorer are forced to use younger and older animals (Daumas, E., 55).

Great care is taken of the mare after breeding and during the last sixty days of pregnancy; wealthy men do not ride them after this time. At birth women help receive the foal and for "the first eight days the foal's neck, ears, breast and legs are rubbed" to correct defects of conformation which may have been noted (Daumas, E., 65–6). Amulets and talismans are applied to the foal and it must become accustomed to drinking camel's milk or ewe's milk (Daumas, E., 68). In Arabia weaning occurs between three and four months of age. When weaned, foals are tied at night to the tent post with a collar around their necks, but during the day or on the march they are allowed to run loose (Wentworth, 103; Blunt, 430). Besides camel's milk, or sometimes ewe's milk, they are fed a few dates and hay, if there is any (Wentworth, 102). In its first autumn the colt is turned out to fend for itself, although it is usually tied. "As a yearling he is like a half-starved cat"

(Wentworth, 103).

Wentworth considers the Arabs good horse breakers because they are extremely patient and do not strike or ill-use horses. She claims Arabs believe it is foolish to lose one's temper with an animal (Wentworth, 161). They may believe this, but the extent to which they practice it is sometimes another matter. Training is a gradual process most often begun in an informal fashion by the time the animal is a year old. At this time small children may often scramble on its back so that by the time serious training in Arabia is begun before the age of three the horse is already "green broke" (Blunt, 430). Saharan Arabs begin training somewhat earlier at eighteen months at which time a child is allowed to ride it, to lead it to water, and accompany it to grazing grounds when a rope halter is used. At between twenty-four and twenty-seven months the animal is bridled and on becoming used to the bridle it is then accustomed to the saddle, after which it is ridden (Daumas, E., 75–77). In the Arabian Nejd it is apparently often bridled with a ring bit, and saddled with the pad saddle about the age of three (Blunt, 1881, 15). Only after a horse has been well trained is it ridden with spurs. Among the Bedouin certain habits are drilled into every horse: to stand without moving when the reins are thrown over the horse's head and rest on the ground; to take off from a standstill at a gallop; to come to a dead stop from a gallop; to make sharp turns to right or left and spin around on its hocks and start off again at a gallop; and to rear against another horse in the battle field. Each of these should be executed at the mere flick of the rider's wrist. Such achievements are deemed essential for the Arab-Bedouin style of raiding activities, but it will be readily noted how important each of these features is, except the last, for the mounted herding of cattle. They are attributes desirable in a good cutting horse.

In the Arabian view the good horse should have "four wide things – forehead, breast, croup and legs; four long things – neck, forearms, belly, and haunches; four short things – loins, pasterns, ears, and tail" (Daumas, E., 42). The ideal stallion is "one that has a long pedigree, whose flesh is firm, who has bare ribs, clean legs, and powerful respiration, when he has been endowed with a good temper and if he has proved that he has great powers of resistance to weariness, hardship, and the rigors of climate" (Daumas, E., 56).

A good mare for the Rwala "has long ears, legs and neck; the croup, the root of the tail and the coronet . . . are short. The nostrils and eyes are large and the distance between the foreknees, broad . . .. The forehead should bulge forward . . ., the breast should be arched, and the forelock, mane and hair of the tail should be thick . . ." (Musil, 372). Dickson says a good horse or mare has "large eyes set well apart".

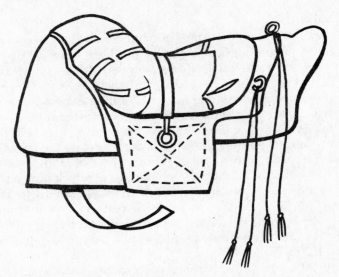

ARAB BEDOUIN STIRRUPLESS PAD SADDLE
From Tweedie

It never holds its tail straight, but always high and well to one side (Dickson, 386).

As among East Indians bad signs are indicated by curly spots or white spots on various parts of a horse's anatomy (Musil, 373). Particular arrangements of hair in one place are evil omens while a similar arrangement elsewhere is an assurance of prosperity. Colour is also important in judging a horse's value. Thus, a chestnut is deemed fastest among Arabs of the Sahara and a bay "the hardiest and most sober" (Daumas, E., 116).

Arabs put their highest value in a mare with staying power and endurance. Such an animal is necessary for raids; there is little interest in fast, short distance horses (Dickson, 385).

Interestingly enough they do not know how to tell the age of a horse by its teeth (Blunt, 1979, 432). Since in the tribe each colt's age is a matter of common knowledge, it is likely there was no reason to develop such a technique (Wentworth, 171).

Ownership

Horses are so valuable among Bedouin that unless one is a very wealthy man or a sheikh, he cannot own a complete horse. "As a rule half a dozen persons own, or have a share in each mare, and the joint-owners often live at great distance from each other . . . ." This therefore makes it difficult, among other things, in purchasing a mare since one must get the approval of all the owners. A prospective European buyer will be told by one owner he can sell the off fore of an animal, but if he wants the other three legs he must consult the owner one hundred miles away (Dickson, 382). Among the Rwala hardly a mare is owned by one man only. A part owner who takes care of the mare is responsible for her health and must give compensation should the animal die or miscarry owing to his negligence. "If the partners want to annul . . . their agreement, they go to the chief's tent and declare it before witnesses, so that they cannot blame each other afterwards . . . .. A partner can be compelled to give up his rights . . . if the other" partner(s) demand "it or have to sell the mare" (Musil, 376). The Rwala apply a specific designation to a horse owned by two owners, another for one owned by three and so forth (Musil, 376–7).

In selling horses the Bedouin of the desert makes no effort to point out an animal's good points nor to conceal its shortcomings, for as far as he is concerned it is the pedigree which counts (Blunt, 1879, 432). Daumas does add that the Arab may often use a flow of words aimed at beguiling the would-be buyer (Daumas, E., 127). Presumably town and village Arabs are less trustworthy as horse dealers. If the purchaser of a mount requests a certificate or pedigree of breeding from the Bedouin he will normally receive a very simple statement such as the following:

"We whose signatures and seals are below, Sheiks of the Suwailimat, a branch of the Aeniza do, testify by Allah, and by Muhammad, son of Abdullah, truly, without compulsion, in respect to the horse of Ma'ashi'l Hashshai of Suwailimat: be a bay, with a mark like the new moon on his forehead; by our stars and fortune, his dam was (of the strain) Wadna Khirsan and his sire Kuhailan Abu Junub – the well known strain. He is a horse used as a sire. It is also known to us that his price has stood Khidhr, the Agel, in 550 ghazis £88 sterling ca.). According to our knowledge and information we have written this certificate" (quoted in Tweedie, 136).

THE BERBERS

The Berbers represent a linguistic and ethnic group in north-western Africa who are largely settled farmers. While they are distinct from the Arabs, both groups share many customs, especially in relation to the horse. Thus much of the following description applies to both Arabs and Berbers in this region. Berbers of the Moroccan Rif and Algerian Kabylia areas, dwelling as they do in mountainous zones, have few horses and keep mules and donkeys instead. Coon says of the Rif that horses are used exclusively for riding and are mostly Barb type. Horses are in their greatest number in the eastern Rif and are rare elsewhere in the Rif because of the rugged terrain. Mules are more common than either donkeys or horses. They are more highly prized because they carry heavier loads and are more surefooted on mountain trails than the horse (Coon, 1931, 38–9). Budgett Meakin also reported that wealthy "Moors" in Morocco prefer mules on account of their smooth pace (Meakin, 67). For riding horses Meakin claimed the military and official classes of early twentieth century Morocco preferred to ride stallions, while the farmers favoured mares (Meakin, 65). Where horses are more plentiful in Morocco, such as in the lowland plains, they along with mules and donkeys, are used to thresh out the grain, to pull carts, and bear packs.

The climatic-geographical conditions in many parts of North Africa are such that horses can be let out to graze on the range far more than is possible in the Sahara or the Arabian Peninsula or the congested Nile Valley. But neither Berbers nor Arabs in North Africa practice the open range maintenance as in Central Asia because a man rarely owns more than one horse and, as such, regularly requires its services. Consequently it must be kept available in the vicinity of the house. If it is put out to graze it is invariably hobbled and taken inside the house compound at night to avoid theft. This system demands more dependence upon stall feeding. Meakin reports that Moroccan horses are fed on straw, barley and beans in season in order to fatten them; they are put out to grass in the spring (Meakin, 65). As among the Bedouin they are treated more like members of the family (Westermarck, II, 283).

Extremely widespread is the belief that the horse is the holiest of animals; it has the greatest concentration of *baraka* or divine grace. The black horse has the most of all, so much that no amulets are necessary to protect it (Westermarck, I, 97). The Mulay Isma'il's horses which had been on the Meccan pilgrimage were so holy they were exempted from all labour including the bearing of the king himself. One who had incurred the king's displeasure assured himself of forgiveness by throwing himself between the legs of these horses (Westermarck, I, 137). Similarly it was believed that by grasping the forelegs of a riderless horse one could command the protection of the owner. Stables – especially those of the Sultan – were places of sacred sanctuary, like a mosque or, in Mediaeval Europe, a church or monastery (Westermarck, I, 520). Oaths might be sworn on one's horse or saddle. In Morocco the 'ar sacrifice is a ritual to force an individual or group to assist the one making the sacrifice. Normally, the sacrifice of a sheep or a goat is sufficient to call forth the desired aid. But under the most awesome conditions a horse might be sacrificed (Westermarck, I, 538).

As horses are the most holy, they are also more sensitive to the evil eye and subject to being defiled by the unclean. Thus, among some Moroccans it is considered bad for the *baraka* for a Jew to ride horseback using a Moorish saddle. A "sexually unclean person"[1] who rode a horse might find himself having trouble or causing trouble to the horse (Westermarck, I, 229–230).

Among some Moroccan tribes when a mare gives birth the event is celebrated on the seventh day like a child's birth; guns are fired off and the owner offers a feast. In one tribe, the Ait Warain, mare's milk is boiled and given to children in the hope that the mare will be prolific. When one purchases a horse the new owner in some areas invites the men of the village to a festive meal and, in others, makes a distribution of food gifts around the village (Westermarck, II, 283–4).

The saddlery and riding style of the Berbers it should be noted does not differ from that of the sedentary Arab population.

The Tuareg are Berber camel herding nomads of the Western Sahara. The camel is their pride and joy even more so than among Arab Bedouin. They do, however, have a breed of horses named Baguezane or Kinaboutout (meaning long penis), famous for its endurance, staying power and speed on hard rocky ground. These are commonly fed camel milk and millet (Doutressoule, 1947).

Horses are nevertheless few among Tuareg and limited to Tuareg nobility. Briggs says that horses were probably never common on the Sahara. He claims they have been given more publicity than their prevalence deserves and their significance to the history of the Sahara has been highly overrated (Briggs, 21). Lhote, on the other hand, has as we have noted already suggested that the Sahara of the first millenium B.C. had been exploited widely by means of the horse. Birket Smith also believes that horses like cattle may once have been more important in the Sahara when the climate was more humid (Birket-Smith, 1960, 133).

Saharan horses have apparently declined in number over the last century. "The Arab nomads around Metlili, Ouargla, and El Golea . . . seem to have had nearly three hundred horses in the middle of the last century, but they have none today. Even the noble Tuareg warriors of the central desert, who apparently never had more than a handful of horses at any time and therefore prized them greatly as symbols of prestige, have had none now for over twenty years" (Briggs, 21). A

[1] Presumably such a person is one who has not performed the ablutions following sexual intercourse as required by Islam. An uncircumcized person would also be unclean in Muslim view.

similar situation obtains in the Spanish Sahara where Robert Adams, in 1810, says that horses were common enough "to be presented as rewards to European captives who accepted conversion to Islam, but there are now almost none left among the northern and central Moors and not many in the south" (Briggs, 223).

THE OSMANLI TURKS OF TURKEY

The largest group of Turks today is that residing in the Anatolian Peninsula, the modern Republic of Turkey. They have been for more than a thousand years separated from their Central Asiatic pastoral roots. As a result of their eventual conquest and settlement of Asia Minor, they adopted many customs of the indigenous Greek population while at the same time introducing Turkish, and some Persian, customs.

The Anatolian Turks are primarily settled peasant peoples engaged in cultivation and to a lesser extent stock rearing. The horse commands only a minor economic position, yet is nevertheless the prestige animal. A Turkish proverb states: "The goat is a devil, the sheep is an angel, the camel is a pilgrim, the horse is a hero" (Szyliowicz, 26). The Turks, as better trained Muslims, no longer eat horseflesh or drink mare's milk or offer horses as funerary sacrifices. Because Turkey is for the most part excellent country for horse breeding and because poverty stricken peasants are often forced by economic circumstances to be more "practical", there are at one and the same time more horses in the country and more that are used for draught purposes than one would find in any Arab nation.

Since most of the horses are small and shabby, their involvement in agriculture is somewhat limited. Until modern times they were universally preferred for threshing out the grain because of their fast and steady pace, but modern technology is beginning to replace them at this task. They are also used for harrowing, for pulling carts and, in towns, still have a role in drawing taxis. They are rarely used for ploughing. Turkish peasants prefer oxen for this purpose and, in lieu of these, believe mules are superior to horses not only for ploughing, but for pulling wagons as well (Kolars, 79). The reason for such beliefs no doubt lies in the fact that oxen are less costly than either horses or mules and, while the purchase price of a mule is as much as twenty-five per cent greater than for a horse, the peasants, like the planters in the southern United States, believe mules require less feed and attention than horses (Kolars, 79). Oxen are likewise far more widely used in stony and hilly parts because they "can be harnessed to the traditional needle plough which is preferred for shallow, rocky soils, where horses cannot be so used" (Kolars, 80). Mountain villages having no roads or wagons also find little need for horses or mules, whereas both of the latter are best suited for the spring-wagons found in more level countryside (Kolars, 80).

The common use of the horse as a riding animal in rural Turkey is now rapidly declining as roads are improved and automobiles become more widespread. They retain their role, however, on festive occasions such as weddings or circumcisions and for purposes of conspicuous display.

The Turks have preserved the Central Asiatic style of riding with short stirrups and extremely bent knee. Their saddles, however, have been modified. Although retaining the basic Central Asiatic pattern of the high pommel and cantle, these are often more pronounced and the saddle in general heavier. Wherever possible a rider desires the most ornate of saddles with embroidered leather or velvet coverings and metal and, even jewel studs on the ball-shaped horn. The extremely colourful *kilim*, the Turkish woollen carpet, is sometimes used on the saddle. Saddles are cinched with a single girth which encompasses both horse and saddle (Vernam, 113). Stirrups are of the shovel-shaped style and bridles are normally equipped with curb type bits. This Turkish saddlery, which does not vary much from the Persian, was diffused among the town and village dwelling Arabs and Berbers, among whom it now prevails.

Whips and spurs are seldom used, a rider controlling his horse by voice and knee pressure and through the bit. Berenger reports Turks riding with a three foot long stick held in the middle so that the rider can tap his mount on right or left side to direct him (Berenger, 130). He does not tell us if the rider also has a guide rope around the animal's neck or a rein of some kind. For the modern Middle East, this fashion of riding with a stick as the only control is restricted to donkeys.

As a general rule, Turkish horses are not well kept; they are often stunted and poorly fed. But again this must be seen in its appropriate context of rural poverty. Since a family rarely has more than one horse it is, especially at certain seasons, in daily demand so that it is kept near the house often in hobbles or stabled in a barn. When working it is hand fed, as is typical of the Middle East. The feed, however, usually consists of straw and a little bran, occasionally vetch.

In a village in central Anatolia Stirling reported that a government veterinary service annually brought two stallions, one of French farm stock and one Arab, to serve the village mares. The villagers appreciated this and sold their colts at a good price, while the government had intended that they should be kept to upgrade local stock (Stirling, 77).

KURDS, PERSIANS AND AFGHANS

In a broad band from south-eastern Turkey and northern Iraq, across Iran and central Afghanistan to the north-western parts of Pakistan, reside several closely related Indo-Iranian peoples. The Kurds dwell in the mountainous area in the western extemities, the Farsi or Persians predominate in Iran and the Pashto or Pathans in central Afghanistan and north-western Pakistan. South of them in the desert of southern Afghanistan and western Pakistan are the camel herding, nomadic Baluchi.

Throughout this area horses are prestige animals and have minimal economic value. They are owned by wealthier individuals and important tribal and political figures and, as a general rule, with the exception of the Baluchi, there is a higher proportion of horses per capita among the nomadic populations than among the sedentary villagers or townsmen.

Horses are primarily riding animals, but especially among grain cultivating Afghans, as among the Turks, they are prized for threshing out the wheat. Nomads employ them as pack animals and in Afghanistan, where pony pack trains have survived to modern times, one breed of small tough pony is noted for its ability to bear great loads (Elphinstone, 142). Universally horses are an important part of festivities and

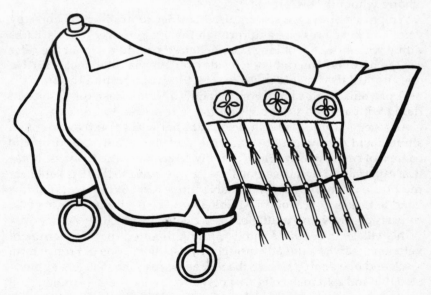

SULIMANIYYA KURDISH SADDLE
From Tweedie

sport. The nomadic Papis, Persian speaking nomads of the western Iranian province of Luristan, perform the fantasia, particularly at weddings (Feilberg, 67). This, it will be recalled is also characteristic of Arabs. Horse racing is most common. Hunting on horseback is a favourite sport of nomadic peoples and of the Afghans in general, among whom a chase is organized involving large numbers on horseback and on foot (Elphinstone, 237). The Afghans have also adopted the Turkic game of *buzkashi*. In Pathan villages in Pakistan horses are sometimes used to draw carts, but are otherwise only used by landlords for riding to the fields to supervise labour, or in sport.

In most parts of this region horses are hobbled and put out to graze. The Papi sometimes tie a leg of the animal to a heavy stone and they and others in more wooded or grassy places turn horses out to graze freely when they are not wanted. Feilberg says the Papi sometimes spend long hours searching for them when they wish to use them (Feilberg, 63). Horses are rarely stabled except for the herds of royalty. In Iran the Turkmen practice of covering a horse with felt blankets is apparently not uncommon among some of the Iranians. Hand feeding of horses with barley and chopped straw occurs when animals are being worked and in the arid zones such as Baluchistan as a regular necessity.

PAPI SADDLE COMMON TO WESTERN IRAN
From Feilberg, 65

Note shovel-shaped stirrups, crupper and pommel which is higher than the cantle.

Iran and Afghanistan encompass many ancient important horse breeding areas. The Kurds reside in parts of what was once the ancient Kingdom of Urartu and the Papi and other Iranians, in western Iran, but horse breeding in these places is today only a shadow of what it once was in Assyrian times, primarily because horses are no longer in economic demand for military purposes. It is also likely that ecological changes during the past two or three thousand years have made these localities less suitable for horse production. The north-eastern part of Afghanistan is the area of old Bactria and, inhabited now by Uzbeks and other Turkic peoples, it remains the most important horse breeding area of that country. Indeed, horses are most numerous among the Turkic people and in the Hindu Kush district of Afghanistan; in southern Afghanistan they are replaced by the ass and to a lesser extent the mule (Humlum, 272–3). In Iran, too, horses tend to prevail over other equines among nomadic peoples whereas in the agricultural villages the donkey is far more important. Fredrik Barth reports one small Kurdish village in northern Iraq of ten households and fifty one people as having twenty-one oxen, twenty-six cows, one hundred and fifty sheep and goats, ten donkeys and two horses – both owned by the richest men of the village (Barth, 1953, 19).

In Iran and Afghanistan three riding gaits are most popular: the walk, amble and gallop. The trot is also found. Short stirrup leathers and bent knee style of riding is universal and, severe curbs are prevalent among Kurds and Iranians. In Afghanistan two types of riding gear are used: that of the Iranian and that of the Turkic, especially Uzbek. Usually the more severe type of bit is associated with the former, and a plain snaffle with the latter (Elphinstone, 241). Elphinstone describes the Iranian saddlery as follows:

"The Persian bridle is a sort of snaffle, which instead of cheeks, has two (or four) large rings passed through holes in the ends of the snaffle, to receive the reins. The snaffle itself sometimes has sharp points to prick the horse's mouth when he pulls. The bridle is adorned with silver chains and other ornaments. The saddle sits near the horse's back, but rises much both before and behind, . . . but the peaks are generally so close, as to make it extremely uncomfortable to those who are not used to it. The peak in front is the highest of the two, and is composed of painted wood, gold and silver curiously embossed, or gold enamelled, according to the circumstances of the owner" (Elphinstone, 241).

In contrast "the Uzbek snaffle is exactly like our own, except that the cheeks are larger in proportion. The headstall is ornamented with a few gold or silver studs at the joinings, and there is an ornament like a flower de luce of the same material in the angle between the nose-band

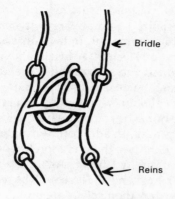

ARAB RING TYPE BIT
From Tweedie

and the cheek-band. There is no band across the forehead. The reins both of the Uzbek and Persian bridles are narrow and very neat." They are of brown and sometimes of green shagreen leather. Martingales are not frequent; when worn they are very loose and the reins fastened to the cheeks of the bit are not run through the martingale. There is also a breast band and generally, a crupper. The Uzbek saddle rises high above the horse's back, is much larger and more commodious than the Persian and not so high in cantle or pommel. "The peak in front is divided and turns down, so as to form two curls like Ionic volutes. Neither of these saddles is stuffed below, both are placed on two or three thick blankets or felts, and tied by a girth which passes through two holes in the lower part of the tree" (Elphinstone, 241).

The commonest stirrups are "like our own, except that the ends of the arch are prolonged beyond the bar on which the foot rests; another, not uncommon, has a flat plate of iron nine inches long, and four to five inches broad . . ." (Elphinstone, 242).

Apparently, horses ridden by nineteenth century Afghan aristocracy were led by mounted grooms and "when the master dismounts at a strange house, the groom mounts his horse till he has finished his visit: this they think good for the horse" (Elphinstone, 242).

Besides their Persian type riding saddles the Papis also ride on their pack saddles. These consist of two pieces of wool stuffed with hay forming a "long sausage like roll" which is placed on the horse's back hanging down on either side (Feilberg, 67).

Kurdish saddles are very flat on top, are covered with straw and padded with blankets. According to Dodge a Kurdish horseman frequently kept his mount saddled day and night, hardly removing it except occasionally to dry off the animal's back (Dodge, 383).

In the Middle East – from Morocco to Afghanistan – we have seen that the horse is a highly specialized animal, largely reserved for the more well to do, in part as a military mount, today, more as a sporting animal. This results from numerous factors: Arid climatic conditions in much of the area are not conducive to ease of horse breeding. Where good rearing conditions do exist, horses are used for more "common" purposes. Nevertheless, cultural values – religious and secular ideology – have been such that the horse has never been considered proper food – either for its meat or its milk. In addition, throughout, even in districts most conducive to the horse, there is a preference for oxen, buffalo or mules for heavy draught labour. For many it is almost shameful to employ horses for such ends. Horses will be used for more common draught work where they themselves are broken-down nags and rejects for riding, or where poverty-stricken owners, desiring a horse as a prestige symbol, must nevertheless put it to practical use, or where European influences – especially French influence in North Africa – have resulted in the employment of the horse as a farm draught animal.

The limited number of horses results in their more continued and frequent use. This, coupled with the generally poor grazing conditions, entails their being kept close to habitations and being more often hand fed.

Universally throughout the area a single riding style, with short stirrups and bent knee prevails, and in the eastern parts of Iran and Afghanistan there is much more frequency of the ambling gait. Except where Central Asiatic influence is evident, as in Afghanistan and north-eastern Iran, snaffle bits are not employed; rather there is a preference for severe curb type bits and, among Bedouin Arabs, the nose band. Similarly, saddlery ranges from the high pommels and cantles and big square stirrups found among most Middle Eastern people to the Bedouin Arab preference for a pad saddle often with no stirrups at all. The importance of this area in the last thousand or so years to horsemanship has primarily been in its effect upon Spanish horsemanship which in turn as a Hispano-Arab complex was transported to America and became a major cornerstone of the cattle ranching industry.

XII

The Horse in Sub-Saharan Africa

OUTSIDE the Arab and Berber areas of Africa the horse has never been of any importance except in Ethiopia, the Western Sudanic zone and, in recent times, in Southern Africa where it was introduced by Europeans and has largely been maintained by them. For the most part the horse has been one of the more recently introduced domestic animals in Sub-Saharan Africa, and, wherever adopted by the indigenous population, has always been a luxury and prestige animal. A considerable part of Africa is totally inhospitable to the horse, including the coastal area of West Africa and the great Congo Basin. This is in part because of the prevalence of the tsetse fly which carries sleeping sickness and ultimate death for horses as well as most cattle. Also this is a tropical rain forest which is poor horse rearing country. The accompanying map indicates the distribution of horses in Africa and distinctly shows, by implication, the areas of tsetse fly infestation. Excluding areas of European habitation, we may discuss three regions of horse husbandry in Africa south of the Sahara: Sudanic, Ethiopian and South African.

THE SUDANIC REGION

The Sudanic region is a grassy steppe whose northern limit is the Sahara while in the south the zone gradually becomes more forested and eventually confronts the tropical rain forest. The Atlantic Ocean delimits the area on the west and the Upper Nile on the east.

There is some question about the introduction of horses into this region. One view is that about the tenth century the Zaghawa from western Darfur and eastern Chad brought some along in their conquests of the western Sudan (Bovill, 221). But Fisher has recently argued that the Zaghawa were mostly camel herders who enlarged their stock of horses on moving west because horses were already there and also because horses were better suited than camels to the Sudan. He links the introduction of the horse with the much earlier trans-Saharan records of horse chariotry in rock art (Fisher, 1972). It does appear somewhat unusual that the horse which had obviously spread to the very heart of the Sahara in the first millenium B.C. would not have passed further to the south to the more fertile western Sudan

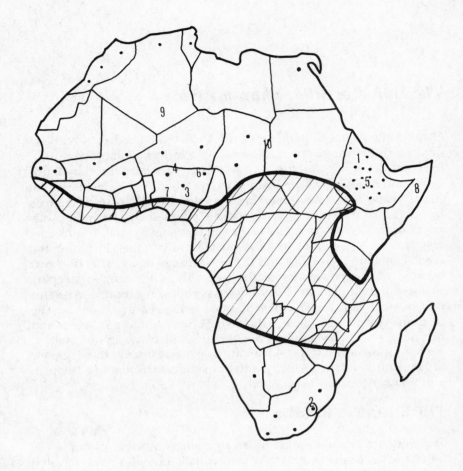

THE DISTRIBUTION OF HORSES IN
PRESENT DAY AFRICA

One dot equals 100,000 horses

 Approximate area where horses are absent

LOCATION OF PEOPLES MENTIONED IN TEXT

1 Amhara	6 Hausa
2 Basuto or Sotho	7 Nupe
3 Bauchi Plateau Peoples	8 Somali
4 Fulani	9 Tuareg
5 Galla	10 Zaghawa

long before the tenth century A.D.

Epstein has noted the distribution of horse breeds in Sudanic west Africa and believes they suggest two different points of origin of the horse in this area. The Fulani introduced the Dongola horse from what is today the Republic of Sudan into western Africa in the thirteenth century and most of the horses, particularly those of the Fulani and Hausa, are mainly Dongola or derived from the Dongola breed (Epstein, 1971a, 453–456). Thus here the presently prevailing breed of horses originates in approximately the same territory as the Zaghawa tribe. Horses of Senegal, Mauritania and immediately adjacent areas, however, are of the Barb breed, clearly pointing to Morocco as the source of horses in this region (Epstein, 1971a, 446–448). Still, both of these breeds represent post-Islamic introductions into West Africa. They are not then the first horses in these parts.

Law, for example, contends that there are two equine periods in West Africa. The first occurred before the fourteenth century and was characterized by the prevalence of small pony-sized horses, possibly ridden without a saddle or stirrups or even a bit, in the Numidian style. In this period horses were of little importance because of their limited effectiveness as cavalry mounts. During the fourteenth century larger horses become the rule and their employment is coupled with the use of the saddle, stirrups, bits and armour. As a consequence, cavalry acquired some significance (Law, R., 116ff.). The date of the fourteenth century for the prevalence of larger horses does not quite square with a presumed thirteenth century introduction of Dongola horses or possibly an earlier introduction of Barbs –both of these breeds being full-sized horses.

It has been argued that the horse in west Africa "made possible the concentration of military force at short notice against foot-bound peasantries, rapid communication of orders from capital to province, and the penetration of uncontrolled areas for slave raiding. Displays of horse riding on ceremonial occasions, the mounting with elaborate trappings of the chief and his emissaries which remain so characteristic today among all these peoples from the Mandingka to Bornu, are not meaningless ostentations, they remain symbols of authority expressed in what was once the key to power over this vast region" (Forde, 1969, 131). Fisher is of the opinion that "the contribution of the horse to state formation and maintenance" was less in purely military activity "than in conspicuous consumption – witching the world, like Henry IV, with noble horsemanship – in facilities for escape and in slaving" (Fisher, 367). Fisher seems to suggest that the horse's role in conquest in the western Sudan was something like its role in the Spanish conquest of America. Cortez and his Conquistadores soon discovered the Amerindians were terrified of their huge beasts and so they capitalized on this as a major vehicle of ultimate conquest.

Partly because western Sudanese kingdoms possessed a weaker economic base, their cavalries were never of the heavy type. Indeed, Fisher states that light cavalry is more suited to hot, dry climate (Fisher, 1973, 360). Cavaliers wore coats of chain mail, kapok or Koranic leather charms, and carried stabbing spears and light swords. The advantage of cavalry was in raiding and in attacks upon pedestrian soldiers (Goody, 35). Fisher finds for the central Sudan little evidence for Goody's claim that horses were only a means of transport to the battlefield (Fisher, 1973, 361 and Goody, 47). As in Mediaeval European armies, the existence of cavalry produced sharply defined strata: the mounted and the foot soldiers. The mounted force, because of its prolonged training and the expense of maintaining and acquiring horses also developed "ideas of nobility and knightly ethic" (Goody, 37).

Law contends that the chief constraining factor on the centralization of military power in the cavalry states of West Africa was not the cost of purchasing horses so much as the expense of upkeep. In West Africa horses rarely grazed on pasture. Rather they were kept in stables in the towns and fed on hay and grain. Presumably this gave greater protection against tsetse flies as well as human predators. Even with the aid of taxes and booty the ruler alone could not afford the expense of maintaining all of the mounts necessary for cavalry use. Thus, he exacted tribute in the form of horse feed and, more important, he distributed animals to the nobility for maintenance (Law, R., 127ff.). Consequently the savannah cavalry-using states were oligarchic as Aristotle would have predicted (Aristotle, 1321a). They were what Goody has called "mass dynasties within segments of which high office often circulated." The "mass dynasty" comprised the cavalry controlling nobility.

The savannah states were said to have arisen "on the backs of horses" (Goody, 49, footnote). "The founding ancestor of the Mossi kingdom of Wagadugu was . . . known as 'the red stallion' and the same surname of Wedroago is still common today among Mossi of the ruling estate" (Goody, 67). Most of these savannah states were founded by immigrant horsemen, often from the north, who established a dominant position over lands of peasant farmers. However, some horse-slave traders were able to ennoble themselves by their trading activities and to build cavalry based states. As Goody says, this is a case of the Yahoos being ennobled by the Houyhnhnms (Goody, 69, footnote.)

Horses and slaves were closely interrelated in these states. The slaves provided a work force for the considerable labour necessary for attending to the horses, but they were most significant as the means of exchange for acquiring more horses. Because of the extent of tsetse fly and other limitations of tropical climate it was necessary to import numbers of horses and all the best ones. Thus a great trade in horses emerged across the Sahara. Caravans included horses taken from Barbary to the Sudan. The ruler of Timbuctoo, who had 3000 horsemen as a cavalry, purchased the best horse from each caravan passing through because he did not raise any of his own (Bovill, 126–7). But horses were a distinct problem on caravans, because of their water demands among other things. G.F. Lyon is quoted by Bovill as saying:"[H]orses generally occasion more trouble to a caravan than anything else" (Bovill, 43). But horses do seem to have been used on some caravans, not only as riding animals for well-to-do merchants, but also for pack purposes. Fisher reports pack horses being used by the traders from Kuka on expeditions to Adamawa, Bagirmi, Kano, and Zinder (Fisher, 1973, 368).

Leo Africanus claimed that horses brought in from Europe for ten ducats were sold again for forty to fifty ducats at Gao, capital of Songhoi on the Upper Niger (Bovill, 129). In Bornu, where they had an excess of slaves due to the constant warfare with weaker neighbours, horses were paid for at the rate of fifteen to twenty slaves per horse (Bovill, 130).

The extent of the tsetse fly and of forests meant that the cavalry-using savannah kingdoms were unable to extend their empires into the forest zone. It meant, further, that kingdoms established in those zones lacked horses in sufficient numbers to establish cavalries. Consequently they organized armies of pedestrians much more cheaply. The acquisition of firearms provided them as well with a military base different from that of the savannah cavalry-using kingdoms. Firearms, once acquired in the forest kingdoms, were placed under the control of the centralized power and slaves and prisoners were employed to man them. Thus these kingdoms were able to maintain "narrower" dynasties with a more autocratic supreme ruler (Goody, 55).

Apart from the horse-based savannah kingdoms and the eventually gun-based forest kingdoms there were also in West Africa many peoples attached to "acephalous" societies. These were highly decentralized, primarily kin based societies in which the power of any one individual was extremely limited and circumscribed. They are sometimes referred to as "chiefless" societies or "tribes without rulers" – a form of functioning anarchy. Such societies lacked the organizational base for either supporting or establishing cavalry; they relied upon the bow and arrow – the "democratic" weapon since it can readily be manufactured and owned by anyone. They were also the chief objects of raids by savannah horsemen. Out of this situation emerged a contrast between invading horsemen and autochthonous pedestrian peasants who soon came to identify the horse with their enemy. Such identification became expressed for example in Gonja, northern Ghana, in various ritual taboos against horses. Particularly, the horse was forbidden to enter the precincts of the shrines dedicated to the Earth in its mystical aspect; this invariably meant as well the entire towns which housed such shrines (Goody, 66ff.). Among the Tallensi of Ghana a "major cleavage" exists within the society between the Namoos, presumably an offshoot from "the horsed invaders who established the Mossi-Dagamba states" and the Talis, "the 'indigenous' agriculturalists, linked with the earth and its shrines." Priests of the Earth cult may not ride horses while chiefs and their clansmen may (Goody, 63–4).

It would appear then that in the western Sudan the identification of the horse with an invading ruling elite was abetted largely by the difficulty in raising and keeping horses and by their limited and specialized role. Under West African ecological conditions horse keeping was especially fostered by an oligarchic state in which surpluses in wealth allowed for a special class of equestrian aristorcrats who alone had horses. But possibly, as Fisher writes, horses were cheaper and more common in the more eastern parts of the Sudanic zone. Hence they were less restricted to a nobility (Fisher, 1973, 372). Subject peoples in West Africa with acephalous social systems could not support such beasts. Because of this and because they were subjected to assault by northern horsemen of the savannah they developed an *anti*-horse complex. This reaction to the horse contrasts with what seems to have happened in most other parts of the earth where those defeated by horsemen themselves therefore sought to acquire and use horses.

The role of the horse among the Sudanic peoples has not been different from that of the Arabs and Berbers to the north. It seems fair to say that, regardless of how horses were introduced, the present horse complex is that of the Arabs, complete, from the conception of the aristocratic role of the horse, to riding style, riding gear, and care and management based on hand feeding rather than open range. If the Hausa are at all exemplary, even the terminology for riding gear is derived from Arabic (Law, R., 116).

The main concentrations of horses in the present day western Sudan are among Fulani, Kanuri, the Tibbus of northern Chad and the peoples of the Senegalese Republic. Among these several peoples there is about one horse for every twenty to twenty-five persons. The horse is also not uncommon among Hausa, Mossi, and those Tuaregs who inhabit the edge of the area – about one horse per fifty to one hundred persons. Probably ninety per cent of the million or so horses in West Africa and the western Sudan are owned by these various people. Elsewhere they are extremely rare or non-existent.

The Fulani are scattered through the western Sudan in a narrow band extending from Senegal to Lake Chad. Numbering about seven million, they are divided between a sedentary village population, which engages in hoe cultivation, and a pastoral nomadic cattle herding population. Fulani exhibit at least one interesting atypical feature. That is, the sedentary farming population was traditionally the primary force behind the aggressive, expansionist Fulani empire, while the pastoralists have been peaceable by comparison. Ordinarily one would predict the reverse to be the case. Nomads and villagers have developed a symbiotic interdependent relationship and among some of the Fulani nomads this kind of a relationship exists with Hausa and other non-Fulani agriculturalists. The Fulani have a patrilinieal tribal structure and are now largely Muslim.

According to Stenning about one adult male in five owns a horse. It is not clear whether he is referring to all Fulani or only the pastoral segment (Stenning, 375). Unlike American cattlemen, the Fulani are pedestrian herders and the horse has no place in the everyday work life of the people. Cattle herds are small enough – with an ordinary family owning fifty or so head – that the cattle can have sufficient personal attention from their masters so that they are used to being handled. Thus, they are docile and readily managed on foot. Furthermore, like the cattle of most African pastoralists they are kept primarily for their milk supply and, thus, must be easily and readily handled on foot. In the last century horses had a role in the cavalry of the Fulani empire. Today they remain as symbols of the past tradition, of aristocracy and wealth. Yet Stenning writes, "A well turned out 'cavalier' is nowadays an anomaly worthy of suspicion" (Stenning, 375). Such a man spends too much time on frills. Horses and saddlery are luxuries for which a man should never sell cattle (Stenning, 375).

Fulani riding gear, like that of the other western Sudanese is modelled after the pattern common to North African Arab towns and villages. The saddle has a high pommel and cantle and is placed on saddle pads, "the topmost of which is highly decorated" (Stenning, 375). Arab style curb bits – usually of the ring type – are characteristic, as are shovel shaped stirrups, the sharp corners of which are used as spurs. A few Fulani have quilted horse armour, even chain mail, which is displayed on ceremonial occasions. "Harness is made of traditionally worked leather, which, because it is inadequately dressed and receives much hard use, is continually breaking" (Stennign, 375). "Men like to own horses and saddlery and weapons, but cannot afford to maintain them; on close inspection they appear old or shoddy or unreliable – and Fulani men are well aware of this"(Stenning, 375).

Speaking of Northern Nigerians without specifying which people, Trench claims they are "perhaps the best African horsemen." They are the only Africans who have taken to polo (Trench, 208).

The Hausa, who are sedentary village farming people and Muslims, for the most part, also keep horses and the horse is a man's pride, although donkeys are the main means of local transportation (Smith, M.G., 124).

The Hausa keep horses for the same reasons as the Fulani and have the same style of riding and horse husbandry and gear. There are a few Hausa and related peoples who have adopted the practice of eating horse flesh. These include the Warjawa Maguza, a mainly pagan people of the Chadic language family, the Ngizim (Bede), a Hausa people who are also predominantly pagan, and the Bassa, Bantoid pagans of the Nigerian Plateau south of the Benue River. If horse meat is eaten by these people it cannot be a very common part of their diet since the number of horses is quite small among them.

In central Nigeria, northern Cameroons, Upper Volta and Guinea a few horses are found, but they are of even less significance than among the peoples immediately to the north. In the central Nigerian Plateau riding with a minimum of saddlery seems to be widespread. The Jukun, who presumably once had more horses than the handful they now own, rode without bits and usually bareback. Several other peoples are reported in Temple's *Notes* as riding in this fashion. The use of some type of noseband and of one rein only appears common (Temple, 254, 269, 280). Another observer adds that people in the Bauchi Plateau frequently own horses and treat them as an American pampers his dog (Wilson, James, 84).

A most fantastic custom is reported for some of the Bauchi Plateau dwellers, including the Angass, Mama and Moroa. They are reported to slit the skin on the backs of their ponies so that calloused pads form to make a "natural saddle" (Temple, 269, 280). Some writers, including Fisher (376), have made the practice more incredible by suggesting that on slitting the back the rider sat on the bleeding flesh so as to glue himself on the horse. As Law has noted this is a misunderstanding of the purpose of the operation (Law, R.). It is also unlikely that anyone could glue himself onto a horse in this fashion.

Along central Nigerians such as the Nupe or Guang, Muslim royal families and aristocracies rule over largely pagan populations and in these cases the horse is very closely associated with the ruling class as a prime symbol of superior status. The Nupe king appears on horseback on all state occasions and for anyone to appear on horseback at any official occasion is a prerogative of rank (Nadel, 124). The Nupe do not ordinarily breed horses but purchase them from Hausa traders (Nadel, 204).

In the Sudanic region the horse has little practical economic importance. While many people are pastoralists they have traditionally herded stock on foot and kept them for milk. So they maintained highly docile herds. Thus, no one would think of herding by horseback; nor would the local population have any model for such a practice from elsewhere. The horse never developed here as a cart animal simply because the cart was never a part of traditional culture and when the horse was introduced it was as a riding animal; no carts accompanied the caravans across the desert. The same may be said regarding harrowing and ploughing. West African agriculture has been horticulture – cultivation with the iron hoe; the plough, the harrow and farm draught animals were traditionally absent. Fisher has shown that the Sudanic horses were not purely military animals. They had a limited use as pack animals; they were often important to governments for rapid communication. Occasionally, hunting parties embarked on horseback. Horses were especially important in trading slaves, in making tribute payments and sometimes for alms giving. They were passed from hand to hand and used in the workaday world "with no more dignity," writes Fisher of the central Sudan, "than slaves, sometimes like slaves reduced to bearing burdens, even suffering the indignity of being eaten." Their moment of glory was in ceremony and circuses wherein they, like their riders, in the course of events became accustomed to noise, confusion and other conditions which stimulate the battlefield (Fisher, 1973, 377). Nevertheless, despite Fisher's somewhat disparaging remarks, the horse did retain the position of the aristocrat among animals.

ETHIOPIA

Nearly all horses in Ethiopia are owned by the two major ethnic groups in the country: the politically dominant Amhara who are Coptic Christians and Semites living in the highland heartland of the country, and the Galla, a mixed Muslim, Christian and pagan people speaking a Cushitic language and living south of the Amhara. The Galla as well as the Danakil and Somali minorities are strongly pastoral in their ways of life, the Amhara less so.

Ethiopia leads all other African countries in numbers of horses, sheep, cattle and goats. In addition, she accounts for over half of the mules in Africa and about a third of all the donkeys and horses in that continent. She easily ranks among the dozen chief equine breeding areas of the world.

The Amhara

Among the Amhara the horse is viewed more as a mount for the young aristocrat or would-be aristocrat, to be used in games and for conspicuous display and, until recently, for warfare. But most Amhara, especially travellers and elderly people, prefer mules because of their surefootedness and even, often ambling pace. Dent quotes a "recent English traveller" as saying "No Ethiopian gentleman would be seen riding a horse" (Dent, 121). Mules are also preferred as the animal of honour ridden by the veiled bride when she is taken to her bridegroom's hamlet. If it can be afforded a white Senaar mule is most desirable for the bridal procession. Such mules are as big as Ethiopian horses and are bred from an Arab-Senaar jack and an Ethiopian mare. The Amhara peasant often owns a mule, while a large landowner owns several. The latter are frequently rented out to caravans or to one's relatives.

Dent believes the priority of the status of the mule among the Amhara derives from their ancient Hebraic cultural ties (Dent, 122). The Ethiopian emperor bore the title, "Lion of Judah" and claimed descent from Solomon and Sheba. In addition, Ethiopian Coptic Christianity incorporates numerous old Hebraic rituals and beliefs not found elsewhere in Christendom. It could be then that the esteem for the mule is another part of this cultural complex which, if not specifically Hebrew, is at least ancient Semitic-Arabian. On the other hand, a more practical explanation for the preference for mules over horses may be that they are a better and more secure mount in the difficult terrain of the Ethiopian Highlands. The Ethiopian horses are small, often pony-sized. While they are wiry and surefooted, according to Rey they are exceedingly nervous and shy easily (Rey, 253). Such characteristics, despite their presumed surefootedness would seem to detract from their desirability on a mountain trail. In the mountains of Morocco there is a preference for mules, especially by the older and more distinguished gentlemen, but such a preference has no relationship to any ancient Hebraic mystique; it results from experience. One gets the impression that the Amhara view of the horse has some parallel to the attitude of most middle aged or elderly Americans towards motor cycles and sports cars – playthings for the young and the show-offs.

Riding animals remain the primary means of transportation in a country such as Ethiopia where there are few roads and where the terrain is rough and mountainous. Because of these factors horse-drawn vehicles are a relative rarity and a recent innovation (Lipsky, 254). They were hardly introduced before they began to be superseded by motorized vehicles.

Apparently livestock is given only minimal attention by the Amhara, a factor which no doubt relates to their more agricultural orientation. The Amhara consider it somewhat inappropriate for a grown man to tend cattle – a job which should be the responsibility of small boys seven or eight years old. Nevertheless cattle are a measure of wealth and the Amhara terms for cattle and wealth are the same (Messing, 123).

Open range grazing is most common since there are few fences. Mixed herds of cattle, horses, sheep and goats are left in the care of young boys and one often sees a number of cattle and horses wandering in the centre of a town in the "thick of automobile traffic, heedless of and unheeded by the municipal police" (Luther, 85). During the rainy season horses are sometimes stabled in the huts of their owners and Rey claims that the smoke from the fires permanently injures their sight (Rey, 254). He further notes that the Ethiopians are not fond of their animals, regarding the horses and mules purely as means of transportation. Nevertheless they are "extremely averse to killing mules or horses for 'religious reasons'", so that diseased animals are usually left to die (Rey, 254).

Despite the rocky and rough terrain, horses are never shod. The traditional rural nobles ride barefoot with iron ring, big toe stirrups derived from India. Bits are invariably of a severe curb type, so that the rider may readily control his mount with his little finger which is passed through a small leather loop fixed to the rein.

Ethiopian saddles, frequently ornamented with silver and gold, have high pommel and cantle with the saddle tree covered with cowhide. Saddles are manufactured by a specialized endogamous caste known as the Faqi.

A century ago Parkyns described the Ethiopian horseman: "Most men pretending to anything like gentility are possessed of [a mule or a horse], or one of each of these animals. The horse is never used on the road, but led before his master, like the war-horse of an ancient knight, while the owner follows on an ambling mule. The price of a mule sometimes exceeds that of a horse. Dejatch Oubi had one that cost 120 dollars, or about £25. The ordinary mule for carrying baggage costs at Adoua about 8 or 10 dollars, while a good ambler may be bought for about 30. In like manner, a horse may be bought for 5 or 6 dollars; a good one will cost 50 to 70; but the price rarely exceeds 100. The horse's head-stall is of white or red leather: a strap, ornamented with circular plates of brass, is placed down his forehead and nose, reaching from his forelock to his nostril . . .. The plates gradually increase in size downwards, the smallest (which is the highest up on the string) being of the size of a crown-piece, or thereabouts, while the one on the nose is perhaps three inches in diameter. Each of them has a brass spike protruding from its centre. The bridle is usually of round plaited leather, nearly an inch in diameter, and covered with scarlet cloth. Like many of the Oriental nations, the Abyssinians have no idea of handling the rein as we do, but merely guide or stop their horses by means of a small leather loop, fixed on the clumsy rein and through which the little finger is passed. The horse's throat is slung round with a set of eight fine copper chains (to which hangs a small bell), and occasionally with a broad set of leathern charms, alternately red and green. The saddles most esteemed are those made in some of the Galla countries. They are of wood, and covered with untanned leather. The pommel and cantle are very high, Arab fashion: the former is furnished with a large knob, which, however, protrudes inwards instead of outwards, thereby endangering the stomach of an awkward rider. The saddle is covered with a shabracque of scarlet cloth, the swallow tails of which hang straight downwards till they nearly touch the ground. By way of stirrups, the Abyssinians use small iron rings, through which the great toe, or at most, the two first toes, are passed.

"The mule's furniture nearly resembles that of the horse: there is a slight difference in the shape of the saddle, and the shabracque is made of leather instead of cloth. Round the neck they wear a 'soullissy', or a band of leather thongs; to this, by means of small chains, are appended a large number of brass plates, the jingling of which makes a pretty noise when the animal is ambling" (Parkyns, 248).

Parkyn's description suggests the Arab influence in the saddle; it also suggests Portuguese influences. The use of the small loop in the reins as a place for the little finger is similar to the style found among ranchers of northern Brazil (Riviere, 50). Brazil, of course, was colonized by the Portuguese and the latter attempted to make a foothold in Ethiopia in the early sixteenth century. Besides the use of this rein ring, the severe curb bit and practice of leading the horse while the master rides after on an ambling mule, just as the Mediaeval knight rode after his charger on an ambling palfrey, are also no doubt of Portuguese origin, especially so, since the Portuguese were one of the few peoples to preserve the basic pattern of Mediaeval style horsemanship. It is usually suggested that the big toe stirrups were introduced to Ethiopia directly by their Indian inventors, but it is also possible that as the

Portuguese carried these from India to Brazil, so they may have also brought them to Ethiopia. In any case, Ethiopian gear is made up of a congeries of Portuguese-Mediaeval, Arab and Indian elements.

The Galla

Like the Fulani, the Galla too are pedestrian herders, but more Galla tribes kept larger numbers of horses. The typical Galla social system possesses a distinct egalitarian and "democratic" quality based as it is upon an elaborate age grading system by which male members of a tribe graduate with fellow class mates through a series of grades, each associated with a specific range of ages and with defined duties and responsibilities. As a result every male can expect to have responsibility in tribal affairs sometime during his life; every male can anticipate becoming a sort of yeoman knight during part of his career.

The horse was not only readily adapted to this role but also to the Galla geographical environment as well. Thus, once introduced by the Amhara between 1554–1562 it spread rapidly among the Galla and became an important male status symbol. But the horse did not become equally important among all Galla peoples. Thus, southern Galla (the Arusi, Bararetta, Boran and Rendele) each had numbers of horses while they were considerably less common among northern Galla. There is some tendency for the more nomadic, savannah Galla to have the larger number of horses. The Arusi Highlands constitute one of the major centres of horse production in Ethiopia. For the Arusi it is important for every man to have a horse and until modern times it was considered dishonourable for a man not to have one (Haberland, 360).

For Galla in general the horse has been a prestigious animal. "So high in their estimation is the horse that people give themselves names derived from their war-horse, such as Abba-Jifar, 'father, i.e., owner, of a dappled horse'" (Huntingford, 26). Killing a horse was punishable, as with a man, by death and "in the scale of murder values a horseman was worth two foot soldiers" (Huntingford, 26). But in recent decades this position of the horse had declined as the mule has acquired pre-eminence presumably because of Amhara influence (Lewis, 53).

Galla horses are largely Dongola-Oriental crossbreds, small and "common looking, rather slow and lazy" (Trench, 207). They do not maintain any sustained gallop (Haberland, 66), but what they may lack in speed they gain in hardiness and the ability to go for long periods with minimum amounts of water and feed (Trench, 207). Yet another observer reported of Galla horses one hundred years ago that they

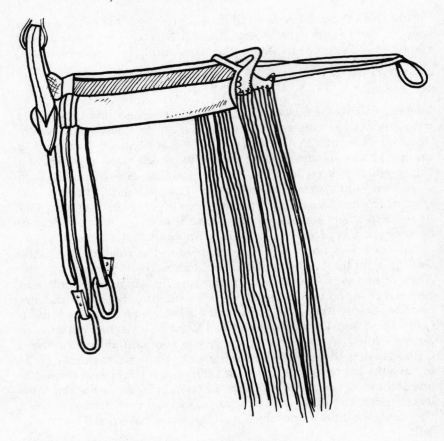

Saddle with crupper and stirrups
and decorative strips of leather

GALLA RIDING GEAR
From Haberland

Saddled Horse

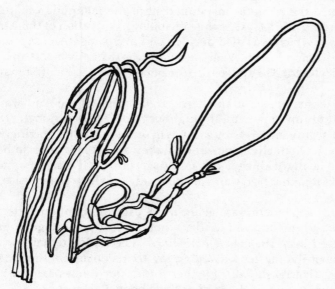

Curb, headstall, bit and reins

were "quite good horses, capable of both speed and extended activity" (Lewis, 53). Colts reared among the Galla are said to be of superior quality.

Galla custom forbids the use of horses for agriculture and they are restricted to riding. Today this amounts to providing a means of transportation whereas in the past they had a crucial military role as part of tribal cavalry. For many Galla hunting from horseback is still important. Thus, the Boran have some note as mounted giraffe hunters. They ride down and spear giraffes like pig stickers, only with less danger. They are said also to train their horses to eat giraffe meat when the grazing is scarce (Trench, 207).

Among the equestrian games played among the Amhara and adopted from them by the Galla is *guks* or *gugs*. A playing field about a kilometer in length is marked off. Players and horses are dressed in festive attire, each player having a round shield and carrying a wooden lance, usually of bamboo, with a rounded or blunted end to prevent serious injury. The aim of the game is for a rider to chase other riders and throw his lance at one of them. That player may ward off the on-coming lance with his shield or attempt to catch it in mid air and wheel his horse around giving pusuit to the one who threw it. Among the Galla violence in the game is strictly frowned upon and there should be no revenge if one is hit by a flying lance. If a player falls from his horse the game is suspended until the fallen man is helped up (Haberland, 535). *Guks* seems obvioulsy a derivation of the Arab game of *el jerid* which was also once played in Spanish America under the name of *canas*. Here as well the object was to hurl canes at an opposing player who tried to dodge them or catch them in the air (Graham, 1949, 18).

Horse management and care parallels that of the Amhara. Horses are left to run in pasture throughout the year. Occasionally they may be fed scanty amounts of straw where there is little grazing available and in the Mati Highlands at least they are given shelter in houses or corrals at night during the rainy season. Both stallions and mares pasture together freely and are allowed to mate as they please (Haberland, 66).

Mules are by contrast given more careful attention. They are fed barley and the best teff fodder when there is a shortage of grass and sheltered from the cold bleak winds. The mule "remains a constant inmate of the master's dwelling, on terms of close intimacy with the family" (Harris, I, 242). Neither mules nor horses are shod and no attention is paid to the care of their hooves (Harris, 241).

Galla riding gear is derived from the Amhara. The names of the parts of the saddle are as well (Haberland, 66). They use toe stirrups and severe ring bits, although some Galla ride with no saddle and only a "halter" (Huntingford, 26). By halter this author may mean some kind of a hackamore.

"The horseman from the Horn of Africa belongs to the flapping legs and waving arms school of equitation, but he can gallop; he can even make his pony gallop, no mean feat" (Trench, 207). One of the distinctive features of Galla and Somali riding is the practice of off-side mounting which arose from the custom of carrying a sword on the right hip, which would therefore hinder near-side or left side mounting. While swords are only carried on ceremonial occasions today the style of mounting persists (Trench, 207).

Harris describes the mounted Galla of over a century ago in a way that, although a caricature, nevertheless is colourful: "[T]he equestrian Galla is an object worthy the pencil of Carle Vernet or Pinelli. Tall and athletic, his manly figure is enveloped in a toga, such as graced the sons of ancient Rome, and his savage, wild and fiery features, are rendered still more ferocious by thick bushy hair arranged either in large lotus-leaved compartments, or streaming over the shoulders in long raven plaits. Grease and filth however form his delight; he sparkles under a liberal coat of the much loved butter, which is unsparingly applied when proceeding to the perpetration of the most dastardly and inhuman deeds. Accoutred with spear, sword, and buckler, and wedded to the rude saddle, whereof he would seem to form a part, the Pagan scours fearlessly over the grassy savannahs which he has usurped from the Christian and is engaged in perpetual desultory strife with all his border neighbours" (Harris, III, 46).

Other People of the Horn of Africa

The Somalis, Danakil and Beja are almost exclusively camel nomads and have as a result only a very few horses. They are of the pony variety, mostly twelve to fourteen hands high. Presumably derived from larger stock such as the Arab, they have become small in adaptation to more difficult environment coupled with less close attention by their owners. Some Somalis use horses in herding and when no water is available they are given camel milk mixed with water brought by camel from the nearest sources. The Somalis are said to lavish great care on their horses (Drake-Brockman, 1912, 200). Until this century horses were employed in warfare and the salute to chiefs was usually made on horseback. In recent years horses have declined in number among the Somali, but they never at any time were very numerous.

The Konso people are reported to keep a few horses in their northern region, but not elsewhere. Particularly outside of the Ethiopian Highlands, horses are a rarity; especially in the south west, climate and insects make horse management extremely difficult, although it should be borne in mind that this is not a satisfactory explanation for their absence and lack of value. The Arab Bedouin live in similarly difficult circumstances for the horse, but it is a prized and favoured animal. An important factor is the absence of any meaningful incorporation of the horse into the cultures of such people as the Konso, Sidamo and others of south-western Ethiopia.

As in other parts of Sub-Saharan Africa, horsemanship and horse husbandry have been adopted from outside sources and little modified by peoples in Ethiopia and Somaliland. Arab influence is noticeable and especially strong among the Somalis; Portuguese and Indian traits are most obvious among Amhara and Galla.

SOUTHERN AFRICA

North of the equator the primary direction of the introduction of a horse complex into Africa was from the north and from Arab and Berber cultures; south of the equator the horse complex was primarily European, with the Dutch and British playing the chief role and the Portuguese a very minor one. Also, south of the equator the horse appears in Africa much later. It is possible that horses were introduced on the east coast of Africa (Kenya and Tanzania) by Arab traders between the eleventh and twelfth centuries. On the other hand, it seems likely that few if any horses were ever introduced by Arabs in these areas, first, because those who moved along this coast were primarily seafarers from south Arabia where the horse is an extreme rarity and where the camel prevails. Secondly, these people were not interested in colonizing and settling, but only in setting up trading stations on the coast which would therefore minimize whatever potential demand there might be for horses.

The Portuguese followed after the Arabs as coastal invaders. Yet here again until the beginning of the twentieth century the Portuguese did not colonize, but maintained small coastal centres for trade and political control. The diffusion of the horse in southern Africa owes most to the Dutch who were the earliest real foreign colonizers, spreading from the south coast on the Cape of Good Hope northward and inland, beginning in the eighteenth century. The Dutch settler-pastoralists carried with them large numbers of horses. They soon encountered Bantu cattle pastoralists who were in the process of gradually moving southward towards the coast.

It is said that one Bantu people, the Basuto or Sotho first acquired horses from bands of Euroafricans (commonly known as Bastaards in

South Africa) engaged in cattle raiding and hunting. About 1830 the Basuto came in contact with a mounted band of these raiders who were drunk on millet beer. The Basuto killed the men and stole their horses and arms. However, before taking the horses they are said to have watched them for several hours to be assured horses had nothing to do with the guns firing off (Coats, 25; Tylden, 1966, 9).

In the case of the American Indian adoption of the horse, it has been argued that a people so ignorant of horses could not be expected to drive off a herd and presumably independently learn to ride and handle them. For the Indians it appears highly likely that some of them first learned to be equestrians from the Spanish and in turn taught their fellow tribesmen. But the case of the Bantu is different in important respects from that of the Amerindian. While the latter was totally unfamiliar with any large domesticated animals, the Bantu were veteran cattle herders. Most of the horses acquired by the Indians were highly spirited, if not unbroken, Spanish horses while the Bantu access was to Boer horses which were well broken and highly docile creatures.

Thus, it is very likely the Bantu might have acquired horses without first learning how to handle them from their European owners. Yet, given the nature of the horse, it would appear feasible that more Africans became acquainted with it through some of their fellows who had learned about these animals while employed by Boers. This is not to suggest that the Boers either gave their Bantu servants horses or taught them to ride. We know that the Spaniards initially attempted to preserve their horses for their exclusive use and to prevent the Indians from riding, but this did not prevent Indian grooms from learning to ride and handle horses.

Of all South Africans the Basuto have become the most interested in horses. But these animals were also adopted by their near kinsmen, the Tswana of Botswana, and to a lesser extent by other Bantu people such as the Swazi and Zulu, and by the Ambo and Herero of Namibia.

The horses acquired by the Basuto were derived from stock imported by the Dutch East India Company from Indonesia. Exposed to the more difficult climatic conditions of Lesotho with its high altitude temperatures, plus indifferent and casual treatment, a breed developed which was the size of a small pony and noted for its endurance, surefootedness and fearlessness. It was even considered superior to the mountain mule since, while the mule is surefooted, it "lacks courage and trust in its owner to face almost impassable conditions, viz.:- rivers in flood, rock ledge trails, etc." (quoted in Epstein, 1971a, 478). The breed came into great demand during the Boer War and in the ensuing World Wars such that its survival was threatened, but government importations of stallions from the Republic of South Africa and from Nigeria in recent years have helped to revive the breed (Ashton, 134).

Among Basuto and other Bantu the horse has a highly specialized role as a riding animal particularly for men. While it is a symbol of prestige it is, especially in more remote areas, an important means of transportation.

Basuto horse management reflects the fact that the Basuto in general are not very eager herdsmen. Livestock as a whole are given only the most minimal attention. In a few cases horses or sick animals receive grain or beer strainings. Most often horses are tied in grassy fields to graze, but others feed with other livestock on open range – a range which is often overgrazed or otherwise not of particularly high quality. Basuto use their horses even though the animals may have serious saddle sores or cuts. They appear indifferent to their being left saddled for long periods in the heat of the day with no food or water. Mares and colts, particularly, are kept at cattle posts the year round except for a short summer break at which time they are brought to the villages for the breeding of the mares and branding and breaking of the young (Ashton, 134ff.).

Basuto riding gear is of a light English type and riding style shows British influence as well, rather than Boer, since they ride with short stirrups, with the reins in the left hand and switch in the right.

The horse never acquired among any Bantu people the central position it achieved among the Indians of the American Plains. One obvious economic reason is that the Plains Indians very quickly perceived the effectiveness of the horse in the hunting of wild buffalo, their main source of food supply. If this was not a product of insight on the part of the Indians at least they had before them a Spanish model of the mounted herding of cattle. In South Africa, as in the rest of that continent, the important cattle herding enterprise is a pedestrian affair. The cattle are docile and easily handled on foot and, indeed, are docile in large part because of the pedestrian pattern and personal attention. The Boer pastoralists, too, never adopted mounted herding. The Boer's servants and labourers, being Blacks, were left to herd the livestock on the farm as they had done in their tribal milieu – on foot. The Plains Indian case provided the opportunity for greatly increasing the efficiency of food acquisition; in South Africa this opportunity was absent.

A less important factor is that horses were introduced into South Africa at a much later time – over a century and a half after they had been introduced into America – and they were never in as great numbers. In South Africa the horse spread *with* European colonizers and settlers; in America the horse was adopted by Indians in direct contact with the Spanish and spread thence northwards in advance of the European colonization of the central and northern Plains. Not only did the Bantu have access to fewer horses, but they had a much shorter period of time in which to develop any horse complex before being ultimately subdued by the Europeans.

In South Africa, tribes such as the Zulu and Swazi came to military prominence in the first part of the nineteenth century. About this time (1808 for the Zulu) they first acquired horses, but these were not plentiful and not much appears to have been made of them. The mighty, militarist Zulu relied upon a spear-bearing infantry until their ultimate defeat.[1] Occasionally, they employed small groups of armed horsemen, but never developed a cavalry, even though they had encountered cavalry forces not only in the form of mounted Boers and formal English cavalry brigades, but also in mounted Basutos. To be sure such forces were not numerous, but one is led to wonder why the Zulu never developed a cavalry. A cursory review of some of the sources on Zulu wars and on the Zulu people fails to deal with this question. Most probably horses in large enough numbers were not readily available to the Zulu. In addition, they had already developed in their infantry a lethal military machine which had proved highly successful. As a result there may have been little motivation to experiment in an untried alternative which was dependent upon a presumably scarce resource – the horse. This is not the entire answer. On suspects that there are unaccounted for factors of value orientation and general outlook which give the Zulu a perspective on the horse which is different from that of the Basuto, for example.

---

[1] They also used the technique of stampeding cattle with sharpened horns before the marching infantry.

XIII

The Horse in Eastern and Southern Asia since the Eighteenth Century

INDIA

THE horse has never been of much importance in the Indian sub-continent. The only horse oriented peoples of any account are the Pathans who live in north-western Pakistan and are culturally oriented to the Middle East, being indistinguishable from their brethren on the other side of the international boundary in Afghanistan. Ridgeway attributes the lack of development of any indigenous breeds of any merit to the climate of the sub-continent (Ridgeway, 150). India possesses too many characteristics unsuited for horsebreeding. Where the country is not semi-tropical or tropical forest it is rugged mountains and where thick forests are kept cleared it is for the cultivation of grains and vegetabls to supply a dense population whose diet is heavily vegetarian. Like south-eastern China and south-east Asia there is literally little room for a horse and it is climatically too hot and humid for its effective use as a draught animal. In addition, water buffalo and cattle have a prior role in this vast area as draught animals. They, too, are more adapted to the geographical conditions, as well as being animals which provide a non-taboo source of milk.

Today horses are chiefly relegated to two roles: for use in ceremonies and the lowly job of drawing taxis in towns and cities. As elsewhere, they once were important for cavalry purposes and as riding animals for members of the military. Indian cavalry, largely derived from the north-western margins including the Pathans, acquired some repute in the development of equestrian games and acrobatics. Like the Cossacks, or Roman circus performers they were great mounted performers. To demonstrate their equestrian skills they rode at a gallop with spear in hand to strike a tent peg on the ground and pick it up with the spear. Several bareback riders would jump a flaming fence, pick up dummies on the other side and ride back over the still burning fence. They rode backwards facing the tail and practiced mounting and dismounting at a full gallop (Aflalo, *passim*).

In rural India the horse is employed as a riding animal for managers of estates and landlords for purposes of overseeing field labour, for pleasure riding, and hunting adventures. The ordinary Pakistani or

Indian peasant may ride a horse once in his lifetime on the occasion of his wedding, although even this opportunity is now disappearing as bridegrooms are increasingly taking to automobiles or even motorcycles. While in Iran it is customary for the bride to ride on horseback to her new home, tradition in northern India and Pakistan requires the bridegroom and his male friends and relatives to ride in proceeding to the bride's house.

The number riding in the procession depends upon the availability of horses, so that in many cases only the groom rides. Among the Hindu population the procession of the groom makes a circuit around the village to stop at shrines for worship (Lewis, O., 1965, 178).

In the Punjab a bridegroom might occasionally receive the gift of a horse from his mother's brother or mother's brother's son, representing a collective gift from his mother's parents' home village (Eglar, 164).

Saddles are based on the wood frame principle with high fork and cantle. The well-to-do once rode in saddles covered with leather or velvet and with fork, horn and cantle inlaid with pearl shell or studded with silver. The saddle skirts consisted of "two large circular leather flaps that hung low over the horse's sides. These skirts were painted or gilded according to the social status of the rider" (Vernam, 83). In the Benares area saddles were frequently covered with quilted woollen fabric. Bits were mainly of the snaffle type (Vernam, 85). While India is the homeland of the toe stirrup, it appears that in recent times, and in north India at least, the full foot stirrup of iron prevails. In the last century Indian riders have tended to adopt English saddlery.

Horses in India have generally been hand fed barley and hay since there is little available grazing land. They are kept in the confines of the owner's compound or stable. There has never been much breeding of horses and until modern times large numbers were imported into India from Arabia and Central Asia.

As in the Arab world, Indians too have paid much attention to the markings and whorls of hair on the horse as a means for judging. A fourteenth century Hindu manual, the *Asva Sastra*, devotes many pages to this subject. There are good whorls and bad whorls, auspicious and inauspicious locations, so that a good whorl in a bad location has its power nullified. Great wealth, fame and happiness will come to the owner of a horse with whorls on the forehead. "[B]lue teeth, spotted testicles, hairy penis, effeminacy, horns on the head, more than four legs, body odour, and a tendency to roam about at night" are among one hundred and seventeen inauspicious marks listed in the manual. Yet all types of unsoundness in the leg and foot are placed under a single heading: "They should not be lame" (Trench, 92).

SOUTHEAST ASIA

The Hindu-Buddhist Indian movement into Indonesia introduced the first horses to the Archipelago, possible as early as the second century A.D. Arab traders and merchants are responsible for major infusions of horses and particularly those of Arabian blood, several centuries later.

Horses are uncommon in Indonesia, as they are in most other parts of southern Asia as well. In the present day one of the chief uses of horses throughout the area, including Indonesia, is for drawing taxis in the towns.

The horse is more widespread in Sumatra and among the Batak peoples in the west central part of the island. There, horses are small and hardy. An observer in the last century noted that rural people brought unbroken ones to market in some numbers (Marsden, 115). They were once used for war, but not as cavalry. According to Marsden the custom of setting out sharp pointed stakes in the passes was a major factor in limiting the use of horses in war. The Bataks consider horseflesh "their most exquisite meat and for this purpose feed them upon grain, and pay great attention to their keep". Horse racing is a common and favourite sport and is associated with gaming and betting. Indeed, Marsden reports that a man who lost more than he was able to pay could be sold into slavery, but if the winner is generous the loser is allowed to kill a horse and offer a public entertainment (Marsden, 381).

Loeb describes horse sacrifice among the Toba, a Batak people of Sumatra. It is a slightly altered form of the Hindu sacrifice. Horses are offered in a great sacrifice for the three gods of the Toba trinity. Every Toba clan possesses three sacred horses each dedicated to one of the divinities. Thus, a black horse is sacred to one god, a brown to another, while a piebald is consecrated to the third god. These horses are "inviolable and non-alienable" and are permitted to graze wherever they choose. Each is sacrificed to its particular god when it becomes old and is replaced by a young one. The two sacred horses – the new one and the old one – are bridled and conducted to the village centre where the older one is slaughtered. Its hide is washed and laid over a crude image of the horse "which is simply a tree trunk, hollowed out on the underside" with a horse's head carved at one end. This is brought to the chief's house where, along with food, the hide is offered to the god. The new horse is then consecrated. Clan members assemble at the chief's house where the god enters his medium, who happens to be one of the chiefs, to inform all that he has received the sacrifice and will give help. After this the horse flesh is divided and everyone takes a portion home to eat (Loeb, 91).

Of saddlery in south-east Asia Vernam writes: "The hard, wooden saddle was also used in Burma, Siam, and Java. There it was usually covered with cloth embroidered in colors. The lower part of the sidebars was commonly left uncovered. It had no built-in rigging, being held in place by a surcingle cinch that went over the seat" (Vernam, 86).

"Stirrups were of wood, iron or cast brass . . .. A knot in a rope-end to fit between the rider's toes often served for a stirrup in" parts of southeast Asia. The Javanese were still using these toe stirrups in the twentieth century (Vernam, 87). The Batak of Sumatra sometimes used wooden bits and headstalls and reins of rattan (Marsden, 381). The Burmese cavalry saddles once were equipped with long flaps or wings hanging down in front to protect a rider's bare legs when going through underbrush, but by the nineteenth century they had become mostly decorative since cavalry were no longer used in the jungles (Yoe, 502).

In the Philippines horses were introduced primarily by the Spanish and Spanish style riding and gear prevails. However, horses on Mindanao, at least, are descendents of those originally acquired from Arab contact. Among the Taboli of Mindanao their small ponies are prestige animals used mostly for bride wealth and in sport. Like the ancient Icelanders they pit stallions against one another in a fight. When one runs away, the other is the victor. Taboli ride bareback and with a bridle.

In Luzon horses are now kept mostly for taxi carriages and are not much used for riding purposes except for a very few managers of estates and landlords to oversee their plantations. In general the Philippines is poor horse country and all horses are concentrated in the lowlands where it is necessary to stall feed and keep them.

On the island of Timor in eastern Indonesia horses have taken on some significance; indeed, Timor is no doubt the most horse oriented part of the eastern Pacific. The horse may have been introduced there by the Hindus. In any case the islanders adopted the habit of riding with toe stirrups. Certainly the Portuguese were instrumental in sparking horse use on the island. Thirty years ago, if not so much today, it could be said that men, women and children alike went everywhere on horseback (St. Clair, 373). Horses were also important as pack animals. They are small, pony sized, sturdy and surefooted with tough hooves that are not shod. For a larger bodied European a long journey necessitates taking two or three extra remounts. Riders are often bareback with a bitted bridle. When toe stirrups are employed they use long stirrup leathers.

One might expect that the climatic and geographic conditions of South-east Asia would indicate a general paucity of horses throughout the region. Indeed, this is to some extent true. Horses are not common, and the geographical conditions are not particularly conducive to extensive horse keeping. However, we find a considerable variation in the relative frequency of horses from one territory to another. The former Portuguese Timor is extremely atypical having an exceptionally high proportion of horses – one horse to six persons as compared to the next, Laos, with one horse to 110 persons while Malaysia has only one horse per 2000 population. Two factors are important to help explain the anomalous situation of Timor. First, the island has extensive savannahs, much of which provide good grassland for grazing purposes. Secondly, the island has been under prolonged Portuguese and Dutch influence. Once horsekeeping was spread by the Portuguese it proved adaptive to the local conditions and a ready means of transportation. The Philippines, no doubt have a relatively high horse population for South east Asia because of the prolonged Spanish control of those islands.

Laos, ranking after Timor in having the highest proportion of horses to population, is at the same time the most sparsely populated of South east Asiatic countries and the least developed economically and technologically. It has less than two thousand miles of all-weather roads and, as a landlocked country most of which is mountainous, water transport is, in contrast to other South Asian nations, at a minimum. Such a combination of demographic, culturo-technological and geographical conditions would seem to encourage greater utilization of pack and riding animals.

CHINA

The primary horse oriented people within what are today the confines of the Chinese nation are the Mongols in Inner Mongolia; next in importance are the Chinese inhabitants of Manchuria and Inner Mongolia. The horse retains a modicum of significance in the northern and western provinces of China proper, but is hardly found in the southeastern part of the country south of the Yangtze River and east of Yunnan. Such a distribution reflects cultural and geographical differences. The northern extremities – Inner Mongolia and Manchuria – have extensive grazing lands; those of the south-east practically none at all, besides being climatically tropical and humid. The northern extremities are inhabited by Mongols, a traditional horse people, and by Chinese who, having lived for ages as close neighbours of nomadic equestrians such as the Mongols, adopted the more extensive use of the horse to resist the northerners.

The northern Chinese employed the horse both as a riding animal for the well-to-do and a draught animal either for the cart or the pack. Apparently today the horse is more frequently put to the plough, although this is a task which has largely been reserved for oxen and buffalo. No doubt one reason for thus preferring cattle is that, despite the fact that the Chinese were the first to develop improved horse harness for draught, their horses were always small in size. Since the Chinese consider milk in general to be unclean food it is understandable that they never adopted the Mongol practice of drinking mare's milk. It is less clear why the Chinese, who once ate horse meat during the Chou period of the first millenium B.C. should no longer do so.

Since the rise of the Communist regime, livestock has been brought increasingly under collective ownership, but there is a distinct tendency for draught animals to be more readily taken out of private hands than for smaller meat animals. Thus in 1956 the percentage of privately owned livestock in China was as follows: oxen 27%, buffalo 20%, horses 29%, asses 30%, mules 24%, camels 92%, sheep 68%, goats 60% and swine 83% (Chen, 1967). Over seventy per cent of each type of draught animal except for the camel were collectively owned, while almost the reverse was true of meat animals. More precisely the division of owners of horses was as follows: state owned 1.7%, collective farm 68.9%, privately owned 29.4% (of which 11.2% were owned by cooperative members and 18.2% by individual peasants and herders).

Apart from altering the entire traditional property system in livestock, the Chinese "new order" has effectively put an end to the use of the horse as a riding and pleasure animal except where used for herding as in Inner Mongolia, for under its Puritan work ethic there is only a place in the system for work horses. Pleasure horses are seen as symbols of aristocratic luxury and useless frivolity.

In a recent work Epstein describes the several types of horses in contemporary China. He finds seven types of which the Mongolian and Manchurian ponies are the most widespread. All Chinese horses are small and light-boned and most must be classed as ponies. Horses are bred over most of China with the exception of the south-eastern provinces where we have already seen that horses are extremely few in number (Epstein, 1971b).

Horses are regularly hand fed and stall kept. In south China they may be fed on broad beans and rice straw (Fei, 209). In some parts of the country mules are highly regarded, kept well fed and groomed, and considered the pride of the family. They are tended only by male members of the family, never by hired labourers or women. Yang states that in contrast to mules there was no sentimental attachment to the donkey. "The poor animal doesn't even have a birthday in the family" (Yang, 49).

Shoeing is common for horses. The process itself is of some interest. The animal is placed in a sling, actually a double sling – one in front and one before the hind legs. Either sling is raised as one wishes to shoe front or hind hooves. As in ancient times the Chinese continued to prefer a riding horse with an ambling gait. Presumably in Marco Polo's time, horsemen in Yunnan differed from the north in riding style, since he said those in Yunnan rode long "after the French fashion" while northern Chinese rode short with bent knee like the Mongols (Polo, 88).

The Chinese had saddles similar to Mongolian design with modifications in particulars. Vernam reproduces a picture of a seventeenth century Chinese saddle with a heavily padded high pommel and a relatively high cantle. The seat is short, but there are extremely large skirts. Seat, flaps and skirt are all embroidered. The unusually large saddle blanket is for decorative effect aimed at protecting the rider's clothing (Vernam, 88). Another style of saddle has no cantle at all providing an extra long seat.

Most bridles had snaffle bits; only a few had curbs. The stirrups were of metal and made in a style similar to European ones, although they were bigger. In some cases stirrups were lined with cork to prevent the foot from slipping. Bridles, stirrups, cruppers, and breast pieces were invariably decorated, many with silver, gold, ivory or bone or cloisonne trim (Vernam, 88).

Today it seems safe to say that the traditional saddlery of the Chinese has been largely relegated to the museums and the junk heaps.

KOREA

The Koreans are neither horsemen nor do they have any important place for them. At best one may say the chief "practical" function for the horse was in the horsehair used in making head-dresses for upper class gentlemen. Horses were once used for cavalry and probably up to modern times had a minor role in weddings and funerary processions of the upper class. As in India it was once common in Korea for the groom to proceed to his bride's village on a horse hired for the occasion. At upper class funerals ten foot high wooden and bamboo horses, covered with paper and painted, were borne in procession to the grave where they were burned to provide the deceased with a means of transportation to the afterworld (Osgood, 150–51). One might suspect that this is a relic of some ancient form of actual horse sacrifice.

Riding on horseback in Korea was exclusively a noble and military exercise except for the procession of the bridegroom mentioned above. But the riding, like that of the ancient Japanese, does not appear to have been a very practical type. The nobleman "was by custom forced to perch himself on an extraordinarily high saddle – presumably a compensation for the smallness of the animal – where he would be safeguarded by a retainer walking on each side, as well as by another retainer leading the horse" (Osgood, 141). Commoners were prohibited from riding in the presence of upper class individuals except where the commoner was in his own wedding procession (Osgood, 141).

Osgood observes that the Korean pony, which is about the size of a Shetland, is "of a temperament not unlike the Koreans themselves" (Osgood, 215). Later he remarks that the ponies have "a savage temper" (Osgood, 328).

JAPAN

Japan is another area where the horse appeared rather late in time as we have already noted. Like South-east Asia most of Japan is unsuited for the horse because of the abundance of mountains and the necessity to utilize all available flatter lands for cultivation and feeding an immense population. Reasonably good horse country in Japan is fairly limited to the northern island of Hokkaido. Also like other East Asians it cannot be said that the Japanese have ever been very outstanding horsemen. But there are interesting parallels between the Japanese Mediaeval period and that of Europe and among these are some that relate to the horse.

There is an early association of the armed knight with the saddled horse. A decree in 682 A.D. proclaimed that: "In a government, military matters are the essential thing. All civil and military officials should therefore sedulously practice the use of arms and riding on horseback" (quoted in Kenrick, 17). Thus, anyone with a horse was to become part of the cavalry and any others were to be infantry (Kenrick, 18). In early Japan the warrior horseman was his clan's leader. "[E]arly aristocrats owed their rank to their mounts." During the tenth and eleventh centuries the noble became an armoured knight and managed an estate (Kenrick, 20). The romantic symbol of the Middle Ages was the "trinity of the horse, the warrior, and the flower" (Kenrick, 35). The foremost accomplishments of the samurai warrior knight were "his skill in horsemanship and archery, fencing and jujitsu." His sons and his sons' sons were born to ride and fight" (Kenrick, 38).

During the Tokugawa period (1603–1868) Engelbert Kaempfer,

Dutch physician to the Dutch Embassy, records in his *History of Japan* taking a journey:

"A plain wooden saddle, not unlike the pack saddles of the Swedish Post-horses, is girded on the Horse with a poitral, or breast leather, and crupper. Two latchets are laid upon the saddle, which hang down on both sides of the Horse, in order to their being conveniently tied about two portmantles, which are put on each side, in that situation, which is thought the most proper to keep them in a due ballance". A trunk or small long box is laid over both portmantles on the horse's back and tied to the saddle and" . . . over the whole is spread the traveller's covering and bedding, the middle cavity between the two trunks, fill'd up with some soft stuff, is the traveller's seat, where he sits . . . either cross leg'd, or with his legs extended hanging down by the Horse's neck, as he pleases . . ." Footmen and stable grooms hold the two side trunks as one proceeds (quoted in Kenrick, 47–8).

The saddle of this time was made of wood with a "cushion underneath, and a caparison behind, lying upon the horse's back, with the traveler's mark, or arms, stitch'd upon it. Another piece of course cloth hangs down on each side, as a safeguard to the horse, to keep it from being daub'd with dirt. Theses two peices are tied together loosely under the horse's belly. The head is cover'd with a net-work of small but strong strings, to defend it, and particularly the eyes, from flies, which are very troublesome to them. The neck, breast, and other parts are hung with small bells" (Kaempfer, quoted in Kenrick, 49).

Tokugawa accoutrements of riding travelers included brass money with holes in the middle, hung in a string behind them "to one of the sashes of their seats", a lantern of "varnish'd and folded paper" and a "brush made of horse's hairs, or black cock feathers, to dust your seat and cloaths. It is put behind your seat on one side, more for shew than use." One also carried a "water pail . . . put on the other side of the seat, opposite the brush." The traveler brings along a large cloak for rain and a large hat to protect himself from the sun. A Japanese on horseback, tuck'd up after this fashion, makes a very odd comical figure at a distance" (quoted in Kenrick, 49–51). The traveler has nothing to do with the bridle since the horse is led by a footman who walks on the horse's right side.

"The Japanese look upon our European way of sitting on horseback, and holding the bridle oneself, as warlike, and properly becoming a soldier." So they rarely take the reins, although it "is more frequent among people of quality in cities, when they go a visiting one another. But even then the rider . . . holds the bridle merely for form, the horse being nevertheless led by one, and sometimes two footmen, who walk on each side of the head, holding it by the bit . . . .

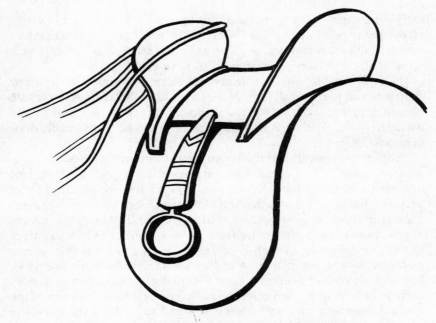

JAPANESE SADDLE WITH RING STIRRUPS
From Kenrick

"The stirrup leathers . . . are very short. A broad round leather
hangs down on both sides, after the fashion of the Tartars, for to
defend the leggs. The stirrup is made of Iron . . . withal very thick and
heavy, not unlike the sole of a foot, and open on one side, for the rider
to get his foot lose with ease in case of a fall. The stirrups are commonly
of an exceeding neat workmanship, and inlaid with silver. The reins
are not of leather, as ours, but of silk, and fasten'd to the bit" (Kaempfer quoted in Kenrick, 52).

The Japanese seem to have gone into elaborate developments in
stirrups since they had a great variety of different forms. Some of them
weighed as much as ten pounds. The earliest style had hooded toes
and later long footplates appeared which were big enough to accommodate the entire foot. One kind of stirrup had perforated footplates to
allow for "the water to escape when crossing streams" (Vernam,
91–93). Bridles were highly decorated and attached usually to snaffle
bits; curbs were rare. Spurs were never used in Japan until modern
times (Vernam, 93).

In Tokugawa, Japan, horseshoes were often apparently made of
twisted straw and since these soon wear out men who care for horses

carried a supply along with them. But they were to be found in every village being peddled by poor children. "Hence it may be said that this country hath more farriers, than perhaps any other, tho' in fact it hath none at all . . ." (Kaempfer quoted in Kenrick, 50).

The traditional Japanese custom required one to mount on the off or right side and to fasten all parts of the harness on that side. A horse was backed into his stall, facing the opposite direction of those in the western world. Further, it was fed from a tub placed by the stable door (Kenrick, 187).

The Japanese developed their own equestrian sports based on models from China and Central Asia but some were quite independent inventions. A circus has been known in Japan for five hundred years and trick horse riding was the first main attraction. Mounted archery, especially shooting at targets while at a gallop and, also, *dakyu*, a form of polo were once important military-related events. *Dakyu* was part of the military training of eighteenth century knights. It involved two teams of four to six players and two kinds of balls with one goal. Between seven and twelve balls were in play at one time on each side, each team having its own coloured balls (red or white). The aim of the game is to throw your own balls into the goal and to keep the opposing team from scoring with theirs (Kenrick, 107). As in the Mediaeval and Middle Eastern world hawking was another horse related activity pursued in Mediaeval Japan.

Horohiki, a kind of show riding, was popular in the seventeenth and eighteenth centuries. Two riders, Masters of the Imperial Household Stables, "each carries on his back a cylinder about three feet in diameter. He rides at a trot, and slowly from the cylinder he extends a silken streamer. Gradually he increases his horse's action, at the same time releasing more and more of the streamer until its entire length of some thirty-three feet floats out behind him. His skill lies in preventing any part of the streamer touching the ground during his performance" (Kenrick, 109).

The early Japanese adopted the ancient Chinese practice of sacrificing horses to the gods. They were especially sacrificed to the water god since the horse was a spirit inhabiting bodies of water.[1] In these ancient sacrifices the head might be cut off or they pretended to cut it off or merely drew blood and smeared it on rocks (Kenrick, 84).

"Within living memory, the country custom was observed of hanging the heads of horses at the entrances of farmhouses. The horse possessed the qualities of an agricultural god, and his head acted as a

[1] Cf. the Greeks and their ancient association of the water god, Poseidon, with the horse. Similar associations occur among the Chinese from whom we may suspect the Japanese acquired the notion.

charm" (Kenrick, 85). The heads were skulls of animals long since sacrificed.

The burial of horses and retainers with noble masters was discontinued in Japan in the early centuries of the first millenium A.D. and replaced by the use of clay figurines (*Haniwa*). At about the same time the practice of presenting horses to shrines began. These then assumed a sanctity because they belonged to the god. They lived at the shrine of the god free of all labour, just as the German tribes kept sacred horses in special groves dedicated to their gods. Apparently some shrines occasionally came to be in danger of being overwhelmed with horse gifts. In addition the poor could not make such offering and so obtain merit. Thus, Kenrick claims it eventually became common practice to give models or pictures of horses to the temple, although the dedication of living horses survived down to modern times (Kenrick, 122–123).

Draught horses were introduced on Japanese farms in the nineteenth century and they were fairly common until after World War II when they began to be replaced very rapidly by tractors. In his ethnography, *Suye Mura*, John Embree gives some idea of the role of the horse in rural Japan during the decade of the 1930's. In this community horses and cattle were the most important forms of livestock, although it should be rememberd that livestock are generally not significant in Japanese agriculture. There were more horses than any other animals in the village. Of 215 househoulds, 155 reported having horses with a total of 205 in the village (Embree, 314). They appear to have been used primarily for hauling carts and wagons. Both cattle and horses were kept in stables when not working. Paper talismans were placed in the barns to cure and prevent horse and cattle diseases. Calves and colts had a naming ceremony on the third day after birth and the name was chosen in the same way as that for babies (Embree, 260). Those who were wagoners and horse-brokers held a special party for Batokwannon, their patron deity, on his holiday (Embree, 282).

During the first third of this century and especially in the militarist period of the 1930's there was a demand for improved horses for cavalry mounts. The government initiated a programme of encouraging farmers to raise horses by paying the sum of two yen for every equine birth registered at the village office in a horse record which was similar to the men's official family record (Embree, 44). Now, of course, there is no longer a Japanese cavalry just as there are also few farm horses. In Hokkaido a few horses are still used to pull sleds and it is said that there may remain an occasional small impoverished coal mine where horses are worked underground hauling coal (Kenrick, 181).

On the whole, the history of the horse in the last century in Japan closely parallels that in the United States; for about a century it was important as a farm draught animal and to a lesser extent for cavalry. After World War II mechanization caused a rapid decline in horse population and the horse became primarily a pleasure animal for the upper class. At the same time, in Japan, European style riding and saddlery have completely superseded the traditional types, but because of the lack of suitable riding areas, hacking is much less important than dressage and riding in a ring (Kenrick, 181). These general changes in the role of the horse represent only a minute part of that immense transformation over the last century which has made Japan a modern industrial society.

In this chapter several different cultures have been reviewed. In general they are similar in being until very recent times what we have called traditional urban-agrarian societies and societies which would not be considered particularly horse oriented. While about two thousand years ago the Chinese made significant contributions to the realm of equine use, it is clear that since that time neither they nor the other people of eastern Asia have displayed any particular achievement in this area. In all these societies the horse has invariably been identified with a military aristocracy. It is noteworthy that the greatest emphasis on the horse as a draught animal appears at two opposite geographical ends of Eurasia: northern Europe and China and Japan.

XIV

Central Asiatic Equestrian Pastoralists of Recent Times

OUR knowledge of the early Mongols and Turkic nomads is considerably sketchy compared to the data available on their more contemporary ways of life. What is known of their early horse husbandry suggests the persistence of many cultural patterns down to modern times.

THE MONGOLS

This discussion of contemporary Mongol peoples draws on four Mongol groups at slightly different times. Chiefly, the materials refer to the Khalkha Mongols of Outer Mongolia for the early part of the twentieth century and the Kalmuk Mongols of the Altai Mountains around 1860 – 1870. Some mention will also be made of the Chahar Mongols of Inner Mongolia and the Dagor Mongols of Manchuria, for the period of the first third of the twentieth century.

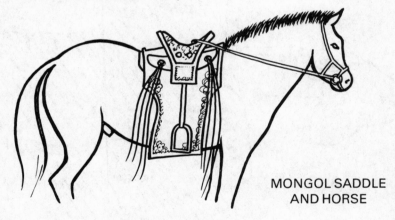

MONGOL SADDLE
AND HORSE

Of the four groups, the Khalkha of Outer Mongolia represents the most nomadic; the Altaian Kalmuks were at best semi-nomadic, moving between a summer and winter camp, and others moved only every few years. The Chahar and Dagor of the early twentieth century both reside in permanent settlements. The Khalkha, Kalmuk and Chahar have economies strongly oriented to livestock while the Dagor are less

ARCT
RUSSIA
SIBERI
CHUVASH
BASHKIR
TARTARS
TARTARS
COSSACKS
BLACK SEA
CASPIAN
KAZAKH
ARAL SEA
ALTAIANS
LAKE BALKHASH
UZBEK
KIRGHIZ
UIGH
TURKMEN
IRAN
TIBETA

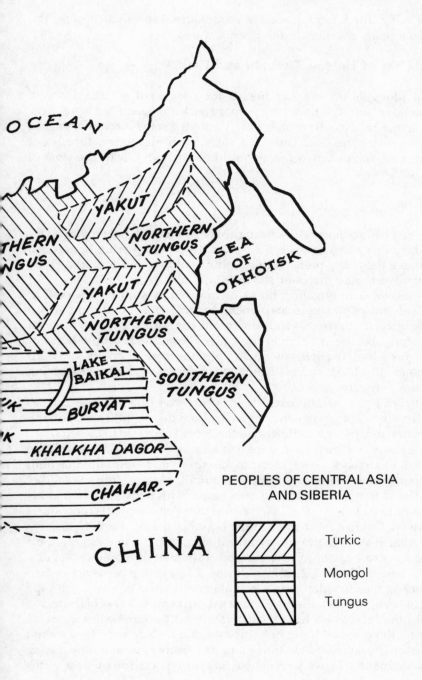

PEOPLES OF CENTRAL ASIA
AND SIBERIA

Turkic

Mongol

Tungus

so. Finally, the Kalmuk reside in mountainous forested country; the remaining are dwellers in the open steppe.

The Uses of Horses: Draught and Pack

Most Mongols do not use horses for pack or draught purposes. Camels, yaks and cattle are the primary pack animals. The Dagor, now a sedentary people, have accordingly adopted some deviant practices. Thus their horses haul carts and sleds, turn millstones, thresh out grain and even plough on occasion although this is mostly the work of the ox.

Riding

The main role of horses is as riding animals. They are not employed for herding sheep and goats, but are used to round up other horses. All Mongols definitely prefer riding geldings although the poor may be compelled to ride mares or stallions.

A fast or a multigaited horse or one which showed off well at festivals brings prestige to its owner. Mongol horses have four paces: a walk, a soft trot, an easy gallop and the amble, which is the favourite of the Mongols. Legend derives the amble "from the favourite horse of Genghis Khan, the spirit of which up to the present enters into born amblers" (Beck, 6). Radloff claimed that among the Kalmuks ambling horses were rare.

Altaian Kalmuks approach their horses from the left side and no horse will "allow anyone to approach it from the right." To mount, the rider first grasps with the left hand the guide "rope tied to the left ring" of the halter, wraps it around his hand, then, "takes the reins with the same hand, places the left foot into the stirrup and, while holding onto the pommel with the right hand . . . quickly swings" into the saddle. "In the saddle he sits with the upper part of his body straight and his arms pressed to the sides". The stirrups are extremely short and knees therefore "form a right angle in the riding position". Radloff portrays the Altaian as ungainly and awkward on foot, but when mounted his whole posture changes as horse and rider melt into one whole, as a true centaur (Radloff, I, 287). "During a fast gallop as well as when riding on the most dangerous mountain trail he quietly takes his pipe out of his right boot, fills it with tobacco, strikes fire, lights his pipe and sticks the fire-steel behind his belt. During this time he lets the reins rest on the pommel horn; only the end of the guide rope he does not release. The course of the horse and its gait concern him little during this occupation. I have seen people ride sitting in saddles whose girths were burst, and yet they did not fall off the horse . . . . The women ride completely like the men and with as much agility, security and endurance" (Radloff, I, 288).

Riding Gear

Kalmuk riding gear includes a halter which is made from woollen rope or tanned leather; to this is attached a guide rope about six feet long. This halter is only removed when the horse is put out to graze in the herd. Bridles and snaffles are put on over it. The bridle consists of two cheek straps passing from the bit rings around behind the ears, a nose strap, and a throat lash. Snaffle bits have side rings which are of moderate size. The guide rope and halter are considered crucial elements of harness; the rider never releases the guide rope while mounted. Should he fall from the horse he holds it so the horse will not desert him; it is also important for tying the horse while dismounted. We encounter this device also among the Bedouin Arabs and American Indians of the Plains.

The Kalmuk saddle consists of a basic wood frame structure of two side pieces, joined by a high pommel and high cantle. The saddle has two girths and they and the stirrup leathers are passed through holes in the side bars of the saddle. Cushions consisting of layers of felt are attached to the frames of the saddle and various felts are affixed underneath the frame as well. Before the saddle is put on several more layers of felt are placed on the back of the horse. The more elegant saddles are finely worked and the cushion is covered in black leather, while the stirrups, ordinarily made of wood, are manufactured of iron. Apparently, however, the more elaborate saddles are rather rare and usually purchased from other Mongols (Radloff, I, 289).

Of the Mongol saddle Vernam writes, that it has changed little since the days of Genghis Khan. "It had a somewhat crude, wooden sidebar tree. Some of them were simply lacquered and gilded in decorative designs. Others were covered with leather, sheepskin, or padded quilt. The high, round-topped forks were almost duplicated by the cantles. They were single-rig affairs, with big, extra-long skirts . . . . The saddle blankets were leather, quilted silk, bearskin, or heavy rugs, usually quite ornate and reaching well down over the horse's sides" (Vernam, 98).

Sport

The three manly sports of the Mongols are horse racing, archery and wrestling. Among the Khalkha summer is the time for racing when pasture is best and there is less work to do. "There are separate races for stallions, amblers, and for age classes (two year olds, three year olds, and so on), but the great race is that for mature horses of age six and upward. Good horses have been known to go on winning races up to the age of about twenty". The Mongol races are long distance affairs of nineteen to thirty-eight miles and the jockeys are children six to nine years old, both girls and boys. Mongols desire young children as riders because they want to bring out the horse's own willingness and capacity and so do not want an older, stronger rider to force the animal, but rather someone to guide it (Lattimore, 1962b, 17).

Ridgeway claimed the Mongol racers used no saddle or seat and that each jockey rolled up his trousers as high as he could clutching "the pony's ribs with his bare legs" (Ridgeway, 138–9).

Winners of races, usually four, canter around the stadium each accompanied by a herald. "They pull up in front of the grandstand and each child is offered a large bowl of fermented mare's milk, from which he drinks, then pours some on the rump of his horse. As he does so, each herald in turn chants, in a poem which he has composed, the name of the horse, the region from which it came, its previous victories, its special qualities of character and courage, the name of the owner, and the name of the child jockey. Then, each in turn, the children are lifted off their horses by their heralds and ushered up into the grandstand . . . to receive their prizes". By their applause the audience indicates which they believe to be the best poem. In Lattimore's example the herald for the horse which came in third place received the greatest acclamation for his poem (Lattimore, 1962b, 19).

Meat and Milk

Horses are not commonly eaten in Outer Mongolia except at a festive or funerary occasion, and when a horse dies the herdsman eats it and saves the hide. Horse hides are made into bags, and shoe soles and the hair is used for rope. This is periodically clipped from the mane and tail. The Kalmuks culled the very thin and weak horses which would be unlikely to survive the winter and slaughtered them in the fall for winter use when there would be no milk available (Radloff, I, 282). One should bear in mind that pastoral people are not ordinarily heavy meat eaters, but depend more upon dairy products from their herds. The bleeding and drinking of the blood of live horses appears to be a practice which is disappearing in Mongolia.

Mare's milk is a favourite beverage, chiefly consumed as koumiss. On the richest pastures a mare can be milked up to twelve times a day, while on drier pastures such as those of western Mongolia there may be eight or fewer milkings. The Chahar of Inner Mongolia milk only twice a day. Both the number of times a day a mare can be milked and the yield depend on pasture conditions. But the yield also depends on the manner in which the mare is milked. Maximum production is obtained by milking very fast and for only a few moments at a time – probably an imitation of the suckling foal. Khalkha Mongol mares require about ten days to break in to being milked. Consequently the Khalkha prefer that the same mares be milked each year. Vreeland calls the mare milking a kind of "rodeo event" since the mares are not very docile during the process (Vreeland, 40).

In Outer Mongolia, mares are milked from about the fourth month to the ninth month. Birket-Smith states that in Mongolia the milking season begins on a definite day which is a common holiday all over the country with offerings of milk to the four corners of the earth and plentiful drunkenness.

In milking season the foals are kept near the house on a line pegged in the ground. Thus, the mares do not stray very far away. When they are to be milked boys and men round them up and as each is caught, a boy or man brings the foal alongside its dam and holds it to induce the flow of milk. Among the Khalkha and Chahar the women do the actual milking, while among the Kalmuks, as also with all the Turkic peoples, this is a job reserved for the men. In Pre-Revolutionary days, the wealthy gentry were assisted by their poorer neighbours who in return were provided with food and clothing (Radloff, I, 286).

In the old days a leather or wooden bucket was used for milking; now the Outer Mongolians use aluminium pails and have adopted the view that anything connected with milk must be clean and sanitary (Lattimore, 1962b, 190).

With the need to milk so frequently and the low yield of from three to five litres a day, it is apparent that acquiring mare's milk is time consuming and therefore a more expensive operation than cow milking. Coupled with the fact that milking mares are not otherwise employed, it is not surprising that the production and consumption of koumiss is more often to be associated with the well-to-do.

Dagor Mongols do not milk their mares. This may be a result of Chinese influences, but also it may be because they employ their horses in more heavy draught work and have fewer of them.

Horse Sacrifice

At a funeral most Mongols sacrifice the deceased's favourite horse as well as a cow, and their meat, along with wine and cakes, "was placed on a table in front of the coffin" and afterwards consumed (Vreeland,

249). The Altaian Kalmuks, however, do not slaughter such horses, but rather the deceased's horse is taken out of service and never ridden again (Rudenko, xxvii). Horses are used as "living sacrifices" as well. Frequently these are sick animals and those which appear to be dying. They are draped with coloured cloth, and strips of cloth, often red or yellow, are braided into the mane. Such horses were relieved of all work. Among the Dagor, horses so dedicated are invariably diseased. If the animal recovers it is put back to work because of the shortage of horses among them (Vreeland, 201). The Mongols likewise dedicate horses to Buddhist lamasaries. Such forms of religious offering are found scattered throughout the world. In Japan, in the past horses were dedicated to Shinto temples; the ancient Germans placed them in sacred graves and Mediaeval Europeans bequeathed horses and harness to churches and monasteries.

Horses are also considered highly prestigious gifts among the Mongols and gifts of horses are made at weddings and for bride wealth. They also have an important place in the payment of fines and debts.

The Types and Numbers of Horses

There are severals types of Mongol horses. For Eastern Mongolia, Beck describes three: One is the ordinary type "with short hook-nosed head, a heavy neck, low fore-quarters, thick legs covered with abundant hair." It is ". . . coarse and ugly." A second "is higher, with a broad chest, a lighter neck, larger shoulders, and low legs with short pasterns." A third is a horse improved by stallions of other bloods imported from the Don by Cossacks and other Russians. It is found in herds belonging to wealthy Mongols. In Western Mongolia there is a type of horse resembling the Arab and throughout the country there are long and lanky horses specifically developed for racing purposes (Beck, 3).

The Mongol horse is known for its endurance. It can be ridden from fifty to sixty miles a day on trips "of not many days". There are even some which make one hundred to one hundred and twenty miles a day (Beck, 6). One Altaian rode from sunrise until sunset and covered one hundred and twenty miles which is made even more an outstanding feat when one considers the difficult terrain which had to be covered. These horses are also known for their ability to negotiate rough mountain trails.

Some have remarked that because Mongols and other Central Asiatic peoples leave their horses to fend for themselves on open range and also have primarily pony-sized animals, they require more horses for the same amount of work that could be accomplished with grain fed, larger horses. These reports of long journeys covered with great speed, then, do not reconcile with such observations. One suspects that the mounts used for these tests of endurance were larger than the ordinary and were given some special feeding. Supplementary feeding on such occasions is implied by Beck (Beck, 119).

A final anecdote from Radloff gives some indication of the intelligence or good training of the Kalmuk horse:

"An Altaian who visited me at the Kengi was so drunk he was unable to stand up. Then his horse was led to him; two men lifted him into the saddle and pushed his feet into the stirrups and someone gave the horse a smack and it ran home with the drunk on its back. [The rider] was swaying and seemed to be about to fall off at any moment. After some time we saw him and the horse up on the mountain path; the rider was still swaying as the horse climbed up the rocks. As I was told next day the drunk reached home safely in the middle of the darkest night. I was even told about another drunken rider who did fall off his horse, but the horse remained standing at his side until he had slept through his hangover and was able to mount again" (Radloff, I, 277).

The main source of wealth for the Mongolian nomads has been in their herds of sheep. Thus, in the Narobanchin Territory of Western Outer Mongolia under pre-Communist conditions a man's status was based on the number of sheep he owned although the number of horses, too, served as a measure since we may assume an owner of extensive sheep herds likewise owned large herds of horses. Four hundred lay families in this territory owned 1300 cattle and 2800 horses. The six wealthiest families accounted for about half of the cattle and each owned several hundred horses. Of the remaining families, all had at least one horse. Most families wanted at least one good riding horse, preferably a gelding. A family owning fifty sheep felt two geldings to be a necessity and one with two hundred sheep desired three geldings and often a mare for milk. Usually a mare was not acquired until the family owned at least three riding geldings. Larger horse herds, including the ownership of stallions, were considered luxuries confined to the well-to-do (Vreedland, 32). Haslund writes that the richest Mongol he met owned fourteen thousand horses (Haslund, 117). Herds owned by Buddhist temples were also extremely large, numbering into the thousands.

Up until 1921 eight per cent of Khalkha Mongol families belonged to the aristocracy and owned 43.5% of all livestock, averaging 2370 head per family. The remaining ninety-two per cent had barely fifty head per family and many none at all. Thus the great majority of people were dependent upon the aristocracy. They herded the lord's cattle, provided him with milk, cheese and koumiss, hides and dressed lambskins, gathered dung for fuel, attended the lord on his journeys and served him at his headquarters. They were obliged as well to provide military service and horses for post-stations for carrying official messages and forwarding official travellers. "Tethered" horses, or horses which were made available at various places for governmental duties, all were provided by the lord's subjects (Lattimore, 1962b, 57). But even the poor Mongol herdsman was not in the same position as the landbound peasant. The herder could flee tyranny and take his small herd with him. If necessary he could stay alive by hunting (Lattimore, 1962b, 58).

Radloff states that in 1860 among the Altaian Kalmuks a man with only fifty horses would be considered poor, but ten years later after a plague had killed most of the livestock, rich men were reduced to herds of fifty head. At the earlier date he had been told of a man who owned 6000 horses but he believed this to be an exaggeration since the Altaians measure their wealth in horses (Radloff, I, 284).

Throughout Outer Mongolia the percentage of horses in the total livestock varies somewhat: The Eastern Steppe in 1954 gave 12.8% of all livestock; the Khangai-Forest Steppe 11.1%, the Gobi Steppe 9.2% and the Altai Steppe 6.5% (Krader, 1955b, 309). The lowest figure is for the mountainous Altai while the most arid zone, the Gobi, has a higher percentage than the mountain area, but less than other steppe regions where there is more rainfall. Rough mountain terrain and desert are not hospitable to horse production, yet in spite of adverse conditions horse population remains impressive. Obviously in the Gobi and the Altai men with values strongly oriented to the horse and possessing specific knowledge of equine husbandry are acting to override "natural" considerations.

The number of horses in Outer Mongolia has remained somewhat static for the last few decades due largely to attempts on the part of the Communist regime to decrease the horses and goats and increase numbers of sheep and cattle (Rupen, 292). Thus, in 1918 there were a million and a half horses. By 1939, there were 2,388,000; 2,334,000 in 1957 and 2,250,000 in 1972. In all, horses make up about nine per cent of the livestock.[1]

Management and Breeding

Mountain Kalmuks of the Altai divide their horses into herds of between twenty and sixty head, including eight to twenty-five mares, five

---

[1] Other livestock in Outer Mongolia included twelve million sheep, 5,600,000 goats, two million cattle and 860,000 camels.

to ten geldings, five to fifteen yearlings, two to eight two year olds, two to six three year olds and one stallion. These graze together and do not intermingle with other herds. The stallion is the lord and master and if the herd is threatened he protects it from all enemies, including wolves and bears. When in danger the mares form a circle facing in with the foals in the centre of the circle and the stallion on the outside who challenges any aggressor (Radloff, I, 278). The stallion knows his own territory and all the members of his herd. He recovers any would-be deserters and, according to the Kalmuks, the stallion tolerates no infidelity on the part of his mares.

Kalmuk horse herds are tended by mounted herdsmen assisted by dogs. Herders must watch that young mares do not seek to flee from the herd to join others. Thieves are not a problem in the Altai since horse theft is presumably an unheard of crime. Herdsmen normally leave the herds alone except to bring them closer to the *yurt* in the evening. Foals, milking mares and riding geldings are picketed by the *yurt*. For a few days the newborn foals remain with their mares who are tied with long ropes. Then halters made of wool or horse hair are put on the foals and they are secured to a line stretched between two pegs in the ground. They are "tied to this line with a very short rope so they cannot injure each other". Here they are left for the day only to have access to their mothers after the latter has been almost completely milked. Riding horses kept by the *yurt* are hobbled with a woollen rope which joins two legs together; another hobbling device is a leather strap used for three legs. It is said that this type prevents all bruising or rubbing of the feet (Radloff, I, 280).

The Altaian Kalmuks are among the least nomadic of central Asiatic pastoralists. At most there is a movement between a summer and winter encampment, but the majority according to Radloff, only move when the dung heaps of their livestock, the garbage and other waste material in the vicinity of the *yurt* accumulates so much that in lieu of cleaning or removing the rubbish the only alternative is to move the homestead. Grass is readily available and in winter it is easily obtainable by the animals because there is not an excessive amount of snow; in addition the winds tend to blow it away. In summer livestock grazed where grass is short leaving areas where it is high for winter feed. In winter also younger stock were grazed nearer the *yurt* and provided with supplements of hay (Radloff, I, 286).

In Outer Mongolia sheep and horses are fed on the same kind of pasture, but horses and sheep are sent out at different distances: mature sheep one mile from camp and horses two miles while cattle are allowed to roam at will (Vreeland, 41). If the horse herd is small, it is often rounded up and quartered in a fold on winter evenings, but if it is a large herd it is guarded on such nights in a sheltered ravine or gorge (Haslund, 117). Herds are organized around stallions each being permitted to select and control his own band of mares and geldings. They are also supervised by a herdsman.

Before foaling time an ordinary herd in Outer Mongolia comprised about forty per cent mares over three years old, twenty-seven per cent stallions and geldings, fourteen per cent two year olds and nineteen per cent yearlings (Beck, 9). Beck claims yearly increases in herds to be thirty per cent while losses were 20.3%. The net almost ten per cent increase appears large considering the relative stability of Mongolia's horse population over the last six decades and the fact that neither exports nor horse slaughter have been sufficiently large to absorb such increments.

The Chahar like the Dagor sometimes employ a watchman for their horses, but often a group of Chahar join together with up to 150 horses and rotate the responsibility of herding among the several owner families (Vreeland, 147). Both Chahar and Dagor cut and store hay for winter use and the Dagor also feed horses on oats, especially those that are to be used for logging and hunting or mares which have just foaled. Supplementary feeding is less common among the Khalkha, but by the nineteenth century Mongols under the influence of the Russians were mowing hay and sowing small quantitites of grain, including oats. Such practices have been considerably increased in the last few decades. Under traditional conditions of open range feeding Mongol horses were stunted because of the bitter winters and lack of supplementary feed (Lattimore, 1962b, 41). On long trips horses have been known to be fed on shrubs and small pieces of dried mutton (Beck, 119). One would suspect that this meat was also salted, thus making it more palatable to the horse. As will be noted below, some Tungus also feed meat to their horses and they do so by introducing them first to salted flesh.

Both Mongols and Turkic people use a kind of lasso, called by the Mongols a *uraga*, a sliding loop of rope or rawhide placed on the end of a long pole which is often made of birch wood. The mounted herdsman with the pole in his arm runs alongside a chosen horse and drops the noose over the animal's head at which point the pursuer's mount, if properly trained, holds back like a Western cow pony until the captured horse becomes subdued and can be mounted by a rider. For the Kalmuks Radloff reports that the pursuer after securing the lasso around the victim's neck, follows him a bit on his horse and then jumps out of the saddle and allows himself to be dragged on the ground until the animal gives in (Radloff, I, 281). In another case he says that the pursuer after throwing the lasso follows the horse and then gradually pulls it nearer and nearer until it remains standing next to his own horse. All Mongols as well as Turkic nomads desire what would in the American West be called a good cutting horse for the capture of horses in the herd.

For identification purposes horses are branded on the haunch with special marks associated with specific kin groups. Among the Altaian Kalmuks Radloff says that only the wealthy branded since the poor easily recognized their few animals (Radloff, I, 279).

For ideal breeding purposes a stallion should serve about fifteen mares – those of his own herd. Among the Outer Mongolians stallions tend to become so vicious with age that they are early gelded and replaced with younger ones. As a consequence most colts are sired by immature stallions (Lattimore, 1962b, 195). The Mongols do not engage in what one could call any rational programme of breeding. They aim at quantity rather than quality. To them the best horses have violent tempers and the hair colour is the primary indicator of a good stallion. Until recent times a respected lama was supposed to select by divination the colour which would bring good luck to the household (Beck, 5). Thus, as might be expected, stallions have all kinds of defects. "Inbreeding, underfeeding, bad management of colts, premature covering and too early work for immature colts" all contribute to poor herds (Beck, 6). In addition horses are ridden until they are lame at which time they are turned out into the herd for another animal (Beck, 48). Under the Communist regime artificial insemination has been introduced so that selective breeding has become more widespread (Lattimore, 1962b, 195). Perhaps this is one of the more positive contributions of that regime.

The Kalmuk believe the young mares, on reaching maturity, are driven out of the herd by the dominant stallion and maturing stallions avoid the caresses of their dams. These young stallions are finally driven away from the herd by the dominant stallion to remain nearby grazing by themselves (Radloff, I, 278). Implied conceptions of incest attributed to horses, similar to those beliefs of the Dagor who hold that horses and dogs, but not cattle and swine, will not mate within the relationship of sibling and parents, are more projections of cultural values onto the horse than empirical fact. Like any other mammal except man, horses have no compunction about mating with their sires or dams. Adequate outbreeding in the herd, as in the wild herd, is attained by circulation of animals among the herds as mares are attracted away from one to join another, and as stallions are driven out to maintain the principle of the single dominant male polygynist to a herd. In addition there is the succession of breeding stock resulting from the natural processes of disease and aging.

Mares are bred between April and August especially in the earlier part of the season so that many foals are born in the end of winter, at the height of feed scarcity. The earliest age for breeding of mares is from two to three years of age. During the foaling season much greater attention must be paid to the herds to prevent colts from being trampled, or devoured by wolves and to see that they do not stray from the herd. After a foal has been with its dam a few days it is kept by the *yurt* for one to two months and then returned to the herd along with its mother, unless the mare is to be used for milking in which case both are kept in the vicinity of the house. In the second year it is branded and unwanted stallions are gelded with the knife that every Kalmuk carries by his side (Radloff, I, 282). Geldings stay with the herd and when they are four years old they are broken to ride; stallions and mares are left in the herd.

Among the Dagor no special care is given to mares who foal in the spring, but close attention is paid to one who foals in the winter and it is taken into the compound for this purpose. Gelding occurs in the spring and the wound is cauterized with a hot iron. For several days after gelding boys ride the animal in the belief that this prevents the development of a hunch and changing its gait before the wound" heals (Vreeland, 209).

Chahar Mongols often make a special party of a gelding operation which is attended by elderly men. The cooked testicles are thought to bring strength and good luck (Vreeland, 148). Beck describes the gelding process in Outer Mongolia as a kind of religious ceremony held in May to which special conjurers are invited.

The New Order

Nearly all Mongol nomads have been exposed to radical social-cultural changes in the past few decades as a result of the establishment of Communist regimes first in the Soviet Union (1917), then in Outer Mongolia (1921) and finally in China (1949). Outer Mongolia represents one of the more unusual types of Communist regime. First, from the point of view of orthodox Marxist doctrine, Outer Mongolia as a pastoral nomadic society with no proletariat – the prescribed primary stimulus for revolutionary change – should not have been conceived as a possible candidate for establishing the socialist state. However, following World War I Mongolian political leaders were seeking national autonomy from China and at the same time found themselves in the shadow of the newly created Soviet Union, equally interested in diminishing the power and influence of China. As a result the Mongolian nationalist movement became an extension of the international

Communist movement. Lenin recommended to the Mongols that as a pastoral nomadic society they should bypass capitalism by expropriating the large herds of the nobility and ecclesiastical authorities and establishing cooperative livestock centres. Thus, secondly, Outer Mongolia is a kind of Communist anomaly since it is still predominantly a land of stock breeders, attempting to apply some kind of socialistic theory to a herding economy.

In the first decade of communist rule, the property of hundreds of noble families was expropriated along with that of over two hundred prominent religious figures. Several hundred household heads were executed or imprisoned and a programme of forced collectivization of livestock was pursued resulting in a decline in the number of animals along with several popular uprisings. Collectivization was then relaxed, but was followed again in 1958–9 by a return to compulsion, requiring individuals to join livestock cooperatives (Lattimore, 1962b, 122).

A livestock cooperative maintains large herds owned by the organization; in addition a member can personally own up to fifty head in the northern steppes and seventy in the southern steppes. Each member is obliged to work a minimum number of days for the cooperative. The cooperative is organized into herding brigades and members herd stock in a quasi to fully nomadic fashion within the new structure much as they always had done. Cooperatives provide a centralized feature previously non-existent, including "centrally located permanent buildings which serve as administrative headquarters and school, stores and warehouses, garages, and offices for doctors and veterinarians". There are also barns which house some of the animals during winter. In general, these innovations have tended to produce a pattern somewhat along the lines of American style ranching, although large numbers of Mongols are still continuing the traditional nomadic life around their cooperative with two to four major moves a year depending upon the type of country. Yet this nomadism too is declining as *yurts* are made in a more permanent, more comfortable and complicated style so they are not so easily moved (Rupen, 296–7).

A total of 337 cooperatives, reported in mid-1961, each had an average of 525 families and 62,000 head of livestock. In 1959, 389 cooperatives reported enrolling 99.3% of the total pastoralist households and owning 75% of all livestock (Rupen, 294–5). The proportion of animals collectively owned to the number owned by cooperative members changed from one to four in 1957 to four to one in 1960. Thus, until 1960 the greater part of all livestock was privately owned even though people belonged to livestock cooperatives. In addition, up to this time there were still a number of "kulaks" or owners of large herds who employed herdsmen to care for their stock. One "kulak" reported owning 10,000 head of livestock in 1954 and engaged forty families to care for his herds (Rupen, 295). Whether any such large herdowners exist today is to be doubted.

TURKIC PEOPLE OF CENTRAL ASIA

From the eastern shores of the Caspian Sea to the Pamir and Altai Mountains in the east and northward to the grasslands of Siberia live several different Turkic peoples. The largest segment constitutes Soviet Turkestan in which live the Kazakhs in the north, and the Uzbeks, Karakalpaks, Kirghiz and Turkmen in the south. The Turkmen extend into north-eastern Iran and Afghanistan and the Uzbeks and Kirghiz are also found in northern Afghanistan. Another Turkic group, the Uighur, live in Sinkiang Province in China while the Tartars inhabit the southern edges of the wooded regions in central Siberia and eastern Russia. Probably the most outstanding difference between these peoples and their kinsmen, the Mongols, is their religious affiliation, for, while the Mongols have largely been converted to Lamaist Buddhism, the Turkic peoples are almost wholly Sunni Muslims. Otherwise their similarities are numerous. The Turkic people were at one time largely pastoral nomads organized in patrilineal tribal structures. Today much of the tribal structure has disappeared and most of the nomadic pattern abandoned, yet stock rearing remains important among them. It is least significant among the Uighur who have been for centuries sedentary agriculturalists dwelling in oasis villages. The Tartars and Uzbeks have also for several generations been settled villagers with a declining interest in stock raising.

Pastoral nomadism has been perpetuated longest and most extensively by the Kasakh, Kirghiz and Turkmen. Yet Soviet policy has been directed to settling nomadic populations in permanent collective farms so that true pastoral nomadism is preserved only among those who live in Iran and Afghanistan.[1]

Kazakh and Kirghiz pastoralism contrasts with that of the Turkmen. The Kirghiz and a large portion of the Kazakh live in grassy semi-arid steppes and mountainous zones, in areas having ten or more inches of precipitation a year. Other Kazakhs, the Karakalpaks, and Uzbeks live in shrub and desert steppe country having less than ten inches of precipitation a year, while the Turkmen exploit a desert steppe with

---

[1] Some Kazakhs and Kirghiz fled to Sinkiang after the Russian Revolution in order to preserve their herds and nomadic pattern of life. It would be expected that under the Maoist regime they too began to have fixed settlements.

less than seven inches of precipitation a year. The type and proportion of different kinds of livestock reflect in many respects these varying conditions. Thus, horses and cattle are greater in number and in proportion to other livestock and to the human population among those inhabitating grassy steppes. This includes northern and eastern Kazakhs and some Kirghiz. As one moves into more arid regions and more mountainous areas the proportion of sheep and goats increases, although the number of horses appears less affected by mountain conditions than that for cattle.

Central Asiatic steppe grasses include high proportions of feather grass and fescue and these afford good feed for horses. Feather grass, extending in an uninterrupted belt from the Urals to what is today Rumania, provided in ancient times a "broad road" to Europe for the steppe pastoralists and their horses (Smith, 22) – thus offering for those who want it, a "greenbelt explanation" of history. The variation in the number of horses in proportion to other livestock can be related broadly to the availability of good horse feed. The southern Kazakhs had fewer horses than their northern kinsmen; at the same time they pastured in grasses and shrubs which are less palatable to and less nutritious for horses, whereas the northern Kazakhs possessed more prairie and excellent horse feed.

The following diagram illustrates the relationship between climate, vegetation, degree of nomadism and horse population for major Turkic central Asian people for the period roughly covering the latter half of the nineteenth century – a time when some statistics are available and preceding the momentous changes of the twentieth century.

Diagram I does not reveal certain important cultural factors which help to clarify why the Turkmen have far fewer horses than the Kazakh or Kirghiz. The Turkmen make more specialized use of horses as riding animals, rarely employing them for other purposes. They have far more mules, donkeys and camels than their kinsmen to the north, and rarely if ever eat horseflesh, drink mare's milk, or sacrifice horses at funerary rites. Thus, they need not reserve part of their herds for these purposes. We cannot say that these habits arise purely out of Muslim zeal or out of scarcity of horses because of adverse ecological conditions. The Turkmen are better Muslims than the Kazakhs or Kirghiz, but they also are desert dwellers. Both factors collectively achieve the result of specialized and limited use of the horse and, hence, a need for fewer numbers. A far less conjectural issue is that the Turkmen have bred large horses which are hand fed with barley and chopped straw, while the Kazakh and Kirghiz rely on horses hardly more than pony size, which are grass fed on open range. As a result the Turkmen require far fewer horses per person for their transportation require-

DIAGRAM I

Climate, Nomadism, & Horses Among Major Turkic People*

	Over 50% nomadic		Less than 50% nomadic	
Horses horses 12% + of livestock & over one per person	Grassy steppe 10″ + precip.	shrub to desert steppe, less than 10″ precip.	wooded steppe 10″ + precip.	grassy steppe 10″ + precip.
	Eastern Kazakh Kirghiz			
Horses 5-11% of livestock & one to ten persons per horse	Northern Kazakh	Caspian Kazakh		Tartar?
		Uzbek		
Horses less than 5% of livestock & over ten persons per horse		Turkmen		
			Uighur	

This diagram shows that the greatest numbers of horses are associated with nomadic conditions on grassy steppes and they are least under those desert conditions where nomadism is no practised (e.g., the Uighur). The Turkmen have more horses than the Uighur, reflecting in part the greater amount of nomadism. One interesting feature not revealed by the diagram is that while, as one might expect, the Caspian Kazakhs had a lower percentage of horses in relation to other livestock than those to the east of them, they, nevertheless, had a higher horse to man ratio.

* Mainly derived from Krader, 1955b and 1963a.

ments than do the Kazakhs or Kirghiz. Thus, when all the various issues are considered, geography, like culture, must be viewed as a factor limiting the extent and type of horse husbandry.

Most of the remaining discussion on the horse in Turkic central Asia focuses on the Kazakhs as described primarily by Radloff in the period of 1860–1870.[1] While the present tense is employed to portray the Kazakhs, the reader must bear in mind that the description applies as in the case of the Kalmuk Mongols dealt with above, to the nineteenth century. What we are dealing with is a way of life that has largely been destroyed in the twentieth century.

[1] Nineteenth century Russian terminology referred erroneously to the Kazakhs as Kirghiz because they did not want "Kazakh" to be confused with Cossack, a totally different people. Nevertheless, the Kazakh and Kirghiz are each separate Turkic people, and while Radloff speaks of the Kirghiz he in fact means the Kazakh. When writing of the Kirghiz *per se* he called them Kara-Kirghiz, again a common erroneous Russian usage.

Kazakh horses are, like other horses of the steppe, renowned for their endurance, but Radloff believes they are not so malicious as the Mongolian horses although they remain stubborn and unpredictable throughout their lives. In the southern part of the steppe there are horses of Arab blood owned by the wealthy and kept as race horses. Since the stallions are used somewhat widely as studs there are many mixed bloods as a result (Radloff, I, 441).

Kazakhs consider the horse the embodiment of all beauty and, like the Arabs, they are said to love their horses more than their women. Horse thieving is a kind of heroic act, whereas stealing other livestock is viewed with contempt (Radloff, I, 441). A riding horse is the pride of both man and woman and in praising one's horse one praises the rider, as also when one finds fault with one's horse he offends the rider. To strike a strange horse is considered the same as hitting its owner (Radloff, I, 449).

Riding horsesback is a symbol also of status so that when a commoner approaches a noble chief he is expected to dismount some distance beforehand and lead his horse. No one would enter a chief's *yurt* with his whip on the wrist, since the chief could then claim his horse (Radloff, I, 526).

Uses of the Horse for Draught

Kazakhs employ camels, oxen and horses in their farming activities. Ploughing is mostly by camel or oxen, although horses are used on occasion. Rather than harrow, they tie the branches of trees to the tails of horses and drive them over the fields. Horses also are driven over the cut grain to thrash it (Radloff, I, 465).

Riding

Like the other Central Asiatic people a Kazakh rides from earliest childhood. As an infant he is tied into a child's saddle; the saddle soon becomes a second home. Radloff believes the horse rarely tires under a Kazakh rider (Radloff, I, 446).

Riding is with short stirrups and with such bent knees they touch the front edge of the saddle, the rider balancing himself in his seat with minimal support. Since the heel of the Kazakh riding boot covers almost half the sole and is directed frontwards like a cowboy boot, only about a third of the foot can rest in the stirrup (Radloff, I, 447).

The amble and the gallop are the primary gaits employed by Kazakhs and when they occasionally trot they stand in the stirrups inclined in a forward direction as compared to the distinctly upright posture observed with the other gaits. Reins are held in the left hand while the right hand holds the guide rope between middle and index finger. Both men and women observe the same style of riding. Quirts are used, but no spurs. The quirt consists of a stick about eighteen to twenty-two inches long at the end of which is a whip about half as long again and about one finger thick. The whip piece is composed of a leather core covered by twenty-four interwoven pieces of strap (Radloff, I, 447).

The bridle attaches to a snaffle bit with rings on either side of the mouth; other bridle parts include a chin strap, headband, cheek straps, throatlash and reins. The guide rope attaches to the right ring of the halter which is worn under the bridle (Radloff, I, 447).

There are three types of saddles: one for men, one for women, and a child's saddle. The design, common to all Eurasian nomads, is a basic wooden frame with a rather high pommel and cantle and a cushion attached to the frame. Men's saddles are a little simpler and have a crescent shaped pommel, while the women's saddle is more massive and has a pointed pommel. Women often have a travelling bag covered in red cloth as well as a cradle in front for carrying a child. Women's saddles are the more richly ornamented, as are their horses' headgear also.

Under the saddle is placed several layers of felt and a leather saddle cloth over these. Two square leather skirts hang from each side of the saddle so that the rider's heels cannot touch the horse's sides. Over the saddle cushion itself a carpet is strapped on and a girth, breast band and crupper hold the saddle on the horse's back. Leather thongs for tying on objects are also attached to the back part of the wooden frame. Saddle bags complete the outfit (Radloff, I, 448).

The wealth of an individual may be displayed by studding the saddle and bridle with silver. When moving their *yurts* women use red saddle cloths and spread a large red blanket over the saddle. The child's saddle is used for children between two and four years of age. As we have already noted, they are tied in it (Radloff, I, 448).

The Turkmen, O'Donovan reports, believe a very loose girth is necessary for a horse and as a result one must take care in mounting and dismounting for the saddle might slide under the horse's belly. Thus, it is common practice especially at dismounting for someone to hold a rider's stirrup. The Turkmen when not so attended "mount and dismount by throwing their whole weight" on the horse's neck (O'Donovan, II, 177–8).

Riding Garb

Traditional Kazakh boots are made of tough hide with pointed toes and a heel which covers half the sole and is studded with iron. For a long trip a man wears, over his cloth trousers, a pair of leather pants which are of a supple leather, dyed yellow, and among the wealthy, often embroidered. A belt made partly of silk and partly of a wide piece of leather studded with metal is also important riding gear as a place to attach one's knife sheath, leather bag for fire steel, and a shearing knife, or, if hunting, ammunition (Radloff, I, 459).

The Horse in Hunting and Sport

The favourite type of hunting among the Kazakh is that which can be conducted on horseback. It seems to be as much an occasion for a wild ride and a demonstration of the capabilities of one's favourite horse as it is for procuring game. One popular hunting technique is to ride after game at a gallop and break the animal's back with a blow from the rider's whip (Fox, 163).

Hawking and racing are the most prized equestrian sports. Racing is an important highlight on any festive occasion especially weddings, and religious holidays. Prizes of livestock and silver are offered, but, apparently from Radloff's observations, there is such a mêlée of racers and spectators at the end of a race that the victors rarely take their prizes. They are grabbed by others in the great confusion. One does not race for the prize, therefore, but for the prestige of having a winning horse (Radloff, I, 491–2). Races are held on a course marked off by poles. As with the Mongols they are long distance affairs usually about seventeen miles with boys between six and ten years of age as the jockeys (Radloff, I, 489–490).

Other games involve acrobatic feats and tests of strength from horseback. A silver piece is placed on the ground and a contestant is required to trot by and, from horseback, pick up the coin with his hand; more often than not he ends in falling off without picking up the coin (Radloff, I, 490). Another contest requires the rider, again from horseback, to grab a sheep by the hind leg and throw it in the air, apparently killing the animal in the process (Radloff, I, 491).

One game is held between boys and girls who pair off and each girl is given a few lengths head start after which the boy sets off after her. If he can catch her, he is allowed to embrace her and touch her breasts. The girl, however, is armed with her whip, so that some boys return unsuccessful and with bloody gashes on their faces much to the rejoicing of the women observers. On other occasions a girl may offer herself freely because she likes the boy and, then, she is considered "prey" (Radloff, I: 492). The Kirghiz and Turkmen have a similar game. At a Turkmen wedding, the bride in her wedding costume rides off carrying the carcass of a sheep or goat which a group of mounted boys try to snatch from her (Vambery, 323). The Kirghiz girl is armed with a whip which she uses on her pursuers, but the Turkmen girl has no such defence (Pahlen, 323).

Bagai or *buzkashi* is without question among the world's most brutal sports and was played in the days of Genghis Khan. It has often been played in conjunction with such rites of passage as marriages and circumcisions as well as at major festivals. Two teams of horsemen are involved. Each is composed of from ten up to several dozen men. The object is to carry a goat or either a live or decapitated calf off to score a team's goal and bring personal glory to one's self. The man with the *buz* or goat may bear it across his saddle or drag it along the ground. He is pursued by all the others, who attempt by almost any means to wrest it from him. In a traditional style game, there was no time limit nor any circumscribed field; players carried knives, chains and whips. The knives have been used to cut opponents' saddle girths, but they and the chains as well as the whips are on occasion used for more violent deeds. More recent refinements of the game have outlawed the knives and chains, established a fixed number of players with umpires and specific time limits as well as boundaries to the game field. Interestingly enough Afghanistan, a predominantly Indo-European land where less than twenty per cent of the population are Turkic and Mongol, has made *buzkashi* its official national sport and, in so doing, it has introduced these various attempts to establish more precise rules and gentlemanly procedures.

Among the Uzbek and Kirghiz of northern Afghanistan there are professional *buzkashi* players who begin their careers participating in local festivities until they can graduate into the status of full time prestigious professionals with their own servant and groom. Horses, selected from offspring of others which have been *buzkashi* players, are the only animals trained for the sport. These horses, which are in their prime between the ages of eight and fifteen, are strictly trained and exercised. They are fed on alfalfa, oats and hay and even, on occasion, eggs and sheep fat in winter.

Meat, Hides and Hair

The Kazakh prefer horseflesh to beef and mutton; it is considered the greatest delicacy. The poorer Kazakhs purchase old horses from the neighbouring Russians in the spring and fatten them up on good pasture to slaughter in the autumn. The wealthy slaughter their own mares which had not foaled, as well as foals. A young, fat mare is considered the best delicacy. Before slaughtering, horses are ridden about until they become covered with foamy sweat at which time they are thrown and dispatched. It is believed that this process much improves the flavour of both the meat and the fat (Radloff, I, 451).

The Kazakhs do not observe Muslim rules regarding animal slaughter. First, of course, horse meat is technically taboo to Muslims of the Hanifi school to which the Kazakhs belong. Secondly, horses which have died are often taken off by poorer Kazakhs and slaughtered sometime after the animal has died, which is also prohibited by Islam, and thirdly, the blood is collected at the slaughter and consumed, anathema to any good Muslim (Radloff, I, 471–2).

The best part of the horse is the fat from the belly, which may be salted and made into sausages and smoked. The horse's intestines are used for sausage manufacture while those of all other livestock are considered inedible and are discarded. Only the lungs of the horse are not eaten.

Horse fat is believed to have very penetrating properties and for this reason it is prized for use on leather (Radloff, I, 451). Horse hides are rarely sold by the Kazakhs since they use the materials themselves. They are particularly suited for cutting into strips for making straps and braiding leather for reins, bridles, girth straps, cruppers, and whips (Radloff, I, 452).

Horse hair is not plentiful among the Kazakhs since they are reluctant to cut the manes or tails. Hair is used for rope making, but hair guide ropes are more commonly acquired from the neighbouring Kalmuks (Radloff, I, 452).

Milking

Kazakh mares provide little milk at one time and are milked from six to seven times a day, yielding only about two quarts total since the foal takes a goodly part of the supply. Because milking is a difficult and sometimes dangerous task it is always reserved for men. Leather buckets are used since one kick from a mare would readily smash a wooden pail (Radloff, I, 445).

Milking mares are carefully chosen and used only for milk since udders become swollen and sore if mares are ridden to any extent (Fox, 157). To milk requires two and, if the mare is wild, three persons. The forelegs are hobbled and a noose is tightened around the mare's neck. One man at least must hold fast to this rope during the milking. The milker kneels beside the mare and rests the bucket on his left knee. Foals are allowed to suckle both before and after milking and may remain beside the tied-up dam if she has been milked dry (Radloff, I, 445).

Mares are milked for four months of the year and remain by the *yurt* during this time, returning to the herd in the fall with their foals. The poor invariably have no milking mares.

Mare's milk is poured raw into large leather bags where it is beaten with a paddle for hours. Koumiss results from four days of fermentation. It is slightly sour and intoxicating and according to Radloff is an agreeable drink "once one gets accustomed to the peculiar smell which comes from the leather bag" (Radloff, I, 450).

Koumiss is a symbol of wealth and prestige and a person's status may be gauged by the amount he serves. The poor come to visit the wealthy in order to drink of the koumiss which they do not have. At feasts great quantitites are drunk, to the extent that some become intoxicated. Radloff states that it takes four to six quarts to reach this state (Radloff, I, 450). Koumiss contains a considerable amount of carbonic acid gas and a very low alcoholic content (from 1.65 to 3.2%) (Montagne, 562).[1]

Koumiss serving is a ritual like the coffee serving of the Arabs or tea ceremony of the Japanese and is one Radloff compares to European wine tasting. Koumiss must be treated with respect and is poured only by men, usually the host or eldest member of the house. It "is placed before the master of the house . . . in the best dish" which has been thoroughly cleaned. During the drinking complete silence should reign as each person savours his brew. "The koumiss is stirred and spooned out to guests with a tin or silver ladle" and offered in wooden or porcelain bowls. "It would be offensive to offer a highly regarded guest any other drink than koumiss" (Radloff, I, 450). Occasionally it may be offered mixed with water, especially when it is in short supply. Radloff observed it eaten mixed with roasted wheat or millet on rare occasions. It is the only dairy product the Kazakhs make from mare's milk (Radloff, I, 451).

The Horse in Rites of Passage: Weddings

Kazakh bride wealth is reckoned in terms of horses since it is held that only the horse is a worthy medium for calculating the value of a person (Radloff, I, 449). After the bride wealth has been fixed the groom's father visits the bride's father and presents him with a horse and a coat and a number of other gifts. When the wedding day arrives the bride is escorted to her groom's house and as she is led to her bridegroom's

---

[1] A koumiss recipe is included in *Larousse Gastronomique* as follows: To prepare the ferment, work a half pound of brewer's yeast and a quarter pound of flour with a little honey and a glass of milk. Next day, add three quarts, plus one cup of milk (Montagne, 562). One would expect that the brew would be allowed to ferment for two or three days thereafter, but Montagne does not mention this.

yurt she is called to thus:

Bride, O bride, you dear little bride,
You, the foal of the dark mare.

The bride's joking and play with the groom are compared to the behaviour of a foal. On arriving at her destination she is veiled and there is yet another song. In it the gifts of animals are named which the relatives will present to her if they may see her face. When such a gift is mentioned the singer raises the bride's veil with a stick showing her face and sings:

If you give a horse, give a grey one!
Give a strong one which ambles!
Greetings to the father-in-law!

Other similar songs are sung for other animals given by lesser relatives (Radloff, I, 478–480).

Funerary and Other Rites

Radloff describes slightly varying forms of funeral sacrifice of horses among the Central Asiatic Turks. In one case when a wealthy Kazakh dies the guests assemble on the seventh day for a feast and the deceased man's saddle is placed backwards upon his horse with his clothes spread over it and his hat on top. So harnessed, the horse is hitched by its halter to the *yurt* of the deceased. As the mourners sing funeral songs the horse's tail is cut off. The horse is now called a widow and is never mounted again. Similarly the horse of a Kazakh who dies on a journey is returned home with an inverted saddle and at the *yurt* its tail and mane are cut (Radloff, I, 449).

"Memorial feasts are held on the seventh, fortieth, and hundredth day after the death" and for an important person these entail the slaughter of large numbers of livestock, including horses, so as to serve hundred of guests for a period of four days. In one instance mentioned by Radloff, thirty horses and one hundred and fifty sheep were slaughtered and between four and five thousand guests were accommodated. Entrails and inferior pieces of slaughtered animals were distributed to the poor as the animals were slaughtered (Radloff, I, 487–8) undoubtedly a custom associated with the Muslim practice of giving part of a sacrifice to the poor. On the fourth day of this funerary memorial, horse races and exhibitions of horsemanship were held (Radloff, I, 489).

The Abakan Tartars between the Eastern and Western Sayan Mountains place a saddle at the foot of the grave and "on the fortieth day after the death the family assemble around the grave and . . . the favourite horse of the deceased is killed". The horse had been given its freedom on the day of the death, but now it is cooked and eaten and the head placed on the end of a pole which is erected at the foot of the grave (Radloff, I, 379).

These Tartars also observe a spring festival in which animals selected for sacrifice are decorated with ribbons as among the Altaian Kalmuks. Sacrificial animals appear to be always stallions or mares. Following the festive meal there are horse races, matches, dancing and singing (Radloff, I, 378).

In pre-Islamic shamanist times the Tartars sacrificed horses to their various deities: white horses to their highest god, the creator being; red horses to one of his four sons and his descendents (Radloff, I, 361). Before their conversion to Islam the Kazakh similarly sacrificed white horses to their divinities and ate the flesh in a sacramental manner. Even after their conversion they sealed their treaties "by parties dipping their hands in the blood of a white horse" (Wardell, 110).

The Kirghiz celebrate the great Muslim Feasts – the Little Feast ending the month of fasting in Ramadan and the Great Feast which follows not long after – with a slaughter of horses. The poor are invited to share in consuming the meat and the hides are donated to the mullahs (Muslim prayer leaders and teachers) (Jochelson, 1926, 131). These feasts, too, are accompanied by games of equestrian sport.

Horses in the System of Fines and Punishment

The cutomary Kazakh legal system was based on the payment of fines which were invariably calculated in numbers of horses. Thus, killing a free man required a fine of one hundred horses or one thousand sheep and for the killing of a woman, or a girl or slave the fine was half that amount, plus nine head of other livestock. The murder of a "sultan", an important tribal chief, however required the payment of seven times the value of a free man by the murderer and his kinsmen. Lesser injuries were also calculated in terms of fines of horses. Thus, a tooth knocked out or a broken leg or wound on the head were each valued at one horse and a coat. One who knocked down a pregnant woman causing her to bear a dead child, had to pay a horse for every month if the foetus were under five months and, if it were older than five months, a camel for every month over that (Radloff, I, 524).

Thievery also was punished by fining. Stealing a horse meant that the horse upon which the thief was riding was confiscated and he had to pay two horses as a fine; one for the neck of the stolen horse and one for the rear end (Radloff, I, 525).

Horse Management

Like the Mongols, most of the nomadic Turkic peoples keep their horses on open range with little or no supplementary feeding, engaging in seasonal movement of herds. Between the wealthy and the poor variations in this pattern of management occur.

The Kazakhs move to their winter grazing quarters with their camels, sheep, and cattle and leave the horse herds behind in the autumn camps which are no more than ten to twenty miles removed from the winter camp. The horses are driven to a summer terrain when there is much snowfall and, especially to places unused during the summer or where new grass has grown because of heavy rains (Radloff, I, 418). Presumably, the resulting higher grass would be easier for the horses to obtain under the snow.

Horses are adept at pawing away snow for winter feed because they are willing to undertake the task and because their single hoof is a better tool for such activity than a cloven one. Central Asiatic horses have tougher hooves than stabled horses yet, nevertheless, they find an accumulation of a foot of snow difficult to paw away and, according to Smith, about sixteen inches is the maximum even for adults. Foals are unable to manage if the snow is more than ten inches deep. The more an animal must work to uncover the grass the more readily exhausted it becomes, so there is a point of diminishing returns where the animal is expending more calories than he is consuming (Smith, 22).

The well-to-do always divide their herds according to type of livestock so that each – sheep, cow, horse and camel – is able to graze in areas most suited to it. Thus horses are grazed in the better pastures rather than on the hard, strong tasting herbage which is left to camels and sheep. However, in winter horses may be moved onto a pasture to break up the snow, and feed on the taller grass after which sheep are driven out to crop the remains. Poor people graze their horses with those of the rich or near their own *yurts* or they may merely turn them out with their other stock. A not uncommon practice among both the Turkic and Mongol peoples of Central Asia was for the wealthy men to distribute their livestock among the poor for tending. In return the poor were permitted to use the horses for riding and the cattle for milk, often also taking a lamb or calf.

A wealthy man divides his horse herds to graze in separate groups, each under the leadership of a single stallion. A band includes about nine mares, nine new born foals, eight two year olds, five to eight three year olds, five or six four year olds and a few older geldings. Each band contains a minimum of fifteen and up to about fifty head (Radloff, I, 442).

The stallion is capable of protecting his group from predators and tolerates no rivals. In addition men may watch over the herd and sometimes hired herdsmen are employed for this purpose (Radloff, I, 463). Particularly once the foals are born and for several months thereafter when the mares are kept for milking, the herds áre not far from the encampment. In addition to the horses kept in herds, a few geldings for riding are hobbled beside the owner's house. Such animals are used for only a short time after which they are sent out into the herd to rest and remounts brought in. This is necessary because of the poor feeding: animals fed on grass alone are not conditioned to sustained work as those with a substantial grain and hay diet. If an owner feeds any hay or grain at all to his mounts it will be a small ration to these geldings while they are in use. When a man goes on a prolonged journey he takes at least one additional mount and changes off periodically.

Some Kazakhs gather wild hay from lands which were left ungrazed, but there is no serious endeavour to raise hay. Grain feeding – mostly barley, but among the Kirghiz, millet – is more restricted than hay feeding. Grain feeding is a practice mostly limited to the wealthy for their favourite horses during winter or when they were working. Especially the Arab riding types owned by wealthy southern Kazakhs are awarded such a privilege.

While horse herds are supervised by mounted men and to some extent the camel herds as well, flocks of sheep and goats are managed by men on foot or mounted on oxen. When it is necessary to round up horses a small group of riders is used, at least one of which carries the lasso described above for the Mongols.

The Turkmen, who, as we have seen, live in the most desert-like conditions and keep fewer horses than other Turkic nomads, observe a pattern of horse husbandry more like that of the Middle East. Some of the Turkmen horses are most likely descended from the famour Ferghana breed sought after by the Emperor Wu and found also in the Pazyryk graves. All horses are very carefully and personally attended by Turkmen. Working mounts are fed barley and chopped straw and owners have been known to share their meal of pilaw with them. Hay is put out for them in baskets as field mangers so that the hay will not be blown away (O'Donovan, I, 267). Horses are rarely stabled, but are kept picketed near the owner's house where they are kept covered with an enormous blanket of felt about an inch thick which totally covers the animal from ear to tail and is tied around two or three times with a broad girth. This is worn in the heat of the day as well as in the cold of the night and it is claimed that the horses prefer this arrangement to a stable (O'Donovan, I, 229). As an animal ages more blankets – up to seven – may be added (Christie, 40 and Dodge, 383).

In the past the Turkmen devoted a great deal of time to raiding and robbing activities and primarily maintained horses for these ends. In the nineteenth century it was said that almost every man no matter how poor possessed at least one horse and devoted a considerable part of his working time to attending it (O'Donovan, II, 62).

Kazakh horses are gelded and branded with a clan mark on the haunch in their second year. As with the Kalmuk there are poor families who do not brand their horses because they can readily identify the handful they own.

Breeding

Stallions are considered ready for breeding use at the age of five; in selecting a stallion for this purpose, the nature and build are considered while colour is ignored, in contrast to the usual Mongol priority on colouration. As a result of this Kazakh horses often have strange colour combinations (Radloff, I: 442). Many stallions are used for breeding purposes for only a year or two when they are gelded.

According to Radloff, young stallions are driven out of the herds by their sires and they graze nearby until the owner adds them to another herd. He also states that stallions never cover their own foals and that a stallion will bite and drive away one of his own that is in heat until she leaves the herd. Further, it is claimed young stallions never cover their own dams and if put in a herd where his mother is present, the mare will be removed (Radloff, I: 443). Most of the above is more Kazakh folklore than anything else, similar to Mongol beliefs mentioned above where it was also pointed out that ideas of incest among horses cannot be reconciled with empirical fact.

Mares usually foal in March and are left unfettered in the herd until May when they are brought to the *yurt* with the foal for milking use. The foals are tied to a foal rope and the mares left to graze freely. Sometimes the young are left free in which case the mares are tied.

THE YAKUT

The Yakut are the most northerly of Turkic pastoralists and inhabit the sub-Arctic taiga, a needle leafed deciduous forest zone. Until modern times they have retained their shamanistic religion. Thus, they diverge from their southern kinsmen in some respects. Nevertheless, they exhibit typical features of nomadic and semi-nomadic horse and cattle breeding tribes of Central Asia (Jochelson, 1933, 197). In the thirteenth century they were located in the region of Lake Baikal after being separated from the main body of Turkic peoples by the Mongol expansions (Jochelson, 1933, 63). In the following centuries they pursued a northerly movement settling along the Lena River and its tributaries and crossing the Verkhoyansk Mountain Range to dwell in the Yana, Indighirka and Kolyma valleys. Others pushed to the north-eastern limits of Siberia to the shores of the Okhotsk Sea.

Horse breeding had been of primary importance in their old and more southerly habitat, but in their present location cattle have increased at the expense of horses to the extent that cow's milk has become a substitute for mare's milk. In the days immediately prior to the Revolution, "droves of horses and mares for milking" were found only in those areas most isolated from Russian influence and, then, only among the well-to-do (Jochelson, 1933, 197).

The average number of livestock in Pre-Revolutionary days (1917) among the southern Yakut was 9.3 cattle and 2.4 horses per household. The Yakuts in the northern two districts, Verkhoyansk and Kolymsk, which extend to the Arctic circle, have adopted more reindeer. Households in these frigid zones averaged about eighteen reindeer, 5.5 horned cattle and 4.9 horses each (Jochelson, 1933, 190). It is these Yakuts who have introduced both horses and cattle to their most northerly and coldest environment: to the Lena and Kolyma Rivers on the Arctic Circle and the northernmost limits of forested zones of Asia. Indeed some of them have settled in the tundra in this vicinity, but this has been a more recent event.

Forde comments: "Among the Yakut the transfer from cattle to reindeer can be observed in progress, for they are adopting reindeer from the Tungus as their horses and cattle die out" (Forde, 1934, 367). This undoubtedly refers to the northern Yakuts only.

Yakut horses are of small pony size and are obviously an extremely hardy breed. Yakut livestock were originally obtained from the Kirghiz (or Kazakhs?) but they have deteriorated in the far north to smaller size and lessened prolificacy (Jochelson, 1933, 190).

Both horses and cattle are used for much the same ends as with other Turkic nomads. They are ridden and used as pack animals. Both the riding saddle and pack saddle follow the general southern Siberian pattern. The pack saddle is essentially two wooden boards secured at an angle while the riding saddle is a wooden frame upon which a pillow is secured. The frame is "usually reinforced at the front with a stamped silver plate with a forged hook in the centre for the reins" (Levin and Potapov, 259). The entire saddle is elaborately decorated with leather tassels and beads, and carved silver and brass (Jochelson, 1933, 176). Side skirts hang down the sides, like the Mongolian saddle. Highly ornamented cloth and leather sweat cloths are placed under the saddle (Levin and Potapov, 260). The stirrups are usually of metal; sometimes wood is bent into a circle for this purpose. They are attached to the front of the saddle and are so short that riding is with the usual extremely bent knee characteristic of Central Asiatic peoples. Ancient Yakut snaffles consisted of two unequal metal parts, but modern bits of two equal sections are derived from the Russians. Other riding accoutrements include whips, mosquito beaters, and curry combs (Jochelson, 1933, 61). As among south Siberian pastoralists horses are not shod.

Before the seventeenth century the Yakut did not hitch horses to sleds or carts, but as a result of their contact with the Russians they have learned how to harness them for these ends (Jochelson, 1933, 61). Sledges are attached to the horse saddle by means of a thong and the individual rides while the horse draws the sledge. Oxen are also ridden while drawing sledges (Jochelson, 1933, 188). The wealthy Yakuts once rode in sleighs drawn by three white horses, wore reindeer skin overcoats, "and carried white staffs in their hands" (Jochelson, 1933, 47).

Horse meat is highly prized, but eaten mostly by the wealthy (Levin & Potapov, 269). Horsehair is widely employed as ornamentation on birchbark and the like. It is braided to make "lassoes, cord, laces and nets, loops", and fly fans. It is used for "stuffing pillows for saddles" and woven for decorative purposes – that is, twisted by hand without a spindle (Levin and Potapov, 259).

Koumiss was once an important part of the diet and associated with ritual. With the decline in horses it has been replaced by milk products from reindeer and cattle. With this has gone the disappearance of the old decorated koumiss pots and goblets and the ceremonial involved in koumiss manufacture and use (Jochelson, 1933, 197).

The Yakut once observed a major koumiss fesitval, which may have survived to the end of the nineteenth century. "During the summer, in olden times, every rich man arranged a kumiss festival at which all members of the clan assembled and were entertained . . . . During the festival defensive and offensive leagues were concluded. Every such ceremony was initiated with sacrifices, which were accompanied with songs, dances, games, horse and foot races, and other contests.

"Two kumiss festivals in honour of the deities were arranged during the year by the owners of large droves of mares . . . . The first milking of mares in the spring is . . . consecrated to the Supreme Being . . . .. In the midst of a large smooth grass meadow is erected a kind of altar, consisting of two posts with a cross beam and three young birch trees with young shoots on them. The altar is hung with sacrificial horsehair; on the ground in front of it are placed ornamented birchbark and oxhide barrels filled with kumiss. The skin barrels are tied to the altar-frame by long ornamented strips of soft elk leather, so that the vessels will not collapse when softened by the liquid in them" (Jochelson, 1933, 202).

Libations of koumiss are offered to the deities and ". . . formerly horses were often consecrated by being driven to the east, the seat of the 'creators'" (Jochelson, 1933, 203). Once the master of ceremonies had scattered the libations of koumiss to the several spirits, koumiss was distributed among those assembled, first to elder and esteemed individuals both men and women and then to the others. There was a preparation of horsemeat and beef and dishes of melted butter for a general feast which followed (Jochelson, 1933, 203).

In addition to the koumiss festival and the blood sacrifice of horses, these animals were also made living sacrifices. "To drive nine horses to a remote place and leave them, constituted a sacrifice. The very rich made this sacrifice three times, the moderately rich twice, and those in ordinary circumstances only once . . . The poor man, trying to imitate these boastingly offered sacrifices [of the rich], often lost all his cattle and despoiled himself of all his possessions, to end in beggary" (Jochelson, 1933, 47).

Horses are left out to graze both in summer and winter. Winter stabling is practiced only for cattle and this to a limited degree only (Levin & Potapov, 248). The long and extreme winters require storage of hay which is however primarily reserved for cattle and foals. No hay was sown in pre-Revolutionary times; all that was cut and put up was wild (Jochelson, 1933, 188).

The general characteristics of pre-Revolutionary horse husbandry among the Turk and Mongol nomads with the exception of the Turkmen may be summarized as follows:

1. Prevalence of open range grassland feeding. Particularly as a result of Russian contact, sporadic, supplementary feeding occurs, usually of hay, in winter.
2. Animals grazed in herds each segmented into bands headed by a stallion, usually with a herdsman but sometimes with none.
3. Multi-purpose function of the horse: riding, packing, draught, milk, meat, hides, hair, blood sacrifice, for gifts, bride wealth and fine payments.
4. Men care for horses, but both men and women ride. Except for

some of the Mongols, men also milk the mares.

5. Preference for geldings for riding; riding style is with short stirrup and at ambling pace, mounted on a saddle with high pommel and cantle and having a bridle with snaffle bit and lead rope as well as reins.
6. Practice of gelding and branding with designs on haunch for identification, and use of rope on end of a pole for lassoing horses.
7. Any systematic and selective breeding programme is minimal.
8. A very high horse to man ratio ranging from 2.5 horses per person to one horse per ten persons. High ratios result in part from small size of horses and open range feeding, necessitating more horses per man, given the reliance upon the horse as the means of transportation.

Today pastoral life in Soviet Turkestan has been radically altered by the relentless programme of the Soviet government to turn its people into collective farm workers. While there was some Russian settlement in the area before the Revolution, a major migration occurred after that under governmental auspices, so that at present close to fifty per cent of the population of Soviet Turkestan is Russian, Ukrainian and Byelo-Russian. These Europeans have been engaged in the development and expansion of irrigation cultivation and especially grain production on collective farms. This alone greatly restricted pastoralism. But, in addition, the nomads themselves have been shunted onto collective farms raising grain and livestock. Bacon estimated ten years ago that within the Soviet Union possibly a half a million Kazakhs are still primarily nomadic (Bacon, 121).

As in Mongolia an attempt has been made to adapt traditional patterns of nomadic pastoralism to collective farming. Only a few farms are, however, exclusively devoted to livestock breeding. Sections of the working population of a collective farm are assigned to herd its stock. There are "brigades" of sheep herders, horse herders, camel herders and cattle herders most of whom migrate throughout the year between summer and winter pastures as was done in pre-Revolutionary times. Bacon believes that "in practice" the brigade does not appear to be very different from the traditional Kazakh kin-based community, the *aul*, since it comprises a family group, the type of livestock it tends, as well as riding horses, pack camels and sheep for its own consumption (Bacon, 128). Animals also appear to be herded in a fashion closely reminiscent of the old tradition (Bacon, 134). The Kazakhs continue to make koumiss and to breed horses extensively. "[T]he continued vitality of horse breeding among the Kazaks is a reflection not of the economic importance of the horse, but of the cultural prediliction of Kazaks for that animal" (Bacon, 122). Statistics do show, however, a marked decline in the number of horses. In 1916 among Kazakhs they numbered 4,340,000; in 1929, 4,200,000. An overall rapid decline in all forms of livestock in the ensuing five years resulted in only 241,000 horses in 1935. A general recovery occurred after this time so that by 1953 they numbered 1,801,000 (Bacon, 119–121). But today they have declined to less than a million.

Collectivization for those who have persisted in nomadism within the Soviet Union seems to have produced three major changes. As in the Mongolian case, the professional herders are tied to a permanent base of supplies and administration. Secondly, the herders constitute a specialized occupational category within a complex and centralized agricultural system. Thirdly, the livestock is mostly the property of the state, not of individual herders.

It is indeed peculiar on several counts that practically the entire world of the equestrian pastoral nomads should have been engulfed by a Marxist system. As in the earlier example of the Mongols, we may inquire out of what *yurts* the Turkic proletariat were expected to arise to implement the socialist revolution? And, of course, the answer to such a rhetorical question is that they did not arise out of any *yurts* since there was no proletariat. Indeed, the socialist state was imposed upon these people from outside by European (Russian-Ukrainian) imperialists disguised as revolutionary working-class leaders. It seems that the Turkic and Mongol nomads in what is now the Soviet Union had little sympathy with the new system. The Kalmuks openly opposed the new order and large numbers of Kazakhs and Uzbeks fled the country.

Secondly, stock breeding is neither culturally nor historically associated with collective ownership; rather, livestock throughout history has been the property of individuals, even where land is communally held. Certainly among the Eurasian nomads individual ownership of livestock has been a time honoured, three thousand year old custom. The Mongolian Communist system represents an attempt to reconcile this deep tradition with Marxist-Leninist ideology. Soviet Turkestan, perhaps because it was administered ultimately by Russians and not "natives", was less given to reconciliations with the old and pursued a more dogmatic course in attempting to stamp out concepts of private ownership.

Horses are, of all animals, most associated with individual ownership; the relationship between horse and rider is an individual one which traditionally has been reinforced by the fact that the rider is the owner and by the widely held view, as among Kazakh and Kirghiz, for example, that a man should not let his horse be ridden by another. The rider has trained his mount in a way suited to him and does not want the horse confused by another's peculiar habits. Of course, in the development of livestock ranching, cowboys rode horses owned by the ranch and cavalry horses similarly were state owned. It is, then, perfectly legitimate to point out that such arrangements are essentially no different from a collective farm which owns all the horses the various "cowboys" might use.

The important issue at stake here is, I believe, that if one is to consider horses for purely utilitarian ends, as is the aim of the Soviet collective system, then that system may be made compatible with a horse breeding programme delimited by those values. If one aims as well to maintain the horse for non-pragmatic, non-utilitarian ends such as personal pleasure, sports, demonstrations of individual skill, or as symbols of manhood and prestige then there will always be at the very least a strong identification of an individual rider with a given horse and this fact exerts strong pressure to individual ownership. In the Soviet system some concessions to individual ownership have been made, but the other side of this coin is that, as in Mongolia, there has been an effort to reduce the horse population. In Soviet Asia this has apparently been more successful than in Mongolia.

XV

Some Peoples Marginal to the Central Asiatic Equestrian Pastoralists

THREE groups which are culturally quite distinct from one another yet peripheral to the Turkic-Mongol equestrian pastoralists are the Tungus, the Tibetan yak herders, and the Cossacks. Each of these people is heavily influenced in its horse husbandry by the Turkic-Mongol peoples, but has developed along divergent cultural lines.

THE TUNGUS

The Tungus, who are culturally and "racially" akin to the Mongols, originate in northern Manchuria and probably two thousand years ago began to spread north and west into Siberia as far as the Yenisei River and the Arctic Circle. In the past five centuries they have lost much of this territory to invading Yakuts, Buryat Mongols, and Russians. Today there are fewer than a hundred thousand in the Soviet Union while the remaining three million inhabit China, presumably nearly all in Manchuria. Most of those in China have become highly Sinified; only the Tungus in the northern extremities of Manchuria have been less affected by Chinese culture. The Northern Tungus are residents of the larch and birch sub-Arctic forests of Siberia where they have traditionally been reindeer herders. The Southern Tungus live in the mountain forest zones and adjacent steppes of northern Manchuria, in much of which reindeer herding is impracticable. Horse breeding and some cattle rearing are carried on instead.

Among the Northern Tungus of the taiga the horse is of little importance. Indeed what few horses there are appear to have an extremely difficult existence. They are left to forage for themselves during the severe winter and are provided with no supplementary feed such as hay. They, as a result, come out of the long winter in a half starved, weakened condition, but are hindered in taking full advantage of summer pastures because of the paucity of good horse feed on the pastures and also because the annoyance of flies inhibits grazing during the day. Because horses are put to work in summer, owners are reluctant to turn them out to pasture at night. Thus, they enter the winter season in a condition not much better than when they left the previous one (Shirokogoroff, 38).

Where reindeer breeding is impossible the horse becomes a substitute. The reliance on horse breeding has provoked certain changes in Tungus organization in that the horse breeders establish definite summer and winter camps with more permanent buildings and supplies of hay. The limited amount of serious horse breeding among Tungus on the taiga has led to the establishment of permanent villages since the horses as we have noted fare poorly here. Shirokogoroff implies they must be stabled.

Those Tungus settled in villages and engaged in some significant horse breeding have two kinds of horses: summer and winter. Summer horses cannot be used in winter since they are exhausted from over-work and underfeeding in summer and those used for winter are rested during the summer. Horses are primarily taken on hunting expeditions and are cared for by the men. Among village dwelling Tungus there are about five or six horses per family at the most (Shirokogoroff, 39).

In the mountain zones of Northern Manchuria, horses are trained to eat meat, in part because of the paucity of feed. They are first given small bits of salted dried flesh and eventually they come to eat raw meat. The Tungus believe meat-fed horses are much stronger and better in all respects than hay-fed animals. Like the reindeer the horses here become accustomed to salt and human urine (Shirokogoroff, 39). In this region women are responsible for tending to the horses which are sometimes left as a herd to graze without a herdsman. Ear marking is the common form of identification.

Riding, harness and general use of the horse among the Tungus as well as much of the vocabulary relating to it are borrowed from the neighbouring Mongols and Buryats. The horse plays little or no role in the Tungus shamanist religion except, as one might expect, where elements have been directly borrowed from the Mongols. Among horse using Tungus, horses serve as bridewealth and for part of the dowry (Shirokogoroff, 226).

Manchurian Tungus generally avoid having stallions since any increase in the number of horses belongs to the owner of the mare and one must infer from Shirokogoroff's remark that there is no such thing as a stud fee (Shirokogoroff, 299). Among the Reindeer Tungus in Manchuria only men inherit horses (Shirokogoroff, 304).

The Tungus of the Khingan Mountains of Manchuria have a reputation as horse thieves among the neighbouring ethnic groups. The Mongols have been known to behead those captured in the act of stealing and exhibit their heads around the countryside for "educational" purposes (Shirokogoroff, 65).

For the most part the Tungus inhabit an area that is poorly suited to the horse and they lack the interest in and love of horses to create any effective horse industry. It is true that the Yakuts of the farthest north have turned more to reindeer, causing a decline in horse production, but those in southern Siberia are still important horsebreeders, living in the same kind of country as the Northern Tungus. The differential role of the horse is not, then, accounted for by geographical factors. Rather it is one of culture. The Yakut know horses, have an interest in them and value them; the Tungus do not.

TIBETANS

Another people marginal to Central Asiatic steppe nomadism are the Tibetans who are primarily mountaineers and sedentary village dwelling agriculturalists with stock rearing as a subsidiary enterprise. However some Tibetans pursue a pastoral nomadic life with an annual cycle of movement that is transhumant – taking advantage of summer to exploit the higher mountain meadows and slopes for grazing and descending in elevation as winter approaches. Herds, as among the Central Asiatic people, are primarily in sheep, although there are yaks which are considered the most important beasts, cattle, hybrid yak-cow crosses, and horses. The nomads are confined to the high pasturage zones of Tibet, beginning at the upper limits of agriculture and ending near the uppermost limits of vegetation. They dwell in tents and have a pattern of social organization not unlike that of the other Eurasian mounted nomads.

Tibetan nomads employ horses primarily as riding animals, for raids, in hunting expeditions, and to some extent in herding yaks and cattle. Horse flesh is never eaten and with one exception Tibetan nomadic people do not milk mares. In the district of Dam north of L'hasa men milk the mares and prepare and drink koumiss despite the disapproval of other Tibetans. This practice originates from an order of the Mongol ruler of Tibet in the seventeenth century for the people of the district to supply his court with koumiss. In the process the people of Dam acquired a taste for the drink (Ekvall, 60).

Manes, tails and the hair of mares are cut off and sold as horsehair, but hides are never sold. The hide of an especially good horse may be stuffed and offered as a religious donation to a monastery. For caravans, mules and yaks are employed, but never horses. This is because each horse has to be led while two or three men can drive a number of mules or yaks over the trails. Raiding for livestock is endemic among Tibetan nomads and anyone who wishes to participate in a raid upon another camp tries to maintain a horse or two in good condition until late spring so that he will be able to attack and flee with greatest speed.

Hunting similarly requires a good horse as well as a gun.

Most Tibetan horses are of two types: those raised in the lowlands in farm districts which are "generally larger and more robust" and those raised among the nomads which are smaller (from twelve to fourteen and a half hands). The lowland horses are less adapted to the harsh weather conditions of the highlands and "have somewhat smaller and tougher feet" for rocky trails. "Nomad horses tend to have wider and thinner hoofs, suitable for the plains and bogs of the uplands. They are also said to be faster and more spirited . . .". Horses of the lowland farmers are stabled and fed grain or turnips when the grazing is poor (Downs and Ekvall, 175). The nomads, on the other hand, rely on open pasture. They make hay near their winter quarters located at lower elevations and feed it to cattle, sheep and horses alike during winter. Meat is regarded by most Tibetans as a necessity for horses especially when pasture is scarce. They may feed them dried meat or hard cheese and even pigs' blood and raw liver in some cases. Despite supplementary feeding all livestock have the "hunger of the half-starved" after a winter (Ekvall, 34). But, of all their animals, Tibetans are most greatly concerned about their horses. They share food with them, including shavings of dried meat. On a cold night they sacrifice their own blankets from their beds to ensure that their horses keep warm.

All horses in one nomad community are driven daily in a single herd to the edges of pastureland. This is because they require the best and untouched grazing lands and, also, should not be grazed near yaks, for an old Tibetan legend of the 'enmity of the horse and yak' is a very real thing especially when cows have calved or it is mating time. An annoyed yak may try to gore a horse (Ekvall, 38).

The breaking of horses is left to very young men who first introduce the colt to the bit by "having ropes attached to both rings of the snaffle bit" and pulling it from side to side and then to a halt. This is practiced "until it responds readily", at which time it is mounted and ridden bareback until it can be ridden quietly. Finally, it is ridden with the saddle (Ekvall, 90).

Geldings and mares are the preferred riding animals. Stallions, because they are often difficult around other horses, are noisy, and "frequently hard to handle" are ridden only when there is nothing else to ride (Ekvall, 45).

Tibetan saddlery and riding style are the same as those of the Turkic-Mongol peoples: snaffle bits, a saddle with high cantle and pommel and short stirrups. When riding in bad weather men wear a huge wide sleeved raincoat made of felt that is more like a tent since it covers the rider, his weapons, saddle gear and saddlebags and most of the horse as well (Ekvall, 90).

Tibetan attitudes towards the horse parallel those of the Arab Bedouin and Turkmen; horses are linked with war and raiding and are a status symbol "of great emotional account" (Ekvall, 90).

THE COSSACKS

The Cossacks are among the more noted horsemen of the world. The name was originally applied to Tartar adventurers on the Russian-Tartar frontier. They were renegades or "free warriors" who had embarked on private expeditions without the permission of their chiefs. The contact between these Tartars and Slavic frontiersmen led to the adoption by the latter of much of Tartar culture. They organized a warrior society along Cossack lines, adopted the horse tail standard as a symbol of authority, Tartar military techniques, Tartar words, and the method of roping horses with a noose hung from the end of a pole. These Slavs, then, also became known as Cossacks. By the late fifteenth century a considerable number of Slavs had joined the growing group. Fugitive peasants from Muscovy swelled the Cossack numbers in the following century. The term Cossack may then be said to refer primarily to a "Tartarized" Slavic population.

Their chief occupation was fighting, eventually becoming professional soldiers in the pay of Russia and, to a lesser extent, Poland. Their major productive activity, however, was fishing especially on the Black Sea where they also gained notoriety as pirates. They never developed farming until the end of the seventeenth century and little attention was paid to stock breeding until more recent times. The constant threat of raiding which faced early Cossack communities tended to curtail these endeavours. Furthermore, the Cossacks despised agriculture as being an occupation of slaves. Horse breeding became important in the eighteenth century especially among the Don River Cossacks. At the same time other Cossacks, such as the Zaporozhian, began to raise sheep.

Early Cossack communities were primarily military, regulated by an assembly of warriors which decided on the division of the community's income, of plunder, hunting, fishing, and pasture rights. Lands were owned by villages as a commune until 1869 when officers and civil servants were allowed to acquire personal holdings. In addition village assemblies were allowed to rent land to outsiders. In this way Cossack territory soon developed social differences.

By the 1840's "some 20,000 Cossack homesteads held an average of only twenty-seven acres of arable land apiece" plus five and a half million acres of pasture "for more than 40,000 horses, nearly 100,000 head of cattle, and over a quarter of a million sheep . . .". By 1851 there were 27,000 households (Longworth, 255). A drastic decline in horse breeding followed a switch after the mid-nineteenth century to the growing of wheat in the Cossack area. "By 1880 there were 140 horses, 362 cattle and 544 sheep per hundred inhabitants in the Ural Host, whereas the Don was down to thirty-one horses per hundred, the Terek to fifteen and the Kuban to seventeen" (Longworth, 272). However, during this period there was an enormous population increase for in 1826 there were about 700,000 Cossacks and in 1880 two and a half million. Thus while horse breeding declined relative to population, the absolute number of horses did apparently increase.

As a kind of military caste in eighteenth and nineteenth century Russia the Cossacks were granted special privileges for their military role. Each Cossack male was obliged to serve in the military for twenty years beginning at the age of eighteen. This was primarily in a cavalry division. In association with this training they became accomplished acrobats on horseback. They mounted and dismounted bareback and at full trot. Reminiscent of the ancient Parthians and Central Asiatic nomads, they shot their rifles to the rear as they jumped fences. Similar to Plains Indians they clung to the underside of their galloping horses while shooting at the same time (Longworth, 266–7).

A battery field competition of Cossacks in World War I "began 'with such simple things as standing upon the saddle at full gallop . . ., two men picking up a third dismounted comrade, and a dismounted man leaping behind a galloping companion.' There followed 'such gymnastics as I have never seen in any circus, the men swinging from the pommel of their saddles while the horses were in full gallop . . . leaping from one side of their horses to the other side, and turning somersaults'. Then, as if this were too tame, a six-foot, 180 pound sergeant 'performed all these things with a sabre clenched in his teeth.'" (quoted in Longworth from an American observer of the Don Guards battery field day competition, 267).

Cossack horses were of the steppe type: small, light and noted for their stamina. Riding style and gear were Central Asiatic with certain later modifications. Older Cossack saddles had the usual high pommel and cantle with a seat consisting of cushions placed over the tree typical of Turkic peoples. The saddle skirts were cut square and stirrups, which were the open variety, were attached to very short straps which for their military role aided the rider in rising in the saddle and striking down a foe. Saddles were not equipped with carbine boots or sabre straps, the rider always carrying his arms on his person (Vernam, 187).

Later Cossack saddlery used in the Russian cavalry in the nineteenth century bore closer similarities to the American Western saddle. And while Cossacks had long preferred snaffle bits, they, also during the nineteenth century, adopted the use of the curb when riding in the regular Russian cavalry (Vernam, 187).

In general the Cossacks represent a peculiar cultural evolution of a frontier-military-stock breeding community which served to protect and extend the frontiers of a major empire.

XVI

Modern Trends in Horse Use

ON the basis of historical and archaeological records it seems that there have been at least five "explosions" in horse population around the world since domestication. The first occurred in the period between 2300 B.C. and 1700 B.C. when the domesticated horse spread in all directions out of its Eurasian heartland. It diffused into China in the east, India in the south, Mesopotamia and the Levant and North Africa in the south-west and into western and northern Europe in the west. A second major explosion occurred between 1200 and 800 B.C. with the adoption of equestrian nomadism in Central Asia and a third between 800 B.C. and 300 B.C. in relation to the replacement of the horse and chariot by cavalry throughout most of the civilized world. The fourth explosion is associated with the introduction of the horse into the Western Hemisphere coupled with its increasing use for farm purposes in Europe from the sixteenth to the eighteenth centuries. The final and greatest explosion occurs in the nineteenth century and first decade of the twentieth when the horse became the dominant source of power in an expanding and more mechanized agriculture in northern and western Europe, United States and Canada, Australasia and South Africa.

After 1920 the number rounded off as the farm tractor and truck began to compete in more technologically developed areas. But these machines did not actually show their adverse effect on horse population until the 1930's when the replacement of the horse by the tractor really began in earnest in northern Europe, the United States and Canada.

World domesticated horse population probably reached its peak about 1910–1920 when it was in the neighbourhood of 110 million. This is probably at least double the number it was a hundred years before. It may have taken most of the previous two centuries for it to double to reach the figure of the beginning of the nineteenth century. In the early part of the twentieth century ratios of horse to man in the major horse using areas of the world, (the United States, Canada, Australia, South Africa, Latin America, Mongolia, and most of Europe including Russia) averaged about one horse to five persons (500 million population and about ninety million horses). In 1500 those parts of this region in which the domestic horse was found had approximately one hundred million people and certainly less than one horse per ten inhabitants, or under ten million horses. Today this same area has hardly forty-five million horses, but one and a quarter billion people – a ratio of about one horse per twenty-eight inhabitants. Clearly this present ratio more closely resembles that of the early days of horse keeping.

The Horse in Modern Mechanized Society

Government livestock censuses disguise the extraordinarily sharp increase from 1860–1920 and decline after 1920 in the number of heavy draught horses. The types of horses are not separately enumerated by the various censuses, but the heavy draught breeds have been fairly concentrated in Anglo-America, north-western Europe, Australasia and South Africa. Löwe presents statistics which show that in north-western European countries between sixty and ninety-five per cent of the horses were heavy draught type two decades ago (Löwe, 1958–61). Scattered evidence also suggests that in United States, Canada and Australia between 75 and 85 per cent of horses were of this type twenty or thirty years ago. It may be estimated that twenty five to thirty per cent of the world's 98 million horses of the early 1930's were of the heavy draught variety. In 1976 hardly five per cent of 64 million were of this type. Thus, we observe a circular trend: until Mediaeval European times the light horse predominated throughout the world. The heavy breeds gradually increased in popularity particularly after the six-teenth century, reaching major proportions with the growth of American and Australian agriculture in the nineteenth century, falling even more rapidly into decline and on the road to extinction since World War II, so that once again we have the universal prevalence of light saddle breeds.

From the statistics in the United States in the 1950's it appeared that the future of the domestic horse belonged with the passenger pigeon and the dodo. Yet beginning about 1960 a remarkable reversal com-menced and is still in progress. The new demand is in the pleasure horse category, stimulated by the growth of a more affluent and leisured upper middle class segment of the population. However, the fact of increased free time and wealth for a larger part of the population does not fully explain why horse production and use should thereby be stimulated. Built into American culture are two important horse tradi-tions. One originates in Great Britain and Northern Europe. It is associated more with the eastern and southern United States, iden-tifies the horse with a leisured landed aristocracy and, thus, makes the horse and rider examples par excellence of higher status. The other tradition is that of the Old American West epitomized by the cowboy.

In one particular at least these two traditions enunciate opposing ideologies: the one is inegalitarian and the other egalitarian. What is distilled from the first tradition is the horse as a symbol of status and prestige. As such it is similar to other symbols which have developed in the technological atmosphere of modern America: the second and third car, motor boat, yacht, snowmobile, auto trailer or motor home. The other tradition, the old American Western, is today inextricably bound up with the nostalgic search for a lost arcadian past. It is symbolized in the house one can call one's own, preferably sur-rounded by a few acres of land, or by the mobile home, camper or camping trip, or the fishing shack in the mountains, or by the horse. The arcadian search, or flight, has been intensified by the increasing complexities, impersonality, crowding and pollution inherent in mod-ern urban industrial living. Yet it is important to bear in mind that there is quite obviously no desire to rely, for example, exclusively upon the horse as a means of transportation or to live permanently in a moun-tain fishing shack or tent without "conveniences". The physical com-fort provided by modern technology is deemed fundamental, but this comfort demands its price in terms of certain psychic discomforts, temporary relief for which may be sought in the flight to the isolated campsite or to a horse's back.

One suspects the arcadian, romantic ideology is stimulated directly as the mechanization and impersonalization of contemporary tech-nological society increases. After all, viewed in the long sweep of history the social life of man has been in the context of the small, intimate and familistic, "rural" setting. Such an enduring and ancient tradition can only be a most persistent and tenacious force, calling men "back" wherever and however it can.

The present importance of the pleasure horse in America, then, derives from the fact that today's affluence and leisure provide the opportunity for the satisfaction of ideological elements embedded in American culture. It derives also from a "reaction formation" against essential aspects of the very techno-economic system which has pro-vided the affluence and leisure. That horses, places to ride them and to keep them are generally readily available compared, say, to Western Europe is also of some economic significance.

Between eighty and ninety per cent of horses in the United States today are pleasure animals, mostly owned by non-farm people.[1] We have already mentioned the general world trend back to light horses and now may note the related circular trend back to the non-farm use of the horse.

The horse as a purely recreational device cannot provide an ever

[1] And the overwhelming majority of "non-pleasure" horses are of the saddle variety employed for ranch work.

expandable market. The great increment in horses in the United States over the last decade and a quarter cannot reasonably be expected to continue for very long. Rapidly increasing world population coupled with limited arable lands suggests there will be in the next thirty years increasing competition between crop growing and livestock raising and the latter will be the one that loses.

Among domesticated animals, the horse is the greatest luxury and most expendable in terms of the practicality of food production. What is more, the pleasure horse is mostly stabled in the vicinity of towns and cities and so competes more directly for prime farmland. If we could graze all the horses in remote marginal and unproductive areas there would be much less of a problem.

The Pleasure Horse in Relation to Other Forms of Recreation

The pleasure use of the horse is largely concentrated in trail riding, dressage and ring riding. There has been also a considerable growth of the number of professional race horses and breeding farms. One measure of the popularity of horseback riding as a form of recreation is of course suggested by the number of horses for this purpose, possibly close to eight million in the United States. Surveys aimed at determining participation in various sports provide another indicator. Thus Gallup Surveys have calculated the percentage of Americans who took part at least once in the year in a major participatory sport. In 1959 five per cent of those queried participated in horseback riding, while in 1972 the percentage doubled to ten per cent, but the activity fell from eighth to ninth place amongst the twelve sports recorded. During the same time, however, the number of pleasure horses increased more than two and a half times.

Canada has somewhere in the vicinity of a third of a million pleasure horses – a lower proportion in relation to total population than the United States. If Canada were to have the same proportion as the United States there would be over two times as many pleasure horses as now – about 700,000. One may suspect then that horseback riding is by no means as popular an activity in Canada as it is in the United States. To some extent this may be a reflection of the lesser affluence and possibly the weather in Canada; more important is that Canadians are less "Western" oriented, more British or French in their tradition – even in their western Provinces.

In Great Britain there are an estimated 250,000 persons who ride to hounds in fox hunting activities and there is some indication that the participation in this endeavour has broadened beyond the narrow confines of a properly attired aristocracy; for many hunts dress is no longer rigidly specified. Icelandic city dwellers are reported to be acquiring pleasure ponies in some numbers, and riding activities are increasing rapidly in the Netherlands and Federal German Republic.

As a general rule it would seem unlikely that horseback riding will ever reach the proportions of importance in continental Europe that it has attained in the United States. Europe does not have the powerful cowboy Western tradition; the pleasure horse remains more closely identified with an aristocracy – and possibly too closely for it to be taken up by the "plebians". While it may be the aim of well-to-do middle class Germans or Swedes to ape the aristocracy – at least in certain respects – they may be discouraged from doing so in terms of the acquisition of horses because of the relative expense and scarcity of such animals in western Europe and because of the greater cost of keeping them, particularly in the more densely settled areas of western Europe. In the United States or Canada it is possible for a man of somewhat modest means to keep a horse or two in the "rurban" fringes of suburbia; in Great Britain or western Europe one would require a country estate.

Among the factors which determine participation in a sport are its accessibility, its cost in terms of financial outlay and in terms of the time to acquire the skill, its fashionableness, and its personal appeal or attraction. In accessibility, horseback riding does not rank high compared to other sports. Walking, jogging and bicycling can be undertaken anywhere. In all urban communities there are ample parks for playing various ball sports; there are usually ice skating rinks and swimming pools easily accessible. The urban horseman invariably must travel outside of town; accessibility is on a par with golfing, often skiing.

The financial outlay involved in horseback riding makes it one of the most expensive sports. Possibly again, only skiing or golfing could compare. At the same time horseback riding requires no little investment in learning and usually imposes on the novice some initial discomfort before the skill is acquired. In these respects it parallels skiing. If not adequately motivated a novice may very rapidly lose his keenness for riding after "bumping" around for a while or after finding himself in a heap on the ground.

Therefore, on the basis of accessibility and financial and time costs alone, it is to be expected that horseback riding would not rank as a highly popular sport.

The subject of fashion is an extremely complex issue clearly related to the factors of accessibility, cost and personal appeal, but also dependent upon one's circle of friends, social class, region, and age as well as being entwined with efforts to achieve a certain style of life. Thus, despite relative inaccessibility and cost, and regardless of whether or not the participant enjoys it, skiing has become fashionable in the last decade among American urban, upper middle class individuals of younger age groups residing in the temperate climatic zone. It has in such circles become the "thing to do" and a person does not "belong" unless he, too, is "in on the action". To a lesser extent, horse riding has become a similar example of this fashion phenomenon. Thus, the *nouveau riche* on taking up residence in expanded premises in an elegant neighbourhood follows the fashion and style of life of his would-be peers, one aspect of which is to join the "horsey" set. But riding has never developed as a popular fashion or fad to the extent that some other sports have. Cost in money and time in the acquisition of the necessary skills as well as the problem of accessibility, as we have indicated, prohibit it from having mass appeal as the "thing to do". In part because of these factors it is further an activity very closely identified with specific segments of society: the wealthy, the old aristocracy, the rural farm and ranch population, and the "rurban" middle class commuters. Riding has simply not been a part of the culture, for example, of the urban middle class of the eastern United States, although one of the recent trends we have noted is that the increasing middle class opulence and leisure have provoked an increase in horse ownership.

The final issue mentioned above – the question of the personal attractiveness of different sports to the individual – is certainly coloured by fashions and the elements which provoke them. But, I propose to discuss this matter in the context of a particular question which is sometimes asked in North America, *viz.*, why is horseback riding, apparently, more appealing to girls than to boys?

In the United States and Canada, particularly in urban and suburban areas and in the eastern parts of these countries where English-style riding prevails it is overwhelmingly girls who join the riding classes, participate in horse shows, and the like. Even in the West and in more rural regions girls outnumber the boy participants. As one random example, 4-H projects in the Province of Alberta for 1971–72 for livestock betray this trend, where in every class of livestock, boys clearly outnumbered girl participants except in the light horse class where more than three fifths of the participants were girls.

There are several factors which may explain this female emphasis in what was once a much more distinctly male enterprise. They are related to three types of explanation: one concerned with horsemanship as a sport, one concerned with the male and female roles in Western society, and one concerned with the changing role of the horse in this society.

The following discussion of these issues relates particularly to urban, suburban areas and the eastern United States and Canada. It applies only to limited extent to the Western rural areas for reasons which it is hoped will become evident.

My first point is that the range of sports open to male participation is broader than for females and that those entailing paid professionals are male dominated sports; paid professional *competitive* games are even more male dominated. Sports open to both sexes obviously will have female participants. Therefore golf, tennis, horsemanship, swimming and skiing all involve high proportions of women. But horsemanship, like skiing and swimming can be a solitary activity and is not a game in the strict sense. More important, when competitive, it, unlike skiing and swimming more often than not does not discriminate between sexes. The usual golf or tennis tournament is between men *or* women; jumping and other horse show competitions less readily discriminate between sexes, but are more apt to pit men against women.

This factor shifts our attention to the relative roles of male and female in Western society where there remains much more than a residue of male dominance and priority. Neither boys nor men like to be outclassed by girls or women. Various observers in horsemanship activities have noted that boys enter horsemanship classes with girls, but on seeing themselves defeated in competition by girls soon withdraw leaving the field almost entirely to the fairer sex. It is not deemed right in our society for girls to defeat boys in sports competitions. Furthermore, boys may begin classes, note that a majority of the participants are girls and withdraw since they do not wish to be involved in what they perceive to be a "sissy" sport.

Why should the girls so readily beat boys in competitions in horsemanship? According to Littauer girls are better horsemen since they are more considerate; they are "softer" yet sufficiently strong to handle the animal (Littauer, 1962). Others have claimed that while girls are initially better horsemen, those males who stick to it eventually become superior. Horsemanship requires, as Littauer implies, consideration, patience, responsibility, as well as an interest in grooming and husbandry. Now in the child training in urban Western society there is much more emphasis on the acquisition of such qualities among girls than among boys. It is not outrageous to suggest, I believe, that playing at dolls, playing at being mother, better conditions a girl for these qualities and thus in the urban non-farm context the girl has at an early age an advantage in these respects over boys.

Boys are almost taught to acquire the opposite traits; at least they are early trained that they ought to engage in competitive team and "contact" sports. Only a minority of those who participate in horsemanship do so as a competitive activity and it is in no sense a contact sport. These features then also favour greater female participation. Horseback riding may appeal to those who are uninterested in competitive or contact forms of recreation or in types of group recreation, but prefer a more solitary activity focusing on the interaction between rider and horse.

Riding demands an ability to control and manage a powerful animal which has a mind of its own and is therefore far more unpredictable and uncontrollable than a machine. If horseback riding gives the individual any psychological effect at all, it is to enhance the feeling of power, independence and mobility. Riding can also give the individual a greater feeling of speed and surging power than a machine, even though the horse may not be going as fast as a machine. Outlets for the experience of independence and power in our society have been more restricted on the female side than on the male. Horseback riding may be viewed as a culturally approved channel by which girls can enjoy such "thrills".

A third type of explanation relates to the changing role of the horse in society. In the ranching regions of the United States and Canada, in the mounted nomadic areas of Mongolia and Turkestan where the horse is still a utilitarian animal identified with the work of men, and in earlier times in Europe and North America when cavalry were an important and prestigeful segment of the military organization, horsemanship is and was identified with men. Where horsemanship then is intimately associated with work and war, i.e., where it is a professional activity, it is associated with male enterprises and sport; where it involves paid professionals in competitive games, as in horse racing and polo, it remains a male activity, but where it is relegated to pure pleasure, female participation becomes common. Thus, given the above considerations regarding relative roles and values associated with the sexes in our society and their relationship to horseback riding as a sport women should exert a major influence.

The Horse in Contemporary "Underdeveloped" Areas

Apart from the United States and its peculiar technological economic situation, there are a number of other countries in which horses continue to show an increase in number. Thus, between 1947/1952 and 1974 forty-one countries recorded increases. Except for the United States, all were among the so called "underdeveloped" nations. One of the areas of most dramatic increase has been in the countries of the Western Sudan of Africa, where their number doubled during this period. (By 1974 a disastrous drought in this area had produced sharp reductions in all livestock.)

How are we to explain this increase in horse numbers in these underdeveloped areas? For one thing, it must be borne in mind that the accumulation of statistical data in such countries is not always reliable. Yet accepting figures as stated there are perfectly good reasons why these countries have experienced an increase in horse population during these decades. Affluence and technology have caused a great increase in the pleasure horse in the United States and in some under-developed countries an increase in affluence accompanied by a continued technological deficiency has served to create a situation in which the high regard for the horse can now be realized by more individuals owning such animals. Horses are still marks of prestige and status and at the same time have some utility as a means of transportation, if not more mundane activity.

In most underdeveloped countries sophisticated agricultural power machinery is still beyond the financial capability of the mass of peasants. Yet various types of simpler modern implements are well suited to horse traction and these the peasant can afford. They include light iron walking ploughs, cultivators, seeders, hay tedders, rakes and mowers. Carting by horse and wagon is much faster than by ox or human porterage, and at the same time also still within the realm of the peasant's economic capability.

Clearly the main impetus for the great increase in horse numbers in Senegal, for example, has been the government policy of trying to encourage peanut farmers to adopt the iron horse drawn walking plough. Thus, one should expect these several factors to produce some contrast in the trend of horse population between "developed" and "underdeveloped" countries. Indeed, we recall that the immense increase in horses in the United States and Canada occurred in the nineteenth century in conjunction with the application of an increasingly sophisticated agricultural technology – a technology especially suited at the time to the horse and prior to the invention of the tractor. We may note likewise the increase of horse numbers with the post-Mediaeval rise of yeomanry – or in other words the increase in peasant affluence in conjunction with a growing agrarian capitalism.

Assuming the continued availability of some kind of fuel for mechanized agriculture, increases in the number of horses in "underdeveloped" countries can not be expected to continue. As these countries improve their productive capability and are enabled to acquire more advanced technology they, too, will abandon the horse. This day may be especially hastened in the Communist countries and other nations which have experimented widely in various forms of collectivized agriculture, since with this mode of organization and state financing they will sooner be able to acquire more complex technology.

The combination of an advance technology and Communist ideology represent in fact a major threat to the survival of the domesticated horse. Aimed as it is at utilitarianism and maximizing efficiency of production and distribution under a collectivist system of property, the Communist social order tolerates the horse in so far as it can labour for the production of wealth for the collectivist society. Unlike the United States, the decline in draught horses in Communist countries can not be expected to be followed or accompanied by an increase in the number of pleasure horses. When Communist societies attain that level of technology where they can dispense with the horse as a work animal, they will experience a rapid decline in its numbers. When capitalist societies reach that condition, the resulting affluence and leisure for part of the society may be diverted to the horse as a pleasure animal. While I make this observation it is not intended thereby to be an endorsement of capitalism, for we should note that the increasing affluence and leisure provided to some in capitalism is invariably at the expense of another segment of the population which has less affluence and less leisure.

The Present Distribution of Horses in Relation to Cultural-ecological Factors

As a general rule a high horse to man ratio suggests that the horse is of considerable importance, although the opposite of this does not necessarily follow. With a low horse-man ratio the horse may still be a most prestigious and coveted animal.

Under what conditions today would we expect to find a high horse-man ratio? First, there must be appropriate grazing conditions. Grassy and wooded steppe from Sub-Arctic through Tropical zones are conducive to horse production and might be expected therefore to have higher horse to man ratios than desert, tropical forest or lands which are intensely cultivated.

But appropriate grazing conditions alone do not provide the necessary and sufficient conditions for a large horse population. The Kenya Highlands, for instance, might be good horse country, but there has never been a tradition of horsemanship to make it so. There must be a positive and high regard for the horse, yet that regard must not be so high as to limit the horse in its use.

Where they may be used by men of all walks of life or where they are employed in a variety of activities are, then, other interrelated factors. Such activity as mounted herding or the use of the horse for the plough, and a belief that every man should ride, each induce a large horse population. These factors are related to yet another, namely, the degree of techno-economic development of a country.

Under modern conditions a relative conservatism in technological and economic development, as we have already seen, should be more associated with high numbers of horses. The most advanced technologically and the wealthiest nations should have fewer horses. However, as has been apparent from our previous discussion it is possible that a country can reach that state of affluence that the horse becomes numerous as a pleasure animal yet this is today, at least, only significant as far as the United States, Canada and Iceland are concerned.

Finally, for the same amount of work a people who depend upon range-fed ponies require more horses than a people who depend upon grain-fed, full-sized horses. A man with a stall-fed Quarter Horse or a Turkman is able to ride further and longer than one with a grass-fed Icelandic pony. A Percheron can do the draught labour of several ponies. Thus the type of horse and the feed management contribute to differences in number. But the full significance of feeding and type of horse in relation to the general question of distribution of their number cannot be as readily considered as the other factors. Thus, for example, range-fed ponies prevail in only two countries – Mongolia and Iceland – which are, incidentally, two of the countries with the highest horse to man ratios. We can also only guess at the proportion of ponies for most of the rest of the world. But the main problem is that the importance of these two factors depends upon the amount and type of work involved. Thus, in order to compare countries in terms of the number of horses in the light of these factors we would first have to know the total work load of the horses in each country.

The issue of feed management and type of horse, therefore, introduces a complexity which is beyond the present scope of this research. It is proposed to consider the four other factors of available grazing lands, high regard for the horse, versatility in use, and relative techno-economic development in relation to horse to man ratios for each country. At the same time some casual note will be made of factors of feeding and horse type.

Nine nations (based on 1974 U.N. figures) have a ratio of one horse to ten persons or less.[1] Of these, all possess extensive grazing conditions conducive to horse rearing; there is a high regard for the horse; there is versatility in the use of the horse; riding horseback is common amongst all classes. Pastoralism is particularly important and is partially or wholly of the mounted type. Horses in two countries are

[1] In order of highest ratio they are Mongolia, Paraguay, Iceland, Argentina, Uruguay, Honduras, Panama, Cuba, and Nicaragua.

largely of the pony type, while in all there is a considerable dependence upon open range feeding. However, on the issue of techno-economic development Iceland is a highly developed country where horses are now used mostly for pleasure riding and meat supply. Argentina and Uruguay may be classed as marginal between "development" and "underdevelopment".

Eleven nations[2] have one horse per eleven to twenty persons. Among these Poland, Costa Rica and Chile conform to our expectations except they are marginal in terms of their degree of techno-economic development. Haiti may also be an exception in that it has little grassy steppe and lacks a well developed pastoral industry. In three of the countries (Lesotho, Ethiopia, Namibia) horses are not much used for heavy draught or for herding of livestock, but they are important means of transportation.

Thus, if we consider the four variables together (grazing, regard for the horse, wide usage, techno-economic underdevelopment) we find that of countries with a ratio of one horse per ten or less persons, six or two-thirds conform to all variables, eight or almost ninety per cent, if we include those countries which are marginally developed. Of eleven countries with ratios of one horse per eleven to twenty persons we find that seven or two-thirds conform to all four variables, ten or ninety per cent, if we include the marginally developed. Percentages fall to fifty-six per cent of countries with ratios of one horse per twenty-one to forty persons and decline drastically for countries with ratios of one horse to forty-one or more persons.

It remains to inquire if there are countries which conform to the four expected criteria but have a low ratio of horse to man. Fifty-eight countries have ratios of one horse to one hundred persons or more. Of these, fifteen are among the most highly developed nations, technologically and in terms of wealth. Thirty-two lack land useful for horse husbandry. Angola, Kenya, Tanzania, Rhodesia, Zambia, Swaziland, and Mozambique have geographical possibilities for horse husbandry, but it was only recently introduced by European colonialist, and for cultural historical reasons has never been much adopted by the native African population. Nigeria, Sudan, Spain and Portugal – the remaining countries – might be expected to fit more the characteristics outlined. They are underdeveloped, or, in the case of Spain and Portugal, marginally developed, have good horse grazing areas and a high regard for the horse (except among some Sudanese and Nigerian tribes). Yet in all four its use is considerably restricted because it is so closely identified with the aristocrat and the warrior, almost wholly

[2] Brazil, Mexico, Haiti, Poland, Lesotho, Bolivia, Costa Rica, Ethiopia, Chile, Colombia, Namibia.

utilized for the saddle. To be sure in Spain there was once a more significant pattern of mounted cattle herding, but this today is unimportant.

In sum, none of the low ratio countries fully conform to all four criteria, for the most part because they lack extensive good grazing facilities for horse husbandry, but also important is the high degree of techno-economic sophistication of some and the restrictive effect of the cultural value on the horse in others.

Lack of technological-economic development is a variable which has correlated with high ratio of horses to man only during the last few decades. In 1900 twenty countries had one horse to nine persons or less and of these, seven ranked as among the economically and technologically most highly developed countries in the world. This is because as we have remarked above at that time the most sophisticated agricultural technology and economy was associated wth the use of horse traction. Several other countries which are today not technologically sophisticated had about the same position and proportion in 1900 as in 1976 and these are countries in which the horse is associated with stock breeding and not with cultivation.

We may therefore conclude that countries which have the highest ratio of horse to man have all the following characteristics: extensive grassy or wooded steppe within the range from Sub-Arctic to Tropical climates; a high regard for the horse; versatility of use or employment by a wide variety of individuals or both. Degree of technological development is of less significance.

XVII

The Role of the Horse: A Summing Up

MAN has made the horse the most versatile of domesticated animals. No other animal quite equals it in the number of uses to which it has been put. Only the reindeer and camel approach it in this respect. But, both reindeer and camel have a highly restricted geographical distribution, being less adaptable than the horse to varying physical conditions.

Apart from its universal use for riding, the horse seems to have a place in the ceremonial and sportive life of all those peoples who possess it. It is, as well, universally viewed wherever found as a prestigious gift and its hide and hair are employed everywhere within the realm of horse keeping. While its exploitation as a pack animal and for light draught is quite common, its role in heavy draught work is much less widespread. Use of the horse in ceremonial sacrifice and as a source of meat and milk have a very limited distribution. The ceremonial sacrifice of the horse was in ancient times more widespread. The milking of mares has been a practice essentially confined to Central Asia. That mare's milk is uncommon as a food undoubtedly arises from the fact that the horse cannot produce milk and work efficiently at the same time. Other animals are readily made into good milk producers, but none equals the horse as a means of transportation. Thus this role is favoured for the horse.

The following table sums up the distribution of major uses of the horse in the cultural areas of the equine using world.

Styles of Horse Riding

Riding styles have varied over time and space, in large part because of different purposes for riding and the varying kinds of riding gear. We may here consider a riding style as including 1) the preferred type of gait for the horse 2) the degree of control by the rider – whether riding is "extended" or "collected" 3) the riding posture, meaning essentially whether one rides "straight-legged" or with bent knee 4) the kind of riding gear employed, a factor which is implicit in any consideration of control or posture.

In terms of gait, we may distinguish between those who prefer some type of lateral gait (like the amble or the rack) and those who rely on a stride based on a diagonal movement of the legs (trot and canter). The

TABLE I

DISTRIBUTION OF SOME SPECIAL USES OF THE HORSE

(riding is universal wherever the horse is employed)

X = present and of some importance. O = absent. / = present but of minor importance

	heavy draught	light draught and pack	ceremonial -sacrifice	meat	milk
Anglo-America	X	X	O	O	O
Latin-America	/	X	O	/	O
North Europe	X	X	O	X	O
South Europe	/	X	O	/	O
East Europe	X	X	O	/	O
Middle East	/	X	O	O	O
Sudanic Africa	O	/	O	/	O
Ethiopia and Horn	O	/	O	O	O
South Africa	X	X	O	O	O
South and South-east Asia	O	X	/	/	O
East Asia	/	X	/	O	O
Central Asia	/	X	X	X	X
Australia	X	X	O	O	O
Plains Indian and Pampas	O	X	X	/	O
Mediaeval Europe	X	X	O	/	O
Roman Europe	/	X	/	/	O
Celts, Germans, etc.	O	X	X	X	O
Ancient Chinese	O	X	X	X	O
Ancient India	O	X	X	O	O
Ancient Near East	O	X	O	/	O

amble or pace has extremely wide distribution. It is preferred by Mongol and Turkic horsemen of Central Asia and has enjoyed wide popularity in Europe. From Europe this preference was carried to America where in the Southern United States, Brazil and large sections of Spanish America it has been highly favoured. The amble is easy on the rider and thus makes long distance riding at a steady pace comfortable for him, although some have questioned how comfortable it is for the horse since it is for most horses not a natural gait. It is not surprising that people who employ the horse primarily for long distance travel such as the Mongols and Turkic nomads should prefer this gait.

The lope or slow canter similarly enjoys considerable popularity, preferred by North American cowboys, large numbers of Spanish Americans, and the Arabs. It has the advantage over the amble in that it is more commonly a natural gait. While it cannot be sustained for as long a period as the amble, the lope is faster.

The trot seems to be a gait which has been more tolerated than favoured. It is best suited for firm and smooth roadways; thus one can appreciate its increase in popularity in Western Europe after the seventeenth century when roads were improved. Most horsemen riding as they do on uneven and rough ground are less given to the trot. It is also uncomfortable for the stirrupless rider and one which is more tiring to the rider than either an amble or a lope.

Another aspect of riding style concerns the rider's control of his mount. Throughout the world an extended riding style has been most common. Here, the horse is less under control by the rider and the animal is allowed to move freely forward with head and neck extended and weight and power thrown on the forehand or forepart of the horse. In contrast, collection entails total submission of the horse, a control such that the mount bends at the poll and has its heels well under it, therefore shortening the stride. It has only a limited distribution and according to Trench probably arose, as in Greece, where hilly and rocky terrain demand more control of the horse than riding on open steppe. Close quarter fighting from horseback is also an impetus to collection (Trench, 42). Collected riding assumes adequate mechanical devices for control of the horse, such as bit or cavesson, whereas extended riding is possible using the gamut of control devices from the most severe sorts of curbs to simple jaw straps.

Until the advent of the stirrup (between 1500 and 2000 years ago) nearly all riding was straight-legged since, without stirrups this affords the best balance. Apparently some early Mesopotamian riders sat bent-kneed on the horse's croup, thus throwing the rider forward and off balance. This technique probably helps explain why horse riding was not very popular there. The introduction of the stirrup allows one to continue the straight-legged posture or alternatively to rely on a bent knee style using the shortened stirrups as purchase so that one may rise to the trot (i.e. "post") or stand in the stirrups.

The kind of saddle or absence of a saddle is likewise contributory to the riding posture. Riding style may be associated with bareback riding, riding with a cloth or a pad secured by a girth, or with a true saddle – that is, a wooden frame seat. The true saddle is essentially one of two basic types: one with high pommel and cantle, as in the Arab, European Mediaeval, Spanish and Western traditions or a light saddle with only a slight cantle and no pommel as in the so-called English saddle. A saddle with high pommel and cantle allows for "sloppiness" in riding posture since one can rely on the greater security of the saddle parts to remain mounted. This is why it is that the best riding habits are acquired by those who learn to ride in the small light English saddle where maintaining the proper "seat" depends more on the rider than on the saddle.

The combination of riding extended and straight-legged with a curb bit, long stirrups, and in a saddle with high pommel and cantle is associated with work from horseback in which the rider must concentrate on affairs other than control of his mount and in conditions where the rider can expect to be easily dislodged. Thus, this is the style of the Mediaeval knight and of the cowboy.

An emphasis on riding for pleasure has resulted in a configuration of short stirrups, bent knee, collected riding on a light saddle more often with a snaffle rather than a curb. Such features are associated with modern "scientific" equestrianism where one is focussing exclusively on riding and jumping. However, there are several exceptions to any apparent tendency for riding with heavy and secure gear to be associated with working from horseback while riding with light tack is associated with pleasure. Thus, Plains Indians, for one, worked and fought with very light gear, either bareback or with a pad seat and short stirrups. Since the Indians manufactured a wooden frame saddle with high pommel and cantle for their women, their reliance on the padded seat for hunting buffalo and fighting did not result from technological inadequacies, but more likely arose out of their preference for a light load to attain speed, rather than an interest in safety and comfort.

It is possible to isolate the several types of riding styles found throughout the world and over the course of history. The oldest, beginning 5–6000 years ago, may be called the Original Eurasian Steppe style. We really know nothing about it but may speculate that it probably entailed the use of the jaw strap, nose band or possibly a snaffle as a means of control and quite definitely it was extended, bareback riding. With the introduction of the riding horse into the ancient Near East – Anatolia and Mesopotamia specifically – by 2300–2000 B.C. another style appears which we may call Archaic Near Eastern. Clay cylinders depict riders sitting either on the croup or astride the back, with bent knees and directing the mount through a nose ring. Girths may also have been used as an aid in riding. This style, did not last for very long, being replaced, possibly by the mid-second millenium B.C. in the Near East by more straight-legged riding and with the aid of the snaffle or nose band. The new technique was associated with bareback riding but also with the use of cloths or padding as a seat. While shared by a number of Near Eastern peoples including the Egyptians we may refer to this as the Assyrian style since the Assyrians best exemplify it. The Assyrian style is historically a more direct descendent from that of the Original Eurasian Steppe while the Archaic Near Eastern style is likely better viewed as a dead-end side development. With the more efficient control and riding seat provided by the Assyrian style, cavalry could ultimately prevail over the horse and chariot in warfare.

The Ancient Greek style differs from the above in that the Greeks attempted to achieve collection in riding and probably were the first to do so. The Numidians of North Africa contributed yet a fifth riding style, employing a neck rope or stick for guidance in place of a bridle even though they knew its use and employed bridles on mules. The Celts are attributed with modifying the bit so as to produce a device which has close similarities to a curb, thus providing a variation on the Assyrian style. The post-Christian invention of the wooden frame saddle provides another variation in riding which we may identify as Roman style. It is a continuation of Greek pattern with the addition of a stirrupless saddle.

With the invention of the stirrup and further developments on bitting devices, including the appearance of the true curb in the early centuries of the Christian era, numerous possibilities for variations in riding style were made available. Central Asians and Chinese employed full foot stirrups on a saddle with high pommel and cantle in riding with snaffle bit in an extended bent-kneed style. They also liked the ambling gait. Mediaeval Europeans used similar kinds of saddles with stirrups, but applied them to extended, straight-legged riding with curb bits and spurs. With this they preferred the canter. While this style was developed especially for the heavily armoured knights another Mediaeval style went in for light saddles and the ambling gait. The modern Boers in South Africa have essentially carried on the old Mediaeval style of the armoured knight except that they have lightened the saddle and, owning rather docile horses, use the snaffle bit.

The East Indians possibly as early as the second century B.C. developed toe stirrups and later added to this some use of curb bits. The Bedouin style of the Arab nomads was characterized by collected riding with straight legs and no stirrups employing a nose band and a padded seat. Other Middle Eastern peoples, including the sedentary Arabs, not long after the advent of Islam adapted the Central Asiatic style to the use of curb bits and spurs. They also employed the canter. This style might be termed Contemporary Middle Eastern. It and the East Indian style combine in producing an Ethiopian style – different from the Middle Eastern in the acquisition of toe stirrups from the East – possibly via the Portuguese. Brazilian style is probably another Portuguese-East Indian product since it entails extended, straight-legged riding using toe stirrups, spurs and a saddle with high pommel and cantle. However, nose bands rather than bits are more commonly found. And the preferred gait is the amble.

The Spanish Western style, a legacy from the Arabs and Mediaeval Europeans, entails extended riding more or less straight-legged in a saddle with high pommel and cantle, stirrups, curb bit and spurs, with a slow canter as the preferred gait. The Modern European or English riding requires collection, bent-knee riding in a saddle with low pommel and cantle and may use either snaffle or curb bit, with trot and canter preferred. American Indian riding allowed for some variety derived in large part from Spanish example. Men invariably rode bareback or with a padded seat. If stirrups were attached they were made short so that the rider bent his knee; in the absence of stirrups riding was more straight-legged. Jaw straps and nose bands were common guidance devices although in the course of time the Indians acquired curbs from the Europeans. Women's riding, in contrast, was on a saddle with high pommel and cantle. A final style developed in America may be called Gaucho, evolved among the cow herders of Argentina. Like the Brazilian it entailed extended, but moderately straight-legged riding with toe stirrups; sometimes nose bands are used but the curb bit is also common as is the use of spurs. The saddle, however, has only the most minimal tree and no pommel or cantle. While Brazilians prefer the amble, Gaucho style, like the Spanish Western, employs the slow canter.

The likely historical relationship between these several types may be shown in a diagram as follows:

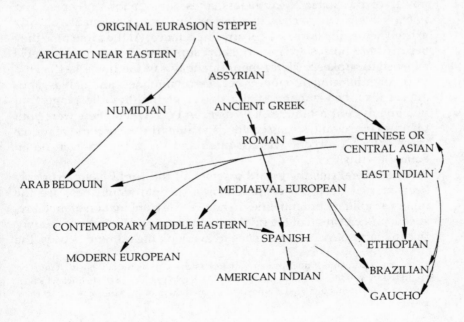

The Horse and the Military

The greatest historical significance of the horse has been as a military machine. The fact that the horse has so often and so widely been associated with aristocracy and the military may lead erroneously to the conclusion that it is a force initiating aristocracy and militarism or that it is always a piece of technology which sustains them. As was suggested in discussing horses among the American Indians, their role can be manipulated in a variety of ways depending upon the values and designs of the people who own them. Indeed, a major theme of this book has been that while horses are invariably esteemed over other domesticated animals they may in one cultural context be kept for the most patrician uses and in another more plebian ones.

Long ago Aristotle pointed out that cavalry are best maintained in oligarchic states because of the expense of purchasing and maintaining horses. Max Weber's statement in his *Religion of India* that horsemen were a major force for preserving European feudalism is interpreted by Wallerstein as suggesting that an emphasis upon horsemen leads to a strengthening of the intermediate warriors in relation to the centres of power (Wallerstein, 58). In more recent times Goody has revived this theme in relation to West Africa in suggesting that cavalries are associated with states in which control is vested in a broad based nobility which collectively shares in sustaining cavalry mounts and, thus, the power of the state. Nevertheless, these associations of horse and nobility occur where class division and values of inequality already existed before the horse was of any importance. At the same time they occur where horses are in very short supply or require considerable expense for upkeep. Here, then, one may say the horse has been a force for enhancing differences between commoners and nobles, and, apparently often enhancing the power of the "middle ranges" of nobility. By contrast in the Old American West where there were both plenty of horses and strong egalitarian values the horse could reinforce those values: everyone was mounted and so, in this respect, on an equal "footing".

As a general rule the great horsemen of the world have invariably been martial people because a martial people would best see the immense military potentialities in horses: the combination of mobility, speed, and elevation of the rider from the ground.[1] Too often, though, this military role is so stressed as to overlook the numerous ways the

[1] The horse's skittishness does present a major disadvantage in the battlefield. It must be countered by conditioning and, particularly, by exploiting the herd instinct which in dangerous situations incites the animal to follow others of his kind – as in a cavalry charge.

horse has contributed to peaceful endeavours.

For more than three millenia (from ca. 1800 B.C.–1400 A.D.) the horse defined victory or defeat in war throughout the greater part of the Eastern Hemisphere. Even after the introduction of gunpowder, cavalry prevailed down to contemporary times as a most effective branch of the military organization. After the mid-nineteenth century the practicality of cavalry came increasingly into question. World War I was the last major international conflict in which cavalry were employed. Trench reports the last use of cavalry for warfare was in the Mau Mau struggle in Kenya between 1952 and 1956 when Kenya mounted troops attacked Mau Mau operations (Trench, 181).

A few countries, Brazil, for example, maintain ceremonial cavalries. The last "functional" cavalry among the modern armies of the Western world, that of Switzerland, was disbanded in 1973 over the protest of a large segment of the population of both right and left wing political persuasions.

Armies have not employed horses solely as cavalry. Probably equal numbers have engaged in less glamourous tasks as draught animals hauling artillery pieces, ammunition and supplies. In sum, it is well to bear in mind that on parade the war horse may thrill the crowd. Yet in keeping with the nature of military organization, this kind of event is merely the grand spectacle which disguises the reality of the situation. For the reality is that there have been few wars employing horses in which the majority of these animals and a high proportion of the attendants did not become fatalities.

In contrast to cavalry, mounted police have managed to survive in the modern world, although they too, have experienced an overall decline in the past few decades. The Royal Canadian Mounted Police is today only mounted behind the wheel of an automobile. A stable of horses for ceremonial occasions and demonstration purposes is still retained. But a "Mountie" is no longer required to learn how to ride and handle a horse. In fact, probably only a minority are able to do so. It is in large city police forces that there has been a recent revival of the use of the horse, where it has been found that the patrol work can be more effective and cheaper on horseback than in a car or on foot.

Sport and Pleasure

Coextensive with the military use of the horse has been its employment in sport and pleasure. In areas where horses are uncommon equestrian sports become identified with nobility and invariably mimic military and hunting activity. Everywhere racing has been a universally appreciated equestrian sport. A second kind includes the various forms of mounted hunting among people who no longer depend upon wild game as a source of meat. Mounted hunting as pure conspicuous display, as an excuse to ride, and as a basis for reaffirming upper class solidarity reaches its epitome in the British fox hunt.

A third major type of equestrian sport is what may loosely be termed equestrian acrobatic competitions ranging from circus performances and othe public acrobatic displays to jumping and dressage competitions. Overlapping with these, but yet distinct from them because they are primarily displays of working from horseback, are such events as rodeos. Finally, competitive team games are a fourth major form of equestrian sport, including *buzkashi*, polo, *jerid* and *guks*. Such games have their origin in Central Asia and the Middle East, although some American Indians may have independently invented similar ones.

The riding and driving of horses and coaching represent three activities which have since disappeared as practical activities in most all of the Western world, but have survived purely as forms of pleasure. Indeed, most horses in the United States and Canada are used for pleasure riding alone. In recent years there has been a limited attempt to revive aspects of old Mediaeval knighthood as a sport including riding in full armour and jousting.

No other domestic animal has been so widely applied to sport activity as the horse. The reasons for this should be apparent since no other domestic animal so combines the necessary qualifications for these events. Only the dog equals the horse in its willingness to work with and abide the commands of its master. The horse possesses the capacity to become immersed in the spirit of a sporting activity.It has the advantage of size and of being the swiftest of domesticated animals.

If the horse is in a dramatic state of decline in terms of its "practical" use, there is certainly no abatement in the interest in horses for sporting purposes. Quite the contrary, as we have noted one of the consequences of modern technological society has been an expansion of affluence and leisure which, coupled with certain values regarding the horse, has resulted in a major resurgence of the horse in the United States, especially, but, now almost exclusively as an object of pleasure and sport.

The Horse in Draught

The extent to which horses are employed for draught work depends upon the prevailing attitude to the horse, the efficiency of harness, the size of the animals, the availability of alternative forms of power, the type of agricultural system as a provider of adequate horse feed and the kinds of implements employed. Horses have been long and widely used as pack animals, but their use in pulling loads has been more restricted. One reason for this was the failure to invent an efficient means for utilization of horse power until around the beginning of the Christian era. The yoke, so effective as a draught harness on cattle is useless on the horse because of the different shoulder structure. For possibly three or four millenia the chief horse harness was a throat strap which in pressing against the windpipe made for considerably reduced efficiency in draught. The invention of a breast strap, possibly independently in both China and North Africa, and of the collar in China provided techniques for good horse traction. Nevertheless, both of these devices were slow in diffusing to the rest of the world. The tardiness of these inventions and of their widespread acceptance, I believe, is in part related to the prevailing attitude towards the horse in many areas. Its association with tasks of an "aristocratic" nature in early Europe, the Middle East and India do not encourage men to tinker with new devices by which it could be turned to heavy mundane labour, especially when alternative forms of such power already existed (e.g., cattle, buffalo, mules).

The size of the horse is another issue which cannot be overlooked. The breeding of large, heavy horses is first associated with the demand for knights' chargers in Mediaeval Europe. Out of this eventually arose even larger horses for heavy draught work. Once a horse specialized for such a function was developed it was easier to bifurcate one's values in relation to the horse so that now the heavy cold-blooded animal could be seen and treated more as a common plebian. Lynn White stresses the need to develop an agricultural system which can supply the added feed necessary to sustain work horses and argues that this occurred in early northern Mediaeval Europe and so provided the base for expansion of horse traction in agriculture and elsewhere. But the breeding of large horses would seem to be of equal importance. There was a considerable increase in the use of horses for draught in northern Europe during Mediaeval times after the introduction of the collar and modification of the agricultural system. However, the draught horse did not prevail there until after the sixteenth century when heavy horses became sufficiently common to combine with the factors of efficient harnessing and agricultural system to allow for maximal use of the horse for heavy draught. Finally, the nineteenth century saw the appearance of agricultural implements which were more suited to the horse, thus, among other things, driving the ox out of existence in the realm of north European and Anglo-American draught activity.

Heavy draught horses were never common in southern Europe

where they were ill-suited to the heat of the region and where the agricultural system was not modified so that it could supply feed for such specialized animals. Lighter horses have occasionally been employed for lighter draught work in southern Europe but until modern times the preference was for oxen and to a lesser extent mules.

In eastern Europe, China and for a short span of time in Japan horses have been commonly used for heavier draught activity, but the big breeds were rarely to be found. Apart from the problem of feeding such large animals, peasants particularly in eastern Europe desired a multipurpose animal which could not only draw a plough, although less efficiently than the heavy horse, but could also pull a farm wagon at some speed. American farmers, for example, were more often able to afford a team of heavy draught horses and at least one light horse for carting and visiting purposes.

While many of us grew up in a time and place when the horse was an expected and normal member of the barnyard community, modern technology has made the draught horse a rarity. Some now suggest that with the energy crisis a revival of the farm horse is to be expected.

Clearly there is a role for increased practical employment of draught horses on the farms of the industrialized world. As one example, more farmers in the colder regions have recognized that it makes better sense to hitch up a team of horses for winter chores than to start and operate a tractor. Obviously, any increase in dependence on horse traction will conserve non-renewable energy resources. Another positive result could mean smaller farms and a curbing of the "agribusiness" mentality. Possibly a day may come when many food stuffs are produced more cheaply on smaller horse powered farms than on large corporate farms dependent on heavy investment in complex gasoline consuming machinery. On the other hand, total dependence on the draught horse in the agriculture of the industrial world would probably necessitate one hundred million more horses and this would entail, among other things, devoting from three to five acres of farmland for each horse. In addition it may be doubted whether such an agriculture could retain the present level of productivity. In sum, while the horse might answer the problem of oil conservation, it would create pressures on another scarce resource – arable land – and would probably not be able to keep pace with the ever increasing demands for more food production by an expanding population.

The Horse in Religious Sacrifice

The incorporation of the horse into religious symbolism, ceremonial and belief goes back to the very beginning of horse domestication and became part of a complex of traits which tended to move with the adoption of the horse. The Indo-European peoples especially are responsible for the spread of the horse sacrifice cult. According to Koppers they had acquired the cult from proto-Turkic peoples in the Eurasian steppes. However, it seems more likely that the reverse is the case, or at least that some proto-Indian-Europeans were responsible for its intrusion among Turkic-Mongol people and among the Chinese.

Koppers considered the elements of the horse cult to be:
1. offering of a young horse (stallion) as sacrifice
2. selection of spring for the event
3. freeing and dedication of offeratory horse
4. white colour especially sacred
5. decoration of offered horse
6. riding and driving races for betting purposes at the feast (Koppers, 1936).

All of these practices and beliefs have widespread distirbution temporally and geographically, although they are not always found together and they vary considerably in their application and meaning. The only major horse using people to largely ignore the cult – at least in its sacrificial aspects – were the Hamito-Semitic people of North Africa and South-west Asia. Quite independently of the Old World influence, the American Indians of the Plains and South American Pampas similarly developed a horse sacrifice cult.

Elements of the horse cult have been perpetuated into modern times among so-called more sophisticated peoples. These include the employment of horse's heads, skulls, skins and shoes or wooden heads as magical protective devices.

Given the late invention of the horseshoe it is obviously a more recent addition to the horse cult complex. Several explanations for the magical significance of the horseshoe have been put forward. As a device applied to a horse's hoof it may be associated with the fleetness of the animal and so come to symbolize a speedy delivery from evil. Hovey stresses the crescent shape of the horseshoe as thus representing the moon and being used to attract the celestial mother goddess. He also points out that iron was a power against fairies and witches so that the iron shoe driven into a wall would serve as protection because of the material of which it was made. This may have associations with the Roman practice "of driving nails into walls of houses . . . as an antidote to the plague" (Hovey, 102–103). Further, since the shoe would be hung open end up it may be designed to catch and hold good luck.

St. Dunstan, an early British bishop who was an accomplished horseshoer, is alleged to have seen the Devil in a horse he was shoeing.

He compelled the Devil to promise "that he would never enter or disturb a building on which a horseshoe had been hung" (Vernam, 81). This story is most likely a Christian rationalization for the older pagan practice.

Relics of earlier sacrifice of horses at funerals of noted men occur in Mediaeval and later European history. Even in modern times the saddles horse of a national leader or a military leader is led in his funeral cortege to the graveside as, for example, with John F. Kennedy. In some cases the saddle has been put on backwards in direct imitation of the Central Asiatic custom where it was believed the rider would enter heaven riding backwards.

The general trend in the nature of the horse cult parallels that in similar cults; they move in time from an emphasis on bloody sacrifice to more symbolic expressions of that sacrifice and often, to the demise of the cult. However, whether or not such a process can be taken as evidence that we of more contemporary times are any more intelligent and less burdened by "superstition" is to be doubted. A more feasible explanation is that the ritual and symbolism of such cults no longer have relevance and they are, therefore, replaced by new cults with rituals and symbolism more appropriate to the times. In addition there is, not infrequently, a revival of ancient cults which were thought to be long-since dead and buried. Note, for example, the recent resurgence of "witchcraft", "Satanism", and astrology in North America.

Care and Management

Horse husbandry is broadly of two types: Horses may be left year round on pasture with little or no provision for shelter, feeding almost wholly on available grasses. Or, they may be kept primarily in stalls and handfed on grain and hay with only limited resort to open pasture. Range-grass maintenance occurs wherever there are extensive grazing possibilities for horses, yet the opposite is not always true. That is, it does not mean that wherever extensive grazing possibilities exist for horses they will be left on the range and grass fed. In some areas horses may be entirely too valuable to chance leaving them out in the open as a temptation to thieves. Owners may possess so few that they must have them always readily at hand for work purposes and so they are kept tied in a stall near the house. In many parts of the temperate zone winter snow is too heavy for any efficient year round range maintenance; thus stall feeding is resorted to. Nomadic desert dwellers of Arabia and the Sahara combine hand feeding with range maintenance.

Prevailing horse feeds have been oats and barley, but with the spread of the horse to America maize was widely adopted for horse feeding especially in Latin America. The training of horses to eat meat or fish has a somewhat surprisingly wide distribution when we consider that the horse is an herbivore.

Gelding is practically universal; apparently only some of the Arabs reject the practice. Geldings are likewise the preference for a majority of riders, while stallions are less desired for this end. Trench has suggested that in ancient times horses may have been considered too valuable to chance the dangerous operation of castration and thus it was not resorted to. Since the majority of mares were kept for breeding purposes, the stallion was the most readily available for riding (Trench, 36). This may have been the case in ancient Egypt, Assyria or Greece where horses were in very short supply, but gelding was practiced by the ancient people of the Eurasiatic steppe who, of course, with their abundance of horses could afford to be less circumspect about the practice. In addition, mares were frequently used in both ancient India and Iran. They are still preferred for riding by Arabs. Yet, a common belief among Spanish speaking peoples is that a mare is only fit for a woman to ride – a likely residue of Mediaeval ideas.

Horseshoeing has a much more limited incidence than does gelding and its prevalence is closely associated with those areas of civilization where iron is more easily obtainable and where there is a highly developed road system: Europe, the Middle East, India, China.

Breeding techniques tend to be of two distinctly different types. A free and permissive arrangement, which allows the stallion to mate with whomever he pleases, is a practice found in conjunction with range-grass maintenance, especially in Central Asia and Ethiopia. A programme of close management of stallions which are segregated from the mares and only bred under control now prevails over most of the world, associated particularly with concerns for purebreeding and pedigreed stock.

Techniques of breaking and training are less related to ecological conditions and more exclusively a product of cultural tradition and diffusion. However, the practice of "green breaking" occurs mainly where individuals raise horses in small numbers so that more intimate associations with young animals arise. Apart from this technique there seem to be two opposing methods of breaking: a "severe" method and a "soft" one. The "severe" procedure is epitomized by some Gaucho and Arab techniques wherein ring or other harsh bits are applied to a completely unbroken horse from the start. Much less traumatic procedures are employed by American Indians and cowboys by the initial application of hackamore.

Horse Complexes of the World

As here employed, a horse complex constitutes a configuration of broadly similar beliefs and practices relating to the use, care and management of the horse. It is a combination of general, rather than highly specific, features shared by different peoples as a result of historical and ecological influences. Our survey indicates a limited number of such complexes.

The earliest domestication of the horse is associated with tribal-horticultural-stock raising sedentary peoples of the Eurasiatic steppes. We know little about the horse in this cultural context except that it seems most to have served as a source of meat. In all likelihood one of the earliest functions of the horse was as a mount for herding other horses. Possibly some were used for packing or drawing a travois-type conveyance or a wheeled vehicle. They may have been early associated with funerary or other religious sacrificial rites. The general character of horse use seems to have been of a multi-purpose nature and the extent to which it was treated by these peoples in any special sense as an expression of an aristocratic theme is a question. In this context horses sometimes comprised a quarter to a third of the total number of livestock, such high proportions no doubt reflecting their use for meat.

The adoption of the horse by the various ancient Near Eastern civilizations introduced a new horse complex, one which was to serve as the general pattern for all urban-agrarian civilizations. The horse was adopted as a war animal, first for the chariot and then for cavalry. As a scarce animal it was reserved for the aristocracy and so a firm identification of the horse with nobility and power was established – a tradition perpetuated in all later urban-agrarian civilizations. It was used only to a limited degree in light draught and for packing. Horses were stable fed and closely managed, in part because they were scarce and valued animals and, in many places because of the lack of adequate open grazing.

Around the end of the second millenium B.C. there arose yet a third major horse complex, that associated with pastoral nomadism on the Eurasiatic steppes. This evolved out of the earliest horse breeding village people of these steppes. The horse was now employed in the greatest variety of uses of any people of any time. While it was a source of milk, meat and hides and was used to some extent as a pack animal and for drawing carts, it was primarily a riding animal, but not merely limited to an aristocracy: every man rode. With an abundance of pasture, horses were grazed on open range and branding became important although shoeing was never adopted. Central Asiatic riding style spread widely and became adopted by the Chinese, Koreans and

Japanese and modifications of it were adopted in South-western Asia and eastern Europe. Horses comprised five to ten per cent of the livestock with a ratio of about one horse per one to ten persons.

The Chinese adapted the horse to more efficient draught work with the chest band and collar harness and so introduced a modification into the pattern of traditional urban-agrarian civilization and its use of the farm horse.

From early Mediaeval times Northern Europe began to deviate from the traditional complex of urban-agrarian civilization in also adapting the horse to draught labour but the Europeans were able to go further than the Chinese because they developed breeds more suited to heavy work along with an agricultural system which could feed numbers of large work animals. The numbers of horses greatly increased in northern Europe, ultimately reaching a high point of about one horse for every five to twenty persons under nineteenth century industrial capitalist conditions. The Circum-Mediterranean, Indian and Ethiopian areas continued to pursue the horse complex of traditional urban-agrarian civilization, reserving the animal primarily for riding, particularly by the aristocratic and military classes.

With settlement of America, the north European complex was extended into British and French held territories while in Spanish and Portuguese colonies the horse was applied to stock raising. As a consequence of this and of increasing demands for beef and hides, a Ranching complex grew and expanded. In this complex which is primarily associated with grassy steppes, horses continue to be used primarily for riding, especially for the herding of livestock. They are maintained on open range with little grain feeding and comprise about five per cent of livestock with a ratio of one horse per two to thirty persons. A British variant of this complex developed in Australia while the Dutch Boers in South Africa practiced an even more divergent form which may be considered a distinct sub-type of ranching because of its reliance on pedestrian herding.

The development of agrarian capitalism is important to the expansion of both the north European and the Ranching complexes as it provided a competitive market for the sale of specialized products and as it made peasants into yeomen who could afford to own carts, carriages and horses.

In the seventeenth century yet another horse complex starts to appear in America, that of the Equestrian Hunting American Indians. This complex proved shortlived, disappearing by the close of the nineteenth century.

The Pleasure complex is the most recent to develop, arising out of the obsolescence of the horse for purposes of transportation and farm labour and in an environment of expanded affluence and leisure. Horses as a result become primarily used for pleasure and a larger proportion of the population are able to take advantage of them in this way. Styles of care and management are drawn from the North American and the Ranching complexes.

For all the different complexes for which we have adequate information – that is, except for the most ancient – the horse has a position of some esteem among men relative to other animals. And except for the Ethiopian complex it seems to be very highly regarded. This is an issue with which I wish to deal more at length below.

In sum we note the following horse complexes:

1. Ancient Tribal-Sedentary-Steppe
2. Later Tribal-Sedentary (e.g. Celtic and Germanic peoples)
3. Urban-Agrarian Centres of Civilization regional variants:
   Circum-Mediterranean
   Indian
   Chinese
   Ethiopian
4. North European (Mediaeval and post-Mediaeval).
5. Eurasiatic Pastoral Steppe
6. Ranching: Mounted and Pedestrian Herding Variants
7. Equestrian Hunting (American Indian).
8. Modern Pleasure

Of the above, the several variants of the Urban-Agrarian Civilization, the Pleasure and Ranching complexes continue to persist, although almost everywhere the Ranching complex has been highly modified so that among other things it has become less dependent upon the horse. The Eurasian Pastoral Steppe complex is rapidly disappearing, tending to converge with the Ranching complex, as in Mongolia. The North European complex emphasizing the farm draught horse is all but dead as a result of twentieth century agricultural mechanization. In the not too distant future we can expect the Pleasure complex to become the most widespread and common horse complex in the world. Such a trend parallels the fate of numerous other elements in human culture which on becoming obsolete as far as practical and mundane usages are concerned assume more exclusively a role in the realms of ceremonial and pleasure. One could construct a long list of such items, but here we may note the fate of sailing boats, sleds, toboggans, skis, canoes, hunting game, camping, or the use of the fireplace or of candles. Among domesticated animals, the dog, once and in some areas, still, important as a hunting or herding aid, as a guard, a scavenger or source of meat, has become primarily a pet, as these other roles have declined for one reason or other.

In the course of this work we have seen how various historical, cultural, ecological, economic and other factors have interrelated with one another to produce these several complexes. While they vary sometimes considerably in their content, one pervasive theme seems to be evident among practically all of them. This theme affirms a high regard for the horse. The horse is recognized as a very special kind of animal, "high born", the aristocrat among domestic animals. In its extreme expression this theme identifies the horse with luxury, leisure and power and involves a restricted use of the horse to the aristocratic class and to "noble" undertakings of war, sport and the hunt, as in the Circum-Mediterranean or (East) Indian complexes.

That the horse is esteemed does not necessarily mean that it is therefore equally well treated. While one must not fall into the cultural relativist "trap" of holding that all things are relative and no absolute standards exist, it is nevertheless difficult to reach any universally agreed upon definition of what would constitute "cruelty" to animals. An important measure of esteem for the horse is that it receives favoured treatment over other animals and, for that matter, in some cases, certain kinds of people as well, not that it is invariably dealt with "kindly". For example, the Spaniards seem to accord their horses preferential treatment over their other domesticated animals, yet in the New World they also exploited feral horses in what would be judged by much of the world as a "cruel" fashion. Apart from this issue, one would suspect that to them feral horses fell into a category totally different from that which included their personal mounts and other domesticated horses.

If we look among other domesticated animals it is difficult to find any but a few isolated examples which parallel the status accorded the horse. Hindu India has sanctified the cow, although this has not prevented cattle from being a beast of burden there. Some African pastoralists also exhibit a high regard for their cattle, but most of these have never known the horse. Beja and Tuareg esteem the camel, probably in large part for reasons that other men esteem the horse, in that it is a device by which by riding one can achieve a sense of power and freedom. However, we note that wherever the choice between camel and horse arises, it is the horse which receives the higher status. Dogs and similar pets have sometimes been treated with luxurious care, yet where this occurs, horses when present, are accorded the same treatment, because it is invariably a practice associated with an aristocracy or a combination of affluence and sentimentalism arising out of the peculiar nature of modern, urban industrial society.

In worldwide terms the high regard for any domestic animal, except for the horse, seems to be extremely limited in its occurrence. The horse in contrast, has almost universally been esteemed as the prize of all domesticated animals. Exceptions to this appear rare; notable examples are the ancient Hebrews and the Amharic people of Ethiopia.

It has been alleged that the ancient Hebrews elevated the donkey and the mule and had less respect for the horse because of its identification with military expansion and oppression. Were the Hebrews a passive people who disdained power and military expansion themselves, one might be more sympathetic to such an argument. But this point of view has the flavour of the mythology which seeks to veil the Hebrews in an unwarranted sanctity and innocence. In addition, countless peoples throughout the world have been frequent victims of military oppression with the aid of cavalry or chariotry, but this did not diminish their esteem for the horse. Why the Hebrews came to regard the donkey or mule over the horse is not a question I am able to answer. Possibly their position as a people long subject to foreign rule in which they were discouraged from having, or were not permitted to have, horses had the consequence of elevating the mule and the ass as symbols of their cultural identity. Max Weber noted two conflicting traditions in ancient Israel, one which was monarchist and another which was anti-monarchist. The latter, supported by the great prophets, identified the horse with the king, while ass riding symbolized the judge and the plain country folk (Weber, 114ff.).

As far as the Amhara are concerned Dent considers their esteem for the mule to be a derivation from their ancient cultural ties with the Hebrews. We have noted it may as probably be a practical result of their experience with both animals in difficult mountain terrain.

A materialist explanation for the widespread aristocratic standing of the horse is simply one of supply and demand. Beginning in the second millenium B.C. Near Eastern civilization saw the potential of the horse and chariot for warfare and imperialist expansion. Horses came into great demand in areas of ancient civilization most of which were not prolific in horse breeding. The combination of their being introduced into these cultures as special animals for war with the fact that the demand was greater than the supply entrenched an aristocratic conception of the role of the horse. From the beginning, horses in ancient civilizations were reserved for the honour of carrying kings, princes and noblemen, bearing them into activities which were deemed honourable and glorious.

Such a materialist thesis has some merit in pointing to the obvious high standing of the horse particularly in the Circum-Mediterranean area, but it does not fully explain why the horse should be highly esteemed in areas where it has been in abundance. It does not explain why there should be such universal expression of this theme when there is a considerable variance in the supply of horses. One suspects then that there are more pervasive causes for this attitude.

We might look at the relationship between man and the horse: the social psychological factor. Since ancient times men of all cultural backgrounds have appreciated certain aesthetic qualities in the horse. No other animal ever domesticated by man so combines grace, "streamlining", intelligence, tractability, power and speed in one body. Because men find this combination of qualities most desirable and because these qualities have a practical utility for men, the horse has been an object of admiration.

The invention of riding lends further impetus to honouring the horse and produces a psychological effect of its own. Indeed, no other single incident was more important in stimulating a high regard for the horse than the invention of horse riding. With this achievement man could now mount this mighty and swift beast and, as a centaur, become one with it in the experience of surging power and speed. The rider had mobility and freedom; he had command over his surroundings; he was raised above and over them. Driving horses has a similar yet lesser effect. With no other animal and, until the very recent invention of mechanical means of transportation, with no other thing could he derive such a "thrill" in speed and control of power.[1] At the same time there is the satisfaction of working or cooperating with a greater and supple living force coupled with the achievement of such mobility and freedom. It would be unusual if men did not immediately perceive in the horse something special and deserving of particular care and regard.

Xenophon has Chrysantas, associate of Cyrus, speak thus: ". . . I think that if I become a horseman I shall be a man on wings. For as we are now, I, at least, am satisfied, when I have an even start in running a race with any man, if I can beat him only by a head; and when I see an animal running along, I am satisfied if I can get a good aim quickly enough to shoot him or spear him before he gets very far away. But if I become a horseman I shall be able to overtake a man though he is as far off as I can see him; and I shall be able to pursue animals and overtake them and either strike them down from close at hand or spear them as they were standing still . . . . Now the creature that I have envied most is, I think, the centaur (if any such being ever existed), able to reason with a man's intelligence and to manufacture with his hands what he needed, while he possessed the fleetness and strength of a horse so as to overtake whatever ran before him and to knock down whatever

[1] For ninety-eight percent of the last 6000 years – that is, up to 1839 – the horse was the fastest vehicle available to man. It is no wonder it represents an archaic archetype for combined power and speed.

stood in his way. Well, all his advantages I combine in myself by becoming a horseman" (Xenophon, *Cryopaedia*, IV, iii).

These social psychological factors may be viewed as pervasive sources for the high positive value on the horse. Obviously, that such an animal has great practical utility and is in short supply can only operate to intensify such feelings. We propose then that the generating force for the high regard for the horse arises out of the admiration for its particular qualities in relation to its practical significance and out of what may be called the centaur effect – the psychological effect derived from horse riding and, to a lesser extent, horse driving. In turn the emergent theme of the horse as the aristocrat of animals may be diverted towards one of two poles by more materialistic factors such as supply and demand.

The "plebian" pole represents the tendency to make the horse a mundane or common farmyard animal. The use of the horse for all kinds of draught work and the consumption of horse meat and milk in other than sacred sacrificial circumstances all signify this orientation. The horse maintains a higher status than other animals, but this status does not confer much that is special.

The opposite to the "plebian" is a "patrician" pole, an intensification of the esteem for the horse so that in its extreme expression the horse is reserved for the most limited and prestigious functions and often only for a special class. The interplay between material factors with the social psychological produce horse complexes which may reflect either "plebian" or "aristocratic" tendencies.

Thus, the particular characteristics of the North European complex with its more plebian orientation arise out of a configuration of material factors as they impinge upon a pervasive admiration for the horse. These factors are: a relative abundance of horses with adequate grazing and an agricultural system capable of providing horse feed, combined with efficient harness for draught use, the development of different breeds specialized for different uses, and of farm implements well suited to horse traction, plus the fact that under these circumstances superior alternative forms of draught power were not present. The development of specialized breeds allowed for some – the heavy draught type – to be employed in a more plebian fashion while others – light breeds – were retained for aristocratic usage, but even the plebian draught horse lent his owner esteem over owners of other lesser animals, because it was, nevertheless, a horse.

China, too, developed a complex which had a plebian flavour. Yet because of the lack of large draught horses, limitations of grazing and feed, and general scarcity in numbers, the Chinese never produced a draught horse complex of the type of the North Europeans. It would appear that the great pressure for sources of draught power in China for supporting an intensive agriculture aimed at feeding a large and densely settled population combined with an early invention of efficient horse harness were important in putting the few horses available to more mundane types of labour. In the Middle East and Europe cattle and buffalo served as a source of milk, meat and draught and so have the advantage over the keeping of horses. In China milk drinking is not customary so that the advantage in this respect for cattle or buffalo over horses is not present.

The Circum-Mediterranean complex is more oriented to the aristocratic pole because of the concatenation of other contrastive factors, including a lower agricultural productive capability, extensive areas where grazing is of poor quality or unavailable, and lack of development of heavy breeds. Further, the general character of the total agricultural complex favoured reliance on alternate sources of draft power such as mules, donkeys, camels, buffalo as well as the ox. Finally, was the widespread taboo on the consumption of horseflesh especially in the North African-South-west Asiatic parts of this area – a taboo which might well have arisen out of the scarcity of horses and their aristocratic-military use, but especially in the Muslim areas had behind it the powerful force of divine law.

In the Indian-South Asian complex we have another stress on the aristocratic role of the horse. For the most part this is a region poorly suited to horse husbandry. Horses are few in number; there has been no specialization into draught and light breeds and other forms of draught power – oxen, buffalo and elephants – are better adapted to working in the humid, hot climate.

Concerning the Ethiopian complex we have already had occasion to observe that the Amhara generally rank the horse below the mule and so in general deviate from the attitude of most other peoples who have maintained horses. The Galla of Ethiopia, by contrast, have traditionally held the horse in highest regard. They abstain from eating horseflesh and reject the use of horses on the plough. With an abundance of horses and ample grazing facilities, they made the horse an integral part of their mounted warrior tradition.

The Central Asian steppe people were at best indifferent cultivators, yet devoted herdsmen and warriors. Thus, the focus was on the riding horse as the common mode of transportation. At the same time, the horse was an object in religious sacrifice, stressing its esteemed position, but it was also kept for the presumably plebian ends of meat and milk consumption. Such consumption, however, differed from that of the eating and drinking of products of cattle, sheep or goats. As a rule, horsemeat was reserved for special festivities or funerals and the drinking of mare's milk, consumed as koumiss, was a ceremonial occasion with parallels to Japanese tea or Arab coffee rituals. Thus, in Central Asia the abundance of horses and of grazing facilities tended to propel the complex in a more "plebian" direction, yet the universal dependence upon the horse and the admiration for its qualities sustained a high regard for the animal.

Both the American Indian and (Mounted) Ranching complexes have many similarities to the Central Asiatic. They were all associated with steppe country, relied primarily on animal resources and paid little heed to cultivation. The pattern of life was very heavily dependent upon the riding horse and these, raised on open range, were in great abundance. Although Ranching and Central Asiatic complexes are associated with herding economies in contrast to the hunting orientation of the Indian, the latter, like the Central Asiatic, was a "subsistence" economy and more nomadic. The role of the horse in gift giving, the payment of fines, funerary sacrifice, sport, and as a measure of man's wealth were elements emphasizing esteem for the horse common to both American Indian and Central Asiatic peoples. The Central Asiatic complex, however, made a more varied use of the horse. Neither among ranchers nor among American Indians was horsemeat usually desirable food and the drinking of mare's milk was unheard of. It is likely that the American Indian and Ranching complexes veer in a slightly more aristocratic direction than the Central Asiatic, but the abundance of horses was a major factor in their never becoming so aristocratic in their orientation as in the Circum-Mediterranean complex.

In large part because of the obsolescence of the horse for draught purposes, the Modern Pleasure complex with its emphasis on the horse for pleasure among those who can afford it again stresses an aristocratic orientation.

In sum, man through the ages as he encountered and adopted the horse has experienced a special admiration for certain of its qualities. This admiration is enhanced with the advent of riding which gives added feeling of power, mobility and freedom not before or otherwise experienced. The psychological orientation so produced forms a basic theme of esteem for the horse whose expression may be diverted and modified by ecological, technological, economic or other cultural factors in either a more aristocratic or plebian direction.

Bibliography

Aflalo, F.G., *The Sports of the World*, London, 1903

Albright, William F., *The Archeology of Palestine*, Harmondsworth, England, Penguin, 1956

Allchin, Raymond, "The Culture Sequence of Bactria," *Antiquity*, 1957

——, "Early Domestication in India and Pakistan" in Ucko and Dimbleby, 1969

Allchin, Bridget and Raymond, *The Birth of Indian Civilization*, Harmondsworth, England, Penguin, 1968

Amschler, R., "The Oldest Pedigree Chart: A Genealogical Table of the Horse and Pictures of Horsemen Dating back 5000 Years," *Journal of Herdity*, XXVI, No. 6, 1935

Anatolian Studies, "Summary of Archeological Research in Turkey in 1960" XI, 1961

Anderson, J.K., *Ancient Greek Horsemanship*, Berkeley, California, 1961

Angress, Shimon and Charles A. Reed, *Annotated Bibliography on the Origin and Descent of Domestic Animals*, Chicago Natural History Museum, LIV, 1962

Antonius, O., Grundzüge einer Stammesgeschichte der Haustiere, Jena, 1922

——, "Zur Frage der Zähmung des Onagers bei dem alten Sumerern," *Bijdragen tot de Dierkunde*, (Leiden), 1938

Antsiferov, Alexis N., A.D. Bilimovich, M.O. Batshev, D.M. Ivanov, *Russian Agriculture During the War*, New Haven, Yale University, 1930

Aristotle, *Politics*, Ernest Barker, transl., Oxford, 1952

Arribas, Antonio, *The Iberians*, London, Thames and Hudson, 1963

Aschmann, Homer, *Indian Pastoralists of the Guajira Peninsula*, Annals of Association of American Geographers, L, 1960

Ashton, Hugh, *The Basuto*, Oxford, 1952

Atherton, Lewis, *The Cattle Kings*, Lincoln, Univ. of Nebraska, 1972

Auboyer, Jeannine, "Animals in India" in Brodrick, 1972

Auden, W.H. and Louis MacNiece, *Letters from Iceland*, New York, Random House, 1969

Aynard, J.M., "Animals in Mesopotamia" in Brodrick, 1972

Bacon, Elizabeth, *Central Asians under Russian Rule*, Ithaca, N.Y. Cornell, 1966

Balfour-Paul, H.G., *History and Antiquities of Darfur*, Sudan Antiquities

Service, Khartoum, 1955

Barnett, R.D., "Assyria and Iran: The Earliest Representation of Persians" in Pope, A.U. and Ackerman, XIV, 1967

Barth, Fredrik, *Principles of Social Organization in Southern Kurdistan*, Brodrene Jorgensen Boktr., Oslo, 1953

Beck, Salim, *The Mongolian Horse*, Tientsin, 1926

Bearcroft, Norma, *The Wild Horses of Canada*, London, J.A. Allen, 1966

Bennett, Russell, H., *The Compleat Rancher*, New York, Rinehart, 1946

Berenger, Richard, *The History and Art of Horsemanship*, London, Vol. I, 1771

Beaumont, Olga & J. Geraint Jenkins, "Farm Tools, Vehicles, and Harness, 1500–1900" in Singer, vol. III, 1954–6

Biesanz, John and Mavis, *The People of Panama*, New York, Columbia, 1955

Birket-Smith, Kaj, *Primitive Man and his Ways*, New York, Mentor 1960
——, *The Paths of Culture*, Madison, University of Wisconsin, 1965

Blishko, Charles, "The Peninsular Background of Latin American cattle Ranching", *Hispanic American Historical Review* XXXII, 1952

Blunt, Anne, *The Bedouin Tribes of the Euphrates*, London, 1879
——, *A Pilgrimage to Nejd*, Vol. II, London, 1881

Boessneck, Joachim and Angela von den Driesch, "Pferde im 4/3 Jahrtausend v. Chr. in Ostanatolien", *Säugetier Kundliche Mitteilungen*, XXIV, 1976

Boettger, Caesar R., *Die Hautiere Afrikas*, Jena, Gustav Fischer, 1958

Bökönyi, Sandor, *Data on Iron Age Horses in Central and Eastern Europe in the Mecklenberg Collection*, Pt. I, Cambridge, Harvard University, 1968
——, "Archaeological Problems and Methods of Recognizing Animal Domestication" in Ucko and Dimblesby, 1969
——, *History of Domestic Mammals in Central and Eastern Europe*, Budapest, Akadamiai Kiado, 1974

Bolinder, Gustaf, *Indians on Horseback*, London, Dobson, 1957

Bovill, E.W., *The Golden Trade of the Moors*, Oxford, 1961

Boyd, Louise, "Polish Countrysides," Special Publication 20, American Geographical Society, 1937

Boyson, H.A., *The Falkland Islands*, Oxford, 1924

Briggs, L. Cabot, *Tribes of the Sahara*, Cambridge, Harvard University, 1960

Brodrick, A. Houghton, *Animals in Archaeology*, London, Barrie and Jenkins, 1972

Brøndstad, J., *The Vikings*, Harmondsworth, England, Penguin, 1970

Brown, William Robinson, *The Horse of the Desert*, New York, Macmillan, 1927

Bruemmer, F., "The Wild Horses of Sable Island," *Animals*, X, 1967
Bryant, A. T., *The Zulu People*, Pietermaritzburg, Shuter & Shooter 1949
Bulliet, Richard, *The Camel and the Wheel*, Cambridge, Mass., Harvard, 1975.
Business Week, "Horses in Demand," August 11, 1945
Byrne, M. St. Clare, *Elizabethan Life in Town and Country*, London, Methuen, 1961
Caesar, Julius, *The Gallic Wars*, H. Edwards, transl., London, Heinemann, 1917
Campbell, Judith, *Horses and Ponies*, London, Hamlyn, 1970
Carter, W.H., "The Story of the Horse," *National Geographic*, XLIV, 1923
Chadwick, Nora, *The Celts*, Harmondsworth, England, Penguin, 1971
Chang, Kwang-chih, *The Archaeology of Ancient China*, New Haven, Yale, 1971
Chapelle, Jean, *Nomades noirs du Sahara*, Paris, Plon, 1958
Chard, Thornton, "An Early Horse Skeleton," *Journal of Heredity*, XXVIII, no. 9, 1937
Chen, Nai Ruenn, *Chinese Economic Statistics*, Chicago, Aldine, 1967
Chevalier, Francois, *Land and Society in Colonial Mexico*, Berkeley, University of California, 1963
Childe, Vere Gordon, *The Danube in Prehistory*, Oxford, 1927
——, *What Happened in History*, Harmondsworth, England, Penguin, 1942
——, "Wheeled Vehicles" in Singer, Charles, E.J. Holmyard and A.R. Hall (eds.) Vol. I, 1954–1956.
——, *The Dawn of European Civilization*, London, Routledge and Kegan Paul, 1958
Christie, Ella R., *Through Kiva to Golden Samarkand*, London, Seeley Service, 1925
Chungshu, Kwei (ed.) *The Chinese Yearbook*, 1935–36, Nendeln, Liechtenstein, Kraus Reprint, 1968
Clark, Grahame, "Horses and Battle Axes," *Antiquity*, XV, 1941
——, *World Prehistory — An Outline*, Cambridge, 1961
Clebert, J., *The Gypsies*, Harmondsworth, England, Penguin, 1963
Cluness, A.T., *The Shetland Islands*, London, Robert Hale, 1951
Cohen, Ronald, *The Kanuri of Nigeria*, New York, Holt, Rinehart, Winston, 1967
Colledge, Malcolm, *The Parthians*, New York, Praeger, 1967
Columella, *On Agriculture*, Cambridge, Harvard University, 1954
Conn, George H., *Horse Selection and Care for Beginners*, No. Hollywood, California, Wilshire, 1971

Coomaraswamy, Ananda K., "Horse Riding in the Rigveda and Atharvaveda", *American Oriental Society Journal*, XLII, June, 1942

Coon, Carleton S., *Tribes of the Rif*, Cambridge, Harvard African Studies, 1931

Cott, Hugh B., "Wonder Islands of the Amazon Delta," *National Geographic*, LXXIV, 1938

Coulton, G.G., *Medieval Village, Manor, and Monastry*, New York, Harper, 1960

Cowen, J.D., "The Halstatt Sword of Bronze on the Continent and in Britain," *Proc. Prehistoric Soc.*, XXXIII, 1967

Creel, Herrlee G., *The Birth of China*, New York, Frederic K. Unger, 1937

——, "The Role of the Horse in Chinese History," *American Historical Review*, LXX, no. 3, 1965

Culican, William, *The Medes and Persians*, London, Thames and Hudson, 1965

Cumont, Franz, *The Mysteries of Mithra*, New York, Dover, 1956

Curtler, W.H.R., *A Short History of English Agriculture*, Oxford, 1909

Curwen, E. Cecil, "Early Agriculture in Denmark," *Antiquity*, 1938

Curwen, E. Cecil and Gudmund Hatt, *Plough and Pasture: The Early History of Farming*, New York, Collier, 1961

Czaplicka, M.A., *Aboriginal Siberia*, Oxford, 1969

DaCunha, Euclides, *Rebellion in the Backlands*, University of Chicago, 1944

Dasent, George W., *The Story of Burnt Njal*, London, Dent, 1971

Daumas, E., *The Horses of the Sahara*, Austin, University of Texas, 1968

Daumas, Maurice (ed.), *A History of Technology and Invention*, New York, Crown, 1969

Davidson, H.R. Ellis, *Pagan Scandinavia*, New York, Praeger, 1967

Davis, William S., *Life in a Medieval Barony*, New Hork, Harper, 1923

Davis, Patrick D.C. and Dent, Anthony, *Animals that Changed the World*, London, Phoenix House, 1966

Denhardt, R.M., *The Horse of the Americas*, Norman, University of Oklahoma, 1947

Dent, Anthony, *Donkey: The Story of the Ass from East to West*, London, George Harrap, 1972

——, *The Horse*, New York, Holt, Rinehart and Winston, 1974

Dickson, H.R.P., *The Arab of the Desert*, London, Allen and Unwin, 1959

Dobie, J. Frank, *The Mustangs*, New York, Bramhill House, 1952

Dodge, Theodore A., *Riders of Many Lands*, New York, Harper, 1894

Doe, D. Brian, *Southern Arabia*, New York, McGraw-Hill, 1971

Doutressoule, G., *L'Elevage en Afrique Occidentale Française*, Paris, 1947

Downs, J.F., "The Origin and Spread of Riding in the Near East and Central Asia," *American Anthropologist*, LXIII, 1961

——, *The Navajo*, New York, Holt, Rinehart, and Winston, 1972

Downs, J.F. and R. Ekvall, "Animals and Social Types in the Exploitation of the Tibetan Plateau" in Leeds, Anthony and Andrew Vayda, 1965

Drake-Brockman, R.F., *British Somaliland*, 1912

Driver, Harold, *Indians of North America*, University of Chicago, 1961

Drower, M.S., "The Domestication of the Horse" in Ucko and Dimbleby, 1969

Ducos, Pierre, *L'origin des animaux domestiques in Palestine*, University of Bordeaux, 1968

——, "The Oriental Institute Excavations at Mureybit, Syria: Preliminary Report of the 1965 Campaign, Part IV: Les restes d'equids," *Journal of Near Eastern Studies*, XXIX, no. 4, 1970

Duerst, J.U., "The Horse of Anau in its Relation to History and the Races of Domestic Horses" in *Exploration in Turkestan*, 1904, Washington D.C., 1908

Dumont, Rene, *Types of Rural Economy*, London, Methuen, 1966

Durham, M. Edith, *High Albania*, London, Edward Arnold, 1909

Dusenberry, William H., *The Mexican Mesta*, Urbana, University of Illionois, 1963

Dussaud, Rene, "The Bronzes of Luristan. A. Types and History" in Pope, A.U. and P. Ackerman (eds.), I, 1938–1967

Dwyer, F., *Seats and Saddles, Bits and Bitting, Draught and Harness*, London, Wittingham, 1886

Editorial Research Reports, "Polo Snobs," June 18, 1971

——, "Leisure Business," February 28, 1973

Eglar, Zekiya, *A Punjabi Village in Pakistan*, New York, Columbia, 1960

Ekvall, Robert, *Fields on the Hoof*, New York, Holt, Rinehart and Winston, 1968

Elphinstone, Mountstuart, *An Account of the Kingdom of Caubul and Its Dependencies in Persia, Tartary and India*, Graz, 1969

Embree, John, *Suye Mura*, University of Chicago, 1967

Epstein, H., *The Origin of the Domestic Animals of Africa*, Vol. II, New York, Africana, 1971a

——, *Domestic Animals of China*, New York, Africana, 1971b

Ernle, Rowland, *English Farming, Past and Present*, London, Heineman, 1961

Ewart, J.C., "On Skulls from the Roman Fort of Newstead near Melrose, with Observations on the Origin of the Domestic Horses," *Transactions*, Royal Society, XLV, Pt. 3, 1907

——, "The Derivation of the Modern Horse," *Quarterly Review*, no.

411, 1907

Ewers, John C., *The Horse in Blackfoot Indian Culture*, Smithsonian Institution, Bureau of American Ethnology, Bulletin 159, 1955

Ezell, Paul H., *The Hispanic Acculturation of the Gila River Pima*, Memoir American Anthropological Assn., no. 90, 1961

Fairservis, Walter, *The Origins of Oriental Civilization*, New York, Mentor, 1959

Fakhry, Ahmed, *An Archaeological Journey to Yemen*, Cairo, Service des Antiquités de l'Egypte, Government Press, 1952

Farshler, Earl, *The American Saddle Horse*, Louisville, Standard Printing Co., 1933

Fei, Hsiao Tung and Chih-i-Chang, *Earthbound China*, London, Routledge and Kegan Paul, 1948

Feilberg, C.G., *Les Papis, tribu persane de nomade montagnards du sudouest de l'Iran*, Copenhagen, Glydendal, 1952

Fel, Edit and Tamas Hofer, *Proper Peasants, Traditional Life in a Hungarian Village*, Chicago, Aldine, 1969

Fernea, Robert, *Shaykh and Effendi; Changing Patterns of Authority Among the El Shabana of Southern Iraq*, Cambridge, Harvard, 1970

Finland, the Country, its People and Institutions, Helsinki, Otava Publ., 1926

Firouz, Louise, *The Caspian Miniature Horses of Iran*, Miami, Florida, Field Research Projects, 1972.

Fisher, Humphrey J., "He Swalloweth the Ground with Fierceness and Rage: The Horse in the Central Sudan," *Journal of African History*, XIII, no. 3, 1972 and XIV, no. 3, 1973

Forbes, J.D., "The Appearance of the Mounted Indian in Northern Mexico and the Southwest to 1680," *Southwest Journal of Anthropology*, XV, 1959

Forde, C. Daryll, *Habitat, Economy and Society*, London, Methuen, 1934

——, "The Cultural Map of West Africa: Successive Adaptations to Tropical Forests and Grasslands" in Ottenberg, Simon and Phoebe (eds.), *Cultures and Societies of Africa*, New York, Random House, 1960

Foster, George M., "Peasant Society and the Image of the Limited Good", *American Anthropologist*, LXVII, 1965

Fox, Ralph, *People of the Steppes*, London, Constable, 1925

Frankfurt, Henri, *The Birth of Civilization in the Near East*, Garden City, New York, Doubleday, n.d.

Frantz, J.B. and J.E. Choate, Jr., *The American Cowboy*, Norman, University of Oklahoma, 1955

Freyre, Gilberto, *The Masters and the Slaves: A Study in the Development of Brazilian Civilization*, New York, Knopf, 1968

Friedl, Ernestine, *Vasilika, A Village in Modern Greece,* New York, Holt, Rinehart and Winston, 1962

von Furer-Haimendorf, Christoph, "Culture History and Cultural Development" in William L. Thomas (ed.), *Yearbook of Anthropology,* New York, Wenner Gren Fdn., 1965

Fussell, G.E., *Farming Techniques from Prehistory to Modern Times,* Oxford, Permagon Press, 1965

Ghirshman, R., *Iran,* Harmondsworth, England, Penguin, 1961.

——, et al, *Dark Ages and Nomads c. 1000 B.C.,* Istanbul, Nederl. Historisc. Inst., 1964

Gianoli, Luigi, *Horses and Horsemanship Through the Ages,* New York, Crown, 1969

Gibbs, James (ed.), *Peoples of Africa,* New York, Holt, Rinehart and Winston, 1965

Gimbutas, Mariya, *The Prehistory of Eastern Europe,* Cambridge, Harvard Peabody Museum, 1956

——, *Bronze Age Cultures in Central and Eastern Europe,* Paris, Mouton, 1965

——, *The Balts,* New York, Praeger, 1963

——, "Proto-Indo-European Culture: The Kurgan Culture during the Fifth, Fourth and Third Millenia B.C.," in Cardona, G., H. Hoenigswald and A. Senn (eds.) *Indo-European and Indo-Europeans,* Philadelphia, University of Pennsylvania, 1970

——, *The Slavs,* New York, Praeger, 1971

Goodale, Daphne, *Horses of the World,* Country Life, 1965

Goodenough, Ward, "The Evolution of Pastoralism and Indo-European Origins," in Cardona, G., H. Hoenigswald and A. Senn (eds.) *Indo-Europe and Indo-Europeans,* Philadelphia, University of Philadelphia, 1970

Goody, Jack, *Technology, Tradition and the State in Africa,* Oxford, 1971

Graham, R.B. Cunninghame, *Horses of the Conquest,* Norman, University of Oaklahoma, 1949

——, *The Conquest of the River Plate,* New York, Greenwood Press, 1968

Grant, I.F., *Highland Folkways,* London, Routledge and Kegan Paul, 1961

Gregson, Ronald, "The Influence of the Horse on Indian Cultures of Lowland South America," *Ethnohistory,* XVI, 1969

Grinnell, George B., *The Cheyenne Indians,* New Haven, Yale, 1923

Gryaznov, Mikhail, *The Ancient Civilizations of Southern Siberia,* New York, Cowles, 1969

Gummere, Francis B., *German Origins: A Study in Primitive Culture,* New York, Scribner, 1892

Gurney, O.R., *The Hittites,* Harmondsworth, England, Penguin, 1954

Haberland, Eike, *Galla Sud Äthiopiens*, Stuttgart, W. Kohlhammer, 1963

Hafez, E.S.E. (ed.), *Adaptation of Domestic Animals*, Philadelphia, Lea and Febriger, 1968

Hahn E., *Die Haustiere und ihre Bezeihungen zur Wirtschaft des Menschen*, Leipzig, 1896

Haines, Francis, *Horses in America*, New York, Crowell, 1971

Hammond, John, "Die Verbreitung der verschiedenen Trerarten in der Welt" in Hammond John, Ivar Johanneson and Fritz Haring, Vol. III, 1958–1961

Hammond, John, Ivar Johanneson, and Fritz Haring, *Handbuch der Tierzüchtung*, Hamburg and Berlin, Paul Parey, 1958–1961

Hancar, Franz, *Das Pferd in prähistoricher und früher historischer Zeit*, Munschen, Herold, Institut für Volkerkunde der Universität Wien, 1956

Harlan, Jack R., "The Plants and Animals that Nourish Man", *Scientific American*, 3, CCXXXV, 1976

Harris, W. Cornwallis, *The Highlands of Ethiopia*, London, Longmans, 1844

Haslund, Henning, *Tents in Mongolia*, New York, Dutton, 1934

Hatt, Gudmund, *Notes on Reindeer Nomadism*, Memoir, American Anthropological Association, vol. VI, 1919

Hawkes, Jacquetta and Christopher, *Prehistoric Britain*, Harmondsworth, England, Penguin, 1958

Hayashi, Minao, "On the Horse of the pre Ch'in Period in China," *Japanese Journal of Ethnology*, XXIII, XXIV, 1959

Hayward, D.E.H., "Transhumance in Southern Norway," Scottish Geographical Magazine, LXIV, 1948

Helmreich, Ernst, *Hungary*, New York, Praeger, 1957

Hencken, Hugh, *Indo-European Languages and Archeology*, Memoir, American Anthropological Association, no. 84, LVII, 1955

Hermes, Gertrude, "Das gezähmte Pferd in neolithischen und früh bronzezeitlichen Europa?" *Anthropos*, XXX, XXXI, 1935 and 1936

Herodotus, *The Histories*, Harmondsworth, England, Penguin, 1971

Herre, Wolf, "Abstimmung und Domestikation der Haustiere" in Hammond, John, Ivar Johanneson, and Fritz Haring, I, 1958–1961

——, "Grundsatzliches zur systematik des Pferdes," *Zeitschrift für Tierzüchtung and Züchtungsbiologie*, LXXV, 1961

——, "The Science and History of Domestic Animals," in Brothwell, D., E. Higgs, (eds.) *Science in Archaeology*, New York, Basic Books, 1963

Herzfeld, Ernst, *The Persian Empire*, Wiesbaden, Steiner, 1968

Hewitt, John, *Ancient Armour and Weapons in Europe*, Graz, Austria:

Akademische Druck-u Verlagsanstatt, 1967

Hill, D.R., "The Role of the Camel and the Horse in the Early Arab Conquests" in Parry, Vernon J. and M.E. Yapp

Hilzheimer, Max, *Natürliche Rassengeschichte der Hausäugtiere*, Berlin, Walter De Gruyter, 1926

——, "The Evolution of the Horse", *Antiquity*, IX, 1935

Hitti, Philip K., *The History of the Arabs*, New York, Macmillan, 1953

Hollis, F.H. "The Horse in Agriculture" in Vesey-Fitzgerald, Brian, *The Book of the Horse*, London, Nicholson and Watson, 1946

Honigmann, John J., *Three Pakistan Villages*, Institute of Social Science Research, Chapel Hill, University of North Carolina, 1958

Hourwich, Isaac A., *The Economics of the Russian Village*, New York, AMS Press, 1970

Howard, R.W., *The Horse in America*, Chicago, Follett, 1965

Howey, M. Oldfield, *The Horse in Magic and Myth*, New York, Castle, 1958

Humlum, Johannes, *La Geographi de l'Afghanistan*, Copenhagen, Gyldendal, 1959

Huntingford, G.W.P., *The Galla of Ethiopia*, London, International African Institute, 1955

Huppertz, Josefine, "Untersuchungen über die Anfange der Haustierzucht unter besonderer Berücksichtung der Pferdezucht," *Anthropos*, LVI, 1961

——, "Die frühe Pferdezuchte in Ostasien," *Zeitschrift für Tierzüchtungsbiologie*, LXXV, 1961

Isaac, Erich, *The Geography of Domestication*, New York, Prentice Hall, 1970

Isenbart, H-H and E.M. Buhrer, *The Kingdom of the Horse*, New York, Time-Life Books, 1971

Jamme, Albert, "Inscriptions on the Sabaean Bronze Horse of the Dumbarton Oaks Collection," *Dumbarton Oaks Papers*, 8, 1954

Jankovich, Miklos, *They Rode into Europe*, London, Harrap, 1971

Jettmar, Karl, "The Altai Before the Turks," Stockholm, *Bulletin of Museum of Far Eastern Antiquities*, no. 23, 1951

——, "Zu den Anfängen der Rentierzucht", *Anthropos*, XLVII, 1952

——, "Zu den Anfängen der Rentierzucht: Nachtrag", *Anthropos*, XLVIII, 1953

Jochelson, Waldemar, *Peoples of Asiatic Russia*, New York, American Museum of Natural History, 1926

——, *The Yakut*, New York, American Museum of Natural History, 1933

Jones, Robert A.C., "The French Canadian Horse: Its History in Canada and the United States," *Canadian Historical Review*, XXVIII, no. 2, 1947

Jope, E.M., "Vehicles and Harness" in Singer, Charles, et al., II, 1954–56

Kammenhuber, Annelies, *Hippologia Hethitica*, Wiesbaden, Otto Harrassowitz, 1961

Kammerman, Eugene, "The Camarque: Land of Cowboys and Gypsies," *National Geographic*, CIX, 1956

Keegan, Terry, *The Heavy Horse*, Cranbury, N.J., A.S. Barnes, 1974

Kenney, Michael, *A Spanish Tapestry*, New York, Harper, 1966

Kenrick, V., *Horses in Japan*, Tokyo, Hokuseido Press, 1964

Keur, John and Dorothy, *The Deeply Rooted: A Study of a Drents Community in the Netherlands*, Seattle, University of Washington, 1955

Kolars, John F., *Tradition, Season and Change in a Turkish Village*, Department of Geography, University of Chicago, 1963

Koppers, Wilhelm, "Pferdeopfer und Pferdekult der Indogermanen," *Forschungen und Fortschritte*, XII, 1936

Krader, Lawrence, "Principle and Structure in the Organization of the Asiatic Steppe Pastoralists," *Southwestern Journal of Anthropology*, XI, no. 2, 1955a

——, "The Ecology of Central Asian Pastoralism", *Southwestern Journal of Anthropology*, XI, no. 4, 1955b

——, Review of Hancar's *Das Pferd in prähistorischer und frühe historischer Zeit*, *American Anthropologist*, LIX, 1957

——, *The Peoples of Central Asia*, Bloomington, Indiana University, 1963

——, *The Social Organization of the Mongol-Turkic Pastoral Nomads*, Paris, Mouton, 1963

——, *The Formation of the State*, New York, Prentice Hall, 1968

Kussmaul, F., "Frühe Nomadenkulturen in Innerasien," *Tribus*, 1952–3

LaBarre, Weston, *The Aymara Indians*, Memoir, American Anthropological Association, no. 68, 1948

Lamb, Robert B., *The Mule in Southern Agriculture*, Berkeley, University of California, 1963

Lamond, Elizabeth, *Walter of Henley's Husbandry*, London, Longmans, Green and Co., 1890

Lane, R.H., "Waggons and their Ancestors," *Antiquity*, 1935

Lattimore, Owen, *The Desert Road to Turkestan*, Boston, Little Brown, 1929

——, *The Inner Asian Frontiers of China*, Boston, Beacon, 1962a

——, *Nomads and Commissars*, Oxford, 1962b

Laufer, Berthold, *The Reindeer and Its Domestication*, Memoir, American Anthropological Association, IV, 1917

Law, L.C.C. "Garamantes and Trans-Saharan Enterprise in Classical

Times," *Journal of African History*, VIII, no. 2, 1967

Law, Robin, "Horses, Firearms, and Political Power in Pre-Colonial West Africa", *Past and Present*, 1976

Leeds, Anthony and Andrew Vayda, *Man, Culture and Animals*, Washington, American Assn. for the Advancement of Science, 1965

Lefebvre des Noëttes, Richard, *L'attelage et le cheval de selle à travers les ages, Contributions à l'histoire de l'esclavage*, Paris, 1931

Leshnik, Lawrence S., "Some Early Indian Horse Bits and Other Bridle Equipment," *American Journal of Archeology*, LXXV, 1971

Levchine, Alexis de, *Description des hordes et des steppes des Kirghiz-Kazaks*, Paris, 1846

Lewin, M.G. and L.P. Potapov, *The Peoples of Siberia*, Chicago, University of Chicago, 1964

Lewis, Herbert, *A Galla Monarchy: Jimma Abba Jefar*, Madison, University of Wisconsin, 1965

Lewis, Oscar, *Village Life in North India*, New York, Knopf, 1965

Linton, Ralph, *The Tree of Culture*, New York, Knopf, 1955

Lipsky, George A., *Ethiopia, Its People, Its Society and Its Culture*, New Haven, Human Relations Area Files, 1962

Littauer, M.A., "Bits and Pieces," *Antiquity*, XLIII, 1969

Littauer, Vladimir, *Horsemen's Progress: The Development of Modern Riding*, Princeton, New Jersey, Van Nostrand, 1962

Livingstone, W.P., *Shetland and the Shetlanders*, London, Thos. Nelson, 1947

Livy, *The History of Rome*, Geo. Baker, transl., Oxford, 1847

Loeb, Edwin, *Sumatra: Its History and People*, Vienna, Inst. für Volkerkunde der Universität Wiens, 1935

Longworth, Philip, *The Cossacks*, New York, Holt, Rinehart and Winston, 1970

Loomis, Frederick, *The Evolution of the Horse*, Boston, Marshall Jones, 1926

Löwe, H., "Kaltblut-Pferderassen in der verschiedenen Landern der Welt" in Hammond, John, Ivan Johanneson and Fritz Haring, III, part 2, 1958–61

Löwe, H. and O. Saenger, "Ponies in den verschiedenen Trerarten in der Welt" in Hammond, John, Ivar Johanneson and Fritz Haring, III, part 2, 1958–61

Lhote, Henri, "Le cheval et le chameau dans les peintures et gravures rupestres du Sahara," *Bull. de l'Institut Francais d'Afrique Noire*, XV, 3, 1953

Lowie, Robert, *The Crow Indians*, New York, Holt, Rinehart and Winston, 1935

——, *The Indians of the Plains*, Garden City, New York, Natural History, 1963

Luther, Ernest, *Ethiopia Today*, Stanford University, 1958

McGovern, William M., *The Early Empires of Central Asia*, Chapel Hill, University of North Carolina, 1939

McWham, Forrest, *The Falkland Islands Today*, Stirling, Scotland, Tract Society, n.d.

Maenchen-Helfen, J. Otto, *The World of the Huns*, Berkeley, Univ. of California, 1973

Mallowan, M.E.L., "The Excavation at Tell Chagar Bazar," *Iraq*. III–IV, 1936, 1937

——, "Excavations at Brak and Chagar, Bazar", *Iraq*, IX, 1947

Marcellinus, Ammianus, *The Roman History*, C.D. Yonge, transl., London, Henry D. Bohn, 1892

Marsden, William, *The History of Sumatra*, Oxford, 1966

Mason, L.L. and J.P. Maule, *The Indigenous Livestock of Eastern and Southern Africa*, Farnham Royal, England, Commonwealth Agricultural Bureaux, 1960

Masson, V.M. and V.I. Sarianidi, *Central Asia: Turkmenia before the Archaemenids*, New York, Praeger, 1972

Meakin, Budgett, *The Land of the Moors*, London, Sonnenschein, 1901

Meek, Charles K., *The Northern Tribes of Nigeria*, London, Frank Cass, 1971

Mellaart, James, *The Chalcolithic and Early Bronze Age in the Near East and Anatolia*, Beirut, Khayat's, 1961

Mellink, Machteld J., "The Archeology of Asia Minor," *American Journal of Archeology*, LXVI, 1962

Mesey-Thompson, R.F., *The Horse*, London, Edward Arnold, 1911

Messenger, John C., *Innis Beag: Isle of Ireland*, New York, Holt, Rinehart and Winston, 1969

Messing, Simon D., *The Highland Plateau Amhara of Ethiopia*, Ph. D. Dissertation, University of Pennsylvania, Ann Arbor, Michigan, University Microfilms, 1957

Minns, Ellis H., *Scythians and Greeks*, New York, Bello and Tannen, 1965

Mirov, N.T., "Notes on Reindeer Domestication," *American Anthropologist*, XLVII, 1945

Mitrany, David, *The Land and the Peasant in Rumania*, New York, Greenwood Press, 1968

Molnar, Imre, *A Manual of Australian Agriculture*, London, Heineman, 1961

Mongait, A.L., *Archaeology of the USSR*, Harmondsworth, England, Penguin, 1961

Montagne, Prosper, *Larousse Gastronomique*, New York, Crown, 1961

Montgomery, E.S., *The Thoroughbred*, New York, A.S. Barnes, 1971

Montgomery, G.G., "Some Aspects of Sociality of the Domestic Horse," *Transactions, Kansas Academy of Science*, LX, 1957

Moorey, P.R.S., "Pictorial Evidence for the History of Horse Riding in Iraq before the Kassite Period," *Iraq*, XXXII, 1970

Muernier, K., "Zur Diskussion über die Typologie des Hauspferdes und deren zoologisch systematische Bedeutung," *Zeitschrift für Tierzüchtung und Züchtungsbiologie*, LXXVI, 1961–2

Murdock, George P., *Our Primitive Contemporaries*, New York, Macmillan, 1934

——, *Africa: Its Peoples and Their Culture History*, New York, McGraw-Hill, 1959

Murray, G.P., *Sons of Ishmael*, London, Routledge, 1935

Murray, Jacqueline, *The First European Agriculture*, Edinburgh University, 1970

Musil, Alois, *Manners and Customs of the Rwala Bedouin*, New York, American Geographical Society, 1928

Nadel, Siegfried F., *Black Byzantium*, Oxford, 1942

Naval Intelligence Division, United Kingdom, Geographical Handbook Series, *Iceland*, 1942

——, *Morocco*, 1942

——, *Tunisia*, 1942

——, *Algeria*, 1944

Needham, Joseph, *Science and Civilization in China*, Cambridge, IV, 1965

Newsweek, "Technology's Seers," March 6, 1972

Nichols, Madaline, "The Spanish Horse of the Pampas," *American Anthropologist*, XLI, 1939

——, *The Gaucho*, New York, Gordian, 1968

Nobis, Gunter, *Vom Wildpferd zum Hauspferd: Studien zur Phylogenie pleistozäner Equiden Eurasiens und das Domestikations-problem unserer Hauspferd*, Cologne, Bohlau, Fundamenta Monogr. zur Urgeschichte, Series B., VI, 1971

Noble, Duncan, "The Mesopotamian Onager as a Draught Animal" in Ucko and Dimbleby, 1969

Norman, A.V.B., *The Medieval Soldier*, New York, T.Y. Crowell, 1971

O'Donovan, Edmond, *The Merv Oasis*, New York, Putnam, 1883

Olmstead, A.T., *The History of the Persian Empire*, University of Chicago, 1970

Oppian in *Oppian, Colluthus and Tryphiodorus*, A.W. Mair, transl., London, Heinemann, 1928

Ortega, Luis, B., *California Hackamore*, Sacramento, Calif., News Publishing Co., 1948

Osgood, Cornelius, *The Koreans and their Culture*, New York, Ronald, 1951

Osgood, Ernest S., *The Day of the Cattleman*, University of Chicago, 1929

Owen, Francis, *The Germanic Peoples*, New York, Bookman Assn., 1960

Pahlen, K.K., *Mission to Turkestan*, Oxford, 1964

Palladius in *Palladius on Husbandrie*, Barton Lodge, trans., London, 1873

Parkyns, G.M., *Life in Abyssinia*, London, John Murray, 1868

Parry, Vernon J. and M.E. Yapp (eds.), *War, Technology and Society in the Middle East*, Oxford University Press, 1975

Pausanius, *Description of Greece*, W.H.S. Jones, transl., Cambridge, Mass., Harvard University, 1935

Pavlovsky, George, *Agricultural Russia on the Eve of the Revolution*, New York, Howard Fertig, 1968

Pehrson, Robert N., *The Social Organization of the Marri Baluch*, Chicago, Aldine, 1966

Phillips, E.D., *The Royal Hordes: Nomadic Peoples of the Steppes*, London, Thames and Hudson, 1965

——, *The Mongols*, New York, Praeger, 1969

Piggott, Stuart, *Prehistoric India*, Harmondsworth, England, Penguin, 1950

——, *Ancient Europe*, Chicago, Aldine, 1965

Pliny, *Natural History*, London, Heinemann, III, 1940

Polo, Marco, *The Travels*, Harmondsworth, England, Penguin, 1972

Polybius, *The Histories*, W.R. Paton, transl., London, Heinemann, 1922

Pope, Arthur, U. (ed.), *A Survey of Persian Art from Prehistoric Times to the Present*, Oxford, 1938–1967

Porada, Edith, "Nomads and Luristan Bronzes" in Ghirshman et al., 1964

——, *Ancient Iran*, London, Methuen, 1965

Powell, T.G.E., *The Celts*, London, Thames and Hudson, 1959

——, "The Introduction of Horse Riding to Temperate Europe: A Contributory Note", *Proc. Prehistoric Society*, XXXVII, Pt. II, 1971

Pumpelly, Raphael, *Explorations in Turkestan*, Washington, D.C., Carnegie Institute, 1905

Rabie, Hassanein, "The Training of the Mamluk Faris" in Parry, Vernon J. and M.E. Yapp

Radloff, Wilhelm, *Aus Sibirien*, Oosterhout, Netherlands, Anthropological Publications, 1968

Raswan, Carl, "Vocabulary of Bedouin Words Concerning Horses", *Journal of Near Eastern Studies*, IV, 1945

Reed, Charles, "A Review of the Archaeological Evidence on Animal Domestication in the Prehistoric Near East" in Braidwood, R.J. and B. Howe, *Prehistoric Investigations in Iraqi Kurdistan*, Oriental Institute of the University of Chicago, no. 31, 1960

Rees, Alwyn D., *Life in a Welsh Countryside*, Cardiff, University of Wales, 1961

Rey, Charles F., *Unconquered Abyssinia as it is Today*, London, Seeley, Service and Co., 1923

Rice, Lee, "A Bit about Old Saddles," *Western Horseman*, XXXIX, nos. 2, 3, 1974

Rice, T.T., *The Scythians*, London, Thames and Hudson, 1961

Ridgeway, William, *The Origins and Influence of the Thoroughbred Horse*, Cambridge, 1905

Riviere, Peter, *The Forgotten Frontier: Ranchers in Northern Brazil*, New York, Holt, Rinehart and Winston, 1972

Robinson, John P., "Daily Participation in Sport Across Twelve Countries" in Lüshen, Günther (ed.), *The Cross Cultural Analysis of Sport and Games*, Champaign, Illinois, Stipes Publ., 1970

Rodriguez, Joe, "Around the Horn," *Western Horseman*, XXXIX, no. 4, 1974

Roe, Frank G., *The Indian and the Horse*, Norman, University of Oklahoma, 1955

Rollins, Philip Ashton, *The Cowboy*, New York, Ballantine, 1973

Rostovtseff, M., "Dieux et Chevaux," *Syria*, XII, 1931

Rudenko, Sergei I., *The Frozen Tombs of Siberia*, London, Dent, 1970

Runyaniev, B.F., "The Origin of the Domestic Horse" (in Russian, English summary), *Bulletin of Akad. Nauk. SSSR*, Biological Series nos. 2–3, 1931

Rupen, Robert A., *Mongols of the Twentieth Century*, Bloomington, Indiana University, 1964

Russell, W.M.S., *Man, Nature and History*, London, Aldus Books, 1967

Ryden, Hope, *America's Last Wild Horses*, New York, Ballantine, 1970

Saggs, H.W.F., *The Greatness that was Babylon*, New York, Mentor, 1968

Saint Clair, Stuart, "Timor: A Key to the Indies", *National Geographic*, LXXXIV, 1943

Salonen, Armas, *Hippologica Accadica*, Helsinki, Suomalaisen Tiedeakatemian Toimituksia, Ser. B., vol. C, 1955

Sahlins, Marshall, *Tribesmen*, New York, Prentice-Hall, 1968

Sauer, Carl, *Agricultural Origins and Dispersals*, New York, American Geographical Society, 1952

Schulman, Alan Richard, "Egyptian Representations of Horsemen and Riding in the New Kingdom," *Journal of Near Eastern Studies*, XVI, 1957

Schuyler, Eugene, *Turkestan*, London, Routledge and Kegan Paul, 1966

Sears, Robert, *A Survey of the Cycle of the Sod and the Livestock Industry*

Here and Abroad, Los Angeles, Wetzel, 1941

Service, Elman and Helen, *Tobati, Paraguayan Town*, Chicago, 1954

Service Bulletin, Education Division, Statistics Canada, Ottawa, no. 1, II, 1973

Settle, Raymond W., and Mary Lund Settle, *Saddles and Spurs: The Pony Express Saga*, Lincoln, Nebr., University of Nebraska, 1955

Shirokogoroff, S.M., *The Social Organization of the Northern Tungus*, Oosterhout, Netherlands, N.B. Anthropological Publications, 1966

Sidney, S., *The Book of Horses*, London, 1892

Sieber, Sylvester and Franz Mueller, *The Social Life of Primitive Man*, St. Louis, B. Herder, 1941

Simpich, Frederick, "Life on the Argentine Pampas," *National Geographic*, LXXIV, 1933

Simpson, George G., *Horses*, Garden City, New York, Doubleday, 1961

Singer, Charles, E.J. Holmyard and A.R. Hall, *A History of Technology*, Oxford, five volumes, 1954–1956

Skendi, Stavro (ed.), *Albania*, New York, Praeger, 1958

Skorkowski, Edward, "Unterarten in den Pferdpopulationen und deren Frühgeschichte, *"Zeitshrift für Tierzüchtungsbiologie*, LXXVI, 1961–2

Slicher van Bath, B.H., *The Agrarian History of Western Europe, 500—1850*, London, Edward Arnold, 1963

Smith, M.G., "The Hausa of Northern Nigeria," in Gibbs, James (ed.), 1965

Smith, R.E.F., *The Origins of Farming in Russia*, Paris, Mouton, 1959

Solanet, C., "The Criolle Horse," *Journal of Heredity*, XXI, 1930

Spengler, Oswald, "Der Streitwagen und seine Bedeutung für den Gang der Geschichte," *Die Welt als Geschichte*, III, 1937

Spicer, Edward H., *Potam; A Yaqui Village in Sonora*, Memoir, American Anthropological Association, no. 77, 1954

Spuler, Bertold, *History of the Mongols*, London, Routledge and Kegan Paul, 1972

Squier, E.G., *Nicaragua: Its Peoples, Scenery and Monuments*, New York, Appleton, 1852

Staffa, Susan J., *Conquest and Fusion: The Social Evolution of Cairo, 642—1850*, Leiden, E.J. Brill, 1977

Statesman's Yearbook, London, Macmillan, various years

Stenning, Derrick J., "The Pastoral Fulani of Northern Nigeria" in Gibbs, James, 1965

Steward, Julian H., *Basin-Plateau Aboriginal Socio-Political Groups*, Washington, Bureau of American Ethnology, Bulletin 120, 1938

Steward, Julian H. and L.C. Faron, *Native Peoples of South America*, New

York, McGraw-Hill, 1959

Stiehler, W., "Landwirtschaft und Seidlungsgeographie äthiopiens," *Erdkunde*, II, 1948

Stirling, Paul, *Turkish Village*, London, Weidenfeld and Nicolson, 1965

Strabo, *The Geography*, H.L. Jones, transl., London, Heinemann, 1917–32

Strickon, Arnold, "Class and Kinship in Argentina," *Ethnology*, I, 1962

——, "The Euro-American Ranching Complex" in Anthony Leeds and Andrew Vayda, 1965

Sulimirski, T., *Prehistoric Russia*, London, J. Baker, 1970a

——, *The Sarmatians*, New York, Praeger, 1970b

Summerhays, R.S., (compiler), *Encyclopaedia for Horsemen*, London, Frederick Warne, 1952

——, *Observer's Book of Horses and Ponies*, London, Frederick Warne, 1968

Swanton, John, *Indians of the Southeastern United States*, Washington, Bureau of American Ethnology, Bulletin 137, 1946

Tacitus, *Historical Works: The Germania*, London, Dutton, 1908

Tarr, Joel A., "Urban Pollution: Many Long Years Ago," *American Heritage*, XXII, 1971

Tarr, Laszlo, *The History of the Carriage*, New York, Arco, 1969

Taylor, Louis, *Bits, Their History, Use and Misuse Plus Practical Advice on the Most Effective Bits for Every Need*, North Hollywood, California, Wilshire Book Co., 1973

Taylor, William B., *Landlord and Peasant in Colonial Oaxaca*, Stanford Univ., 1972

Temple, O., *Notes on the Tribes, Provinces, Emirates and States of the Northern Provinces of Nigeria*, London, Frank Cass, 1965

Thaliath, Joseph, "Present Day Relics of the Vedic Horse Sacrifice?", *Anthropos*, XLVII, 1952

Thevenin, Rene, *L'origine des animaux domestiques*, Paris, 1960

Thirsk, Joan, *English Peasant Farming*, London, Routledge and Kegan Paul, 1957

Tinker, E. Larocque, *Centaurs of Many Lands*, London, J.A. Allen, 1964

Tothill, J.D. (ed.), *Agriculture in the Sudan*, Oxford, 1948

Tozer, B., *The Horse in History*, London, Methuen, 1908

Treloar, D.W.G., "Investors and Kimberley Cattle," *Australian Journal of Agricultural Economics*, IX, 1965

Trench, Charles C., *A History of Horsemanship*, London, Longman, 1970

Trow-Smith, Robert, *History of British Livestock Husbandry*, London, Routledge and Kegan Paul, 1959

Tweedie, W., *The Arabian Horse: His Country and People*, Edinburgh and

London, Blackwood, 1894

Tylden, G., *The Rise of the Basuto*, Cape Town, Juta, 1966

——, *Discovering Harness and Saddlery*, Tring, Herts., Shire, 1971

Tyler, Stephanie, J., *The Behaviour and Social Organization of the New Forest Ponies*, London, Bailliere Tindall, Animal Behavior Monographs, V, pt. 2, 1972

Ucko, Peter J. and G.W. Dimbleby (eds.), *Domestication and Exploitation of Plants and Animals*, Chicago, Aldine, 1969

Underhill, Ruth, *Red Man's America*, Univ. of Chicago, 1953

United Nations (FAO), *Production Yearbook*, Rome, 1961–1971

Uppenhorn, W., "Warmblut pferderassen in den verschiedenen Landern der Welt" in Hammond, John, Ivar Johanneson, and Fritz Haring, III, 1958–61

Vajda, Laszlo, *Untersuchungen zur Geschichte der Hirtenkulteren*, Wiesbaden, Otto Harrassowitz, 1968

Vambery, Arminius, *Travels in Central Asia*, London, John Murray, 1864

Varro in *Roman Farm Management: The Treatises of Cato and Varro*, V. Farmer, transl., New York, Macmillan, 1913

Vernam, Glenn, *Man on Horseback*, New York, Harper and Row, 1964

Vernon, A., *The Horse and the Romance of the Horse*, Ann Arbor, Finch, 1939

Vesey-Fitzgerald, Brian, *The Book of the Horse*, London, Nicholson and Watson, 1946

Vialles, Andre, "The Camargue: The Cowboy Country of Southern France," *National Geographic*, XLII, 1922

Vigneron, Paul, *Le cheval dans l'antiquité graeco romaine*, University of Nancy, 1968

Virgil, *The Georgics*, London, Benn, 1928

Vives, James Vicens, *An Economic History of Spain*, Princeton University, 1969

Vreeland, H.H. *Mongol Community and Kinship Structure*, New Haven, Human Relations Area Files, 1957

Vuorela, Toivo, *The Finno-Ugric Peoples*, Bloomington, Indiana University, 1964

Wagley, Charles and Marvin Harris, "A Typology of Latin American Subcultures," *American Anthropologist*, no. 1., LVII, 1955

Waley, Arthur, "The Heavenly Horses of Ferghana: A New View," *History Today*, V, 1955

Walker, Eric, *The Great Trek*, London, Black, 1965

Wallace, Ernest and E.A. Hoebel, *The Comanches: Lords of the Plains*, Norman, University of Oklahoma, 1952

Wallerstein, Immanuel, *The Modern World System*, New York,

Academic Press, 1974

Walle, Paul, *Bolivia: Its People and Its Resources*, London, Unwin, 1914

Wardell, John, W., *The Kirghiz Steppe*, London, Galley, 1961

Waring, G., S. Wierzbowski, and E. Hafez, "The Behaviour of Horses" in Hafez, E.S.E., *The Behaviour of Domestic Animals*, London, Bailliere Tindall, 1975.

Warriner, Doreen, *Economics of Peasant Farming*, London, Frank Cass, 1964

Webb, Walter P., *The Great Plains*, New York, Grosset and Dunlap, 1931

Weber, Max, *Ancient Judaism*, New York, Free Press, 1952

Weir, Thomas R., *Ranching in the Southern Interior Plateau of British Columbia*, Ottawa, Dept. of Mines and Technical Services, Geographical Memoir 4, 1964

Wentworth, Judith, *The Authentic Arabian Horse*, London, George Allen and Unwin, 1962

Westermarck, Edward, *Ritual and Belief in Morocco*, London, Macmillan, 1926

White, Lynn, *Medieval Technology and Social Change*, Oxford, 1962

Wilkinson, Paul F., "Oomingmak: A Model for Man Animal Relationships in Prehistory," *Current Anthropology*, XIII, 1, 1972

Wilson, David, *The Anglo-Saxons*, Hammondsworth, England, Penguin, 1971

Wilson, James, "Three Wheeling Through Africa," *National Geographic*, LXV, 1934

Wilson, John, *The Culture of Ancient Egypt*, Chicago, 1951

Winner, Irene, "Some Problems of Nomadism and Social Organization among recently settled Kazakhs" *Central Asiatic Review*, XI, 1963

Wissler, Clark, "The Influence of the Horse in the Development of Plains Culture," *American Anthropologist*, XVI, 1914

——, "Riding Gear of the North American Indians," *American Museum of Natural History Anthropological Papers*, XVII, 1915

World Almanac, New York, Newspaper Enterprise Association, various years

Xenophon, *The Art of Horsemanship*, with notes by Morris H. Morgan, Boston, Little Brown, 1893

——, *Cyropaedia*, Walter Miller, transl., Cambridge, Mass., Harvard University, 1914

——, *The Art of Horsemanship*, Zoltan Sztehlo, transl., New York, Vintage, 1968

Yang, Martin C., *A Chinese Village: Taitou, Shantung Province*, New York, Columbia University, 1945

Yetts, W. Percival, "The Horse: A Factor in Early Chinese History,"

Eurasia Septentrionales Antiqua, IV, 1934

Yoe, Shway, *The Burman: His Life and Notions*, New York, Norton, 1963

Zelmar, Sandra, *Alberta Light Horse Study*, Farm Management Br., Alberta Department of Agriculture, 1973

Zeuner, A., *History of Domesticated Animals*, New York, Harper and Row, 1963

Index